# UNFORGIVEN

*The American Economic System
Sold for Debt and War*

# ABOUT THE AUTHOR

Charles Walters was born in Ness County, Kansas in 1926. A veteran of WWII and the Korean activity, he holds a bachelor's degree from Creighton University, Omaha, and a graduate degree from the University of Denver. He is noted for his works on agriculture and agricultural economics, having authored thousands of articles on the subject. He is also the founder and executive editor of *Acres U.S.A.*, North America's largest, oldest journal for ecological agriculture.

Also by Charles Walters

*Holding Action*
*Angry Testament*
*A Farmer's Guide to the Bottom Line*
*The Case for Eco-Agriculture*
*Eco-Farm, An Acres U.S.A. Primer*
*A Life in the Day of an Editor*
*Raw Materials Economics*
*Weeds, Control Without Poisons*
*Fletcher Sims' Compost*
*Socrates — The Lost Dialogues*
*A Farmer's Guide to the Bottom Line*

Editor

*The Albrecht Papers, Volumes I-IV*

Co-Author

*A Farmer's Guide to Homestead Rights*
*The Carbon Connection*
*Mainline Farming for Century 21*
*The Economics of Convulsion*
*Hands-On Agronomy*
*The Carbon Cycle*

# UNFORGIVEN

*The American Economic System
Sold for Debt and War*

## Charles Walters

Revised second edition

Acres U.S.A.
Austin, Texas

# UNFORGIVEN

Acres U.S.A.
P.O. Box 91299
Austin, Texas 78709 U.S.A.
(512) 892-4400 • fax (512) 892-4448
info@acresusa.com • www.acresusa.com

*Printed in the United States of America*

Publisher's Cataloging-in-Publication

Walters, Charles, 1926-
    Unforgiven; the American economic system sold for debt and war/Charles Walters
    Austin, TX: ACRES U.S.A. 2003

    xvii, 432 p, charts, tables.
    2nd edition, revised
    Includes index.

    ISBN: 0-911311-67-X

    1. United States—Rural conditions. 2. United States—Economic policy. 3. United States—Economic conditions. I. Walters, Charles, 1926- II. Title

                HN58.W28                        330.973

Originally published by Economics Library, Kansas City, Missouri in cooperation with Citizens Congress for Private Enterprise, Granite Falls, Minnesota, 1971.

*Dedicated to the memory of*
*Carl H. Wilken*

*The people is a beast of muddy brain*
    *That knows not its own force, and therefore stands*
    *Loaded with wood and stone, the powerless hands*
    *Of a mere child guide it with bit and rein.*

*One kick would be enough to break the chain;*
    *But the beast fears, and what the child demands,*
    *It does; nor its own terror understands,*
    *Confused and stupefied by bugbears vain.*

*Most wonderful! with its own hands it ties*
    *And gags itself—gives itself death and war*
    *For pence doled out by kings from its own stores.*

*Its own are all things between earth and heaven,*
    *But this it knows not; and if one arise*
    *To tell this truth, it kills him unforgiven.*

— Tomasso Campanella,
from the Italian poem, "The People,"
translated by John Addington Symonds

# CONTENTS

# FOREWORD

As we enter Century 21 anyone who reads or listens is aware of the fact that America's so-called progress and prosperity has been kept alive with deficits, war and defense spending, debt expansion, and foreign give-aways on the broadest scale in history. Millions of family farmers have been driven from the land in this process. The smaller businesses of the nation have been taken over or driven from the Main Streets of both rural and urban communities, closing one door after another to the ambitions of our youth and making millions of men, women and children either directly or indirectly dependent on city, county, or state or federal trea-suries for existence.

The title and subtitle of this book suggests a link to institutional ar-rangements of a yesteryear that hangs on today. The industrial age, which properly started before the American Revolution, had terminated the in-dividual influence of the French physiocrats for good, or so it seemed. Yet those ideas and their codified slogan—"all new wealth comes from the soil"—stayed on to color the thinking of men like Thomas Jefferson, James Madison, and not least, George Washington.

Washington's *aide-de-camp* was Alexander Hamilton, a discerning pa-triot who came to comprehend the reality of the physical economy and the nuances of business. Once the wry epigrams were swept away, there was the reality: *trade as plunder*, with the people—"a beast of muddy brain"—being deprived of "their own stores" by the power of institutional arrangements.

Before he accepted command of the Continental army, Washington tallied his receipts for tobacco sent to England, and watched with abject disbelief as his debts mounted. The King's corporation argued for free trade, and some support was forthcoming because there was urban sup-port for breaking the landowner Lord's grip on the food supply. In Eu-rope the farm worker was a peasant or serf. In America he was a free-holder, a farmer.

Still a farmer produced only raw materials. It took manufactures to create added value, but the world traders—meaning the King's corpora-tions—did not permit this profitable enterprise in the colonies or conquered lands. Therein rested a truth, revelation of which was always *unforgiven*.

# [1] GENIUS AT RISK

The Madison constitution did not achieve its genius by accident. Each line was debated and examined under the lens of scholarship never seen before or since. A free people had to protect themselves, not only from pirates and Indians, but also from commercial predators.

Richard Cobden's type of thinking was afloat long before that famous calico printer set them down on paper. By the time the United States Constitution was written, the fire of the physiocrats as spokesmen for agriculture had largely spent itself. In command were the speakers for rising industrialists in England and on the Continent.

A revolution needs a system of ideas to justify itself. The reality of private enterprise and manufactures needed such a system to justify itself, not against landed aristocracy, but against the self-same merchants. The fact that Adam Smith's *The Wealth of Nations* appeared in the year of the American Declaration of Independence has been seen as no coincidence. The situation that brought on the revolution in economics was precisely the situation that brought on revolution in the colonies.

There was the new liberal doctrine of enlightenment in France, all of it confirmed by David Hume, John Locke and Jacques Rousseau. Thus there were the four terms: *inalienable rights* coming from *nature's God*, and the rights to *life, liberty and the pursuit of happiness,* and perhaps *property* as proposed by Benjamin Franklin. This language was based on the ethic found in the Bible and on legal and economic perspective best expressed in *The Federalist*.

Even a peace treaty was no protection from the King's predator corporations. Sugar producers would be annihilated by producer costs based on lower than slave wages, and industry could be strangled in its infancy by import invasion. This, indeed, was the proposal made in the British Parliament.

The first several American administrations answered by imposing tariffs on imports. Thus protected, infant industries and resultant innovations literally jump started the nation. Under the Articles of Confederation, the President of the United States in Congress Assembled was helpless. That is why a meeting to deal with the Northwest Ordinance resolved itself into a Committee of the Whole, the result being the Madison constitution and the language that set the stage for political, social and economic stability.

In England, Richard Cobden could pamphlet to his heart's content about free trade. The United States merely shrugged a collective shoulder and passed tariff laws. With an internal market capable of buying most of its production, why should the foreigner be allowed to dismantle farm solvency, budding manufactures, technical inventions and structural equity as a bow to speculators and predators?

## [2] UNRESOLVED ISSUE

A recital of this historical inventory constitutes the platform from which *Unforgiven* truth can be resolved. Carl Wilken was more than a farmer and statistical analyst. He was an acceptable historian. In the story that unfolds he never once dismisses the sequence of events that led the nation into the depression of the 1930s or the economic remedy found in the Stabilization Act of 1942 and the Steagall Amendment, both parity measures that complied with the tenets of the Madison constitution.

Indeed, the history of the United States is a veritable roller coaster ride, passage of tariff laws, repeal of tariff laws, prosperity attending the former and depression always a consequence of the latter.

Only the correct use of logic to satisfy facts makes it possible to look back or see ahead, and those facts are always colored by the laws, the state of the arts and the culture upon which a civilization rests.

Fisher Ames, one of the ablest men in the American Congress in 1789, said as follows: "I conceive that the present Constitution was dictated by commercial necessity more than by any other cause. For want of an efficient government to secure the manufacturing interests to advance our commerce was long seen by men of judgement and pointed out by patriots [as] solutions to promote our general welfare."

The historian Bancroft said, "The necessity for regulating commerce, *i.e.,* for providing a proper tariff, gave the immediate impulse for a more perfect Constitution." The great Daniel Webster, historically known as the greatest expounder of the Constitution, in a speech at Buffalo, New York, in June 1833, declared that the protection of American labor against the injurious competition of foreign labor so far at least [as] to general handicraft production, is known to have been one end designed to be gained by establishing the Constitution.

Indeed, the tariff question was the very first to be discussed by the first Congress, and for over two centuries of our existence remains the single subject never settled. Nullification, slavery, secession, reconstruction, all have had their discussions and all have been forever settled. The tariff remained the vital question many years later during the Roosevelt administration and remains unsettled to this day—world trade, NAFTA, and congressional nonfeasance notwithstanding.

It was a case of piracy and international business conducted by the King's corporations—the first internationalists—that gave the American statesmen the impulse and analysis required to support a protection instrument for government. After all, the threats from England were blatant, and their history was deep-seated.

## [3] CAUSES WHICH IMPEL SEPARATION

I have yet to read an historian who could explain why the industrial revolution came to Europe and England in its trader form. Not even Arnold Toynbee the elder, who coined the term "industrial revolution," had an answer. Why didn't it happen in China, or in ancient Greece? Why didn't parenthood for industrialization take place in the Dyak culture of Borneo, or among the Ainu culture of northern Japan, or even out among the Andaman Islanders?

I have my answer, if asked. The industrial revolution must have responded to a special philosophy not available among the civilizations just mentioned.

There was a mythology that remained afloat to the effect that Columbus proved the Earth was as round as the Sun. In fact the Greeks knew the Earth was a sphere long before medieval mapmakers surmised as much. But it was not until Magellan circumnavigated the globe that the Earth was perceived to be finite, its resources limited.

Queen Elizabeth founded the East India Company for the purpose of plundering the planet in A.D. 1600. England elevated herself above all others based on John Locke's philosophy called "the rights of conquest."

The American nation came into being during the late 16th century. Two philosophies clashed, one serving England, one tailored for America.

The East India Company founded Haileybury College for the purpose of staffing the Empire. It trained the soldiers, businessmen, and missionaries who came to log the pages of history within 200 years. Haileybury College was called upon to inventory the planet and its resources. The man in charge was the head of the Department of Economics, one Thomas Robert Malthus, philosopher, a minister of Christian doctrine.

Malthus had a population theory based on the idea the planet would be overtaxed with population. New life, he held, expanded geometrically, whereas food supply acquired new efficiency only on an arithmetic basis. Therefore some life was superfluous. Malthus was soon joined by followers of Charles Darwin, who argued survival of the fittest. The fittest had the divine right to survive. This was the philosophy that set the Dutch, French,

Spanish, Portuguese, and finally the English on a course of conquest until each coveted each acre, each sandbar, each spit of land on earth.

Finally the English pronounced expendable any population they could bully. Except for Continental wars, the British rarely fought an enemy that wore shoes, the American colonies excepted.

In 1699 the English Parliament decreed that no wool, yarn or cloth or manufactures of plantations in America "shall be shipped by sail from any plantation or sent to any place whatsoever" under penalty of forfeiting both ship and cargo, a heavy fine accompanying each offense. It was the role of a few traders to control manufacturing for the entire world and to monopolize its reproductive power, and—as one historian put it—to keep all other countries in a state of industrial vassalage.

This public policy, enacted from the top of the political spectrum, Lord Brougham, in 1816, told the House of Commons, "It is well worthwhile to incur a loss upon the first exportation in order by the flood to stifle in the cradle those infant manufacturers in the United States which the war has forced into existence."

As every school child knows, the Founding Fathers drew up a Constitution, but it is less known that the Constitutional Convention was called to protect America from a grasping foreign power. The Founding Fathers had directed the Revolutionary War, of course, and they strived to maintain the power via the status quo. Here is what the contemporary George Mann had to say.

"And so the years from 1783 to 1789 were lovely, halcyon days for the merchants of Great Britain. In about three years time money of the country passed into the pockets of British merchants and manufacturers. And we were left poor indeed. For not only did they take from us our money, but they took also our good name for integrity, independence and common sense which we had won in the Revolutionary War. As there was no tariff to prevent it, foreign nations poured in their products of every kind and description in such quantities and such prices that our people could not compete with them. Domestic industries were suspended. The weaver, the shoemaker, the hatter, the saddler, the rope maker and many others were reduced to bankruptcy. Our markets were glutted with foreign goods. Prices fell. Our manufacturers generally were ruined, our laborers beggared, our artisans without employment, our merchants insolvent and our farmers followed all the classes into the vortex of general financial destruction. Depreciation seized upon every species of property. Legal pressure to enforce payment of debts caused alarming sacrifices . . . "

In Massachusetts, fully a third of the people joined Shay's rebellion due to the poverty and distress visited upon them by free trade. In sparsely populated Connecticut some 500 farms were seized for taxes, the owners being too poor to pay, and the situation was hardly better in New England. There was no market for real estate. Debtors were compelled to sell their land. They were ruined. Men distrusted each other.

Historian Mann wrote, "Had there been no free trade, there would have been no inundation of foreign goods. There would have been no drain of specie. Had there been no drain of specie, there would have been no lack of circulating medium. Had there been no such disaster, there would have been no insurrection to the state."

Ruin came to the people hard on the heels of the Revolutionary War, free trade being the destruction engine unchained. Free trade as managed by the forebears of our transnational corporations was followed rather quickly by imports in excess of exports. Without business in domestic trade, labor fell idle. Without earnings, property declined in value and became worthless.

So over a span of 200 years agriculture served as a precursor going into and emerging from depression. The Secretary of Treasury during the James K. Polk administration was Robert J. Walker of Mississippi. The South under slavery was dedicated to free trade. "We have more fertile land," said Walker, "than any other nation. We can raise a greater variety of products and, it may be said, we can clothe nearly all the people of the world. Agriculture is our chief employment. It is best adapted to one section. We can raise a larger surplus of agricultural products and a greater variety than almost any other nation and at cheaper rates. Remove from agriculture all our restrictions and by its own unfettered power it will break down all foreign resistance, would feed the hungry and clothe the poor of our world."

Ezra Taft Benson and Earl Butz continued to echo that conceit even as the chapters of the *Unforgiven* saga were being written.

## [4] BENEFITS AND BENEFACTORS

Looking back we can recall that the very first act of the first Congress was a tariff, signed, sealed and delivered by George Washington, July 4, 1789. The great majority of that first Congress were farmers. They lived close to the soil and they understood the physical economy. No less than five Founding Fathers became presidents, while the Tariff of 1789 was anchored in the statute books.

George Washington spoke for the free people he led. Their safety and interests required the nation to promote the manufacturing they needed for self-sufficiency, otherwise they would surrender their independence and sovereignty. The suggestion that foreigners could provide military supplies was a reflection on the mental acuity of those holding such an opinion, according to Washington.

John Adams, Thomas Jefferson, James Madison, James Monroe, none found a bit of dissatisfaction with protection. Indeed, Andrew Jackson, Abraham Lincoln, and presidents down the line to Theodore Roosevelt and William Howard Taft agreed with the American System. To the very edge of the Wilson administration, to the 1910-1914 parity base period in fact, agriculture became more extensive and prosperous. Many new industries sprang up. The merchant navy was revived and multiplied. All branches of domestic trade were made prosperous. Revenues became sufficient to pay the expense of the government. The whole country was on the high road to wealth and prosperity.

There were a few discordant voices that attacked the Washington protection measure. There was a shift to free trade in 1812-1816 when Cobdenites installed their thinking into the capitol. Richard Cobden of England first conjured up the fantasy that free trade could erase cultural differences, national boundary lines, the world's disputes and finally wars on the planet.

The scheme was sold on the basis that people could increase their comfort by buying cheaper from the foreigner. Yet by sleight of hand this cure for poverty seems to increase poverty. In 1824 the general tariff was restored.

From the age of Jackson to the eve of the Wilson administration, it was always a case of the South linking arms with the Northern bankers to remove tariff protection and promote unregulated free trade. In 1833 free trade prevailed again. A new word entered the American vocabulary, *panic!*

Protection returned again in 1842, and financial gloom disappeared as if by magic. Business recovered. There was full employment and therefore an improved market.

In 1844 the Democratic Party again embraced free trade, James K. Polk the candidate. Polk prevailed. Once the election was over, the meaning of free trade came in clear, although it was delayed by the Mexican War and hostilities in the Crimea.

Not many people could win a debate with Daniel Webster. On July 25, 26 and 27—over three days running—he intoned the arguments that are as valid today as they were a century and a half ago.

"You indulge in the luxury of taxing the poor man and the laborer. That is the whole tendency, the whole character, the whole effect of the bill. One may see everywhere the desire to revel and delight in taking away man's employment.

"It is not a bill for the people or the masses. It is not a bill to add to the comfort of those in middle life or the poor. It is not a bill for employment."

He might as well have been speaking about NAFTA and the World Trade Organization. The scheme was, Webster said, " a bill for the relief of the highest and most luxurious classes of the country, and a bill imposing onerous duties on the great industrious masses, and for taking away the means of living from labor everywhere throughout the land.

Then as now, the same tired argument about feeding the poor of the Earth and driving foreign industries to the wall with superior skills and better technology, the slave argument, using cheaper labor, prevailed. The free trade pledge was reiterated by the Democratic Party in 1860. It mattered not. The voters had had their fill.

## [5] 1913

It is here that the *Unforgiven* story starts. For the Wilson administration truly compromised the American System—with an income tax to replace tariffs, with a Federal Reserve to accommodate the internationalists, with a Foundations law to protect the super-rich, and with the emasculation of the Senate so that power money could do the electing—dismantling the Constitution to a marked degree.

True, there were more administrations between Wilson and Franklin D. Roosevelt, but their brains had been softened so that by 1929 the wind had spawned the whirlwind.

While I was writing the manuscript that follows, Carl H. Wilken told me how Herbert Hoover hated Roosevelt. The bank run could have been cured, but Hoover chose not to intervene, and Roosevelt wanted the economy to get as bad as possible before he took over. The immediate cure would have been to pay depositors and the long-term remedy would have been to restore farm prices.

# FOR THE RECORD

The Cassandras of history always rise so that this truth be given, and the beast of muddy brain always kills them, "unforgiven!" Those who stand up to be "unforgiven" can be found at almost any stopping point along the way.

Ferdinand Lundberg was forced to ask, in the opening lines of *The Rich and the Super-Rich*, "How has this process been contrived of stripping threadbare most of the populace, which once at least owned small patches of virgin land?"

This is a story of death and wars and inflations and depressions. At one point I started to tell it in an epistolary manner, that is, as a series of documents with only a rare assist from the editorial pencil, as the following few entries suggest.

## [6] THE RECORD

*Extract of testimony by Georgia Commissioner of Agriculture Tom Linder before the House Ways and Means Committee, 1947, as reprinted in a Georgia Department of Agriculture booklet entitled,* TRADE TREATIES AND INTERNATIONAL CONTROL.

When England, France, Holland and Italy became involved in World War I against the central powers, the international bankers, especially J.P. Morgan and Company of America, the Rothschilds of England [and other international bankers] together with their associates, were called upon to loan large sums of money to the Allies, including England, France, Holland and Italy. Loans from these international bankers totaled approximately $15 billion in American money. At that time $15 billion was almost an unheard of sum of money.

By the summer of 1916, it became apparent that left to themselves, the Allies would lose the war and the central powers would be victorious. In the summer of 1916, the campaign for the election of a President for the United States got under way. . . .

Wilson was elected in November with great shouts of rejoicing among the people that America would not be involved in a war. . . .

When the United States entered World War I, in addition to the great loss of wealth, human life and suffering involved by the United States, we were called upon to loan approximately another $15 billion from the public treasury to these same European countries. The net result was that the Allies were indebted to the international bankers $15 billion and to the United States government another $15 billion. They could not pay either at that time.

The international bankers looked over the world and saw the hopelessness of collecting the money from the hungry and naked people of Europe. The only place the international bankers could get their money was from the taxpayers of the United States.

Accordingly, in 1919, while Mr. Wilson was still President, the newspapers of this country, with one accord, began a campaign demanding that the war-torn countries of Europe pay US what they owed US. . . . The cry that "Europe pay US what she owes US" was a very popular cry. The newspapers did not take the trouble to explain who the "US" was who was to be paid. The burdened taxpayer of America naturally thought that he was the "US" that was to be paid.

No one took the trouble to explain to the taxpayer that he would be worse off if he got paid than he would if he did not get paid. No one took the trouble to explain that this country having a balanced economy could not collect in goods without having to pay for those goods all over again.

The taxpayer was accustomed, when someone paid him a debt, to go to the bank and get the money. He had no conception of the vast difference between collecting a debt here at home and the collection of a debt from a foreign country.

Consequently, the taxpayer who believing that he was the "US" that was to get the money fell for the trap, and became himself one of the loudest to demand payment of those debts.

The United States had no need for foreign goods. Our factories were capable of turning out all the manufactures that we needed. Our farmers were capable of producing all the food, fiber and feed that we needed. Our labor supply was adequate for every purpose. Our economy had become adjusted to a high level of prices and volume.

We were enjoying the best economical experience of our history. Nobody was being hurt except the international bankers who had loaned their money to England, France, Holland and Italy. If we had followed the sane course, we could have marked off those war debts and kept our own national economy on a high scale and have told the international bankers to go jump in the ocean.

Instead of doing this, we lowered the tariff bars and we started importing goods, merchandise and commodities to collect the war debts. From 1919 to 1929, over a period of 11 years, according to government figures, we imported goods to a total of more than $43 billion. By the time Mr. Coolidge was going out of office, it was apparent to all students of national and international economy that the American economic setup had been wrecked by these wild imports. Mr. Coolidge, being an astute student of national and international economy, stepped out from under with the memorable phrase, "I do not choose to run."

Mr. Hoover came into office and inherited a condition which was bound to blow up in his face. . . .

Naturally, $43 billion worth of foreign imports closed down, or put on part-time, our manufacturing industry and created an army of unemployed which we said was 12 million strong. Nobody knows how many. Imports of agricultural products took away the American market from the American farmer and he was faced with crops he could not sell.

The administration called the American farmers' crops surplus and sought to deal with them as surplus. Actually, the surplus consisted of imports which replaced the American market, and actually, the American farmer, in the overall picture, did not have a surplus. . . .

Mr. Hoover took office on the 4th day of March 1929. Mr. Hoover took a most proper action in passing an Executive Order declaring a moratorium on the collection of war debts.

In the meantime, out of the sale of the $43 billion worth of imports, the international bankers received their money. The international bankers were the "US" that was going to be paid all the time. . . .

One thing Mr. Hoover overlooked was that England, France, Holland and Italy had credits in American banks in the amount roughly of $3.5 billion . . . he overlooked this most vital matter when his Executive Order went into effect. The $3.5 billion credit was left subject to draft. . . . At that time we could not spare $3.5 billion worth of gold and still maintain the legal gold reserve. When the gold supply was depleted $3.5 billion, it became necessary for United States banks to reduce their deposits.

But the banks could not reduce their deposits without first making collections from their customers to whom the depositors' money had been loaned; therefore, the banks were under the necessity of enforcing collection. When they went out to collect they found their customers could not raise the funds with which to pay.

The banks were compelled to unload stocks and bonds which they held as security against loans and the natural result was the great stock market crash in New York in October 1929.

# [7] REPARATIONS

*Direct quotation notes from speeches by Congressman Louis T. McFadden of Pennsylvania, delivered before the Government Club, New York City, April 7, 1930; before the Bethesda, Maryland, Chamber of Commerce, December 7, 1931; and before the House of Representatives, December 20, 1930, February 14, 1931 and May 4, 1933, as printed in the* CONGRESSIONAL RECORD *and in* COLLECTIVE SPEECHES OF CONGRESSMAN LOUIS T. MCFADDEN.

The Germans signed the armistice agreement after a long series of negotiations between President Wilson and the German Chancellor in October. These negotiations ended in a peace agreement which was binding on both sides when the armistice came into effect. It provided for reparation payments which were less than a fourth of the sum afterwards fixed by the London Ultimatum. . . .

The official peace conference convened late in January, and in the meantime . . . conquest of Germany by the slow pressure of a food blockade, carefully concealed from the President and the trans-Atlantic audience, was well under way. . . . By the end of March the land and sea blockade of Germany was doing its work. The German government asked upon what terms the blockade would be lifted and food supplied, and a conference was arranged at Brussels to fix these terms. Germany delivered up all the gold in the Reichsbank and all the negotiable securities . . . and accepted the obligation to pay reparations in an indefinite sum and for an indefinite future to be fixed by her conquerors. In return she received a contract for the delivery in her ports of a fixed quantity of grain and foodstuffs per month for a definite number of months. Thomas Lamont and Norman Davis were the American members of this commission. . . .

The Germans carried out the terms of this agreement, but the peace conference did not. There was fear that if food now reached Germany she might reject some of the terms agreed upon and those yet to be imposed. No food ships, therefore, were allowed to dock at German ports until after the Treaty of Versailles was signed on June 28, 1919. . . .

[The U.S.] Senate did not ratify the Treaty of Versailles, and in declining to ratify the Treaty it incidentally declined to ratify the war settlement with Germany. . . . But as the years passed, the Supreme War Council, not discouraged, continued to stage the elaborate drama of German reparations for the benefit of the trans-Atlantic audience . . . the London Ultimatum of 1921 . . . created negotiable German reparation bonds in the sum of $33 billion belonging to the Allied States with a view to disposing of them chiefly in the United States. . . .

It was to the American public then that the bulk of the German reparation bonds were to be sold, and to accomplish this purpose a systematic falsification of historical, financial and economic fact was necessary in order to create in America a state of mind that would make the sale of the bonds successful. . . .

The hypnotic trance in which the paid American publicists, the political college professors have lived . . . enabled the international financiers to use their voices and pens to keep the political deception alive. Because the definite allied postwar policy has been to secure the quick return from America of the gold stock lost by Europe in the war. . . .

In proportion, as the United States increas[ed] its holdings of German reparation bonds, the allied Governments decreas[ed] their holdings of them, for it [was] from the allied Governments that the American investors [bought] bonds. . . . What was done in the London Ultimatum, the Dawes Plan, and the Young Plan leaves small doubt that it was the intention of the makers of the Treaty of Versailles that American investors in these bonds should pay the German indemnity to the allied states in cash. . . .

Someone had asked Mr. Ogden Mills what caused the Depression [of the 1930s]. He answered quite truthfully, "The Federal Reserve lent so much money abroad that it broke down the system."

## [8] FOUNDATIONS

*Extract from* TAX EXEMPT FOUNDATIONS, *Report of the Special Committee to Investigate Tax-Exempt Foundations and Comparable Organizations, House of Representatives, 83rd Congress, 2nd Session, 1954, pps. 18-19.*

As indicated by their arrogance in dealing with this Committee, the major foundations and their associated intermediary organizations have intrenched themselves behind a totality of power which presumes to place them beyond serious criticism and attack. . . .

Research in the social sciences plays a key part in the evolution of our society. Such research is now almost wholly in the control of the professional employees of the large foundations and their obedient satellites. Even the great sums allotted by the federal government for social science research have come into the virtual control of this professional group. . . . [This] concentration of power has tended to support the dangerous "cultural lag" theory and to promote "moral relativity" to the detriment of our basic moral, religious, and governmental principles. It has tended to support the concept of "social engineering"—that "social scientists" and they alone are capable of guiding us into better ways of living and improved or substituted fundamental principles of action. . . .

In the so-called Walsh Investigation, which took place in 1917, both

Samuel Untermyer and Louis D. Brandeis concluded that the foundation as a perpetuity was 'inconsistent with democratic conceptions."

## [9] ALIEN INFLUENCES

*Extract from* ALIEN INFLUENCES IN AMERICA, *by George N. Peek and John Lee Coulter, Economic Council Papers, Vol. II, No. 8, December 1943, p. 13.*

In passing, it is to be noted that the explanation usually given for producing and exporting mineral and agricultural products has been in order to create foreign exchange balances needed to finance imports of exotic foreign materials such as tea, coffee, cocoa, spices, sugar, rubber, silk, jute, wool and other fibers, special strategic and critical materials not readily available in quantity or quality desired for use within this country (including freight, marine insurance and other charges). Slight emphasis has been placed upon the large amount of dollar exchange absorbed in capital transactions which, prior to 1940, equalled or exceeded the amount absorbed by merchandise transactions . . . in 1919 the balance of all capital transactions absorbed less than 9% of the volume of our total dollar settlements for trade and all other current transactions; in 1935 over half; in 1939 approximately two-thirds. . . . As capital transactions increased merchandise transactions declined.

## [10] THE PAGEANT OF CUBA

*Extract from* THE PAGEANT OF CUBA, *by Hudson Strode, 1934, pps. 248-279.*

By no means did sugar prosperity affect only the cities and the business centers of that island. Like a good angel and a nemesis, like a double-edged sword which the Cubans lacked the skill to handle, the sugar boom also penetrated the civilization of the *bohio* and the very depths of the jungle. Everything bowed before the royal decree, "Clear more land to plant cane." And the magnificent primeval forests, bowing beneath the dread command, assumed a prominent but sorrowful role in the Cuban pageant. No country on earth is more rich in the blessings of its woods than the Pearl of the Antilles. Forty excellent cabinet and building woods are grown in Cuban forests: mahogany, rosewood, logwood, ebony, the fragrant Spanish elm. In clearing up land to make way for sugar, Cubans felled and burned phalanxes of century-old royal palms, which yielded food, milk, rope and numerous necessities of pleasant life, [and they] were sacrificed to the Great God Sugar.

And with more subtle significance the coming of the sugar industry on a large scale changed the world of the peasant. Formerly the rural Cuban had squatted so contentedly on his square of land which produced about everything he wanted, that a German peddler coined the immortal phrase: The "damned wantlessness" of the Cuban countryman.

Now with his land sold to the sugar corporations, he found himself a part of a great industrial enterprise, which provided him with a house and wages on its own terms. Temperamentally he was unsuited to this stream of modern industrial progress in which he found himself. And as Mr. Jenks [another writer] quotes from a sympathetic American, "He has no part in directing this industrial giant; he has no voice in its management. Yet to it he must look for education, recreation, and bread. He has, willy-nilly, exchanged a simple life for a vassalage to a foreign colossus. His future is not his own. It is determined for him in a director's room in New York."

As wealth accumulated and the Cubans indulged their pleasure loving instincts in an orgy of extravagance, men decayed, and education and worthwhile activities degenerated. As if Cuba were the only spot on the globe where sugar could be raised, more and more cane land was put into cultivation. At the peak of the prosperity delirium, in the summer of 1920, economic reports revealed an overproduction of sugar in various parts of the world.

The market, satiated with sugar, turned sick with nausea and fright. The price of sugar began to slide. It shot from 22½ cents to three percent in 1921. . . . Speculation was in a frenzy of dismay. The fabric of business crumbled. The American banks which had made enormous loans to finance the sugar crop on the basis of high prices, found themselves with their security wiped out. Virtually all the Cuban banks collapsed. Wall Street stepped into the breach and American capital dominated Cuban economic life. Cuba woke from its hangover to find itself in the hands of absentee landlords. Three-fourths of the sugar industry was owned by American stockholders. During the next decade the railways, the public utilities, the tobacco industry, and the mines came under the control of American corporations.

## [11] RAW MATERIALS

*Extract from* INTERNATIONAL CONTROL OF MINERALS, *Studies made by the Committee of the Mining and Metallurgical Society of America on Foreign and Domestic Mining Policy and the Committee of the American Institute of Mining and Metallurgical Engineers on Industrial Preparedness, 1925, page 10.*

5. Freedom Of Exploration is to be Preserved in Backward Countries.

Where backward countries possess important mineral supplies needed by the world we can see no escape from the conclusion, whatever the ethical merits of the case, that demand will make itself felt through political pressure of other countries. In such cases we favor joint action by governments to secure equal opportunities for all nationals. If circumstances require that pressure be brought by one government, the end to be sought should be the opening up of the territory not only to the government bringing the pressure for its exclusive benefit, but to all nationals. Disregard of this principle has been the cause of much international friction.

## [12] OIL

*Extract from* THE POLITICS OF OIL, *by Robert Engler, 1961 pps. 69-73, 202, 204-206, and 265.*

[Iranian Oil] had been the largest Middle Eastern crude source and Abadan the world's largest refinery. Great Britain was receiving more in taxes from the profits than was Iran [for selling the oil], a smoldering source of contention in all oil producing countries. . . . When in 1951 the group headed by Premier Mohammed Mossadegh moved zealously for nationalization of the Anglo-Iranian Oil Company operations; the Americans were presented with a new opportunity as a result of actions in which they were participants and beneficiaries. . . . Iran had been the first country to receive Point Four aid. Now the limited assistance of $1 million for the fiscal year 1951 was increased to $23 million in 1952 and in 1953. But the Western nations and companies expected that Mossadegh could not last in office. They grew tougher in their determination to break him or force a settlement on their terms. At one point the State Department apparently advised him to make arrangements with Shell if he could not allow the return of Anglo-Iranian. The premier grew increasingly intransigent as he learned more about the realities of an integrated world industry. He wanted Iran to be able to sell its oil in abundant quantities, not set by the dictates of the industry's private production plans. The large-scale purchasers he needed could not be found. Iran had the oil, but without the technicians, the markets, and the transportation it was caught by a system of power that, at least for the short run, was able to get along without these supplies.

Requests to the United States by Mossadegh for additional loans to meet budgetary needs aggravated by the complete loss of oil revenues were turned down. In the closing days of the regime, President Eisenhower made clear the position of the United States in support of Anglo-Iranian:

"There is a strong feeling in the United States . . . that it would not be fair to the American taxpayers for the United States Government to extend any considerable amount of economic aid to Iran so long as Iran could have access to funds derived from the sale of its oil and oil products if a reasonable agreement were reached. . . ."

There is evidence that the United States also worked behind the scenes for the overthrow of Mossadegh that came in August 1953, with the Central Intelligence Agency playing a key part. Questions about the United States' role in Iran and about the activities of this secret arm of the United States—which operates with a budget and personnel concealed from the Congress and the public—are generally shunted aside or remarks placed "off the record."

When Mossadegh was being replaced, it was the American-trained and equipped army of the Shah that supported his military successor who was pledged to come to terms with the Western private and public powers. Major General George C. Stewart, Director of the United States Office of Military Assistance of the Department of Defense, later testified that— ". . . when this crisis came on and the thing was about to collapse, we violated our normal criteria and among the other things we did, we provided the army immediately on an emergency basis blankets, boots, uniforms, electric generators, and medical supplies that permitted and created an atmosphere in which they could support the Shah. . . . The guns that they had in their hands, the trucks that they rode in, the armored cars that they drove through the streets, and the radio communications that permitted their control, were all furnished through the military defense assistance program . . . had it not been for this program, a government unfriendly to the United States probably would now be in power."

I have included these several notes without comment for reasons that will become clear to readers as they follow the rest of this book.

Nevertheless, the central theme of this book is stranger than fiction. I have developed it exactly as I found it—first a stray clue or two, then hours of taped interviews with Carl H. Wilken, finally the research that made the economic riddle come clear. My tapes are edited, of course, yet after several reviews I am satisfied that they retain their intellectual honesty. My sources and footnotes—in the main—are cited in the running text. Any intelligent student can locate published works and citations with the information provided. Other sources, such as field notes, private papers, correspondence, and photographs have been turned over to the University of Iowa.

There are several sections in this book. Each depends on the other, and yet each can stand alone.

Students will want to read the entire book. Casual readers may want to start on page 151 in order to enjoy continuity, and read through to the end before studying pages 1 to 150.

In the final analysis, this is not an uncritical tract. It is, rather, the biography of an idea that has withstood every scholarly assault for over 70 years.

Certainly, this might have been an epistolary presentation, one given with abstracts and extracts only, each entry a direct quote and a structured part of the whole. So it is, in a manner of speaking. I have merely assembled the papers and records and written out nonfiction lines. These lines tell about decline and fall, but they tell a great deal more. Indeed, as Will Durant has noted, power in kingdoms rests with kings, in theocracies with priests, and in democracies with money. This is the story of how money rules through raw materials.

*— Charles Walters*
Raytown, Missouri

# CHAPTER 1: THE INTERVIEW

An interview requires preparation, and the interview for which I had traveled to Miami, Florida required more than most. Carl H. Wilken was then the surviving member of a fantastic triumvirate, the last active worker of the old Raw Materials National Council. For a span of almost a decade Carl H. Wilken, Charles B. Ray and Dr. John Lee Coulter gave more testimony to various committees of Congress than all other non-government experts combined. It was their testimony which resulted in the famous Steagall Amendment, the one that established a 90-92.5% of parity floor under basic farm crops in 1942, and for the "two year period beginning with the first day of January immediately following the date . . . that hostilities in the present war [have been declared] terminated."

The Raw Materials National Council had issued certain claims about all this, and I was familiar with many of them. At a time when President Harry S. Truman was predicting 5 to 6 million unemployed and a national income below that of 1946, Carl Wilken and his associates argued to the contrary. A slump, they said, was impossible because the Steagall Amendment was still in force, and a depression could not develop as long as farm income maintained its parity. A big question in 1947 was over a tax reduction bill, one that President Truman did not want and therefore twice vetoed, and one that Congress passed over Truman's veto largely on the basis of testimony by Wilken, Ray and Coulter.

Though the economic climate changed rapidly after that, 1947 and 1948 were years during which the Council of Economic Advisers thought chiefly in terms of the proper relationship between wages, profits and farm income. Both Edwin Nourse, the first economic chief under the Employment Act of 1946, and his Vice Chairman and successor, Leon Keyserling, argued structural balance, not *laissez faire*. "The long-range agricultural policy of the Government should be aimed at preserving the family-sized farm and preventing another agricultural depression as we go through the readjustments following the Second World War," read the section marked *Agriculture* in the first *Economic Report of the President*. "It should help to see that farmers' incomes do not fall below those earned by other comparable productive groups." Never really at home with abstract ideas, Truman leaned more to the kind of thinking then coming out of Secretary of Treasury John Snyder's office—hence the first toe-hold for forces that had brought the country to near ruin in the late 20s and early 30s.

Much of Carl Wilken's thought had been refined before the late 1930s, when he appeared before a Sioux City, Iowa based hearing on the Pope-McGill Bill, October 19, 1937. Although Wilken styled himself as a corn and livestock farmer at the time, he was testifying as President of the Progressive Farmers of Iowa, a 7,000 member group, 99% of which, he said, were active farmers. He filed two briefs with the Committee that day, one a critique of legislation then being offered, the second a farm bill Wilken believed statesmanship required. Calling attention to his first brief, Wilken noted "that under our present marketing system there is no relationship whatever between quantity of production and price. . . ." Of the 26 grain crops produced between 1909 and 1934, the 13 largest sold for more per bushel than the 13 smallest. Wilken also established beyond doubt that the credit system was chiefly responsible for fluctuation in farm prices, "because the farmer is compelled to depend upon private capital and world markets in the liquidation of his crops."

There were certain principles, Wilken said, that were essential to legislation dealing with agriculture. Any measure must—

1. Be constitutional.
2. Yield parity or equal exchange value prices for farm products.
3. Provide for storage of seasonal and periodical surpluses.
4. Provide means for disposal of surpluses.
5. Protect the American farmer and keep him in possession of the American market.
6. Provide for new uses of farm crops and encourage new industries to consume them.
7. Promote sound land-use policies.
8. Be operative without regimentation of land or men.
9. Protect taxpayers and consumers.
10. Divorce commodities from gold as the base for credit.

"We have a right to criticize, because we have something better to offer," Wilken told both Senators James P. Pope and George McGill at that hearing. The two conflicting philosophies of economics—"that based on scarcity of domestic production supplemented by imports, and the opposing economy which calls for plentiful production and utilization became the best argument for "something better" until Carl Wilken passed from the scene in December 1968.

It was during the Pope-McGill Hearings of 1937 that Wilken and his associates unveiled the 1-7 theorem. O.L. Brownlee, the editor of the *Sioux City Tribune*, and a member of the Wilken team, was there to testify. He stated the proposition thus: "We find that there is a very definite relationship of about 1 to 7 between the farm income and the national income. . . ."

By the time the Pope-McGill Hearings had ended, the record had come clear on one point. Two more or less conflicting theories of economics claimed attention. Both relied on precepts that were seldom stated openly. Both called to witness the facts of history, and both appealed to what everyone believed to be common knowledge. The trouble was that both could not be right.

Almost all economists—including John Maynard Keynes and Milton Friedman—had signed on with the proposition that investment was the engine that drove the economy, even if it was debt-based. The raw materials economists anwered, "No, the real economics engine is earned income based on the parity monetization of raw materials.

In the late '30s, the standard bearers for a parity economy set the stage for a grand sweep. Yet hardly a decade later the drive seemed to have spent itself, leaving the old way of thinking in command of the field. Why? Perhaps Wilken could answer the questions and explain the answers! As I viewed it, the clash was over much more than rural fundamentalism. It was over a foundation concept. Scholarship and proof seemed to favor this small band of Cassandras who started their crusade as the Raw Materials National Council. But those opposed to a full income for rural America had the weight of institutional power in their camp.

In 1946 the nation's banking fraternity organized its Committee for a New Public Debt Policy, W. Randolph Burgess, chairman. Out in California, also, the Bank of America sparked a Committee of 100 drive to "get Jerry Voorhis," a friend of farm parity and an advocate of low interest rates. Thus while Richard M. Nixon was swinging into orbit in 1946, Carl H. Wilken and his associates were already on the way down. The last of the big battles were fought while an unsuspecting public cheered its own undoing.

The Aiken Bill came on strong in 1948, riding high on misspent ingenuity and carrying its flag of a 60-90% sliding scale for agriculture. Again, relying on testimony by Wilken and his associate the House refused to approve the Aiken Bill. Thus in the last hours of the 80th Congress (the one Truman characterized as the "worst in history"), the House revealed at least some statesmanship by accepting the Aiken Bill only after restoring a 90% farm price support feature temporarily. As a matter of compromise the Senate agreed to go along for one more year, and the predicted slump of 1948 did not appear.

My notes on the passage of events were cryptic enough. In the interview, I hoped to develop them further. There was the 81st Congress and the Brannan plan to socialize agriculture, a plan that was checked in part with facts presented by Carl H. Wilken. Finally, the one year extension of 90% price supports for farm crops expired, and the new generals were winning. Foundations and various shades of pitch men were funding confusion with minions while a few friends of agriculture were trying to scratch together a budget of $25,000—enough to keep Carl Wilken and a secretary on the job in 1950.

The job was staggering. Its ramifications ran beyond instant comprehension. If Wilken and his associates were right, then economic literature would have to be rewritten almost from scratch, and the few hardy souls who had questioned the establishment and its bought and paid for education machine would have to be reinvested with academic status. The consequences of Wilken's findings would help millions and dethrone a few thousand.

Outside of the hearing halls, the metes and bounds of Wilken's thought emerged as "The Key to Prosperity" in the December 1944 issue of *Country Gentleman*. America, Wilken argued, could have any level of prosperity it wanted. As reported by E.H. Taylor, the basic premises emerged thus: "All the major interests in our economy are geared to the same controlling factor. The value of manufacturers, labor, payrolls and employment, retail sales, transportation income and volume of construction work are limited by farm income. They follow its course, for better or worse, at an interval of roughly three to six months."

Taylor reported these findings as flowing from the National Association of Commissioners, Secretaries and Directors of Agriculture of the 48 states, and they did, but the trail led straight to Carl Wilken of the Raw Materials National Council of Sioux City and Washington, Charles B. Ray, an engineer and business counsellor of Chicago, and Dr. John Lee Coulter, former president of North Dakota A&M and a one-time head and member of the U.S. Tariff Commission.

In summary form, "The Key to Prosperity" stated that "raw material income, most potently that of agriculture, is the prime mover in our national economy." Further, the research findings "demonstrate, for the first time, that there is a natural law—the law of exchange—which controls the whole complex system by which we live."

"What the research men found," the *Country Gentleman* article continued, "is that there is a rate of turnover to this raw-material income as it passes through the various stages of economic use. This is the key to the whole matter. For the national income is then simply the amount of raw material income times the rate of turnover. The nation's wage fund, the manufacturing output possible and the amount of public purchasing power are fixed by this turn of raw-material dollars."

The records of a century of economic activity proved, Taylor wrote, that the nation's income is bounded by this factor. "The rule did not vary, but the rate of turn has accelerated, due to the increased efficiency in both raw-material production and manufacturing. In 1850 one half of our labor force was required in the production of raw materials and the turnover was only twice. By 1925-29 our national efficiency had risen so that a much smaller part of our population was required to produce the raw materials and the turn for the five-year period averaged 3.9. It is now up to a five-fold turn, with only one fifth of our working population engaged in raw-material production."

Two other paragraphs more or less summed up the gist of what Wilken and his associates were saying and they both deserved circulation well beyond anything they were likely to receive.

One read as follows:

"Thus farm income appears to be a key factor in our system of making a living. It becomes of tremendous importance to all our after war plans for the full use of our machines and tools and the employment of an increased labor force. These plans cannot work unless an adequate farm income is provided. For this research shows that the total fund to be distributed among all working groups and to finance the Government's obligations will approximate only seven times the total farm income."

And the last paragraph I noted said:

"A parity—or equal exchange—price level for farm products, it thus becomes obvious, is not simply a matter of fairness to the people engaged in agriculture. It is a matter of direct self-interest to those in every other group in America. What they make, sell and earn is equally at stake."

One other item was fitted into the dossier I carried to Miami early in January 1967. It was a reprint of an article by Wilken, "The Way to Maintain Prosperity," which had appeared in the June 1950 issue of *Country Gentleman*. As a restatement of "Key to Prosperity," it merely brought things up to date, but as an example of Wilken speaking for himself it drove home points that had become the foundation concepts behind all of Wilken's thinking.

"Raw material income," wrote Wilken, "the new wealth annually created by production, is the start of this cycle of exchange. The study revealed that there is a constant rate of turnover and pyramiding of this raw material income as it passes through the various stages of our economic cycle. It is the key to the whole matter, for it sets the limits to the amount of national income that can be distributed among the different working groups. This rate of turnover is five times the raw material income, seven times that of agriculture.

"It is really a labor turn. One worker out of five is now engaged in producing raw materials, one farmer averages enough production to supply himself and six others. Our economy in practical reality becomes an exchange between these and other groups producing the goods and services necessary for our standard of living, with the initial raw material and farm income fixing the volume this exchange can attain."

Wilken went on to state that a drop in farm income meant a drop in national income on a ratio of 7. In all this research the farmer came off as a biological person, one no better than other human beings, true, *but his money was much better*. Agriculture supplied the best part of the raw material income, and its income was the "most sensitive and active part of this combination. Its products are mostly the kind that quickly enter into use, generating a rapid turnover. Also farm income is distributed among a large number of individuals, while more than one half our labor force is engaged in processing and distributing the products of agriculture. A drop in farm prices is carried through this whole economic circuit."

By chapter and verse Wilken detailed the cause and the effect as he perceived them. 'The nation, he wrote, always enjoyed prosperity when farm prices were at parity. Economic trouble always arrived after agricultural prices fell out of line. The recent depression of the 1930s matched cause with effect. When farm prices rose in 1937, the Depression seemed over. When they dropped in the last part of that year, the sliding aspects of 1938 were already in the making. As a result, fully 1 million workers found themselves out of work that year, and the Depression seemed to have a new lease on life.

"As a matter of fact," wrote Wilken, "for the 10-year period, 1930-1939, farm prices averaged 82% of their 1929 parity and factory employment averaged 81%. Our volume of farm production and its price levels were too low to generate the income necessary for full employment."

Then came the war and following the war came 1946. At that time the nation's economists were routinely predicting a depression. Congress, scared half out of its wits, passed the "full" Employment Act of 1946 that year, and the powers that be were busily at work structuring lower farm prices "so people could eat." Yet at that time Wilken and his associates made a different forecast. On the basis of high farm production and strong price level, using its natural trade turn, he calculated a national income and buying power large enough to assure full employment. This was the actual result.

If Wilken was right, and the new breed with their new economic theory period were wrong, then the Brannan Plan—the principles of which were highly touted in the *Journal of Farm Economics*—was dead wrong, and would lead straight into a business depression or a wild inflation supported by debt. Briefly, the Brannan Plan that came on after Truman humbled

Dewey, called for dollar payments to farmers themselves, with actual farm prices determined at the market.

".. . the Secretary fails to realize the significance of the trade turn of the farm dollar. It is the value at which it enters the system of exchange that is all important. Its turnover determines the total income that will be available to other interests in the economy. . . . The dollars paid to the farmers in production payments would have performed none of the work of generating new income in passing through the various stages of the economic cycle."

Everything Wilken said seemed clear enough, yet I doubted that one person in a thousand understood him. There was a bit of Henry George here, it seemed, and I made a note of a passage in *Progress and Poverty* in which George spoke of "cessation in demand for some commodities, which marks the depression of trade," and another in which he sought a solution that was too easily cut down by the revolving teeth of existing institutions—the single land tax! But it was the approach of the physiocrat that struck home: "The primary and fundamental occupations, which create a demand for all others, are evidently those which extract wealth from nature, and hence, if we trace from one exchange to another, this check to production feeds itself into every level of the economy."

And there was a bit of Say's Law of Markets in Wilken, Jean Baptiste Say, whose Chapter 15, Book I of *Treatise on Political Economy* had been quoted, paraphrased and analyzed for over a century because it seemed so obviously true and so obviously false. Say's Law might be stated as follows: The act of production creates the credits that enable consumption of that production, ergo supply creates demand because human wants are insatiable. Perhaps Wilken could explain in detail what many thinkers understood less than perfectly as an abstraction. Yet nowhere in my notes could I find a Wilken appeal to economic theory, technocracy, or the ever recurring call for a fundamental restructuring of the nation's economic institutions. Wilken's appeals were almost always for informed political action. "At the present time the world is threatened with communism," was the message Congressman Ben F. Jensen caused to be published in *The Congressional Record*, April 14, 1947. "The cure for communism is prosperity and there is no other. The formula of $1 of gross farm income which creates $7 of national income is the yardstick which Mr. Wilken has uncovered in his research work and given to us for guidance."

Wilken, it seemed, discussed more than exchange, and the parity laws of the 1940s involved more than fair prices for farmers. Nothing less than the creation of money was involved in the Wilken system, and yet the subject was being barely mentioned.

I expected high drama in that interview. That public policy had taken a different turn did not trouble me. I knew that politicians were imprisoned by ideas just as were the economists who tried to explain away the fact of depressions and rash inequities without examining cause and effect on the proper plane of observation. I knew too that more good ideas die each year than are preserved simply because the community is incapable of evaluating an idea on its own merits. Not a little press agentry has to accompany the sale of any idea, and press agents are not often on the side of the angels. The few scraps of information on Wilken already indicated that powerful concepts had become the planks for a system he didn't even style as a "theory."

# CHAPTER 2: TAPE NO. 1

*The questions proceed in my best Studs Terkel style. I now allow Carl Wilken's answers to speak for themselves, always setting the stage for the chapters that follow.*

Q. Mr. Wilken, in the *Country Gentleman* articles it was stated that all major interests in the economy are geared to the same controlling factor, and that national income is limited by farm income. Can you explain that line of reasoning a little more?

WILKEN. Every farm is a factory—for milk, meat, grain. That's the farmers manufactured product. How did he manufacture it? By means of combining the soil and moisture and sunshine with his labor and capital. This farm production becomes a big share of industry's raw materials. One of the big questions economists pose is, "Which comes first?" Common sense ought to tell them the answer. The farmer really precedes the rest of the economy by 16 years for the simple reason that the products of the farm have to feed labor from the time of birth to 16 years of age before the new human being goes into the labor supply.

Q. In your published statements, you and your associates made reference to a trade turn or multiplier. According to these findings, you say that national income is nothing more than raw material income times 5, or farm income times 7. What in fact governs this ratio or trade turn?

WILKEN. It starts with efficiency. Going back to 1787, some nine out of ten people were farmers. But by 1850 only half the people were farming and mining and so on. So the trade turn moved up to 2—or one farmer was required to feed two people. In the 1910-1914 period, the turn came to about 5. If the trade turn is computed in terms of all raw materials, that ratio still holds today [1970]. If you compute earned national income on the basis of farm income, then the ratio is 7. To illustrate the point—from 1929 to 1933, gross farm income fell off $6.8 billion, and the national income fell $47.6 billion, or $7 of national income was lost for every dollar of farm income lost. This ratio still holds. In 1945, when the farmer got $14.2 billion net income, it was a trade turn of 7.01. From 1928 to 1953, the trade turn averaged 7.04. In other words, for a ten year period that involved both war years and a post-war period—and when we had

90% price supports for basic farm crops—the trade turn proved out at $6.97 of national income for every dollar of farm income. Now agricultural income has continued to turn out an *earned income* on the ratio of approximately 7, but this is hardly half enough income to operate the economy. I call this a *shortage*. The rest of the income—the *unearned income*—has been developed by injecting borrowed money into the economy. Between 1951 [and] 1964 the national economy sustained an operating loss of $3,300 billion. This happens to duplicate what happened between 1929 and 1942, when we lost $563 billion of income because we didn't maintain the 1929 price level on farm products. During the Depression years we absorbed the loss by doing without $563 billion of goods. During that period, also, we started with the Keynesian theory and government programs, but by not getting farm income back up to the appropriate level, we simply liquidated just about as much private debt between 1929 and 1940 as we added to federal debt through government programs. The total debt at the end of 1940 was almost exactly the same as it was in 1929. It was not until 1941, when our income got back to the 1929 level, that the 12 central states got back to the 1929 income level.

Q. When you say *earned income* and *income generated by debt*, exactly what do you mean?

WILKEN. It takes about $5.50 of national income to pay $1.00 interest made necessary by capital debt creation. Don't confuse this with operating debt. You see, the idea behind the Fed was that money could be created and extinguished when the crop came in. When you borrow to put in a crop or stock inventory, you have what amounts to a floor plan debt. It has to be paid off as soon as the crop is in or the merchandise sold. The lending institution has a claim against income generated this way, and it has that claim first. In other words, the bank takes repayment for the loan off the top. I'm not talking about that kind of debt. I'm talking about *capital debt*— the kind of debt that is being injected into this economy because income has been short due to underpayment to agriculture. An economy can only expand its production facilities, or its capital investment, out of profit. It cannot borrow capital beyond its ability to generate profits to pay it off. Operating debt has to be paid on an as-you-go basis. So do expenses and other costs in doing business. This means capital has to come out of profits, and repayment of capital debt has to come out of profits. And interest has to be paid out of profits. Now here is what is happening. By injecting debt into the economy—capital debt—the nation manages to earn about $4 of national income for every dollar of new capital debt. That's income generated by debt. But it takes about $5.50 of national income to generate a single dollar of profit with which to either pay interest or liquidate any part of that capital debt. As a result, we now [circa 1967] have over $1.5 trillion public and private debt, and it will be very near $2 trillion* by the end of the decade. At 7%, money doubles itself once every 10 years on compound interest. The thing that's wrong with income generated by debt is that it cannot be paid, and eventually it cannot be carried. That's the situation in the country right now.

Q. Within this framework, what is the situation in farming?

WILKEN. About the same. Halfway through the '60s, in spite of all the prosperity you hear about, this economy lacked $73 billion of having enough income to balance with wages and interest. Some $68 billion of that was the shortage of income for farm operators, farm business, and corporate profit after taxes. Without earned income, here's what happens. A young man inherits a farm or business. He goes out, he wants to expand to stay even, so he borrows some money, and then he borrows some more. Pretty soon he's in over his head, and he can't borrow enough to cover the interest on the loans as they fall due. Finally he loses the entire business. That's what we're doing to the United States.

Q. Does this multiplier you call a trade turn prevail in all economies? Does it hold in the Russian socialist economy, for instance?

WILKEN. They all have a trade turn, but they all have different trade turns. In Russia, I believe they have a trade turn of about 2.

Q. What accounts for the difference?

WILKEN. Efficiency of agricultural production, basically. We talk a lot about efficiency—farm efficiency and labor efficiency. Well, most of our labor efficiency is brought about by capital investment in machines. In other words, the average workman in a factory works less in terms of physical energy than he did 20 years ago. Labor organizations have taken this machine efficiency and bargained it into twice as much increase as labor is entitled to receive. On the other hand, agriculture—because of its efficiency, machine efficiency included—has been penalized with a reduction in prices. When agriculture produces enough to release a man to work in another field the trade turn goes up. Now to illustrate this: in 1787 nine out of every ten people in the country were farmers, and it was farmers who drafted the Constitution of the United States. I don't think the present group of intellectuals could draft a constitution equal to the one our forebears drafted.** Nowadays, they've got too many theories involved. They haven't got the practical common sense and down-to-earth thinking to write a constitution. The Constitution of the United States

---

* Gross public and private debt came to $1.9351 trillion by the end of the decade, or $44.9 billion short of Wilken's off-hand estimate.

** Rexford G. Tugwell, a former member of FDR's New Deal brain trust, has written a 10,000-word, 11-article model under the auspices of the Center for the Study of Democratic Institutions. It recommends a single term for the president, life terms for Senators, and

is a wonderful document. And the whole economy is tied up in Article 1, Section 8, in which Congress was given the right to establish a monetary system and to issue money, which became the dollar, and to regulate the value thereof, which is price. And—also—to protect it with import duties, or whatever it might take. This is the same article that gives Congress the right and duty to regulate weights and measures. This is significant. In Europe, they set up the metric system. Well, in the first session of Congress they set up our weights and measures system, and our money system. They had two purposes in mind. One, to start to protect the development of industry in the United States. Two, to maintain the value of money and to run the government. At first we supported the federal government with import fees and two excise taxes. From 1797 we ran the government that way. In 1914 we brought in the income tax. To illustrate: in 1910 it took $680 million to operate the government of the United States. In 1966 it took $137 billion. Well, where are these additional dollars going to come from? There are only two sources. One is production, and the second is the price of that production. In 1789 we passed a sugar tariff. At that time it was 2 cents a pound. At 2 cents a pound with wages at about 50 cents a day, it was a pretty high tariff. Why? We wanted sugar. We wanted to bring about domestic sugar production.

Q. When did the development of American agriculture start to deliver a trade turn of more than 1 for 1?

WILKEN. About 1850. At that time we had developed our resources to the point where we could release one man to go into other lines of endeavor. We had a 2 times trade turn.

Q. But the United States was not a leader in international trade?

WILKEN. We were not a big trading nation. When Lincoln was president the question came up whether we should import the steel from Europe to build our railroad system, or whether we should produce the steel ourselves. And Lincoln said something like this: I don't know much about rails and tariffs and I don't know much about railroads, but here's one thing I do know. If we produce the steel ourselves, then we'll have both the rails and the money. So the United States built up its steel industry. Starting from that time, and up to 1929, we built a steel industry that was producing half the steel in the world. And most of that production was being used in the United States.

Q. What was the multiplier, or trade turn, around the pre-World War I era?

---

republics to take over the states. Tugwell was quoted by *The Wall Street Journal*, September 9, 1970, as characterizing the old Constitution as "primitive in the extreme." One of the heads at the Center has been Paul Hoffman, the same Paul Hoffman who helped launch the Committee for Economic Development (CED).

WILKEN. In the 1910-1914 period, we had a trade turn of about 4.5 to 1. In short the national income was about 4.5 times bigger than the gross farm income. It was during this period that we brought in most of the big machinery on farms. We brought in the horse-drawn gang plow and the horse-drawn eight-foot binder, all big equipment. We developed the harvesting of grain by running it through a binder and tying it in bundles. We developed the threshing machine. It was moving fast. By 1921, and until 1953, the trade turn in terms of agriculture reached 7.

Q. We understand, according to your calculations, that this trade turn has pretty much stabilized itself since that time.

WILKEN. Well, in 1929 we had $87.8 billion of national income and we had $13.9 billion of gross farm income. In making calculation, you have to be careful to use the gross realized farm income figure. You see, there are half a dozen different kinds of farm income, according to the statisticians. Now in 1933 the gross farm income was $7.1 billion. If you subtract that from $13.9 billion, you'll have a drop of $6.8 billion. According to the economic theories, that kind of a drop would have been a great benefit because it made food cheaper, and people presumably could buy more. That's the supply and demand idea, but it does not take into account how income is created in the first place. You have an illustration of how it works in the records. When that farm income drop took place, national income dropped from $87.8 billion down to $40.2 billion, a drop of $47.6 billion. If you'll divide the $6.8 billion into $47.6, you'll find how we get this 7 times ratio. Remember, because of low payment to agriculture, we continued to lose national income all through the Depression and through 1940. Then in the pickup from 1940 to 1943, we increased our gross farm income $11 billion to $23.4 billion, and we increased our national income seven times that amount from $81.6 billion to $170.3 billion. That's how the Depression ended. The survival of the nation required stabilization of the economy. We did it in one year because a war threatened survival of the system. We could have done it without a war just as well.

Q. Was it the added income that made the surpluses of the 1930s?

WILKEN. Yes. Surpluses vanished into thin air. At that time we brought into being the 90% price support program. And for ten years we maintained farm prices at parity. It is this ten-year period—a documented period—that gives us the real clue to how stability can be maintained. In that period we averaged $6.97 of national income for every dollar of farm production.

Q. The pragmatic observation the businessman makes is that if he can drive prices down and buy cheap, then he will make his dear sale and make a profit. What you're saying is that this is a short-circuit situation, because when you do drive that price down, you also dry up the purchasing power of your customers in a roundabout way?

WILKEN. Well, as I pointed out, here's your gross value of your farm production, say in Kansas. These communities, 1,000-1,500 of them, don't have any source of income except from the agricultural industry surrounding that town. That's the fact of the situation. So when the farmer doesn't get the money he can't come in and spend it with a machinery dealer or a lumberyard. And, when he doesn't have any income, the whole circulation right in that community is stopped. The state of Arizona issued a report in 1951. They developed six counties with public underground water tables and made a survey of the situation. They pointed out that for every dollar additional farm income that came into that county it increased the income $2.27. Now this 7 times turn is an average. Some of the dollars turn more. The farmer in Kansas gets $5,000 for wheat or cattle or whatever it is and then goes to an implement dealer and wants to buy a new tractor. Well the implement dealer lives off the markup between the price he pays for that tractor at the factory. He doesn't get money from the factory. When he sells, he has the money to order a new tractor from the factory to replace the one he sold. That implement manufacturer gets the order and immediately has to have more steel. The average turn is 7 times. Now you have the same thing in your product market. As we speak, they only make about one cent a pound on your dressed meat. That's all they make. They get it on volume. In your petroleum industry half a cent a gallon too little on the bulk product will practically wipe out the profit. There again it's based on volume gallons. And your supermarkets—they only make about 2 cents on a dollar, perhaps less. In a clothing store the markup is about 50%, because the turnover is less. If farm states are going to grow and expand with the rest of the country, they've got to have an income that is in balance with the overall nation. Wages and interest in the '46-'50 period increased on an average of 12.5% a year, income of private enterprise the way I use it—net farm income and small businesses and corporate profit after taxes—increased 3.6% a year. In other words, the value of the farm production produced in those communities could only buy 94% as much goods as they could buy in the '46-'50 period.

Q. Is there any possibility of gaining equity for agriculture before an institutional structure geared to accomplishing this is developed?

WILKEN. Not really. The farmer has never had any control in the market. His market has always been set by public auction and by speculators. Certainly, the farmer always has a situation where he can sell, but he has to sell cheaper. He has to sell at distress prices most of the time.

Q. The farmer generally has a place to sell, but at the same time he is being processed into bankruptcy, is he not?

WILKEN. True, rural America is being liquidated. Here's what's going to happen in my opinion. If we have corporation farms we're going to lose much of our livestock industry, because your corporate farm can't be bothered with hogs. Even if scientists succeed in keeping hogs alive, nature will have its say in time, and the industrial farrowing will fail. Livestock takes personal attention. Dairy, sometimes 24 hours a day, sometimes seven days a week. Kill off your livestock industry and you pave the road to world starvation. Let me give you a picture of the livestock industry. We have about a 1,180 million acres of farmland in the United States, improved and unimproved. About half of it is unimproved. We have a lot of area where there is subnormal rainfall—grazing land in the Western plains. Half the acreage would be complete wilderness if it wasn't for the livestock industry going out and walking over 20 to 25 acres of grazing land for a mouthful of grass and food to raise a calf. This livestock labor force processes all of the production from those acres. There are about 75 million acres in hay, which we use to carry the livestock force through the winter season, when there is no grass. Livestock processes this hay. It processes perhaps 88% of the corn crop. It processes linseed and cottonseed and soybeans. In so doing, it helps create the trade turn that stands between raw materials and national income. If we lose our production, or if we don't pay for it, then we lose national income. Lack of parity is just as bad as lack of production.

Q. This sniping at parity—is it done deliberately?

WILKEN. Yes. *Capper's* in 1959 reproduced some testimony that I gave before the House Committee on Appropriations. At that time I pointed out that agriculture ran behind the economy some $71 billion dollars. And they used it in an editorial, and the title of it was "Who Is Subsidizing Who?" They pointed out that agriculture, by taking this loss was subsidizing the rest of the society. The national advertising raised the devil. There wasn't a word after that.

Q. You hear the complaint that if farmers got the prices they were asking for, people would have to go hungry. Can you comment on that?

WILKEN. The American people could pay the farmer full parity and buy 40% more with an hour's work today than they could back in the 1946-'50 period because they'd earn that much more.

Q. This cause and effect relationship between income at the farm level and the national level—can you prove that it is more than just a ratio that might be happenstance?

WILKEN. Look—the aim of all science is to predict. When we get enough evidence together to predict, we join the observations together into working relationships called laws. These laws enable men not only to predict, but to design the outcome. Cause and effect, natural or managed, must be understood. This goes back to earned income, and draws a distinction between it and income that pretends to be *earned*. Now Kansas City has a Federal Reserve Bank. If you'll go to the Federal Reserve Bank there and get the bank turns from 1929 to 1932 you'll really get an eye-opener. It will prove to you that your bank turns dropped in direct proportion to the drop in the value of farm production and income level.

Q. But they're not doing that now?

WILKEN. They're not doing that now because of the injection of borrowed money.

Q. In other words, to keep the national level from dipping in harmony with the farm level, we've injected credit to keep the economic kite flying?

WILKEN. Right. For every dollar income you've increased in the last six years, you've added $2 to your debt.

Q. You say the income is created, but the mounting debt is still owed. But the Keynesian economists say, "So what, we owe it to ourselves."

WILKEN. That's the trouble. Let's just take the debt that we've added since 1950. If you'll take a lead pencil and figure 5% interest, that's $50 billion interest that has to be paid on $1 trillion. Now you have a 20% operating profit for the United States as a whole, so it takes well over $5 of national income to generate $1 of profit to pay that interest. We may owe it to ourselves, but *ourselves* is really a few millionaires.

Q. What you're describing here is a geometrical progression. You'd be doubling this debt in a decade and doubling it just on the basis of interest. Can anything—people, hummingbirds or debt—stand geometric redoubling?

WILKEN. Absolutely not. Let me illustrate this thing. In 1929 we had $214 billion gross debt, federal, state, local and private. In 1940, after 11 years of operation, we had $215 billion. In other words, practically no increase in the total debt. Now the private debt had been reduced through liquidation, repudiation, foreclosure, but in carrying on the New Deal policies we injected almost an equivalent amount of federal debt. We created new debt about as fast as we repudiated or liquidated the old, and we got nowhere. In this period we lost $563 billion dollars of income, or roughly 7 times the underpayment for farm products below the 1929 level. How did we absorb this loss? We went without the goods that $563 billion would have purchased at the 1929 price level. That was during the depression. This time we've done things differently. Since the end of 1950 we have lost $7 of the national income that should have been earned, or 7 times the underpayment to agriculture. But to offset it we've poured in this additional debt. And we've used the backward roll of this money to offset the loss in income. We've called it prosperity.

Q. The nation's profit is determined, according to what you're describing here, by the valuation you put on raw materials at the beginning of each cycle?

WILKEN. That's right. Then you end up in this position. It takes $250 billion of income in 1967 to earn the interest on the debt expansion from the end of 1950 to 1967. Saying it another way—if we didn't have this $1 trillion additional debt in 1967, we could operate the United States with $250 billion less income during the year.

Q. Could you set up a table showing—say from 1929 to the present—that the money paid for farm raw materials, oil, shale, stone, lumber and other raw materials became the earned income (that is, the income not created by debt injection), and then make a projection to illustrate exactly how much debt creation became mandatory in order to sustain the national income at a socially acceptable level?

WILKEN. That could be done, surely. [See the Interlude chapter]

Q. Is the information the government makes available suitable for easy translation into such a table?

WILKEN. Not at all. In my publication, *All New Wealth Comes from the Soil*, I tabulated the record of all raw material income from 1929 to 1953. To finish the table from 1948 to 1953, I had to send a special request to the Bureau of Mines for tabulations on mineral raw material income so that it would be expressed the same as it had been in 1948. In 1948 they discontinued the tabulation on metals recovered by smelting or recycling and translated the figures into manufactured income.

Q. Why did they do that?

WILKEN. Well, it made manufacturing income look bigger, and helped make corporations look capable of paying bargained wages. In any case, I got a special statement from the Bureau of Mines finishing the period I was interested in. In that period your value of farm production plus your other raw materials were equal to 95% of the profit in operating the United States. Now what happened to the other 5%. The other 5% was *standing expansion*. That's where you got your money to expand.

Q. But this table could be brought up to date?

WILKEN. With revised figures, yes. You see, you have to start with raw materials. What do you do with a ton of ore? You fabricate it into different parts. But you don't add one ton of ore. You don't add one pound. You do add value in terms of dollars, because of the capital cost factor in transporting and in paying processing labor, and so on, and all this is added on to the raw material, finally ending in your consumer price level. Let's take the full raw material equation. The record proves you have a five times turn. You have the initial dollars of raw materials. Now through your system of private enterprise, you carry this thing through transportation, processing, and so on. What does private enterprise have to do to accomplish all this? It has to borrow the money—the operating account to pay for the cost of transportation, to pay for processing, to pay labor cost, to pay return on capital and that value in terms of dollars is added to the consumer price. And it is sold at the consumer level.

Q. What you're saying then is that the amount paid for the raw material when it is brought out of Mother Earth becomes the total profit, the total saving available to all those who touch it, fabricate it, sell it or have anything to do with it from the time it leaves Mother Earth until it is consumed?

WILKEN. That's right.

Q. So therefore if I'm a processor I'll get the idea that if I can get the raw product cheaper, then I can have his share of the profit as well as my own. And if I can beat somebody up the line a ways I'll have three shares of that profit instead of one. Oversimplification, of course?

WILKEN. But the general concept.

Q. But you're also saying the economy outsmarts itself the minute it starts cheating the raw material producer, or even the laborer, because it breaks down the mechanism that enables it to reap any profit at all? You break down Say's Law of Markets?

WILKEN. The minute you underpay the raw material producer a dollar you lose approximately $5 of what could or should be earned income to utilize the end product, and you lose $1 of profit.

Q. Let's say the economy underpays its labor a dollar?

WILKEN. You'd have the same principle in operation. There's a parity for labor just as there is a parity for agriculture. There's a parity for small business and for big business.

Q. What is the parity for labor?

WILKEN. Labor must have a price that is in balance with the consumer price level. And this concept is being reflected in some labor contracts.

Q. Can labor have a parity greater than farm parity?

WILKEN. No, not without taking away from the other segments. And that's exactly what has been going on. Take your percentage increases from 1950 to 1966, you'll find that wages and interest have increased 207.7%. Now divide that by 16 and you have over 14% increase per year in the cost factors in operating the United States. To balance, private enterprise should have had a similar increase. Small business, agriculture, corporations—they have to earn it before they pay it out. Their part of the whole has not gone up accordingly. So we added to the gross debt consistently to pay the wages and interest bill. In spite of the injection of this credit, we lacked $90 billion of having enough income in 1966 to balance income with costs—using 1948-1950 as the base period. This means there's $90 billion of market that just didn't exist. All right, how did we offset that $90 billion? We had to borrow the money because we didn't earn it.

Q. Was the post Korean War debt expansion justified?

WILKEN. On the basis of $300 billion of income and the profits from it, a $72 billion expansion in 1955 was twice as much money as we had any right to borrow based on profits and savings. So with savings running out in 1957, this debt expansion was moved down to $36 billion, half as much as in 1955. So we had the 1958 depression. At that time I had a meeting with 12 Republican Senators (arranged by Senator Capehart) and pointed out to them that if they didn't restore farm prices they'd lose the election and have some more depression. Well, we had the depression in 1958 and they lost the election. Then in 1959 we injected another $69 billion. By that time the operating loss had increased to a point where this was just barely enough to keep the economy going and in 1960 when it fell back to $51 billion we had the 1960 recession. As you know, Kennedy used it to say *we've got to get the country moving again.*

Q. Can you extend this pattern into the Kennedy years?

WILKEN. Yes, and beyond. Kennedy had the same advice from the Harvard boys. In 1961 we increased the debt $61 billion. In 1962 we increased it $79 billion. Then we increased it $80 billion. Johnson took over and increased $84 billion. And then $94 billion. Then $104 billion. And in 1966, about $115 billion. And if you keep going like that for ten years, you'll have to have $250 billion dollars of debt injection to keep this thing operating.*

Q. Where's the point when you can't carry it anymore?

WILKEN. Well, you can't carry it now as far as that is concerned.

Q. Where's the point at which the kite won't even fly?

WILKEN. When people stop borrowing. There's no law that forces people to borrow.

Q. But war—for an economic point of view—keeps the credit coming, doesn't it?

WILKEN. It just throws everything out of the window. Let me illustrate this thing from the debt point of view. I can take the 1966 *Economic Report of the President* and the 1967 report, prepared by the same Council for the same president and it'll show that in 1967 they had to adjust the net debt expansion for the year 1966 by $10 billion above what they showed in

---

* These figures will vary from those published in *The Economic Report of the President*, depending on which *Economic Report* is viewed, because government statisticians are constantly revising figures all the way back to 1929. Wilken's figures used here conform to the era of the observation.

the 1966 report for the year 1966. They are that much behind. Now the joker in the whole thing is that debts are easy to acquire, but hard to retire. Besides that, the American people are not being trained to save. They have no intention of saving to buy a house because they can buy a house for $500 down. They even borrow the money for the down payment, and they don't try to pay it off. They just keep making the payments as rent. So the minute you have a little depression cycle and people lose their jobs, they can't keep their homes. About 20% of the disposable income after taxes [circa 1967] has to go to make payments on money people spent earlier. So that's subtracted from today's earnings. And it has to offset with debt expansion. All the information is available in the *Economic Report of the President*, but nobody uses it. Why not? I don't know. We can spend billions to figure out the operation of a space ship to the *nth* degree, and we have to use arithmetic to do that. But we simply won't set up an income equation on the economy as a whole to find out how to operate.

Q. Many people complain it's too complicated. The USDA Secretary says your system is too simple. Is it really too complicated or too simple?

WILKEN. Look at it this way. It would be easy if every family could go out and spend $1,400 or $1,500 a year more on a family basis than the family earns. They can't. So they borrow what they've overspent or dissaved. That'd be an easy way to operate an economy, wouldn't it?

Q. That's the way a lot of families operate.

WILKEN. Yes, and that's the way we've been operating the economy for a decade and a half. Now this thing started out with a shortage of national income of about $3 billion the first year, in 1951, according to the income equation that I set up. And it's moved up to a shortage of national income of $90 billion in 1966. Common sense should tell the American people that the national income increase must increase in ratio to wages and interest—the chief cost factors in operating the economy.

Q. But people are not listening to this analysis. They read in the papers that we're having the greatest boom in history. And they look around and see lots of evidence—roads, hotels, motels, houses.

WILKEN. But it isn't paid for. We've done it all with borrowed money.

Q. You also have a lot of people who say, "So what. If the debt is repudiated, you've still got the roads and you still have, the buildings." In short, we owe it to ourselves.

WILKEN. There's no question about it. But if this thing goes on, in the final analysis, we'd have about 10% of the people owning all the farms and all the corporations and all the finances. These are the conditions that bring on revolution.

Q. Would you say, then, that the balance wheel to "We owe it to ourselves" is the proposition that the first fact of economic life is people?

WILKEN. You could say that. And that's exactly the reason why the struggle today is with the Keynesian theory and why the struggle today is over whether we'll have Keynesian socialism all the way—and don't forget the communistic system is also socialism, but we never think of it as socialism. Don't forget one very important man we had in the United States. That was Ben Franklin. He said there are three ways for a nation to become wealthy. First, by war, and taking away the wealth of another by force. Second, by trade, which to make a profit requires something cheap. Third, by agriculture, where by planting a seed you create new wealth as if by a miracle. Let me analyze that for you. The farmer can take a grain of corn and put it in the ground and in 120 days it will send up a stalk and an ear of corn, maybe two ears of corn, with 700 or 800 grains. And each one of those grains will have as much food value as the initial grain planted. In other words, in agriculture you have the source of continued reproduction of the energy absolutely essential to human existence. Now you don't have that situation in other raw materials. You can't plant a pound of copper and grow 500 pounds of copper. Agriculture is the only renewable source. Approximately 30% of the raw materials used in operating the American economy come from mines and pits—gravel, stone, coal, petroleum, and so on. Some 70% of the raw materials used to operate the economy come from farms. These are the raw materials needed to operate industrial America. The cycle starts with raw material production. Why? *It all has its origin in the laws of energy, and the whole of human existence has to do with using energy.*

# CHAPTER 3: LAWS OF ENERGY

*It all has its origin in the laws of energy, and the whole of human existence has to do with using energy.* As the technocrats of the Depression era correctly argued, "energy enters into the production of all goods and services . . . energy is the common denominator of all production."

W. H. Smyth, writing in 1919 (*Industrial Management*), noted that during World War I America "became for the time being an industrial nation. This we did by organizing and coordinating the scientific knowledge, the technical talent, the practical skill and the manpower of the entire community." The government accomplished this great thing, he said, simply by setting aside democracy and replacing it with technocracy, and with that Smyth coined a term certain promoters believed to be good for a buck or two. The word "technocracy" took on a capital letter and an organized, dues-paying following.

And at times the Technocrats of the Depression era even talked sense. But their curious energy certificates failed to properly consider the institutional arrangements under which an economy operated, and thus shared with Say's Law of Markets a fatal fault, that of defining and projecting economic reality in terms either eons away or not available at all.

## [1] PHYSICAL LAWS

The origin of production has to do with physics, certainly. But distribution deals with strange unfathomable impulses, social ceremonies, and "economic laws" perceived by the simple-minded and the schoolmen to exist independent of human will when in fact they are merely ploys for the cunning who rule, and the crafty who exploit.

By common consent, historians and economists nowadays hang their hats on Black Thursday, October 23, 1929 as the day it happened. "There has been a little distress selling," commented Thomas W. Lamont, Sr., a "partner" of J.P. Morgan & Company, when $5 billion in paper values went down the drain. Six days later another $30 billion in paper values were washed out as a frantic public scrambled to unload 16 million shares on the New York Stock Exchange, and another 7 million on the curb.

The Great Depression pinpointed the problem of glut and want and served up nostrums. These "solutions" were as different as Howard Scott's $20,000 a year for a four-hour day and Dr. Francis E. Townsend's $200 a month for all Americans over 60. Townsend lifted his plan out of Edward Bellamy's perfect state in *Looking Backward*, and Scott—before Dr. Murray Butler ordered him and his Technocrats off Columbia University campus—certainly picked up the angle for his gray-suited brigade from the 1919 work by engineer William Henry Smyth, and from Frederick Soddy's *Wealth, Virtual Wealth and Debt, the Solution of the Economic Paradox.**

Carl Wilken hardly considered as real the concept that an egotist turned Messiah might lead the people to a promised land, mumbling something about *ergs* and *joules* all the while. He believed, first, last and always, in democracy's brand of collective bargaining. "We will not accept the defeatist philosophy that assumes that Booms and Busts are inevitable and inherent in the Capitalistic system," was the expression that went out under the imprimatur of the Raw Materials National Council. "We insist the shortcomings of our system can and therefore must be corrected."

Nevertheless, Wilken's concept of a raw materials base for an economy came from writings as far back as the French physiocrats. Its modern adaptation was first expressed as the energy theory of Frederick Soddy in 1926. And Soddy both stated and implied some pretty fundamental laws, all of which sooner or later found expression in the work and proof of Carl H. Wilken. Energy was a key—"the constantly accelerating increase of energy from the twelfth century to the twentieth," as Lewis Mumford put it in *The Myth of the Machine*. The grab for dominance over the fruits of an improved energy tap had caused Henry Adams to speak of the consequences as early as 1904. "The assumption of unity, which was the mark of human thought in the Middle Ages," Adams wrote to historian Henry Osborn Taylor, "has yielded very slowly to the proofs of complexity. The stupor of science before radium is a proof of it. Yet it is quite sure, according to my score of ratios and curves that, at the accelerated rate of progression since 1600, it will not need another century and a half to turn thought upside down. Law in that case would disappear as theory or *a priori* principle and give place to force. Morality would become police. Explosives would reach cosmic violence. Disintegration would overcome integration."

The generalizations of Henry Adams were confirmed within a year of his death. Indeed, by 1919 Baron Ernest Rutherford and his associates

---

* I cannot tell you whether [*Wealth, Virtual Wealth and Debt*] is one of the most important [books] ever written, although it may well be," wrote Stuart Chase in a review of the book. [Soddy's] "analysis of the going structure is clear, penetrating, and for me at least, "exciting. I did not miss a word or an idea, as he looked at production, distribution, and physical plant in the light of the first and second law of thermodynamics."

had developed the theory for breaking the atom and paved the way for Einstein's E=Mc². Rutherford's chief assistant was Frederick Soddy, the same Soddy who was to write *Wealth, Virtual Wealth and Debt.*

Soddy saw the economic consequences of an energy tap as have few others. Writing in *The Interpretation of Radium* he unloaded this observation:

"The problem of transmutation and the liberation of atomic energy to carry on the labour of the world is no longer surrounded with mystery and ignorance, but is daily being reduced to a form capable of exact quantitative reasoning. It may be that it will remain forever unsolved. But we are advancing along the only road likely to bring success at a rate which makes it probable that one day will see its achievement. Should that day ever arrive, let no one be blind to the magnitude of the issues at stake, or suppose that such an acquisition of the physical resources of humanity can be safely entrusted to those who in the past have converted the blessings already conferred by science into a curse."

The curse that modern technology showered down on mankind troubled Soddy no end. It caused him to apply the principles of physics to economics. "His anticipatory insight . . . remains highly creditable," noted Lewis Mumford, despite his "single factor analysis."*

The original entry of Soddy's "anticipatory insight" in *Wealth, Virtual Wealth and Debt* remains as meaningful today as when first issued.

Life, after all, continues to obey physical laws. It "works according to, not against the principles of the physical sciences," wrote Frederick Soddy shortly after winning a Nobel Prize. "Neither individuals nor communities can escape conforming to the laws of matter and energy, however they may apply them to their own ends."

Pierre Lecomte du Nouy, the brilliant French scientist who perfected a mathematical expression for the process of healing of wounds, once defined science as the method for "foretelling." The general method, he held, had to be statistical and respondent to the calculus of probabilities. As with Poincare, du Nouy saw in the kinetic theory of gases the best available expression of how physical laws operate, and how the concept of a scientific system discovers laws without first calibrating every movement of molecules. Any gas is composed of free molecules which are in perpetual motion. These molecules move at different speeds, drive in all directions, collide with each other and against the sides of a container. Pressure is nothing more than the measurable result of impacts, the calibration of energy of molecules striking the walls of a container. No one

---

* I do not think Soddy relied as much on "single factor analysis" as he did on the proposition that control of money and credit, and distribution of income, had to be honest and balanced before the many other aspects of economic direction could be dealt with. C.W.

could possibly calculate the path of each molecule. "If by ill-luck I happened to know the laws which govern them I should be helpless," said Jules Henri Poincare. "I should be lost in endless calculations and could never supply you with an answer to your questions. Fortunately for both of us, I am completely ignorant about the matter. I can therefore supply you with an answer at once. That may seem odd; but there is something odder still, namely that my answer will be right."

Wilken knew a great deal about sciences, more than he generally imposed on others in his conversations. He was aware of the "endless calculations" any survey of business transactions involved. He was adept at numbers, small numbers and large numbers, and could expound on handling astronomical figures as easily as he could take a lead pencil to the inescapable fact that 2 and 2 are 4. The laws of energy became incomprehensible to many people because numerical expression of the facts often disappeared into high level meaninglessness. The number of molecules in a cubic centimeter of gas might be written as 30,000,000,000,000,000,000, a totally unreadable figure. Written as $3 \times 10^{19}$ that same expression meant three times 10 to the power of 19, with the power figure simply expressing the number of zeroes. Thus $10^3$ simply means $10 \times 10 \times 10 = 1,000$ or $3 \times 10^3 = 3,000$.

Figures to a power increase quite rapidly, whether they represent hummingbirds or dollars, and ultimately have to conform to the laws of physics, the laws of matter and energy. A few expressions should illustrate the point. Scientists up to a few years ago agreed that the Earth was probably no older than 2,000 million years, or $2 \times 10^9$. In terms of centuries, the age of the Earth would be written thus: $2 \times 10^7$. There are only $10^5$ days (actually 100,000) in a century, thus no more than $2 \times 10^{12}$ days have elapsed since the Earth was first spun off, established, or created. [This figure has been enlarged during recent years, and may be changed next year. The arithmatic nevertheless has to obey the laws of nature.] Lecomte du Nouy once calculated that there are $10^{19}$ molecules in one cubic centimeter of gas, but that there are only $10^{79}$ molecules in the entire universe, including the farthest stars.

The age of the Sun, the source of all energy, is probably no more than $5 \times 10^{12}$ (5,000 billion) years.

During the recent decades, inanimate energy has become the workaday substitute for animal labor. Almost from the dawn of the industrial revolution, inventions piled on inventions started tapping a "capital store of energy" that wasn't "entirely dependent on the revenue of sunshine," mentions Soddy. The mere act of burning a lump of coal releases sunshine that may have reached the earth during the Archean Age, 1,200 million years ago. Once used, however, that same lump of coal is gone, and there is no way anyone can earn interest from it in perpetuity.

# [2] THE ORIGINAL CAPITALIST

From the chair of a theory of energy, chlorophyll, the green coloring matter of vegetation that is built around a single atom of magnesium, is the original capitalist. Plants are man's key to natural energy because the dye chlorophyll is the principal transformer of solar energy into the kind of power human beings can use.

Soddy detailed the flow of energy with fantastic brevity. Man, he said, had to be wound up like a clock, and "the economics of life deals primarily with the ways in which Nature winds up man." Food is the prime requisite and the dominant factor. "Possibly future races of men may feed their internal fires in the same way as we perform external labour, with inanimate energy. But until entirely new discoveries are made, agriculture remains still the key industry of life. All that science has been able to do has been of indirect assistance. Fundamentally it remains unchanged, as the collection of sunlight by the agency of chlorophyll and its transformation into the chemical energy of foodstuffs, either directly or through the intermediate transforming agency of animals."

"Energy cannot be created or destroyed" is usually the way teachers put it to pupils in elementary science classes. Yet for all practical purposes, energy tends to become "unavailable," a polite way of saying it achieves the same temperature as its surroundings. The fundamental Carnot-Clausius law (frequently called the second law of thermodynamics) puts it thus: *an isolated material system never passes twice through the same state. Each state decreases the available energy.* In short, there can be no perpetual motion.

The life process ranks first in efficiency when it comes to harnessing energy. Machines, though not insignificant, come in second, and rate as imitations of the life process. In terms of translating energy intake into heat without capital loss, the human body is the most magnificent mechanism of all.

Natural and man-made systems for getting solar income need not be presented here in any great detail. Every grade school child knows how solar energy falls on water and causes vapor to undergo "adiabatic cooling and expansion," how rain collects in rivers to fill dams, how the internal heat of the Earth or the oil and coal and gas deliver revenue for which man is debited, the Sun credited. Nature's accounting system deals with fantastic entries, both because they are so large and because they are so small. The moment man discovers some rule of reason, behold, a scientific law is established. Without exception, these laws have always met the same requirements—that is, they have conformed to the laws of matter and energy.

It was not by accident that the first economists looked to nature—and physical reality—in developing their line of thought. "All new wealth comes from the soil" became a maxim both before and after Richard Cantillon published his *Essai sur la Nature du Commerce en Général*.

During the years that followed, the physical basis for economics rated recognition. Adam Smith could tell his peers that a nation had to devote its resources to agriculture first, manufacture second, trade third, but by the time David Ricardo and the other classical economists arrived, legalities of title and institutions of property wrote the scenario, and the question of whether there were physical laws that might pertain to economics survived only in the abstractions of J.B. Say and the rhetoric of seers who were more quoted than believed.

## [3] THE ARENA OF ETHICS

The never ending search for a planetary system of the markets did yield principles, and they were understood. At the time of Andrew Jackson, John Stuart Mill wrote his scholarly *Principles of Political Economy*, a two-volume treatise that surveyed the entire field of economics—rents, wages, prices, taxes. Say's Law of Markets still reigned supreme, as it would for a hundred years. And institutional interplay still upset the Law of Markets so regularly that to be an economist in the minds of the common folk was to be a big joke. Yet Mill did more than codify the academic thought of the hour, he brought on a principle all his own—one that has been regularly forgotten and regularly mis-placed ever since. In effect, Mill argued that distribution in an institutional world had nothing to do with economics.

"The things are there," wrote Mill. "Mankind, individually or collectively, can do with them as they please. They can place them at the disposal of whomever they please, and on whatever terms. . . . Even what a person has produced by his individual toil, unaided by anyone, he cannot keep, unless by the permission of society. Not only can society take it from him but individuals could and would take it from him, if society . . . did not . . . employ and pay people for the purpose of preventing him from being disturbed of his possession. The distribution of wealth, therefore, depends on the laws and customs of society. The rules by which it is determined are what the opinions and feelings of the ruling portion of the community make them, and are very different in different ages and countries, and might be still more different, if mankind so choose. . . ."

Vince Rossiter, a banker from Hartington, Nebraska and a supporter of Carl Wilken, used the above quotation in a talk before a group of bankers in 1965, because it pin-pointed a problem, and guided the thinking and the system of thought Carl H. Wilken sought to prove out mathematically. "For what Mill said," noted Rossiter, "was transparently obvious—once it had been said. Never mind if the *natural* action of society was to depress wages, or to equalize profits or to raise rents or whatever. If society did not like the *natural* results of its activities, it had only to change them. Society could tax, subsidize. It could even expropriate and redistribute. It could give away all of its wealth to a king, or it could run a gigantic charity ward. It could give due heed to incentives, or it could—at its own risk—ignore them. But whatever it did, there was no correct distribution—at least none that economics had any claim to fathom. There was no appeal to laws to justify how society shared its fruits. There were only men sharing their wealth as they saw fit. It was a discovery of profound consequences, for it lifted the whole economic debate from the stifling realm of impersonal and inevitable law and brought it back into the arena of ethics and morality."

Yet even ethics and morality cannot insulate a society from the laws of matter and energy, even though socialists and communists imply as much.

I believe it was this realization that provided Carl Wilken with rare insight, that prompted him to hunt cause and effect in the observed facts of the situation. Records, figures, data meant everything to Wilken. Although he knew the theories, he scoffed at them because he more or less expected conclusions to flow logically from the facts. The laws of exchange, therefore, had to be physical laws. Society could ignore them only at its own risk. Moreover it could *not* obey them in order to achieve stability and full employment unless it understood them in the first place.

Wilken believed Say understood. He believed internationalists, also understood, but chose to ignore the laws of matter and energy in order to apply benefits *to their own ends.*

Although the seeds of sound economics were laced together throughout Adam Smith's *The Wealth of Nations,* the entire discipline of economics got lost in the horse latitudes even as it emerged into the English speaking world. After that, except for a few brief underworld tries, few bothered to define wealth in terms of physics, and so the "science" evaporated, and the value system of the day regurgitated economic "laws" suitable to those who had invented, and benefited from, standing legal conventions, the transfer system of the exchange economy—that is, debt.

It would be all too simple to assume that this dilemma was born in the thick-rimmed heads of schoolmen alone. Perhaps the psychology of the community had something to do with it. From cave days onward, men have sought to make secure their existence by gaining income without working. The concept of an annuity to tide one past old age and to set up the children forever is not one average men abandon easily. Indeed, it seems difficult to question the fact that—with foundations, trusts, legal wills and the like—many men rule from the grave, thereby hanging the albatross of ancient decisions around the necks of those who follow. With legal devices, some men have prevented erosion of their fortunes, and these fortunes have had only to increase and multiply, compound themselves, and proceed to bring the laws of mathematics into conflict with the laws of physics. Toynbee and Pierenne and Durant notwithstanding, it can be stated as a clear observation that all human history is finally a showdown between the human psychology of acquisition and the possibilities of physics. Physics, of course, permits no perpetual motion. How to circumvent this fact has become the name of the economic game.

Once upon a time the nobles of Europe believed they had accomplished the physical impossibility of perpetual interest simply by owning all the land and raking in tribute from the peasantry, and when death finally pulled down an economic maggot, then there was always the heir. The historical showdown arrived, of course, and the "new nobles" were forced to invent a more subtle form of tribute taking. It came on as debt, interest, compound interest, and all the institutional arrangements required to make the producing community share its income with the creditor. For centuries the details have stacked up, but economists (men like Wilken excepted) have failed to draw the appropriate conclusions.

Wilken grew up close to the soil. He understood the physical reality of wealth creation. This enabled him to reconstruct economic theory so that it complied with reality. Wilken believed in handing this knowledge to the only possible place for safekeeping—to the man on the street, the same one who stood guard over the fact that two and two were still four. Soddy's clear thinking helped.

There were a few things people who aren't blind, deaf or dumb could observe. Even cavemen didn't think in terms of art and lace curtains until they had first provided for the material necessities of life—food, garments, shelter. The farmer who could provide enough to feed two families might talk things over with his neighbor, and the two might decide that one would do the food growing, and the other might devote his energies to being, say, a furniture maker or a teacher. But no one ever deluded himself into thinking that the furniture maker or teacher wasn't being sustained by the farmer.

# [4] ONE MILLION CALORIES A YEAR

Then as now, it took about one million calories a year to feed a hard-working human being adequately. Food was the first requirement of human life, and life itself demanded a constant flow of energy. Only after it had been supplied could men devote themselves to writing books, painting pictures or creating the baubles of the good life. The economic process found its origin in the laws of energy, not exchange. Fortunately, the life process demanded more. It demanded stylish clothes, comfortable homes, efficient transportation, tools to extend man's puny efforts, and plant and equipment to harness technology. The life process required production, and production of food and tools and machines required a tap into the flow of nature's available energy. Indeed, the manner in which production tapped into the flow of available energy held the key for economic balance, that single achievement that could put to pasture both war and depression, unemployment and want, unearned wealth and extreme poverty.

There are certain characteristics of wealth that are often observed, but seldom understood. There are the various commodities that warehouse energy—food, coal, petroleum, sulphur, and so on. When these commodities are consumed, they release energy. It is the function of these commodities to be consumed, to be converted into waste—in a word, destroyed. Consumption (and destruction) is not only necessary for economic balance, but a prime requirement. Commodities that warehouse energy are produced simply by combining work and raw materials. And when these commodities are consumed, they yield life energy, waste energy and waste materials. Production of such commodities x price = income. Obviously, production of commodities that warehouse energy is helped along by tools, inventions, automation. When all a man can do is feed himself and no one else, then he cannot develop the good life with theatres, automobiles and vacation homes. Yet the development of tools and equipment cannot outrun the consumption (destruction) of perishable commodities—that is, those that give up energy and suffer annihilation by being what, say, a lump of coal ought to be.

Wealth, also, comes in other forms. The fibers we wear, the tools we use, the machines that spin wood and iron—none of these suffer quick destruction in serving their purpose. Still, no machine or building or suit of clothes is really permanent. It is, in terms of energy, consumed as soon as it has been produced. Its creation requires abstinence from regular consumption—a condition that makes creation of capital debt beyond income a physical impossibility. At best, only a brief time can separate it from being washed out. The energy that has gone into its production has—in the very process of production—already been degraded to its final stage. Still, production of fibers, tools, equipment x price = income also, exactly as in the case of commodities, that warehouse energy. Permanent wealth is already consumed in terms of energy the minute it is created but it must pass from the scene (destruction, planned obsolescence, etc.) before there is room for more such production. At a final point, permanent wealth is the same as perishable wealth.

## [5] PERMANENT WEALTH CANNOT ACCUMULATE

Despite the fact that some types of production take on the air of permanence, there is no such thing. The Empire State Building must one day disappear. The clothes we wear will be gone within a year or two. The multi-million dollar airplane won't last two decades. But many forms of the more permanent sort of wealth are, when used, productive—that is, they allow man to extend his arm, strength, or memory power—and this has enchanted economic planners no end. As machine (kinetic) energy replaces human (metabolic) energy, the human contribution to production changes, chiefly from that of expending energy to that of guiding non-human energy. This might be the difference between digging a ditch and riding a ditch-digging machine. Yet the economic process has a stem requirement. Permanent wealth cannot accumulate faster than the consumption of perishable wealth for reasons Soddy best explained by allegory.

A water tank high in the mountains might take in water from the melting snows much faster than outlet pipes could carry it off. As the water-head builds, pressure will drive water from the tank, and at some given point water will flow out as fast as it enters.

The flow of inventions, machines, automation (even better yielding corn strains) is subject to the same laws of physics. Each influx brings on accumulation, but in the end the inflow of production must balance with the outflow or consumption of production. In short, production and monetization of consumable wealth have to be fine-tuned to the production of capital goods, so that capital goods production proceeds only as fast as required to produce perishable wealth.

It is for this reason that agriculture and red meat production are of such fantastic importance. After all, agriculture produces raw materials that suffer destruction in consumption. A man eats at noon, and a few hours later he is ready to put on the feed bag again. The food that is consumed has to be replaced at once. The lion's share of the nation's foundation income has to come from the farms, because it is chiefly in farm raw material production that the more permanent sort of wealth can be put to use producing wealth that is destroyed quickly in consumption.

It takes about a million calories a year to feed a farm hand. How shall these calories be delivered? People who style themselves as "eminent scholars and world planners" frequently ask: "Should we be eating the soybean meal or feeding it to animals and then eating the meat and eggs?" At seminars and public platform presentations, many of these eminent scholars and world planners call for liquidation of cattle, hog and poultry production. They point to the spectre of world famine and remind their audiences that one calorie of animal meat requires seven calories from a vegetable source. Isn't it a shameful waste then to feed so much protein to animals when man is starving, they say. The platform performance of confusing the world's production problem with the exchange problem of American agriculture is, of course, more than a harmless exercise. It muddies the water, confuses the issue, and feeds the common sense public full of common nonsense. The American economic problem is to consume more, not less, food and to consume it all at full parity prices.

In translating feed grain production into meat, America consumes about six or seven times more production while filling its caloric needs than if the country ate corn mush, Wilken said. Indeed, the corn crop alone could probably furnish enough calories to more than feed the American population. Each pound of corn has approximately 1,500 calories (which is very near the level of daily consumption in China).

This is what Wilken meant when he cited the gullibility of the American people for thinking cheap farm prices were beneficial. The economic law that requires permanent wealth to produce wealth that is destroyed quickly in consumption is the key. It is exactly this law that requires the public works project called war. In war, as in pyramid building and space probes, the more permanent sort of wealth is destroyed, and takes up the economic role once held by parity food. Although each of these destructive activities remains a dwarf when compared with the constructive activity of feeding the people, it is true that the nation that degrades either the production or the income of its agriculture thereby condemns itself to war. "The fact that war is 'wasteful' is what enables it to serve this function," wrote Leonard Levin in *Report From Iron Mountain,* a novel that depicted a Kennedy *ad hoc* committee set up to study the war syndrome. "And the faster the economy advances, the heavier this balance wheel must be."

# [6] FIGURE KEEPING

A reasoned approach yields a theory. But a theory can be proved only with observed facts. In the main, Carl Wilken devoted his life to tracing figures, proving out equations, and pointing up the laws of exchange that had to be followed if harsh consequences were to be avoided.

Figure keeping has come a long way since Sir William Petty first dealt with *Political Arithmetick*, and since John Marshall published his *Digest of all the Accounts Relating to the Population, Productions, Revenues, Financial Operations, Manufacturer*, etc.—the rest a title that consumes six full lines of print. Commodity prices have never been difficult to get, not since Thomas Jefferson and a few farmer intellectuals formed a government. Still, it was 1921 before the Department of Commerce established *The Survey of Current Business*, the figure bible for economics until its contents became absorbed in the *Economic Report of the President* with the passage of the Employment Act in 1946.

Economic data, Wilken soon discovered, have built-in defects, defects that are often managed, and frequently misunderstood. There is no year No. 1 for economists, as there is for historians. Thus most data are presented in terms of base periods. Some of those that surface now and again leave the novice far afield because a sound base period has to comply with certain requisites.

Much the same is true of income totals, profits, GNP, GDP—and the precepts behind many aggregates. Nevertheless, certain principles enjoy universal acceptance. No responsible economist—whether capitalist, socialist, or a combination thereof—will argue against the principle of the multiplier (or trade turn, as Wilken had it) and few will question that all saving except hoarding means spending. But there is a big question: *to what extent can an economy save?* Economists also agree that profits and savings are the same, that

Savings = current income - (current consumption + capital consumption allowances).

Savings = change in assets - change in liabilities.

Savings = change in net worth.

Add the word national in front of each of the above equations, and you have national saving.

The most comprehensive work yet to be issued in an attempt to solve the earnings/savings ratio came styled *A Study of Saving in the United States* by Raymond W. Goldsmith. Issued in late 1953, *The Savings Study* filled some 1,138 pages in Volume 1 alone, only to find that in 50 years "the estimates of saving developed by this study tend to be somewhat above other estimators' figures (of course after adjustment for differences in concept and coverage) particularly for the period after World War II." In comparisons limited to the national level, the study showed "virtually no difference between saving and investment for the period as a whole."

Goldsmith pointed out that several accounting approaches figure in almost all national records. The most common, of course, is the business accounting system, the one that calculates depreciation at the end of a period by prorating an asset's cost over its calculated life. Social statisticians object to this because assets are often written off before their useful life is over. Another system, the cash flow method, simply ignores capital consumption and other accruals. This makes cash savings equal to gross expenditures on durable goods (cash expenditures less proceeds from sales). This system is useful in money flow studies, but has built-in defects otherwise.

Social accounting generally figures replacement cost instead of original cost.

Not many figure wranglers bother to spell out every nuance in the gathering game, and this can easily account for variations that often affect details, seldom overall results.

Goldsmith and his co-workers summarized as follows:

From 1897 to 1949, households—including farms and unincorporated enterprises—saved 1/8 of their incomes. During so-called normal years, that is 1897-1916, 1919-1929, 1934-1941, 1946-1949, savings came to 1/8 of income. During periods of full employment, 1902, 1905, 1925, 1929, 1948, the ratio was 1/7—that is, savings for this group came to 1/7 of income. Goldsmith further found that national savings during a "normal period" differed but little from the personal saving ratio.

The ramifications, as with most statistical studies that run into thousands of pages, cannot be summarized briefly, except that they seemed to match precepts of earlier workers, Carl Wilken and his associates included.

In *Business Cycles,* Wesley Clair Mitchell detailed the work of Willford I. King, an economist who scrutinized the national earnings/savings ratio with attention to adjustments for foreign debits and credits and price fluctuation. For the period 1909 to 1918, he concluded that "The normal fraction of the national income saved is about one-seventh." Another worker of that era, Walter Renton Ingalls, confirmed King's results. Ingalls computed savings at about 15% of national income, year in and year out, thus substantiating King's findings—savings = 1/7 of income.

# [7] MAN IS DEBITED, NATURE CREDITED

The mystery of double entry bookkeeping came on in 1494, when it was first published as an Italian invention. It represented a technical advance on the level of writing itself. Yet its meaningful transition to national economics is still to be had. This shortfall has made it difficult for many to find the source of savings or profits. It has caused others to overlook entirely the proposition that profit is really the free revenue of raw materials for which man is debited, nature credited (but never paid). Certainly the flow of energy requires man to be debited, and the source of energy to be credited with every primary transaction. As Frederick Soddy correctly stated, "the economics cycle properly boils down to two interlocked operations, payments by producers to their employees and themselves for producing new wealth, and then the payment of the same money by the same people and other consumers to get the wealth out of the production system after it is made. All simple exchanges of finished property are only of individual importance." In the trade turn, they add to the price, but not to the product. Velocity of money can become affected by the frenzy at which people gamble on the stock market, by how they go about getting and spending, buying and selling, none of which affects the gestation period of a beef cow, the germination time for a seed, or any of a thousand industrial equivalents. All these things, merely deal with distribution, not the creation of new wealth. Speculators getting money—created for themselves and destroyed for their own advantage—simply add to the price, and not to the product.

Among those who worked with the tired problem of the Depression years, Carl Wilken and his associates saw the real meaning of new wealth, and how its creation could be translated into national income. The ratio worked out was no figment of an imagination. Farm income, because it represented the lion's share of raw material income, was new wealth—man debited, nature credited. The revenue of energy in a corn crop—except for the out-of-pocket cost of bringing it in—did not have to be paid back. The renewable resource of agriculture thus stood as a perpetual source of energy revenue. It was there for the taking. Properly debited, it became the foundation for a trade turn that (under the existing state of the arts) developed national income approximately sevenfold.

Farm income, Wilken held, had a duality that other types of income did not have. It served as the basic operating income for the farmer, and it provided the foundation income for rural townspeople who provided services to the farmer. But it meant more. Farm income was the lion's share of the total new wealth created in any given year, and therefore the total addition to the existing money supply. It, with other raw materials, was the source of investment for expansion and the total savings of the economy.

Wilken knew all about paper money, gold and silver, and the printing press equivalents thereof. He asked, why didn't the socialist regimes make good their word, print money, and create metropolitan communities as if by magic? Why were there underdeveloped areas in the world if it were merely a matter of printing money, bonds, and other such certificates?

In truth, it took generations—each adding annually the gross value of the raw material production, one year atop the last—to bring on savings. And with these savings (savings which reflected a holdback from consumption) so many schools and homes were built, so many churches and miles of highways were constructed, and so many other permanent capital improvements were made. In earlier times, people actually waited for the next crop to finish a job started the season before.

It's bigger now. It's more glamorous. Economies have learned how to buy the pews the same year they build a church because they've learned how to use credit. But ultimately they still have to harvest the next crop and bring in the next cart load of coal to pay the bill. It has never been any different. It will never be any different.

There was no use looking to a keelhauling of the society, or creation of curious energy certificates, to bring on the proper relationship between raw materials and other sectors in the economy. It took an honest price to keep the new wealth production coming, that's all. That was both the root of the farm problem and the national economic problem. And Carl Wilken expressed it with a formula that was as simple and as accurate as the kinetic law of gases.

# CHAPTER 4: TAPE NO. 2

Q. Mr. Wilken, in the February 1951 issue of *The Economic Search Light* [the official bulletin of the Sioux City Advisory Committee of the Raw Materials National Council] editor John O. Knutson comments on your 1-1-7 formula, that the farm dollar generates the dollar for industrial payroll, and ultimately produces $7 of national income. Quote: "This economic phenomenon is so consistent and constant that Mr. Wilken has been able to project the national income with better than 98% accuracy for the past 14 years, six months prior to their official publication. This is not guess work."

WILKEN. You can go on quoting from *Search Light* because the statements are essentially my own. The boom and bust part of the capital system is not inherent. We do not have to have depressions. Now in cutting these tapes, I'm going to give you the material that will make it possible for you to write a review of the basic economic factors that determine the income of the United States or any other nation, and whether or not a depression is inevitable. The income of a nation boils down very simply to two parts, both equally important. One is the production of goods and services for human use. The second is the price goods sell for at the consumer level. When you multiply production times price you generate income, the monetary measure of value. This money then delivers the ability to exchange the products that you produce. If somewhere along the line you fail to generate enough income from production to utilize it, something is wrong. And striking a balance points up exactly what is wrong. If you strike a balance you find that there is either not enough production to generate income, or not enough price. There are these two multiples. Now in the case of physical production we have very accurate measurements. We have pounds, inches, we have the yardstick, all units of measure that are accurate. In other words, when a farmer takes corn to market he has to deliver 56 pounds to a bushel regardless of whether he's had a short crop or a big crop. But this is not true of the money factor. I've witnessed the change of price of corn from 10 cents a bushel to $2.50 a bushel in my lifetime. Yet with the change of prices there has been no change in the physical value of the corn. It has just as many calories at 10 cents a bushel as it had at $2.50 a bushel. But if the price is too low for the initial producer, then it moves through trade channels without generating adequate income for the exchange economy. A study of the record proves that we did not have a surplus in the early '30s, but as a result of the low price we had a shortage of income. To illustrate this very simply, suppose you have a level of 100% production, or enough to supply the needs of the population. If your prices are 100%, or at full parity, your income will be 100%. And you will have generated the income necessary to utilize the production. That's really what Say meant with the Law of Markets. Now if for any reason the price falls off 10%, then your income equation is 100% production times 90% of a full price, or only 90% of the income required to consume the production. You're 10% short. If you try to cure that by cutting back production 10% to balance with income, then your income equation becomes 90% production times 90% price, or only 81% of the income will be generated to utilize the production created by the economy. When you reduce production, you destroy the physical production required to employ the labor force. So you create unemployment by cutting back production in an attempt to offset the failure to maintain a proper price level.

Q. You're using the term balance sheet a little differently than it is generally used in normal accounting procedures, aren't you?

WILKEN. Not necessarily. In your normal accounting procedures, you have income on one side of your ledger and you have cost factors on the other. And the difference makes up your profit and loss. However, when I talk about a balance sheet I'm talking about income equations.

100% production  x  100% price  =  100% income.
100% production  x  90% price  =  90% income.
90% production  x  90% price  =  81% income.

Let's say you have full production, or 100% of what's required, and you only pay 90% of a parity price for it. What happens? The population can either do without, lower its standard of living, or it can dissave, or borrow the money lost by failing to maintain proper price relationships.

Q. Is that what you mean when you use terms such as shortage of income, or *we lacked so and so much of having enough income to balance with wages and interest?*

WILKEN. You have to bring all the separate records together and strike a balance to know whether an economy is generating enough income to consume its production. We have all the separate records in the government, and we end up with a record of national income as published in the *Economic Report of the President,* but we fail to create a balance sheet—or income equation—of the economy as a whole. And to illustrate that—I'll use General Motors as an example. Suppose General Motors never set up an income equation. The president of the corporation could be compared to the President of the United States, the board of directors can be compared to the Congress, the stockholders can be compared to the American people. Without a balance sheet we wouldn't have the slightest conception of the actual state of affairs in General Motors. Now that's our situation as far as our country is concerned today. On the other hand, different segments have used parts of the record to go before Congress to get special legislation without regard to the effect it would have on the whole. The same thing could happen in General Motors. Supposing they called in an auditor and said now we want you to look at this record and the auditor would pick out five or six departments which were showing a good growth and profit and total them up and find a good profit—and tell the directors and the president that everything was fine—and fail completely to look at the other departments, many of which might be operating at a loss. He couldn't give them a true picture unless he brought all the departments together. I think that you will admit after reading the newspapers that our so-called experts have completely ignored agriculture—the raw materials producers and all of the people in rural America who depend upon the value of our agriculture and other raw material production for income. In other words, you read of meetings of experts and they never mention agriculture. They never mention raw material production. It's all in terms of wages and so on. Well, as a result of this they have ignored 50% of the national market which exists in rural America. And the reason I say 50%—we have this interesting situation: because of the importance of small business and the farm operators in rural communities, these communities spend 70% of their income for goods at retail. Now you can compare this to 50% in the state of Pennsylvania and the state of New York. They spend more of their money for recreation and other things. Now the farmer, in addition to being a buyer of food, clothing, and so on, is also a buyer at retail of machinery, gasoline and other fuels to operate his machinery. He buys fertilizers, fencing, and other materials which the average individual doesn't have to buy. The same is true of the small businessman in rural towns. He buys a lot of things at retail for his own particular business. Our experts miss completely the importance of this market.

Q. How is this income equation constructed for the entire economy? In the first tape you said that during the mid-'60s we lacked $73 billion of having enough income to balance with wages and interest. Exactly how does an income equation reveal that fact?

WILKEN. The United States government reports national income statistics in six component parts. These are compensation of employees (wages), income of unincorporated enterprise, income of farm proprietors (net farm income), rental income of persons, corporate profits before taxes (which can be converted to corporate profits after taxes), and net interest. Here's the process. In producing, distributing and consuming the national product, our unincorporated private enterprise, our corporations and our farm proprietors advance the money for wages and interest, and then they recover costs plus a profit in the process of selling the production. In terms of accounting, and in terms of common denominators this means net interest and wages are the chief cost factors in operating the economy. On a profit and loss statement, sometimes called income statement, the first line is usually called *income*. In terms of an income equation (which is what my balance sheet really is), our private enterprise sector—corporations, unincorporated enterprise, farms and private rental units—accounts for the economy's entire income. This is the income that must feed the working mechanism of this economy. Now what are the costs involved in operating this economy and producing this income? These are chiefly labor and interest (or capital costs). Obviously, no company or country can continue to operate if costs outrun income. Yet this is precisely what has happened in the U.S. To offset the underpayment on the income side of the equation, not only to agriculture, but to all of private enterprise, we have resorted to debt injection. This is no solution at all because interest compounds the debt. It doubles the debt in a decade. If you put an income figure behind each item, you'll find that private enterprise, in terms of parity to balance with wages and capital costs, has been consistently short since the early 1950s. As a sector, private enterprise has been earning little more than 50% when it should have earned a dollar.

Q. What is the key to understanding all this?

WILKEN. If there is a key, it has to be the fact that you have to save to capitalize. You can't create capital debt beyond narrow limits as an economy—no more than you can have everyone win in a lottery drawing. This brings us back to how an economy operates. What is an economy? Really little more than the production of goods and services. Goods and services are produced, and if they are priced properly then the act of production generates the income necessary to consume or buy back the product. By pricing raw materials at parity—that is, to balance with labor costs and interest costs in the rest of the economy—we require industry to borrow working capital for the processing job. Of course a business can be its own banker for working capital if capital investment does not require the funds. After the raw materials are fabricated and transported, and so on, the middlemen recover their costs from the market, plus a profit. When an economy tries to expand beyond what it has a right to borrow based on savings, then capital costs start running away from income.

Q. And the income equation points up dislocation between the various sectors? Can you explain this in a T account?

WILKEN. Very simply. Remember, this is an income equation, not a bookkeeping debit and credit account. [Here Wilken drew out this presentation.]

| INCOME | COSTS |
|---|---|
| Unincorporated Enterprise | Wages |
| Incorporated Enterprise | Interest |
| Agriculture | |
| Rents | |

To offset the underpayment on the income side, not only to agriculture, but to all of private enterprise, this injection of debt since 1950 has been no solution. Interest on the right-hand side compounds the debt, doubling it on the basis of interest alone in terms of ten years. If you put an income figure behind each item, you'll find that private enterprise in terms of parity of income to balance with wages and interest is around 56%—or 56% enough to pay the bill. In other words, private enterprise as a whole is getting 56 cents when it should have a dollar.

Q. Would you illustrate what this has meant to, say, Iowa?

WILKEN. In 1946-1950, the value of farm production in Iowa was equal to 65% of the entire income in the state. Here you had one industry producing products equal to 65% of the entire income of the state. Yet it wasn't being considered an industry. In the period between 1946 and 1950, we permitted an industry that was creating income equal to 65% of the state income to be liquidated by reducing the income from this industry fully 50%. So you're not going to solve this thing by passing revenue bonds or bringing in a trailer factory. You can't even begin to make up the loss. To go a little further, any new industry has to take three factors into consideration. One is the availability of labor. Another is the availability of markets. And there is the transportation cost. Now if you liquidate agriculture, and liquidate the population in rural America, where are these new industries going to market their production? The point I want to make is that we're not only losing income, but we're losing people, or the potential market necessary if we're going to operate any industry.

Q. Businesswise, how does the feedback work?

WILKEN. The state of Iowa is short in income in terms of the income equation for the state. In other words the income of Iowa comes in short of the minimum required to pay the increase in wages and interest. Iowa businessmen lose sales because of this shortage. Merchants lose operating profit. When you finally get to the end of the line we lose the profit needed to further develop the economy of Iowa. In the same way, nations that have low prices and international investments bleeding profits out of the country can't possibly build capital to develop themselves.

Q. If this is the case, how do they get along?

WILKEN. There are all those corporations with all those brains—they added $365 billion to their gross corporate debt from the end of 1950 to the end of 1965 alone. Now why did they add it? For one thing, they wanted to build machines which would cut down their labor costs. They wanted to stay in business and compete. And, strange as it seems, different corporations wanted to see their competitors go broke, then absorb them.

Q. If a corporation is losing money, it can make up a good part of the loss by dominating a specific market, or by avoiding taxes. I have in mind airlines handing part of the real operating bill to the taxpayer. Or it can find a differential advantage as long as the game lasts. Isn't that what all the mergers are about?

WILKEN. It's the basic reason. They think they can diversify their operations, and in case of a depression some of the operations will do well and alleviate some of the effect.

Q. Can it work out that way?

WILKEN. It didn't work out in 1929.

Q. You will concede, won't you, that the effects of imbalance as you define it can be hidden for a long time. Business can merge, take over a money-losing plant, and pay for it with money the tax man might get. In effect it is possible to acquire the corporation for nothing. This in turn can help the bigs dominate the market. By dominating the market they can recover by adjusting upward the price structure?

WILKEN. Sometimes. But frequently they have the overall market, or the general economic climate, in a position that makes it impossible. Let me illustrate this thing. In 1966, we were short $90 billion in having enough income to balance with wages and interest. If you figure it out you'll find that if we had been able to sell 14% more goods we could have had $90 billion more income out of the sale of production. Or by a 14% increase in the price we could have had $90 billion. Or by a combination of both, roughly 7% increase in production and 7% increase in price, we would have had the $90 billion. It's not hard to solve. Of course, you have two sides to an equation.

Q. What you're saying runs counter to a theory of low prices?

WILKEN. If low prices provided an answer, then the ultimate of efficiency would be full production times zero price—and no income. This is possible on an island where everyone picks his own fruit, but nowhere else. If there are production costs, there has to be a price.

Q. Parity, then, has the cost of production figured in?

WILKEN. That is correct. Now here's how the whole theory as presently applied to agriculture is wrong. They have penalized agriculture for efficiency. On the other hand, they've overpaid labor for efficiency created by capital investment. For example, we've had an increase in the hourly wage every year without exception from 1934 up to the present. Now if there's anything to the idea of efficiency in labor, our price structure would be less than it was in 1946-1950. That would be the case if the theory were correct. But instead of that, our price structure is 43% [circa 1967] higher than it was in 1946-1950.

Q. We have, then a double standard. Prices are supposed to go down in agriculture, and up in everything else?

WILKEN. That's right, exactly. Now in reducing the price of farm products we really attack private enterprise. You see, business enterprise is tied to agriculture. Agriculture is the foundation of private enterprise because agriculture is the principal source of new income and new profits and new capital which private enterprise must use. Wages and interest are operating costs which private enterprise has to pay.

Q. How does a parity base year affect the calculations as to what wheat or corn should be?

WILKEN. If it is the wrong year, it compounds the degree of imbalance. You can't use a base year if capital costs and interest that year are not in balance with the rest of the economy.

Q. Why, then, has the farm parity base been changed from 1947-'49 to 1957-'59, *etc.*?

WILKEN. The proper parity formula told too much, and that's the reason the formula has become rigged. The government established what they called modernized parity. It's a very complicated formula. The purpose of it is to get parity prices down, and to fix it so farmers can't tell what honest parity is.

Q. What was the justification for this change?

WILKEN. No justification. They wanted a lower figure on wheat and corn, and so on. They had to have a lower figure to prove the efficiency theory, or the idea that efficiency on the farm was outrunning efficiency in the factory. But they forgot one thing—arithmetic does not change. According to the record, corn in 1910-1914 averaged 64.2 cents a bushel. Now the price that the farmer has to pay in order to be able to produce that corn has advanced 340% over what it was in 1910-1914. So the parity price for corn today [circa 1967] should be calculated at $2.19 a bushel.

But they claim 1910-1914 is out of date. It sounds out of date because it was a long time ago. But we're not talking about cars or buggies. We're talking about arithmetic and a basic commodity. OK, let's take a later date—let's take 1946-1950. In that five-year period our farm prices were at parity. The price of corn averaged $1.54 a bushel. Since that time consumer prices have moved up 43%. So your parity should be 143% times $1.54. You have to add the base period, which is 100. This calculation would give you about $2.20 a bushel. If you take the effective parity of that time, $1.82 a bushel, and calculate parity in terms of the fact that the consumer price level has gone up 22%—you have $1.82 times 122%, and that would give you $2.22. The point I want to make is that no matter what method you use to calculate it, if you adjust to the consumer price level you have an accurate yardstick.

Q. What have the lower prices really delivered?

WILKEN. Debt. And that's what financial organizations wanted. Anyone in debt has to pay interest. Here's what we're facing. Even now we've mortgaged the country up to 60%, and we're down to the other 40% without equity. In other words, we're reaching the point of diminishing returns. The top man always gets the best cut—he's the man with the best bank statement. If you have the financial statement, you can get money today in spite of anything. If you have the security, the bank can loan you $2,000 and then immediately set it up on the other side of the ledger as $2,000 deposit. The Fed testified to this effect in 1945. They pointed out that if they released a billion credit, it would translate itself into five or six times that much in deposits throughout the banking system. That's because you have two sides of the ledger. If you borrow from the bank, you borrow a thousand dollars, then your deposit of loans move up.

Q. Where does the guarantee of deposits fit into the picture?

WILKEN. They had a bankers' guarantee law in Nebraska and it worked fine in the 1920s. But following 1929, the state of Nebraska didn't have the power to protect the income of the people of Nebraska, and when we had the Depression 1929-1933, income in Nebraska fell off 55%. So this little dribble of money in the reserve evaporated into thin air. The main reason we have the bank guarantee in the United States is for its psychological effect. There isn't even 1% of the money available to pay out as a guarantee.

Q. If there isn't a satisfactory reserve to pay out a deposit guarantee, why did they raise the guarantee?

WILKEN. Psychological.

Q. Why did they raise the Social Security benefits?

WILKEN. One of the reasons why they raised the Social Security benefits is that they haven't got the money coming in to pay the Social Security benefits now. They used this money as a flow-in and replaced it with IOUs. So they've raised the Social Security payments and then turned around and increased the tax on the premium for the people who are working. So now there's more money flowing in. If our insurance companies operated that way, we'd put them in the pen.

Q. One Wall Street researcher has stated that no nation has ever been able to take more than 25% of the national income in taxes without heading into a massive adjustment in political and economic institutions. Is this true, and if so, why?

WILKEN. It's true because you lived on borrowed money and borrowed time under such conditions. Remember, it takes well over $5 of income to pay back $1 of debt. We would have to have over ten times the annual national income of the nation to pay the debt, that's how deep in hock this economy is.

Q. Dr. Kline, an American Keynesian, says, "So what. We owe it to ourselves." Heilbroner and Bernstein [in *A Primer on Government Spending*] say the same thing. They say, ". . . find a nation whose domestic debts are mounting, whose mortgages year by year are increasing, whose corporate debentures are proliferating, whose local and state and federal bond issues are growing, and the chances are that you have found a nation whose rate of growth is high, whose economy is buoyant, whose savings are abundant, whose business is booming." End quote.

WILKEN. One part of the statement is true. For example, we had the Depression in 1929-1932. All the homes and facilities didn't disappear. But we lost our liquidity, our ability to function. When a business can't meet the payroll, it may well have plenty of accounts on the books—all uncollected. But the doors close. When the same thing happened to the American economy in 1929, we broke down, and we didn't get going again until we restored the 1929 level. The second part is false. You need profit to invest for expansion, and after you invest the profit you've got to have a return on capital out of the price of goods sold. You can't pull it out of the pipeline or the poker game because if you do you lose your liquidity.

Q. So what we're talking about is simply that an economy has to run like a car, and if it doesn't run, what good is it?

WILKEN. OK. Take a car. Now what operates that car. You have an engine. The engine is the same as private enterprise. But what is the thing that drives it? Fuel. You put fuel into the economy and you run it until you stop. Farm production is the basic fuel. It has continually a three-times-a-day turnover or disappearance factor. That's the fuel. Now after driving the car a while, you find that you can make 15 miles per gallon. Well, that's the ratio of your automobile. If you want to drive 150 miles, you have to put in ten gallons of gas. If you try to save and put in only half of that much when you get half the distance you'll stop and walk the rest of the way, or you'll have to borrow gasoline to finish. And if you borrow gasoline to finish, you are obligated to pay it back. All the other parts of that automobile will not turn it without fuel. Every nation has a ratio of raw materials intake. We have the highest ratio. I would imagine the Common Market countries have about a 4 times ratio. They can't ever have the trade turn of the United States because they haven't the resources. Look at your raw material intake and look at your income equation as it affects the various segments of the economy. That's where you'll find an answer to why we have business cycles and depressions.

# CHAPTER 5: INCOME EQUATION

*Look at your raw material intake and look at your income equation as it affects the various segments of the economy. That's where you'll find an answer to why we have business cycles and depressions.*

## [1] BUSINESS CYCLES

For almost two centuries the concept of business cycles has undergone investigation. One of the first to present cycles graphically was Leonard P. Ayers of the Cleveland Trust company. His charts reached back to 1790, depicting 23 depressions, with the Depression of the 1930s the worst of the lot. Even casual scrutiny revealed that there were really very few normal years. There seemed to be an almost equal division between years that could be termed "prosperity" and years that can be called "depression." The strange association of wars with prosperity and then depression became at once apparent. And aside from the fact of wars, good years seemed to be associated with new industrial opportunities. The depression of 1893 seemed to be overcome by the birth of the mass production industries, and this stimulant again seemed to be in evidence in 1907 because of new technology, chiefly automobiles. Recovery from the 1920-1922 depression correlated with the development of radio, a sensational invention that mushroomed into a billion dollar business in about five years. Other developments included railroads, corporate enterprise, and mining. Still, periods in which there was full employment turned out to be rare and of short duration, sometimes only a few months. During such periods, however, food surpluses vanished as if by magic, and when a downturn came a drop in commodity prices always led the way.

The classic Depression of them all came on in 1929. For fully a decade after the great collapse, those in command of the academic world hashed and rehashed the cause of the cause, and historians have concerned themselves with the "great bath" ever since.

In *The Oxford History of the American People*, Samuel Eliot Morison, an eminent American historian, stated: "The stock market crash of October 1929 (which of course continued its downward spiral until late 1932) was a natural consequence of the greatest orgy of speculation and overoptimism since the South Sea bubble of 1720." Morison correctly noted that speculation began to reach a "giddy height" by 1925, and "when speculation began to get out of hand, neither the federal nor the state governments did anything effective to check it."

Viewed from that vantage point, it was not the first time in history that an entire nation took leave of its senses. Dr. Charles Mackay, writing in *Extraordinary Popular Delusions and the Madness of Crowds*, detailed how nation after nation has "become simultaneously impressed with one delusion, and run after it, till their attention is caught by some new folly more captivating than the first. We see one nation suddenly seized, from its highest to its lowest members, with a fierce desire of military glory; another as suddenly becoming crazed upon a religious scruple, and neither of them recovering its senses until it has shed rivers of blood and sowed a harvest of groans and tears, to be reaped by its posterity.

"Money, again, has often been a cause of the delusion of multitudes. Sober nations have all at once become desperate gamblers, and risked almost their existence upon the turn of a piece of paper. . . . Men, it has been well said, think in herds; it will be seen they go mad in herds, while they only recover their senses slowly" one at a time.

Did the American nation take leave of its senses before or after the 1929 crash? Could the American people have kept the boom by obeying the injunction of leaders to "have confidence?" More important, could collective confidence have been a substitute for basic errors in economic planning? These questions were important to Wilken because he could almost hear the gentlemen of yesteryear speaking just before the 1929 crash.

President Herbert Hoover: "Any lack of confidence in the economic future or the basic strength of business in the United States is foolish."

Charles M. Schwab (Bethlehem Steel): "I do not feel that there is any danger to the public in the present situation. Money is now being lent in Wall Street by people who never lent it before. As long as the people remain enthusiastic and interested the market will hold up."

Irving T. Bush (Bush Terminal Company): "We are only at the beginning of a period that will go down in history as the golden age."

Among those who saw no depression coming (at least in their public pronouncements) were Calvin Coolidge, Charles Evans Hughes, Irving Fisher, Roger Babson, John D. Rockefeller Sr., Andrew Mellon, Robert P. Lamont, Arthur M. Hyde, Henry Ford, Arthur Brisbane, Sir Josiah Stamp, W. Randolph Burgess, and Leonard P. Ayres.

When Franklin D. Roosevelt took the oath of office on that bleak inauguration day in Washington, unemployment had climbed above 12 million—25% of the labor force. The gross national product had tumbled from $104.4 billion at the end of 1929 to about $25 billion in 1933. Prices on such basic commodities as wheat, corn, cotton, wool, tobacco—all had started their nosedive in 1929. They hit their lowest point in 1932 and 1933, and for every dollar that farm production went down, the national income followed by going down approximately $7. Banks failed. By inauguration day 1933 the governors of 22 states had ordered them closed. By March 4, 1933, almost 5,000 banks had collapsed.

## [2] A COLLECTION

In a collection of causes that filled a several inch thick set of file cards, I once codified many of the prime ideas behind cycles. Questioned, Carl Wilken knew of and could discuss them all.

The causes ran full circle. J.C.L. Sismondi argued that purchasing power for the production of one year was simply the income of the previous year, and that therefore inequitable distribution of income was the culprit. John Stuart Mill explained the phenomenon was psychological, this at the time W. Stanley Jevons* calculated his involved sunspot theory, one that linked crops to weather and weather to sunspots. Cycle spotters have seldom been bashful in either touting their conclusions, or assigning definitive status to them. A man named John Wade, in 1833, put it thus: "The commercial cycle is ordinarily completed in five or seven years, within which terms it will be found, by reference to our commercial history during the last seven years, alternate periods of prosperity and depression have been experienced."

Others picked up some of the physical ideas, notably Henry L. Moore, who in 1914 announced a rainfall theory and 33 and 8 year cycles respectively. Why not? By the dozens, economists were getting into the act, even before the 1920s. "The statistics from 1870 to the Great War," wrote one Ellsworth Huntington in 1919, "show that a high death rate regularly precedes hard times, while a low death rate precedes prosperity," both depending on the prevailing mental attitude, because mental weather and health go together!

There were curious theories—Werner Sombart's organic and inorganic goods theory—and theories that had to do with businessman cunning—Charles O. Hardy's "tendency to alternations of over and under production." A.C. Pigou of Cambridge saw "business confidence" or the lack

---

* Elaborating on a theory suggested by an English worthy, Sir William Herschel writing in 1801.

thereof as the cause of boom and bust, whereas Joseph Schumpeter scored innovations brought on by energetic businessmen changing the pace and scope of activity, bringing on a flurry of activity, high interest, and slow-down in turn. No, said Emanuel H. Vogel of Vienna University, crises are caused by "accidents." They happen in a growing society.

The elite of the "cycles" corp were the savings-investment people, Tugan-Baranovski, for instance, who hammered out the concept that at times the loan-fund is uninvested, largely because of concentration in the hands of a few. "Oversaving," said John A. Hobson, bowing to that popular concept—certainly the same one entertained by the Senate Committee on Banking and Currency when it timidly investigated the great Houses of Kuhn, Loeb and Company, J.P. Morgan and the handful that controlled investments because, as Committee counsel Ferdinand Pecora wrote in *Wall Street Under Oath*, "If this smooth flow of investment is impeded for any reason, the paralyzing effects are soon felt throughout all branches of trade and industry."

"Over-construction," said Malcolm C. Rorty, and "over-commitment." "Over-production," emphasized economists from Tiflis to Moscow, al-though the Russian N.D. Kondratieff dealt with long-term wholesale price indexes and ended up with a look-see at the tempo of prospecting probes for gold, because the creation of money figured, whether legal tender came off the printing press or from the cold, cold Earth.

Cycles, it has been said, all tie to the vault of heavens. Isaac Newton said it all. He could, he said, calculate the swing of the planets, but he could not compute the madness of crowds.

It is also said that while the swing of the stars can be calulated, psycho-logical measurements cannot. They cannot claim addability. There are no exact uinits with equal intervals and there is no absolute zero, although things like IQ scores pretend as much. You almost have to read the philosophers, Socrates, Plato, Aquinas, Kant, Spinoza, Schopenhauer, Spengler, even John Dewey and George Bernard Shaw to confront the reality that Newtonian physics has been supplanted, that measurable im-pulses literally pulse the planet, and if the connection has been elusive, the scattered pixels are being connected rapidly.

Cycles such as Kondratieff and Kitchin owe their image to Joseph Schum-peter, an Austrian trained economist who taught at Harvard.

Kondratieff was a Russion economist during the Stalin era. His original cycle was essentially a commodity cycle with all the weather conditions basic storable grains suggest. He enlarged his study to take in inudstries, finaince, the free world and socialist systems. Here he ran afoul Soviet theory and wishful thinking. Kondratieff published in 1926. He predicted the economic depression of the 1930s and resurrection of the capitalist word. He also predicted the demise of what Lincoln Steffens called "the future now," communism. Stalin had him trundled aboard a train for Siberia. Solzhenitsyn tells us Kondratieff died in solitary confinement, his mind tormented into madness.

The long wave survived largely because Schumpeter picked up on the idea and made it part of his Harvard study course and his text entitled *Business Cycles*.

One of Schumpeter's associates was a man named Joseph Kitchin, thus the subdivision known as the Kitchin cycle. The Kondratieff was defined as 50 to 60 years, but latitude has to be granted for elongation and contraction because of the psychic propensity that annoints human conduct. The hunt for absolutes is taken to be a moral imperative.

Wilken was well aware of ice ages, global warming, volcanoes, droughts and floods. These were nature's toys. More lethal in delivering instability was man's intervention that kept the laws of physical balance from working. Thus cycles became an aside, mere arcane knowledge compared to the exchange equation he illustrated with facts and numbers.

Nevertheless, if the key to prosperity unlimited is commodities, and commodities tilt the scale in a hierarchy of cycles, the arcane has its place in fine-tuning an understanding, a fact Wilken always conceded before returning to observed data.

Banking has been singled out almost as much as the weather in the hunt for depression causes. Still many agree with A.C. Pigou in the *Economics of Welfare* that bank credits were merely mechanisms through which more basic forces worked effects. On this some economists begged to disagree.

"Demand," wrote Alvin H. Hansen, "is based on purchasing power. The source of purchasing power is income, and the source of income is the production of material goods and services. . . . In short, goods and services are exchanged against goods and services. On this basis one would expect production to run an even course, and not to run in cycles." Banks, however, have a rather unique power. They can create money by granting credit. "The nominal incomes of people generally are as before, but their real purchasing power is reduced because of the increase in prices. The issuance of bank credit simply redistributes purchasing power, reducing the real purchasing power of income receivers generally, and increasing the purchasing power of entrepreneurs able to secure bank credit. It is this redistribution of purchasing power, accomplished through the instrumentality of banking institutions, that changes demand, upsets prices, affects the profit margin, and therefore production. Here, in short, wrote Hansen in *Cycles of Prosperity and Depression in the United*

*States, Great Britain and Germany*, "may be found the fundamental cause of the business cycle."

Wesley C. Mitchell, writing in *Business Cycles*, catalogued theories as physical, emotional and institutional, with special emphasis on institutional, since weather cycles, variations in solar radiation and the push and pull of organic industries were few, and emotional processes fewer still. Institutional causes meant banking, government, and power, just as institutional arrangements meant the power one sector of an economy could exercise over another.

R.G. Hawtrey of the British Treasury touched on some of this because he saw "an inherent tendency toward fluctuations in the banking institutions which prevail in the world as it is," and his on-scene citations sounded sensible enough, because high prices stimulate imports, check exports, cause an outflow of gold, hence less credit, hence depression.

Production and the money flow popped up again and again in the tomes of William T. Foster and Waddill Catchings who said simply that depressions resulted from a lack of markets brought on by a lack of buying power.

Again and again the lack of equilibrium between incomes and money values of goods, between liquid capital and savings, between saving, spending and employment bookmark any catalog of depression causes. It would take many volumes the size of this one to recite in abstract form the many ideas. There are hundreds that can be judged by themselves and not compared with others, and each contains a germ of plausibility. Juxtaposed next to each other, they often seem contradictory. Taken in the aggregate, they all suggest a missing link. Among those that deal with economics in an industrial age, few consider raw materials, just as those with vintage status consider little else.

Through most of his adult years, Wilken lived in the underworld of economics, a limbo from which there was no escape. Had he accomplished his research under the auspices of Harvard or M.I.T. and then endured a lifetime subservient to the canons of acceptable economic thought, he might have survived to gain a hearing replete with academic trappings. As it happened, Wilken took to economic analysis in the depth of the Depression. He and his associates were interested in causes and solutions.

For fully a decade after the great collapse, the academic economists rated somewhere near absolute zero in some government circles. They had known all the answers, and yet the economy had collapsed. A few Congressmen in the late 1930s wanted new and daring ideas.

Those who had been mistaken fought valiantly. They dismissed men like Wilken as "colorful cranks" or "talented amateurs." Foster and Catchings weren't considered "pros." Frederick Soddy wasn't a graduate economist. And Gertrude M. Coogan rated attention only as a monetary meddler.

In the final analysis, however the intellectual failures of the 1930s and the outbreak of war accounted for Wilken getting his chance. Practical Congressmen wanted practical answers, not more of the taxonomy associated with Marshall's *Principles*, which was then standard college text-book fare.

Wilken saw that all the standard explanations lacked something. They accepted the economy as a going concern, but failed to explain how it got going in the first place. They did not explain profit. They did not explain the creation of real purchasing power. They did not bridge the gap between physical production at the foundation level and national income.

Wilken agreed with Soddy that income for a nation boiled down simply to two parts, each equally important. One was the production of goods and services for human use. The other was the pricing of goods and services at the consumer level. Production times price meant income. Here is an exchange from one of my interviews with Wilken.

WILKEN. The first thing I did was to take up the farm production because the low prices were being blamed on surpluses. So I set up the record of crop production in 1928 and 1932 and found that our crop production in 1932 was less than it was in 1928. And we had 4 million more people in 1932 than in 1928. Having operated a farm I knew that most of the grain was processed through livestock, so I set up a record of the production of livestock in 1932. I found that we had less meat production in 1932 than we had in 1928. So the surplus theory went out the window.

Q. The 1928 production was all consumed, was it not?

WILKEN. We were going great guns. I have a chart which covers a period from 1910 through 1950. It shows that during the time span represented, our consumption has pretty much equaled our production. In other words, we didn't have a surplus other than seasonal between 1910 and 1950. Now—due to our crop cycle, the law of supply and demand can't possibly maintain farm prices at harvest because at harvest we have full year supply and one day of demand. Even with half a crop, we'll have 180 days' supply and one day of demand. And without support prices everybody takes advantage of the farmer because they know he's got to bring it in and get some money to pay off his banker at harvest time. The next step was to take a look at the import-export situation. Because the theoretical economists blamed low prices on high tariffs. Then I checked the imports and exports. And after deducting the imports, many of which were the same products as those we exported, I found that 98% of our production is consumed in the United States. So it didn't seem possible to me that this small 2%, and the tariff situation, could have broken the price of the 98%.

## [3] IRREDUCIBLE AND STUBBORN FACTS

"I have to forge every sentence in the teeth of irreducible and stubborn facts," wrote William James when he was finishing his great work on the *Principles of Psychology*. This was the challenge Wilken faced, to find the relationship between general principles and "irreducible and stubborn facts." How did the stubborn facts square with abstract generalizations? Could economic occurrences be correlated with antecedents? And if the cause were directed, could the result be controlled?

Others have pondered the problem.

When Thorstein Veblen detailed his concept of evolutionary capitalism, he added insight to the riddle of economic life. When John R. Commons took on Veblen's teachings to become a social reformer and public administrator, he dealt with symptoms and signs and avoided construction of a theory. But when Wesley Clair Mitchell resolved to test each hypothesis against stubborn arithmetic, he uncorked the beginning of the answer to the booming, buzzing confusion. The three became known as institutional economists. They became the intellectual descendents of Cantillon, Quesnay and the physiocrats. They reasoned with a fine singleness of purpose, and they taught their students lessons that the institutional *powers that be* had a hard time putting down.

One student out of the Wisconsin of John R. Commons was John Lee Coulter, later Dean of North Dakota A. & M., later a member of the U.S. Tariff Commission, still later an associate of Carl H. Wilken. The information flow between Coulter and Wilken drew constant nourishment from Veblen, Commons and Wesley Clair Mitchell. And Mitchell was an economist who believed in arithmetic.

In the process of writing a *History of the Greenbacks*, Mitchell observed the paucity of good statistical information. His career thus became a scholar's search for statistical techniques. Working on the problem Mitchell visualized a work entitled, *The Money Economy*, but when it was published in 1913 it went forth as *Business Cycles*. Hard on the heels of World War I, Mitchell gave direction to the business of statistics gathering at the National Bureau of Economic Research. Today, the finest set of statistics in the history of man—those gathered by the U.S. government—can correctly be counted as a monument to the career of Wesley Clair Mitchell.

The income equation used by Wilken might never have been developed without the data gathering apparatus Mitchell and his associates accounted for.

# [4] THE INCOME EQUATION

Although it wasn't accomplished in 24 hours, those early researchers finally set up the elements for an income equation for the American economy. In short, the total national income had to be the sum of the component parts. A cost to one segment was income to another, and vice versa.

It did not take an astute seer to observe the relationships. The gushing well that kept the system moving was the private enterprise system. Individual capitalists save, borrow, beg or steal, and capitalize businesses or farms. They pay out the wages and capital costs to do a job, and recover from the market if they are successful. Today, the *Economic Report of the President* expresses all this as six component parts. These are common denominators. All forms of income finally telescope until they fall under one of these heads, and the total of all six becomes the national income.

The segments are:

1. Compensation of employees (wages).
2. Income of unincorporated enterprises.
3. Income of farm operators (net farm income).
4. Corporate profits.
5. Net interest.
6. Rental income of persons.

In terms of an equation, Wilken explained, the balance had to line up this way. In other words, the national income division has to move at a rate governed by the raw material intake and the state of the arts.

| INCOME | COSTS |
|---|---|
| Income of unincorporated enterprises | Compensation of employees (wages) |
| Income of farm proprietors | Net interest |
| Rental income of persons | |
| Corporate profits | |

The income achieved on one side of the equation has to stay at parity with the costs on the other side, even in a static economy. The correct ratio for a stable economy is approximately 33.3% on the income side and 66.6% on the cost side of the equation. Thus corporate profits, income from unincorporated enterprise, farm income and rentals have to maintain parity in order to pay wages and interest. Each of the sectors must advance at approximately the same rate unless some compensating factor becomes evident.

The relationship between segments on either side of the equation can be changed with impunity only when warranted by technological development, efficiency of capital or a change in the state of the arts. Indeed, an entire segment can be erased as long as it is absorbed by a segment on the same side.

Wilken frequently calculated the exact posture of national balance. And at the time of my first basic interview with Wilken he noted that since the last balanced base period, 1946-1950,

| | |
|---|---|
| National income increased | 130.0% |
| Corporation profits before taxes increased | 93.9% |
| Small business income increased | 67.9% |
| Rental income increased | 97.8% |
| Farm income (gross) increased | 5.9% |
| Wages increased | 153.4% |
| Interests (capital costs) increased | 725.0% |

All of his calculations were made on the basis of the *Economic Report of the President*, 1966.

The logic of the Wilken system and its proof were contained in that income equation. Beyond that, all else was elaboration. The equation and the equation alone pointed out how each sector was managing, how close the nation's brinkmanship was taking it toward depression or wild inflation.

In truth, labor and interest could not have a higher parity than corporations, farmers, or unincorporated enterprise. The above percentages translated into dollars revealed how short income on the first side of the equation had become. The kite had been kept flying by paying farmers for less wealth than they produced, by short-changing both corporations and private enterprise, and by creating debt. The surface manifestations could be seen by anyone: mergers and bankruptcy on the one hand, bargained wages and high interest costs on the other. High interest costs were made mandatory by debt expansion. For 15 years a deficit on the earnings side of the income equation had been hidden under an umbrella of expanded debt (hence the 725% interest note). Private enterprise (including farming) had continued to function by consuming its capital, scaling back its earnings, and substituting debt for earnings.

Without understanding the significance of farm income, public policy managers seemed free to fund placebo "solutions" to the poverty that imbalance created, just as they felt free to solve the farm problem by feeding it into the cities.

Wilken argued that there are only two ways a nation can turn a profit. One is to produce, to take raw materials and create wealth where none existed before. The other is to best another nation in trade, and to maintain the favorable balance of trade and payments. It is impossible for a nation to turn a profit by besting any segment of its own economy. Yet this is what four administrations had been trying to do. If continued, Wilken pointed out, this practice would bring on the consequences that boom and bust always account for.

## [5] IN PROCESS

All the many other "systems" of observation overlook the quite obvious, Wilken pointed out again and again. The starting point of the economy "in process" is raw materials, because all new wealth must come from nature. The state of the arts, the refinement of tools, the education of the people, all figure mightily in wresting this wealth from nature and giving it utility, but in the end the proximate source remains unchanged.

The "in process" economy thus subjected itself to accounting principles not unlike accounting principles used in any business. It may be argued that the economy is always in motion, therefore no one can make calculations and tabulations of any meaningful nature because by the time they are made the situation is no longer the same. This, of course, is foolish. An operating business goes on even while accountants compile profit and loss statements and balance sheets. Still the accounting record enables a business to stop the motion long enough for a good look. One need not know the ancient history of a furniture manufacturing business in order to view an annual operating statement. The process starts with raw materials and ends up with sales and deliveries. The earth orbits the sun in $365^1/_4$ days, and this time sequence has appropriately been chosen for the accounting period.

The accounting period is dictated for even another reason. The days of a year come in seasons, and the four seasons allow a nation to grow the food required for its commissary on an annual basis. The raw materials used for food can be pinpointed on an annual basis, and render defensible the annual cycle as the appropriate record period.

Agriculture produces in advance of the rest of the economy. On the short run, at least $^1/_{12}$ of food production is produced fully a year in advance. The rest of the production is produced from one to 11 months in advance of use. In the long run, food production precedes the rest of the economy by the number of years prevailing culture requires before a youth enters the labor market.

Indian tribes on the American frontier hunted for their food, and with the planned destruction of their commissary by frontier military leaders these Indians were reduced to being wards of the state. Survival required it. Unable to solve the most elementary problem of any society, the American Indian was easily defeated by encroaching settlers and their power backed mentors in the east. It is simple to visualize the play of events in the passing of the frontier, yet the role of farm production in developing civilizations is all too easily overlooked.

The annual food production cycle not only dictates the scope of development, it figures heavily in determining how fast a level of prosperity proceeds and maintains itself. Wilken calculated the wealth that comes from farms to be 70% of the raw materials consumed in the process of running the economy. The Italian who discovered double entry bookkeeping proceeded from philosophy—"for every thing you gain, you part with something of equal value"—and now accountants who have never heard of this philosophical principle build on its premise without hesitation. Still the basic premise of accounting, both to the effect that debits must equal credits, and the appropriateness of the annual record period, have been spurned as a valuable tool in understanding the causes of depression.

"In process," the economy starts with raw materials. It starts with raw materials in each accounting period, and through one period flows into the next—like a creek emptying into a river—the process can be defined in sections, analyzed in sections, and effect traced to cause within the framework of the section invoked. The earned income of an economy and the profits of an economy can thus be traced to their fountainhead with the certainty that the stubborn facts must square well with abstract generalizations.

There are certain rules in the accounting game, just as there are principles in the discipline called economics. Violation of rules or ignorance of principles does not absolve the results from being in error.

## [6] TO GO BROKE

The world understands what it means to go broke, but there seems to be an elusiveness about "the process" of going broke, just as earning one's way is one of those concepts people misplace from time to time. The main reason officials have no clear cut idea on why a national economy fails to earn its way is because they have no clear cut idea of what "earning its own way" is in the first place. Because there is so little understanding about earning the income of an economy in the first place, it has become a matter of simple expediency to inject borrowed money against profits and savings—relying on the turnover of borrowed money to create prosperity. Similarly, there is no real understanding nowadays of how unearned income can be spent and still be owed for, and accordingly there gets to be a psychology that leads people to believe that they can enjoy prosperity indefinitely by mortgaging the future of their children, grandchildren and great grandchildren.

Earned income, then, means economy debited, nature credited, and the income equation instantly pinpoints any imbalance and the sector in which it occurs. Unearned income means income based on borrowed capital, because in the end it involves economy debited, economy credited, and makes impossible a net profit—the multiplier notwithstanding.

No expenditure in an economy can be calculated as a simple expenditure. It compounds itself as it turns and generates income. To put the Keynesian multiplier to work, it is necessary first of all to set in motion an expansion of purchasing power. Once the expansion is under way, the multiplier goes into motion, just as it goes into motion when raw materials are paid for at full parity.

As propounded by Keynesian economists, an increase in capital formulation causes a cumulative effect in the national income. An injection of, say, $4 million (the figure Keynes recommended to Roosevelt as a monthly injection in the 1930s) by way of investment adds $4 million to the national income through the rubrics of rent, profit, wages, etc. The journey of the new capital injection does not end there, however. Depending on "the propensity to consume," the same sum is turned again and again. If such a propensity is 70% then only 70% of the $4 million continues to turn in the second stage of the multiplier—or $3 million. If the propensity to consume remained the same, the formula would ultimately yield $11,428,571 of new national income as a result of the investment injection of $4 million. Even at full "propensity," the system made no provision for profit, or the wherewithal to pay debt.

## [7] GENERAL THEORY

Years ago when I was a student studying the economics of John Maynard Keynes, I noted in seven points the dominating message of his *General Theory*. These are:

1. When employment increases, aggregate real income is increased.

2. The psychology of the community is such that when aggregate real income is increased, aggregate consumption is increased but not by so much as income.

3. Hence employers would make a loss if the whole of the increased employment were to be devoted to satisfying the increased demand for immediate consumption.

4. Thus, to justify any given amount of employment there must be an amount of current investment sufficient to absorb the excess of total out-

put over what the community chooses to consume when employment is at a given level. For unless there is this amount of investment, the receipts of the entrepreneurs will be less than is required to induce them to offer the given amount of employment.

5. It follows, therefore, that, given the community's propensity to consume, the equilibrium level of employment, *i.e.*, the level at which there is no inducement to employers as a whole either to expand or to contract employment, will depend on the amount of current investment. The amount of current investment will depend in turn, on what we shall call the inducement to invest; and the inducement to invest will be found to depend on the relation between the schedule of the marginal efficiency of capital and the complex of rates of interest on loans of various maturities and risks.

6. Thus, given the propensity to consume and the rate of new investment, there will be only one level of employment consistent with equilibrium; since any other level will lead to inequality between the aggregate supply price of output as a whole and its aggregate demand price.

7. This level cannot be greater than full employment, *i.e.*, the real wage cannot be less than the marginal disutility of labor. But there is no reason in general for expecting it to be equal to full employment.

In short, the highly special theory which begged the existence of extreme poverty and depressions due to disequilibrium between supply and demand did not find a patient listener in Keynes. Keynes held that there was always equilibrium. It was not the lack of balance between supply and demand that was the cause of such extreme and disastrous distress as was being experienced in the great Depression. Keynes believed it would be necessary to look to other than the supply and demand forces of the classicists. Man-made devices, government spending, control of the rate of interest, adjustment of exaggerated contrasts in the level of income, and the comprehensive socialization of the rate of investment were perceived to contain the answer. Keynes more or less ignored raw materials as the foundation for an economy. He touted another approach, one more pleasing to the powers that be, that is the great lending houses and mature fortunes.

Keynes was fully aware of the fact that an economy had to operate in balance, and he knew that balance could occur at less than full employment, and he had an idea of how credit injection could rock an economy out of a stabilized depression, but the big engagement of continually servicing an ever-aging and compounded debt remained forever unanswered.

# [8] UNEARNED INCOME

Credit injected into the economy could create unearned income, but at what price? A dollar invested (via the multiplier) would produce nearly four dollars of national income, but it would be profitless income, because the process meant economy debited, economy credited, with the borrowed capital plus interest still to be paid back. This made the system nothing more than a device for pushing the wealth of the nation into the hands of a few.

The profit end of raw material production did not have to be paid back. Nature could be credited *ad infinitum* until all energy was leveled—a very distant possibility—and it was this revenue that in fact became the profit of the economy.

"The operation of an economy is made up to two parts," wrote Wilken in *All New Wealth Comes From the Soil*. First the production and second the price which the production is sold for, thus translating the production into income, the determining factor in whether we earned the money to utilize what we produced.

"To illustrate, if we start with 100% production and maintain a price in balance with cost factors, we generate 100% of the income required to market the production. If for some reason or other we permit the overall price level to fall off 10%, we lost 10% of the income and we have a 10% surplus of production. Then instead of correcting the price factor, we cut back production 10% to balance with the shortage of income, our income equation becomes 90% production times 90% of the price we should have and our income is only 81% and we move into a downward spiral of unemployment, shortages of income in what we term a depression."

The confusion between whether a lack of buying power triggers a depression, or whether holders of investment funds fail to sense opportunities (as touted by the rate of interest, liquidity preference, and the like) must be framed by a concept of cause and effect. It seems difficult to argue that in a society where tools are developed, factories built, and the state of the arts advanced, that investment leads the way.

The assertion that agriculture and other raw materials are the foundation of the economy seems to be a hard bite to swallow nowadays, largely because intellectual advisors have become unduly impressed with gadgets, utility creation, and the happy standard of living that an industrial society seems responsible for. Still, without bountiful agriculture, without efficiency of production preceding the rest of the economy, nations remain undeveloped. Credit-injection and pump-priming—

by making use of the multiplier—can rock an economy off low equilibrium, but unless raw material production is priced at a level of parity with all segments, an economy can starve in the midst of plenty, or it can tune-up the engine of credit expansion until it explodes.

The significance of the family farm in America is seldom understood because writers find it difficult to tie small details into the grand picture, and end up with meaningful presentation. Yet it remains a matter of responsible observation that the preservation of the family farm has to be equated with the preservation of the private enterprise system itself.

Those who fail to see the need for farm parity argue quite simply that the situation has changed, that $x$ number of people have left the farm, that mechanization has altered patterns—and there is some credence in all this. But it must be remembered that the rest of the economy has not stood still either, that there have been shifts, and this change in the state of the arts is duly reflected in the multiplier between raw material production and the national income *when the economy operates at a profit*. There is every reason to hold that economic balance between the several sectors has not shifted as much in wealth creation as indicated by payments for wealth (money). Raw material producers—particularly farm producers—are paid for less wealth than they produce. This is the consideration even casual inspection of the record reveals.

## [9] EXPAND IN ADVANCE

Raw materials production ideally should expand in advance of the rest of the economy, particularly food production, which is geared to weather cycles, and must be made available a year in advance. Balance can be changed with impunity only when warranted by technological development, efficiency of capital, and in general the state of the arts. Thus still another premise must be considered. There was a time when medicine lagged behind mechanical engineering, or farming lagged behind industrial production, but after the mid-20th century in America it must be noted that technology has affected the economy more or less evenly, visiting no special favors on one sector over another. Labor in the factory is no more efficient than labor on the farm. This assumption must be openly stated, because labor is being paid for machine efficiency in factories, and penalized for machine efficiency on the farm.

Wilken's income equation (or balance sheet) became a cornerstone that would permit the man on the street to understand economics even before WWII. His "elaboration" on how to compute parity proved his point so powerfully that it prompted revision of the record.

# [10] THE BASIC CALL FOR FARM PARITY

When George Peek and Hugh S. Johnson left Bernard Baruch's old War Office after WWI, they sounded the basic call for farm parity. The year was 1922. It was the era of the Capper-Volstead Act and the Ford-ney-McCumber Tariff Bill, and farm welfare was very much in the news. Parity insisted that there should be a fair relationship between the prices for which the farmer sold, and the prices on things the farmer had to buy. The farmer sold his production at wholesale. He bought his tools and equipment at retail. If the prices on farm production at wholesale were not in balance with prices on tools and equipment at retail, farmers would either consume their capital and go bankrupt, or work for nothing, or both. When parity was first calculated, it was obvious that the mechanism through which a farmer got his income was simply "sale of farm production." Either a farmer on the average well-managed farm gained enough on the sale of farm production to cover costs, or he didn't. It didn't take a fancy formula to compute whether wheat, corn, or rye were high enough in the market at wholesale to cover the costs incurred by a farmer in producing them. It took simple arithmetic.

Thorold Rogers' *History of Agriculture and Prices* was eminently correct in seeking out a base from which projections can be made. Such a year had to hone close to an era in which there was no debasement of money, and no rupture of the price structure through imports. Should we follow Thorold Rogers, using 100 as the index price for 1541—a year before Henry VIII's debasement of coins—we can read the sorry results, prices hitting 213.5 by 1556. Debasement, of course, is no different in principle than credit creation as practiced by the Federal Reserve System. Debasement, coupled with the flow of imports to the "high market," produces a double inflation, one that visits a heavy hand on the unorganized who are less able to fend for themselves.

Peek and Johnson knew this. It was not by accident that the first parity figures were calculated in terms of 1910-1914 as 100. It was a period when farm prices at wholesale were in balance with the commodities the farmer had to buy. For many farm products, the base period selected meant the 60 months from August 1909 to July 1914. The earliest calculations simply took the index number of the things farmers needed to buy, using the base period as 100. The index number was then multiplied by the average base period price—thus the parity price at any particular time. In time, new, old, and transitional parity were added to the lexicon, with USDA making calculations few lawmakers could understand.*

Wilken's calculation thus became simple in the extreme:

1910-1914 average price = base of 100
CORN        $ .642 per bushel
WHEAT       $ .884 per bushel

Since 1910-1914, up to 1967, prices of goods the farmer had to buy increased 240%. To compute true parity prices as of year-end 1966, one had simply to multiply 1910-1914 farm prices times the increase in commodity prices, or 240%. Thus the multiplier became 340% (3.40), because it was necessary to add the base period of 100.

Thus:

|  | CORN per bushel | WHEAT per bushel |
|---|---|---|
| 1910-1914 | $ .642 | $ .884 |
|  | x 3.400 | x 3.400 |
| Honest parity, year-end 1966 | $2.18 | $3.00 |
| 1910-1914 | $ .642 | $ .884 |
|  | x 18.320 | x 18.320 |
| Honest parity, year-end 2000 | $11.76 | $16.19 |

Therefore, the true 100% of parity prices as of year-end 1966 for corn should have been $2.18 per bushel and $3.00 per bushel for wheat. During the base period years of 1910-1914 the total national income averaged $33 billion per year and industrial wages averaged 23 cents per hour. In short, it took several hours of wages to buy the equivalent of a bushel of wheat.

The span of time since the original 1910-1914 parity period has often been used to discredit the calculations, but this is an argument lacking in logical content. Indeed, many of the nation's leading educators pooh-pooh the idea of farm parity on grounds that the world has turned over many times since 1910-1914, that price relationships at that time might not have been satisfactory, that changes in production costs might have affected different sectors of the economy differently, that demand for food may have given way to demand for TV sets and other consumer goods, that farm production in kind and quality may have changed materially over a particular base period used for a parity projection.

These criticisms deserve to be answered. It is no argument at all that the modern John-Deere tractor far outpaces the Rumley Oil Pull of many years ago, or that antiques on display at the Agricultural Hall of Fame

---

* See Parity Handbook, Senate Document No. 129, 1952.

have been replaced by more modern equipment, or even that beef and cotton and corn production nowadays are superior to the types of a few years back. The fact that the ratio between any sector of the economy and the whole moves but slowly indicates how slowly technological improvement puts one sector ahead of the rest.

This is clearly shown by calculating farm parity on a later period, when, again, farm prices at wholesale were in balance with prices of goods the farmer had to buy. By using a series of balanced base periods, Carl Wilken clearly proved the honest parity idea as being one of enduring importance.

Taking 1946-1950 as a base period, farm prices averaged 99.5% of parity. Corn averaged $1.54 per bushel and wheat averaged $2.01 per bushel. From 1946-1950 through year-end 1966, the consumer price level adjusted 43%. Therefore, it is necessary to multiply the base prices of corn at $1.54 per bushel and wheat at $2.01 per bushel times 143% (1.43), and thus determine the honest parity that corn and wheat should have been at year end 1966.

|  | CORN per bushel | WHEAT per bushel |
|---|---|---|
| 1946-1950 | $1.54 | $2.01 |
|  | x 1.43 | x 1.43 |
| Honest parity, year-end 1966 | $2.20 | $2.87 |
| 1946-1950 | $1.54 | $ 2.01 |
|  | x 7.57 | x 7.57 |
| Honest parity, year-end 2000 | $11.70 | $15.21 |

During the 1946-1950 period the national income averaged $212.4 billion per year. The average industrial wage averaged $1.287 per hour.

In June, 1965, Carl Wilken published a study on the 12 central Midwestern states covering the period 1951-1964, using prices from 1946-1950 as 100. Wilken at that time pointed out that as a result of America's failure to maintain parity prices for agriculture, the nation as a whole was short some $570 billion in income. Of this shortage, $225 billion took place in the 12 states that produced 43% of all the farm production. In the publication itself, Wilken published a letter from then Under-Secretary of Agriculture John A. Schnittker to Congressman H. R. Gross of Iowa. In the letter Schnittker admitted that the parity price paid for corn had been reduced from $2.04 under the old formula to $1.55 a bushel under the so-called modernized parity, 1947-1949 = 100. In changing the method of computing parity, government statisticians took 49 cents off each bushel of corn, in Wilken's words, "with a lead pencil."

Today, the strange manipulations in government records and systems must surely be the work of intellectual embezzlers, who are hiding behind the complexities of their craft. Having put the economy on a ruinous tack, they have sought to cover their miscalculations. Without a plausible theory or a meaningful story, USDA experts relocated the base period for calculating parity. The balanced years of 1947-1949 were perceived to be ancient, and therefore a new period 1957-1959 was called 100 and substituted in its place. The problem was, however, that 1957-1959 was not a balanced period, either in terms of farm commodities at wholesale or consumer indexes at retail.

$$\$2.20 \overline{\smash{\big)}\ \$1.55}\ \ 70.5\%$$

Therefore, the support price for corn was only 70.5% of honest parity. The following table shows the wholesale commodity prices for the base period 1947-1949.

| YEAR | ALL COMMODITIES | FARM PRODUCTS | PROCESSED FOODS |
|---|---|---|---|
| 1947 | 96.4 | 100.0 | 98.2 |
| 1948 | 104.4 | 107.3 | 106.1 |
| 1949 | 99.2 | 92.8 | 95.7 |
| Total: | 300.0 | 300.0 | 300.0 |

By dividing each commodity by the three years one arrives at 100. During the three-year base period 1947-1949, all commodity prices at wholesale were in balance at 100.

Using the same source of reference, the *Economic Report of the President*, 1962, the commodity prices for the years 1957-1959 are as follows:

| YEAR | ALL COMMODITIES | FARM PRODUCTS | PROCESSED FOODS |
|---|---|---|---|
| 1957 | 117.6 | 90.9 | 105.6 |
| 1958 | 119.2 | 94.9 | 110.9 |
| 1959 | 119.5 | 89.1 | 107.0 |
| Total: | 356.3 | 274.9 | 323.5 |
| Avg. per year | 118.7 | 91.8 | 107.8 |

Prices were not in balance during the period 1957-1959. Farm prices were 26.9% lower than all commodity prices, and 16.0% lower than processed food prices. Farm prices were below prices on all other commodities.

Such lavish dishonesty could not possibly stop at the farm price manipulation level. It had to feed its way into the national records.

In any case, some elements in the government became so dissatisfied with the figures in the *Economic Report of the President* that revision was indicated. Starting with the *Report* of January 1966, all national income figures from 1929 on were revised. Every figure for interest for every year was changed all the way back to 1929. In the prospectus on the *Report*, no mention was made of the revisions. Yet revisions of this nature make it all but impossible for citizens to calibrate real values and results.

The adjustments had the effect of making the income equation look better than it happened to be, just as the rigged parity figures made farm income look better than it was. In one maneuver, interest was transposed from one side of the income equation to the other, thus raising corporate profits from $57.0 billion in the old report to $64.5 billion in the new, and when Wilken asked, "If this is a reality, why haven't the corporations paid taxes on this income?" he was ignored.

The adjustment for net farm income delivered $14.3 billion for 1965 to agriculture—a big gain. The fact that farmers never got this big gain was abstracted away, sent back into the thin air from which it came.

The following statistics are taken from the *Economic Report of the President*, 1966. They reveal how the price index was manipulated. This was the period being used at decade end—that is, the years 1957-1959=100.

| YEAR | ALL COMMODITIES | FARM PRODUCTS | PROCESSED FOODS |
|------|------|------|------|
| 1957 | 99.0 | 99.2 | 97.9 |
| 1958 | 100.4 | 103.6 | 102.9 |
| 1959 | 100.6 | 97.2 | 99.2 |
| Totals: | 300.0 | 300.0 | 300.0 |

Divided by three, everything averaged out at 100. Farm prices were brought into balance with all commodity prices with a lead pencil. Farm prices were actually 26.9% below all commodity prices, but evidently USDA figured the farmers would never check, so they called everything even at 100.

This periodic leveling of the figures continues. The Bureau of Labor Statistics (BLS), the current keeper of these series, now uses 1982 = 100 as the base year. Their numbers can be readjusted mathematically to get an idea of the imbalance buried in the statistics. Using 1947-1949 = 100 as the base for recalculating their numbers, 1982 actually looked like this:

| YEAR | ALL COMMODITIES | FARM PRODUCTS | PROCESSED FOODS | |
|------|------|------|------|------|
| 1982 BLS | 100.0 | 100.0 | 100.0 | (1982 = 100) |
| 1982 reindexed | 377.1 | 221.4 | 300.6 | (1947-1949 = 100) |

And the picture is even more distorted the further along we go. Year 2000, according to the BLS, and the same year calculated from a balanced base period reveal the Farm Products index value hasn't moved since 1982 while the All Commodities index has risen over 130 points and the Processed Foods index has risen about 100 points.

| YEAR | ALL COMMODITIES | FARM PRODUCTS | PROCESSED FOODS | |
|------|-----------------|---------------|-----------------|--|
| 2000 BLS | 132.7 | 99.5 | 133.1 | (1982 = 100) |
| 2000 reindexed | 500.5 | 220.3 | 400.0 | (1947-1949 = 100) |

Wilken's explanation of parity was unveiled in the form presented here at a Sioux City Seminar, February 17, 1967. By mid-1967, USDA had taken the position that the parity price standard used in agriculture for 30 years was deficient because it measured only price, and not quantities. According to USDA, farms grossing $20,000 and up were making 129% of parity during 1966. Top operators were computed to have made 168% of parity for the same period compared to returns operators might have made working for pay and investing in stocks. USDA also revealed that farms grossing $10,000 to $20,000 made 85% of parity compared to a landlord, and 98% of parity returns compared to a stockholder-investor. Farms with $5,000 to $10,000 gross were making 62% of parity, and farms grossing under $5,000 got merely 31% of parity in terms of landlord standards, and 35% in terms of stockholder standards. Although highly suspect because of the substandard accounting procedures involved, findings such as these became the basis for the government's "empty the countryside" mandate. "Small farmers had better get big and efficient or get out," became the translation.

Shortly before my interview with Wilken, All Commodities stood at 105.7; Farm Products were 102.0; Processed Foods were 110.2. Farm prices were within 3.7 of being in balance with All Commodity prices, according to the rigged figures, when actually the spread was 30.6 compared to 1947-1949 level.

At the end of the decade, farm prices were approximately 56% of full honest parity. The following table, computed by Former USDA General Sales Manager Frank M. LeRoux for publication in *The Farmers' Worst Nine Years*, tells the story:

| | 1910-1914 =100 | 1970 Honest Parity | Rigged Parity | Mid-1970 Market | Difference Between Rigged Parity and Honest Parity | Today's Price Short of Honest Parity |
|---|---|---|---|---|---|---|
| Corn (bu.) | .642 | $2.50 | 1.77 | 1.21 | -.73 | -1.29 |
| Wheat (bu.) | .884 | 3.44 | 2.82 | 1.23 | -.62 | -2.21 |
| Soybeans (bu.) | 1.03 | 4.01 | 3.78 | 2.6 | -.23 | -1.41 |
| Oats (bu.) | .305 | 1.19 | .956 | .613 | -.234 | -.577 |
| Sorghum (cwt.) | .897 | 3.49 | 2.90 | 1.80 | -.59 | -1.69 |
| Barley (bu.) | .45 | 1.85 | 1.45 | .994 | -.40 | -.856 |
| Rice (cwt.) | 1.93 | 7.53 | 7.49 | 5.08 | -.04 | -2.45 |
| Dry Edible Beans (cwt.) | 3.21 | 12.52 | 11.60 | 8.86 | -.92 | -3.66 |
| Cotton (American Upland-cwt.) | 12.40 | 48.36 | 49.06 | 22.31 | +.70 | -26.05 |
| Potatoes (cwt.) (all grades) | .861 | 3.35 | 3.20 | 2.97 | -.15 | -.38 |

No figures are available for choice hogs or cattle for the 1910-1914 period. However, at the start of the 1970s farmers were being encouraged to produce choice animals. To do so, farmers should have been paid at least $35.97 per hundredweight for hogs and $45.34 for cattle at the start of the 1970s, not prices well over $10 less per hundredweight for each category.

# CHAPTER 6: TAPE NO. 3

Q. Mr. Wilken, in one of your publications you said President McKinley hated the word cheap. He said cheap prices meant cheap income and cheap people. He was, of course, in favor of a tariff to protect American producers. But now we have preachers, rabbis, priests, economists all talking of one world, free international trade, and they talk of this as if to equate cultural exchange with economic intercourse. In other words, no tariffs. Yet you seem to favor tariffs at a time when the Kennedy Round has cemented the concept of free international trade into place. What is the basis for free trade?

WILKEN. Well, fundamentally, there's no basis for free trade for the simple reason that different nations do not have the same raw materials. In other words, they have a difference in natural resources. As a result, every country has a different economy. We have the same thing in our 50 states. We are all in the United States, that's true, and we like to think we have no tariffs—but we do have tariffs. An internal tax is a tariff. Now take my home state, Iowa. We have no petroleum. We have a 7-cent tax on gas in Iowa, which is a tariff against the production in Kansas.

Q. Lauren Soth, who has a great hand in formulating *Des Moines Register* agricultural policy, was formerly an associate professor of economics at Iowa State College, and I understand he once edited *Agricultural Situation* for the USDA. In his book *Farm Trouble** he argues that farmers should logically vote against high tariffs because the U. S. has never imported much meat, lard or grain at world prices. The real effect of *Des Moines Register* farm policy would seem to be to drive farm prices down

---

* The difficulty many people had in handling Wilken's concepts was expressed by Lauren Soth in *Farm Trouble*, p. 69. After quoting Wilken's farm income-national income ratio, Soth notes: "Common sense quickly shows the fallacy of this line of reasoning. Practically all segments of the economy bear fixed ratios to the total." Soth then illustrated that the ratio of the fishing industry to the national income was virtually constant at 1,800 to 1. Soth pointed out that fishing was at least as basic as agriculture, and "if seven times turn of farm income will create prosperity, why not an even greater multiplier?" Soth has recently materialized on government study committees (such as the National Advisory Commission on Food and Fiber) with the regularity of Wimpy refereeing a boxing match in the *Popeye* comic strip.

to world levels. Soth concedes, however, that when U. S. farm prices are above world prices, import control becomes mandatory. Now I read in the newspapers that Iowa's governor and an entourage of experts are in the Orient looking for foreign markets for farm production. Can we find those markets?

WILKEN. We can't compete there. We can't sell at world prices. For example, you can go into Mexico, you can go into South America—the rural worker there is getting $100 a year. India—per capita income, $70 a year. They can't even pay our present prices. You have to give it to them. Now the Common Market has established support prices higher than our parity on a lot of items. But they protect those prices with a tariff. And we've been trying to get those prices down ever since the Kennedy Trade Expansion Act.

Q. Economically, then, you'd have to protect a nation's farm prices with a tariff?

WILKEN. We've got to. It is the only way we can operate. With the per capita income in the United States around $2,400 compared to $500 outside of the United States, we'll buy the stuff away from the rest of the world even if they starve to death, because it will flow to the highest market. You can go into your chain stores in Washington, Miami, you've got a lot of Polish and Dutch hams coming in, canned hams. They're underselling our hams 10 to 12 cents a pound, but they're getting far more than the Dutch people can afford to pay. It's the same way with the steel. This steel is coming in here. Why? For the simple reason that Germany and Japan can undersell the American producer around $35 a ton, delivered in Chicago through the Great Lakes, and delivered to New Orleans and San Francisco by freighter. The steel industry in the U. S. has been heavily subsidized—not intentionally, but indirectly—by the expansion of government spending for military equipment, and road building, and the housing program, and borrowed money to build motels and hotels and office buildings. These devices have created a market for a lot of steel. Steel labor has been demanding an increase in wages. I'll take you back to when Kennedy was president. They wanted to increase the price of steel $6.00 a ton. Suppose it had been permitted. That would have increased corporate profits $600 million on 100 million tons of steel for the industry. Half of that would have gone to the government in tax revenue. The other $300 million would have gone to the steel industry as new capital for expansion and development. They couldn't do it when Kennedy was president. Now take Japan and West Germany. They can undersell our steel industry. They can land the steel in New Orleans or San Francisco, or, come in through the St. Lawrence seaway, and we import steel equivalent to 10% of our production. You can see, facing that sort of competition, it is pretty hard for the steel industry to increase its prices because of the competitive situation. Now just supposing that as a result of that competition the steel industry would have to cut its price $35 a ton to meet the competition. Then on 100 million tons of steel that would be $3.5 billion. It would wreck the steel industry in the U. S. because they couldn't take it. It's not only the steel industry—we have the same situation in a lot of manufactures. We can't pay the wages we are paying and compete with the price of manufactured products from other countries. If we don't have enough sense to correct this, then we'll pour in import production until we break our own prices, and we'll probably suffer the consequences and go through a liquidation, that's all. But the depression today would be seven times harder because there is seven times more debt involved, and seven times more income would go down the drain. A depression under the conditions we have in the United States today would really curl your hair.

Q. In other words, it might bring on an adjustment in our political and economic institutions?

WILKEN. This is a possibility.

Q. In international trade, what would correct this fundamental error?

WILKEN. The thing the world needs to apply is the principle called equity of trade. This would mean paying for imports in terms of high market parity, not world parity. Even with equity of trade you're not going to be able to equalize the income of different countries because basically the income of any country is determined by its basic resources. You don't have economies in deserts unless you find diamonds or oil or something of that nature. We just happened to be fortunate enough in the continental United States to have raw materials in great abundance. In fact, we have enough to operate a complete economy, and that is why the economic record of the United States should be used to find the answer for the rest of the world.

Q. What could we do with this record?

WILKEN. We could tell the world that we were going to stabilize the prices of 25 leading raw materials and—if we want—we could include gold and silver. By adjusting 25 leading raw materials to cost factors, we could write the ticket for stability at home first. As a matter of fact, I prepared a tentative bill to do that in 1959.

Q. Supposing that you had a law that fixed the price you had to pay if you bought products from out of the country. How would it operate?

WILKEN. Well, if you had a policy of equity of trade, in other words, if it cost 40 cents to produce a pound of copper in the U. S., then that's what you pay wherever you buy copper. If you don't do that, how can you expect the country that you buy it from to buy your product?

Q. Couldn't an equity of trade policy be made part of a tariff structure?

WILKEN. It could if you took about 25 commodities and stabilized them and kept them there like we've done with gold and silver for years and years.

Q. If we would demand from the Japanese people a fair price for soybeans, then in turn we could pay them this extra $35 per ton for the 10% of steel that we're going to buy from them?

WILKEN. If you paid Japan comparable price for the steel that you bought from them and required them to buy American goods for this money, they could buy more soybeans than they're buying now. And pay the price!

Q. Wouldn't this make international trade strictly barter?

WILKEN. Not barter. Equity of exchange. Equity of exchange value.

Q. You wouldn't allow an unfavorable balance of trade, or unfavorable balance of payments to develop. Is that what you mean?

WILKEN. Just let me illustrate. Here's a Common Market in western Europe, set up in '54. It kept farm prices balanced with internal cost factors. Now they've got a support price for wheat, $2.64. Per capita income is less than half of ours. And we've got a support price for our farmers of $1.25 for wheat. Less than half as much. Now if they were to follow our leadership and reduce their wheat price to our $1.25, the Common Market countries would collapse, because they're based on their earnings, not on trade. Now to show you the complete lack of information in regard to trade we have: In 1925-'29, our exports averaged about 5% of our national income. When you deduct like imports from like exports, we were 98% self-sufficient.

Q. You mean "like" imports such as, say, sending beef out and importing beef.

WILKEN. That's right. In 1935 we passed the trade agreements under which we promised the world we were going to reduce our tariffs. However, since 1935 our national income has moved up considerably. Yet your exports in 1965 didn't average 5% of national income. So we haven't increased our export trade in ratio to our national income. But we've subjected ourselves to having the world determine the price we're going to get. There's the key to the whole thing. That's what they have done to us through this process. Deliberately moved us down, down, down!

Q. What is the nature of the dislocation in the Common Market?

WILKEN. The only quarrel in the Common Market was between France and Germany. Germany had a support price for wheat at $3.05 a bushel. France was the only surplus producing wheat country in the Common Market. So they all wanted some equalization. They wanted the price of wheat the same in these market countries. Germany didn't want to cut her support price, so that became the quarrel. On the other hand, we're over there trying to get them to reduce their tariff so that our stuff can get in. Their tariff on broiler chickens is as much as our farmer gets. That's to protect their own internal economy. Now why do they have to protect their internal product? Barley is the nearest thing to corn in Germany. They had it supported at about $1.97. In other words, feed grain costs in Germany and France are higher than here. We want to ship them chickens, and they have as much duty on chickens coming into Germany as our farmer gets. Any man with common sense ought to know that our farm prices are pushed way down. Yet out of the 12 chief states you haven't got a single Senator or Congressman who's introducing legislation to help farmers get parity. Not one! Yet those 12 states produce 43% of the farm products.

Q. What would be the obvious solution as far as the U. S. is concerned in the case of the Common Market?

WILKEN. Well, when they set up the Common Market we should have wrapped our arms around them and said, "Now we'll work with you and make the American parity the world price." In the last 15 years, however, through misrepresentation—in spite of the fact that we have labor legislation specifically providing for wages, in spite of the fact that we have legislation setting a specific price on postage stamps, on railroad rates, airplane rates, income taxes, real estate taxes, telephones—it's a crime to maintain a price on farm products to keep them in balance.

Q. The prices of food commodities in France right now are approximately 100% of the parity they'd be in this country if American farmers were getting parity income. The French prices for agricultural commodities in France are evidently quite close to balance right now, are they not?

WILKEN. If you want to make a distinction between what the farmer gets and what the retailer gets. Now in France it only costs half as much to take it from the farmer to the retail counter as it does in the U. S. That's because of the wages.

Q. Nevertheless, France is enjoying a pretty healthy economy as a result of this. And so is West Germany?

WILKEN. True. To give you an idea about not only tariffs, but just a simple tax proposition, when I was over in Cannes, France last summer, a gallon of gasoline was 45 cents. Now why the difference between the price in France and here? It's the internal tax which goes to support the revenue of the French government. You've got the same thing right here in the U. S. For example, I can buy a package of cigarettes in one of the supermarkets in Washington for 23 cents and that same pack of cigarettes in the state of New York will cost 45 cents. When we talk about tariffs we forget that any tax is a tariff. It increases the cost of an item, the cost of produc-

## COMPARISON OF NATIONAL INCOME
## TO ANNUAL IMPORTS OF ALL GOODS

|  | NATIONAL INCOME (BILLIONS $) | IMPORTS \1\ (BILLIONS $) | PERCENTAGE OF NATIONAL INCOME FOR IMPORTS |
|---|---|---|---|
| 1929 | 86.8 | 4.5 | 5.2% |
| 1930 | 75.6 | 3.1 | 4.1% |
| 1931 | 60.4 | 2.1 | 3.5% |
| 1932 | 43.9 | 1.3 | 3.0% |
| 1933 | 41.4 | 1.5 | 3.6% |
| 1934 | 50.2 | 1.8 | 3.6% |
| 1935 | 57.9 | 2.5 | 4.3% |
| 1936 | 65.8 | 2.5 | 3.8% |
| 1937 | 74.0 | 3.2 | 4.3% |
| 1938 | 67.4 | 2.2 | 3.3% |
| 1939 | 72.9 | 2.4 | 3.3% |
| 1940 | 81.1 | 2.7 | 3.3% |
| 1941 | 104.3 | 3.4 | 3.3% |
| 1942 | 137.6 | 2.7 | 2.0% |
| 1943 | 171.4 | 3.4 | 2.0% |
| 1944 | 184.3 | 3.8 | 2.1% |
| 1945 | 183.3 | 3.9 | 2.1% |
| 1946 | 182.3 | 5.1 | 2.8% |
| 1947 | 198.6 | 6.0 | 3.0% |
| 1948 | 223.3 | 7.6 | 3.4% |
| 1949 | 216.7 | 6.9 | 3.2% |
| 1950 | 241.0 | 9.1 | 3.8% |
| 1951 | 278.7 | 11.2 | 4.0% |
| 1952 | 293.3 | 10.8 | 3.7% |
| 1953 | 308.2 | 11.0 | 3.6% |
| 1954 | 308.4 | 10.4 | 3.4% |
| 1955 | 338.5 | 11.5 | 3.4% |
| 1956 | 358.7 | 12.8 | 3.6% |
| 1957 | 375.0 | 13.3 | 3.5% |
| 1958 | 377.3 | 13.0 | 3.4% |
| 1959 | 411.5 | 15.3 | 3.7% |
| 1960 | 427.5 | 15.2 | 3.6% |
| 1961 | 442.5 | 15.1 | 3.4% |
| 1962 | 477.1 | 16.9 | 3.5% |
| 1963 | 504.4 | 17.7 | 3.5% |
| 1964 | 542.1 | 19.4 | 3.6% |
| 1965 | 589.6 | 22.2 | 3.8% |
| 1966 | 646.7 | 26.3 | 4.1% |
| 1967 | 681.7 | 27.8 | 4.1% |
| 1968 | 743.6 | 33.9 | 4.6% |

| | | | |
|---|---|---|---|
| 1969 | 802.7 | 36.8 | 4.6% |
| 1970 | 837.5 | 40.9 | 4.9% |
| 1971 | 903.9 | 46.6 | 5.2% |
| 1972 | 1000.4 | 56.9 | 5.7% |
| 1973 | 1127.4 | 71.8 | 6.4% |
| 1974 | 1211.9 | 104.5 | 8.6% |
| 1975 | 1302.2 | 99.0 | 7.6% |
| 1976 | 1456.4 | 124.6 | 8.6% |
| 1977 | 1635.8 | 152.6 | 9.3% |
| 1978 | 1860.2 | 177.4 | 9.5% |
| 1979 | 2075.6 | 212.8 | 10.3% |
| 1980 | 2243.0 | 248.6 | 11.1% |
| 1981 | 2497.1 | 267.8 | 10.7% |
| 1982 | 2603.0 | 250.5 | 9.6% |
| 1983 | 2796.5 | 272.7 | 9.8% |
| 1984 | 3162.3 | 336.3 | 10.6% |
| 1985 | 3380.4 | 343.3 | 10.2% |
| 1986 | 3525.8 | 370.0 | 10.5% |
| 1987 | 3803.4 | 414.8 | 10.9% |
| 1988 | 4151.1 | 452.1 | 10.9% |
| 1989 | 4392.1 | 484.5 | 11.0% |
| 1990 | 4642.1 | 508.0 | 10.9% |
| 1991 | 4756.6 | 500.7 | 10.5% |
| 1992 | 4994.9 | 544.9 | 10.9% |
| 1993 | 5251.9 | 592.8 | 11.3% |
| 1994 | 5556.8 | 676.7 | 12.2% |
| 1995 | 5876.7 | 757.6 | 12.9% |
| 1996 | 6210.4 | 808.3 | 13.0% |
| 1997 | 6618.4 | 885.1 | 13.4% |
| 1998 | 7041.4 | 930.0 | 13.2% |
| 1999 | 7462.1 | 1046.9 | 14.0% |
| 2000 | 7980.9 | 1244.9 | 15.6% |
| | | | |
| '46-'50 Avg. | 212.4 | 6.9 | 3.3% |

National Income data from:
Table 1.14. National Income by Type of Income Imported Goods data from:
Table 4.1. Foreign Transactions in the National Income and Product Accounts U.S. Dept. of Commerce, Bureau of Economic Analysis
Published date is 10/31/2001
1. Exports and imports of certain goods, primarily military equipment purchased and sold by the Federal Government, are included in services. Beginning with 1986, repairs and alterations of equipment are reclassified from goods to services. Provided by NORM, 11/01

ing an item. I saw an article in *The Wall Street Journal* that the taxes on land in New Jersey are up to $12 an acre real estate taxes. Why have they gone up? The value of that land has gone up not because of what it produces in the way of farm products, but because of real estate development and speculation on the acreage.

Q. With or without tariffs, how were we competing in international markets in 1953?

WILKEN. In 1953 the dislocation had just started. I'll show you what brought it on. In the '46-'50 period, American parity was the world price. That was because we had moved up from $80 billion of income in 1940 (pre-war) to level off at $121 billion in '46-'50. Great Britain felt she couldn't afford to pay that price. She devalued the pound from $4.05 to $3.80. It hasn't been worth over $3.80 since the price of gold went up to $35. That broke commodity prices 30% for the rest of the world. And in the first five years of that devaluation, we shipped in $6 billion more farm products than we exported. Now that started taking effect in 1953.

Q. What could you have done to offset this devaluation?

WILKEN. You couldn't have done anything except set tariffs or import quotas. That's the only constitutional authority you've got.

Q. If you had direct convertibility to gold what effect would that have?

WILKEN. The trouble is gold is a lot like silver. We've got gold, but it takes $70 to produce gold in the United States paying American wages. So there's a shortage of gold throughout the world.

Q. Should gold be repriced? What could be done to keep gold up to more or less what it ought to be?

WILKEN. I suggested this in a bill I prepared in 1959. I would have established the price of gold at $70 at that time. But only in the United States. Then in exchange of goods with other countries, I'd have paid them a comparable price either for gold or any other product. In other words, establish equity of trade instead of free trade.

Q. Would you make the American buck convertible to gold here?

WILKEN. Yes. At $70 an ounce, here!

Q. Let people have it if they want it?

WILKEN. Yes. But you can't do that now, because you haven't got it.

Q. Isn't there some way gold could be revalued up to reality without this tremendous jump at great intervals?

WILKEN. Go back to 1910-'14. Our economy was very much in balance. We had adjusted from the drop in silver prices from 1873 to 1896. At that point we were producing 4.5 million ounces of gold. Wages were 23 cents an hour. In World War I, wages went up to 50 cents an hour, and our gold production fell off in the post-war period. The internationalists broke the price of metal, so we had a depression in the 20s. Henry Ford came out and told the American people if the working man was going to drive a car, he'd have to have 50 cents an hour. And the manufacturers felt that with 50 cents an hour wages, they could sell more goods than by going back to 23 cents. So we passed a tariff bill, and from 1922 to 1929 we leveled off into a period of approximate balance again. And our income moved up from $33 billion in 1910-'14 to an average of $82 billion. During that period the price of gold had not been increased. So our gold production fell off to 2.5 million ounces from 4.5 million.

Q. What should gold be? Should it be increased a dollar at a time, or what?

WILKEN. The price of gold or any commodity—I don't care what it is— has got to increase with the cost factor or you can't produce it.

Q. Why can't a government raise the price of gold a dollar at a time as needed, instead of waiting for this big, tremendous jump?

WILKEN. It can, but you see we forget that we're only 6% of the world's population here in the United States. Now we forgot that in 1934 we increased the price of gold to $35. We could very safely have increased the price of gold to $35 produced in the United States, but we did it for the whole world. So what did they do? They sold us the gold at $35, and we made our people turn it in at $20.67. And in the process of selling us the gold, it devalued world currencies, and commodity prices couldn't recover in the '30s, and didn't.

Q. Aren't foreigners (France particularly) draining gold out because they realize we're going to have to raise the price of gold?

WILKEN. They are buying this gold as a hedge against deflation.

Q. Are they correct in doing that?

WILKEN. Well, the way we've been deflating commodity prices, sure they're right, because this whole thing will collapse and the only thing with a fixed value will be gold.

Q. What happens when we can't meet the international credits anymore?

WILKEN. You'll just have complete world chaos for the simple reason that we cannot devalue the American dollar because we're the high nation.

Q. If we can't make good our gold commitment, what's going to happen?

WILKEN. We'll have to go off the gold*, just like we've gone off silver, and get down to paper money. Let me ask you this. We've got billions of dollars set up for social security payments, unemployment compensation, and that money has been spent. Supposing we have a depression? Where is the government going to get the money to pay the social secu-

---

* Which we did, first by breaking the governor relationship between gold and currency and deposits, and next by adopting international funny money—Special Drawing Rights.

rity payments except by issuing paper money? If I were doing it, I'd just tell the world we're going to maintain American prices for all farm products, raw materials, and manufactured goods at the American parity level. And then from there on I'd be willing to help the world up. How would I help them up? I'd pay them a comparable price for whatever I bought from them.

Q. In other words, you wouldn't buy the raw materials out of South America at world prices, but at an American parity?

WILKEN. That's right.

Q. Now this is what you meant by the Cuban sugar example?

WILKEN. In 1946 we passed the Sugar Bill. Now sugar is an interesting example of how we developed this country.

The first sugar tariff was passed in 1789—2 cents a pound—in a day when the wage was 50 cents a day. It was a very high duty. That was to induce sugar production in the United States. We're up to where we produce about 50% of our sugar now. We could produce it all if we wanted to since we have sugar beets and cane. But in 1946, under the agreement, we established a quota to bring in so much sugar from Cuba, the Philippines, different countries. Outside of a small fee of about 50 cents per hundredweight, which was to make adjustment of production in the United States, we paid them the same price. Here's what happened in Cuba. The land was consolidated on the basis of debt that couldn't be paid. The international financiers simply foreclosed on the Cubans after World War I. About 57% of the Cuban sugar land was owned by American interests; about 25% by European interests. So Castro had an easy go of it. The Cuban economy was based on sugar. Those poor devils had work about three months a year, and the rest of the time starve to death. So Castro made the promise he'd divide up the sugar lands. He took over Cuba and got Batista out with practically no effort. When he finally got too "leftist" for us, to punish him we cut off his sugar deals. Cuba had the big part of the sugar quota because of the workings of the big financiers in New York who owned the sugar plantations. The world price at the time was about $3. And we were paying Cuba a little over $6. Then Russia stepped in and told Cuba she'd pay her 6 cents a pound. Castro turned to Russia. Losing that big quota of sugar from Cuba, the supply in the United States ran us into the problem of trying to get sugar to replace it. The speculators got into the thing and ran the price of sugar up to 12 cents a pound in 1963. Then we got quotas with other countries. Today the price we pay in the United is more than double the world price. We're paying approximately the same price for the sugar we bring in as we're paying the American producers. Now we produce about 50% of the copper. We could produce it all, but we like cheap copper. I'd put a price on copper to protect the American production and whatever copper I imported I'd pay the same price.

Q. Is there any way of achieving equity of trade by making use of the market mechanism?

WILKEN. You've got to do it through your quota system. The government is the only authority that has the power. It is the only authority with power to regulate the dollar, which is what you're doing when you're talking about prices. I think we're leading with our chin toward labor socialism patterned after Fabian socialism, the origin of the Keynesian theory. You've got to liquidate agriculture and private enterprise before you can have labor socialism. We've been doing the best job of liquidating private enterprise in the history of the world without knowing it.

Q. From an economic point of view, what does this war do?

WILKEN. It forces and makes psychologically possible the addition of even more borrowed money.

Q. In other words, the war enables the borrowing to keep right on?

WILKEN. That's right. Now, what's been the effect on the farmers? From the '46-'50 period, you had an increase in the hourly wage rates. But as fast as that wage increase took place, there was more installment credit, more home buying credit to mortgage that money, and in the mortgage they agreed to pay not only the interest but also the principal. People have had to balance their budgets at the grocery counter, and the farmer has gotten what was left. If this thing in Vietnam is ever over, we're headed for a heavy import of all manufactured goods, because our wage rate is way up. That's how cattle prices were broken. In 1964 we brought in 10% of the beef and veal. This was all cheap beef coming in from New Zealand and Australia and Ireland. It went into hamburger, sausage, and so on. Congress said that's not competitive. But it is.

Q. What is the difference?

WILKEN. With a buying public mortgaged up to the hilt, people go to hamburger. The advice of all four Presidents—Truman, Eisenhower, Kennedy and Johnson—has been exactly the same. They've all been in favor of getting farm prices down to what they call a world level. Free trade! To conform to the trade agreement act we passed in 1935, when we took the advice of the classical economists.

Q. With farm prices at a world level, how does this affect the rest of the economy?

WILKEN. The thing that has happened—when we drove farm prices down, business lost its markets. And it lost its new capital for expansion. So it turned to borrowed capital generation. When it borrowed the capital it had to pay interest on it. And after paying the increase in wages and interest, you have business only paying a 3% dividend on the average stocks. The minute agricultural prices go down, private enterprise—in other words your business operation which is your mechanism—loses money for the simple reason it loses the volume of market necessary to earn the profit to meet wages and interest .

Q. In other words the factor really out of line is the wages and interest. It's out of line not only with agriculture, it's also out of line with corporate profits. Is that what you mean?

WILKEN. Labor is also out of line with itself. For example, you range all of the way from about 95 cents an hour in the agricultural industry to $5 and more an hour for electrical workers in cities. And to give you a concrete illustration—we have practically lost our merchant marine—because it costs twice as much to build a ship and it costs twice as much for American labor to operate the ship as other countries are paying. A lot of our merchant marine have enlisted their ships under foreign flags—Panamanian flags—to get away from the high wages that American seamen are asking. When I'm talking about American wages, don't think for a minute that I'm against the wage level. I never criticize the wage level. The point that I make is that whatever the wage level is, the income of private enterprise in terms of net farm income, small business income and corporate profits after taxes, must be in balance with it, or we can't have a solvent economy.

Q. Supposing that you had agriculture in balance with today's wage level. Does this mean the interest and wage level automatically balance themselves.

WILKEN. No, but they're the principal cost factors.

Q. Let's say that you had corporate and small business and agriculture in balance with wages and interest. Would this allow you to compete in international markets?

WILKEN. No. You'd have to have the differential between your price and the price of your imports. It would take a tariff, or quota, or whatever you wish.

Q. Is it possible to bring farm prices up in view of the fact that half the world is starving?

WILKEN. It's pretty hard for 6% of the world's population with half of the world's debt to take on such a job at world prices. Here we are, 6% of the world's population. We've got ourselves engaged in the cost of policing the world, financing the world, and keeping it on relief, and letting the world set the price on what we produce.

Q. You're saying, keep our own house in order first?

WILKEN. If we don't do that we will lose our ability to help anyone. I'll give you two examples. In Formosa, Chiang started with agriculture. They've had a good, sound expansion. They don't need any relief. They're earning their own way. The Common Market set up in 1954—what did they do? They balanced agricultural prices with income-cost factors. And Germany and France and all those countries are in better shape than we are, and are buying up our gold. We've got the finest economy from the point of natural resources and production of any nation in the world. If we ever got sense enough to realize that when you sell your production you must have a price level to generate the income due, we wouldn't have so many problems.

Q. How do international economics and internationals fit into this picture?

WILKEN. We get so far ahead they have to knock us down once in a while and do. But you see their whole aim in the '20s was to maintain that international exchange ratio $20.67 on gold; now it's $35. And to illustrate that they succeeded in their purpose, note that your support price on corn today is $1.05 compared to $1.09 a bushel in 1953. They got agriculture back to a prewar level but your hourly wages have gone up from 95.7 cents an hour to $2.64 by 1966. There's your dislocation. And they are not earning half the income they're spending in the United States. How long it's going to last, I don't know. The reckoning will come. The other part of it is that we got so far above the rest of the world, it's pitiful. In Vietnam a native soldier gets a dollar a month wages. The rural citizens of many South American countries are getting $100 a year. With $100 a year, how can they buy a tool for production or fertilizer to produce more farm products? What are they doing? They're migrating to the city because they're starving, and in the city they hope to get on relief. Who's furnishing the relief? We are. They can't buy, so we kid ourselves on this kind of exchange. You see, no country can afford to let its profit leave the country, or its raw materials leave except under conditions of equity. In the late 1930s, Mexico expropriated the American oil properties. You've had more governmental stability in Mexico than in any South American country since that time. You can see the pattern everywhere. The Egyptians took over the Suez Canal for the same reason. Everybody said the Egyptians couldn't run the canal, but they did run it and made a profit [until the war]. Why did Egypt say the canal belonged to them? Well, it's their country. Much of the world, is no longer going to put up with this so-called free trade. In order to knock down American prices we have tried to wet-nurse the world, keep it on relief, fight its wars—all by adding to our debt. Now who is going to have to pay this debt? Those other countries aren't going to pay it. The U. S. is going to have to pay it. That's why this debt is a mortgage against the income of future generations. As a result of this mode of operation, here we are today with 6% of the world's population, and we're saddled with 50% of the entire debt of the world.

There is something tragic about a debt that can't be paid. There is something tragic about a debt that can't be serviced. Free international trade causes both. There is no basis for free trade at all.

# CHAPTER 7: THE GHOST OF FREE TRADE

*There is no basis for free trade at all.*

Even Herbert Hoover, before he became Secretary of Commerce, no longer believed in *laissez faire*. He complained bitterly in his memoirs how "Mr. Mellon had only one formula: 'Liquidate labor, liquidate stocks, liquidate the farmers, liquidate real estate. . .' In fact Hoover, after 1929, called in industrial leaders in an effort to forestall wage rate cuts. *Laissez faire* was dead, dead, dead, even then!

And yet after World War II its ghost walked again.

This realization caused Carl Wilken to fairly crackle with indignation. In early 1967 the American State Department was taking the lead in lowering farm prices for the world market, and these lower prices would be translated into low American farm prices. "We import our depressions," Wilken said, as he busied himself exposing the fallacy of a low world commodity price concept.

The big stumbling block during the GATT talks in Geneva that year was simply that USDA (and the millers and traders civil servicing that agency) wanted wheat lower than a world price other producing nations seemed ready to accept. "Lower!" Yes, but why?

As a matter of fact, the big banks in New York, and the commodity groups that took a rake-off whenever a bushel of anything moved into trade channels, had sold the bill of goods called *free trade* again. *Laissez faire* economics was picking up where the trade agreement under Cordell Hull had left off.

When the American nation was founded, the basic idea of *laissez faire* was scrapped, chiefly at the insistence of old Ben Franklin. As industrialization took hold, economist Henry C. Carey provided the renewed thinking for scrapping *free trade* still more. A few generations had to be born and die before people would allow the old system, one dedicated to maintaining low raw material prices, in the saddle again.

Wilken liked to cite *The Breakdown of Money*, by Christopher Hollis, to explain his point when he said there was no basis for free trade, because Hollis best detailed the premises and explained the conclusions. And they all added up to the fact that free trade and its many manipulations caused debts to be created, debts that could neither be serviced nor paid.

## [1] FOUR BASIC CONDITIONS

There are four basic conditions under which *laissez faire* has to operate, Hollis said, and fulfillment of these conditions is always fatal to world economic stability.

The first of these is *"free contract between employer and employee"*—or, no unions! Jeremy Bentham and David Ricardo found economic laws to justify the harsh realities of labor conditions, but on the firing line of business low wages simply meant that workers could not consume the production their economy had accounted for. Thus low wages made necessary the trader nation, the one forever on the hunt for markets elsewhere.

The first law of *laissez faire* led to the second law: *free exportation of goods*. There never has been a time when *laissez faire* held sway completely. Human conscience could not allow for long some of the conditions that developed in the industrial state. Thus there were laws to raise wages. But, said the Benthamite, that did no good at all, because you can't raise the wages of a foreigner. Any attempt to raise wages in one country results in foreign competition capturing the market. The loincloth producer by definition was the low cost producer, and his goods would flow to the high market!

The traders and manipulators of Adam Smith's day understood all this. They knew that unless laborers and farmers and service trades earned enough to consume their own production, the economy would be forced to look to foreign markets for outlets. *Free import required free export.*

(Bargained wages in the United States, during the 1960s, coupled with free imports indeed made it possible for foreigners to capture American markets. And world prices for farm commodities produced under the American cost of production schedule—one twice as high as that evident in the rest of the world—were driving American farmers into bankruptcy.)

All this, it was reasoned, could be avoided with tariffs. But again, *laissez faire* has its condition No. 3—*free export of capital*. Export of capital has never been challenged, not seriously anyway, and in the long haul it can bring back into play the first two conditions of *laissez faire* simply by starving local capital markets in the same way that low wages and low farm income starve local markets.

The last condition of laissez faire and free trade is *the existence of international money,* because Eurodollars and gold make money the only real citizen of the world. International money makes free export of capital a working reality.

## [2] EUROPEAN ECONOMIC COMMUNITY

The 1967 discussions in Geneva proceeded with the basic requirements of *laissez faire* in mind. One thing had changed, if only temporarily. The Common Market nations had turned their backs on at least three of the conditions necessary to *laissez faire*. They no longer looked for a profit by exploiting labor, just as they no longer looked for a profit by exploiting the farm producer. Variable levies (tariffs) on imports had been constructed to protect European Economic Community countries from low cost (*and low price*) producers from other sections of the world. The levies of the late 1960s required a higher price for wheat and corn than the price a cornbelt farmer dared hope for. The Common Market, for at least one bright, shining moment in history, realized that the ultimate consequence of low world commodity prices was to subject every developed economy to having to accept the same rate of wages as those being accepted by the lowest paid country involved in world trade. This, it was generally conceded, could not be accomplished without a depression, and therefore the policies designed to drive world commodity prices into the ground were fairly tuned in on creating such a world depression.

It was to Wilken a matter for common observation that the internal market of the U.S. has become limited because too much of the earned income has gone to the far corners of the world, either as foreign investment or as a governmental attempt to wet-nurse much of the world, or, to fight the world's wars and keep it on relief. The natural decline in purchasing power has been stalled these many years simply by floating more debt. In the meantime, Bulgarian cheese, Japanese electronic equipment, European manufactured goods—all produced under an income structure hardly $500 per capita a year vied with American production produced under a per capita income structure of $2,400 a year (circa 1967).

The shock waves had become intensified because American farm production rode along at world prices, whereas manufactured goods commanded a price closer to American cost of production parity. But the shock waves had to be absorbed as best possible. This had come to mean that American farmers had to be processed into bankruptcy, business had to operate with a declining rate of profit, and corporations had to protect themselves with wave after wave of mergers, elimination of competition through market domination, and also through removal of bargained wages with automation.

As businesses and farms continued to be consumed by bankruptcy during the '60s, those who were paying the price for free trade started coming to their senses, one at a time.

## [3] LOW COST MARKETS

There is nothing very complicated about international trade. The low cost producer has to end up with the market. It's that simple. When world markets move higher than the wage and capital cost level in the United States, as they do when a depression has knocked the American economy down a few notches, then American producers can export their unemployment by underselling in foreign markets. When the wage and capital cost level in the United States rises well above the world level, then foreign production will flow to the high market. This means that the United States under such conditions simply imports its depressions. Needless to say, an economy only rarely moves as a whole. Usually, the various sectors manage to mangle each other first, creating an imbalance. Trouble is usually manufactured through imbalance at home, and unfavorable climate abroad—both at the same time.

The underdeveloped nations of the world have only raw materials to sell, and even among the most unsophisticated there is a growing realization that these nations cannot permit profits from business enterprise to leave the country—because without capital profits the so-called emerging nations cannot develop.

## [4] INTERNATIONAL INSTITUTIONS

In the workaday play of international trade, raw materials are the first to field the pressures of economic imbalance. This pressure at the raw material level short-circuits purchasing power through the full length of any economy, because in the final analysis gold and silver (the money) are really wheat, corn, lead, zinc—the basic raw materials that become the wealth of nations. If gold (the international money) is to remain stable in a dynamic world, then there must be constant pressure to bring wheat and corn in line with the price of gold. If wheat and corn are to line up with the price of gold, then the wage and capital cost structure must submit to the same pressure, and line up with the price of gold.

Thus an unadjusted price for gold speaks of a static world, but almost all economic pursuits of man speak of a dynamic world, one that will not be laid to rest at the level of a certain year in history.

To illustrate this point: The British pound was $4.86 in terms of $20.67 gold. When the price of gold for the world was raised to $35 during the Roosevelt administration, the British pound sterling became worth $2.80.

Pride, the "going concern" of England as the world's financial house, and not a little tradition figured in England's decision not to devalue the pound at that time. Through the rest of the 1930s and all through World War II, England kept the pound sterling at $4.05. Some $10 billion in lend lease from the United States extended the British an assist in this endeavor.

The world is organized by countries. This is so obvious that to repeat it here might seem a reflection on the intelligence of a reader. Nevertheless, were this fact to be repeated about four times a day together with "two and two still make four," most of the economic ills associated with depressions could be avoided.

Many economists like to think of Country A and Country B in terms of "the most efficient producer," but the fact is that all these countries have different shapes, different resources, different stages of development, different labor costs, different institutional "going concerns." From the economic point of view, a country such as the United States must control its own destiny.

In 1948, the United States House of Representatives extended the 90% parity bill for agriculture, but an attempt was made in the Senate to put agriculture under a 60-90% parity sliding scale. The psychological impact caused speculators to break farm prices 13% almost overnight. The national income dropped $23 billion in the wake of this farm price break.

In 1949, Senator Russell and Senator Young joined hands in sponsoring 90% parity. The measure carried and became law as President Harry S. Truman moved into his second term.

It must be remembered that ever since the Roosevelt administration pegged the world's gold at $35 an ounce in 1934, England had refused to bring the pound in line with $35 gold. During WWII, England expropriated foreign-held securities of its citizens to keep from making this monetary adjustment, and after the war England showed more than academic interest in the removal of the American farm parity program. Thus when the U.S. Congress returned to 90% parity in 1949, English financiers must have abandoned hope of maintaining the pound at $4.05. The British pound was devalued to $2.80—or 30%. This action reduced the price of goods being produced in England by 30% to the rest of the world. Such a maneuver, however, could have only a short run effect, because after devaluation Britain could only buy 70% as much as previously for the pound.

As a result of the devaluation, the U.S. became the high market in the world. In the five years following the devaluation of the British pound, the U.S. imported over $6 billion more in farm products than were exported. The American economy imported its surplus. As a result of the British devaluation, and as a result of imports prompted by Britain's lead in devaluing its pound, American farm raw material prices were reduced to the world price level—where they have been ever since.

In the meantime, Europe set up a Common Market. The Common Market protected itself from import invasion of its price level by setting up a support price for agricultural raw materials at approximately the 1948 level. And the Common Market kept it there (although the Rome Treaty—a CED nostrum—was destined to take EEC nations the low cost raw materials route, the same as the United States).

Needless to say, this support program has not been accomplished painlessly, or without micro-economic distortion. The rigmarole of subsidy bureaucracy in France is frightful to behold, but few can deny that the Common Market achieved a level of unity and prosperity never envisioned during the dark days of WWII.

## [5] THE OVERPRODUCTION THEORY

On the blackboards and in the journals, economists work out complicated looking formulas illustrating the nature of inelastic demand, and at the same time governors and farm spokesmen look the world over to discover export markets for farm products. Yet world income is at a level that makes it impossible for foreign nations to buy American farm production at world prices, much less at prices that would return to the farm producer his cost of production as balanced with the rest of the American economy.

The records of the Department of Agriculture amply refute the overproduction theory. In 1954 the United States imported 1.6% of the beef and veal supply. By 1963 the economy was importing 10% of the total supply. Imports laid in at less than the American cost of production broke cattle prices that year. The economic consequences were visited on the grain trade. With 10% of the meat supply imported, some 600 million bushels of corn were no longer needed to feed our domestic animals on American farms or in feedlots. The market for corn tumbled accordingly.

The individual records of "going concerns" illustrate how greed and exploitation walk hand in hand with the power to depress raw material prices. Among the many programs used by the American government to aid underdeveloped countries, one made use of the so-called Cooley dollars (after the then House Committee on Agriculture Chairman Harold D. Cooley). Cooley dollars were federal dollars given to foreign countries in payment of purchases. These dollars could not be returned to the United States, but they could be used in the country involved.

American packing plants, industrialists and movie actors, according to documented record, sent pilot companies to these foreign countries—

New Zealand, Australia, Colombia, etc.—for the purpose of borrowing Cooley dollars, buying land, creating red meat production, and bringing this production into the American market, where it drove domestic prices down. In the final analysis, the taxpayer financed his own destruction, because between 1950 and 1967 the nearly $800 billion added to the private debt of the United States had been occasioned by failure of the economy to earn its way.

## [6] POLICY PAPERS

As prices continued to sink, one wave of pundits after another hit farmers with the productivity bit. The Committee for Economic Development, with Goldsmith's *A Study of Saving in the United States* in tow much of the time, did its hatchet work on a continuing basis, starting immediately after WWII. Policy papers such as *Toward a Realistic Farm Program, Economic Policy for American Agriculture* and *An Adaptive Program for Agriculture* explained to hoemen how they had to get bigger, more efficient, and finally depart the scene. The Bible-style texts of Messrs. Don Paarlberg and Dale Hathaway also arrived to help style public policy so that the job of liquidating agriculture might proceed without bringing on open revolt from the farmers, and by the time those volumes had been thumbed to death in the learning halls, Johns Hopkins Press struck off another entry, this one titled *Policy Directions for U.S. Agriculture*. The last was issued under the auspices of Resources for the Future, Inc., a non-profit organization based in Washington for the altruistic purpose of serving the powers that be. The writer, one Marion Clawson, came to the Resources for the Future foundation via the customary route—out of USDA and the Interior Department. His message came to the public from the mature fortunes of the nation by way of the tax supported instrumentalities that no longer knew which hand did the long-range feeding.

The message was the same. *Look, we're producing too much. Conclusion, agriculture is still overmanned. Hurry, grow more to stay even. Worry, because by the year 2000 production will have doubled and there will be too many farmers anyway. The painful process of decline and decay will involve human costs. Sorry about that!*

Instead of support programs, Clawson fell back on the Brannan idea, direct payments to older farmers, or institutionalized poverty, so those who remained could double their production, enjoy prices held down by imports, and starve to death in the end.

Pensioning farmers and speeding the exodus from the countryside could not solve either the farm problem or the city problem because rural America required the gross dollar, and without the gross dollar rural towns would starve as well. The sore of low farm income thus became the cancer that consumed fully a third of the American population by the end of the 1960s.

The "too many resources in agriculture" pitch failed to express or prove a concept of economic growth, because too many resources in agriculture could become too many resources in widget-making, entertainment or professoring, for that matter. Unfortunately the gut agriculture seers dismissed this problem with a "we'll get to that later" gesture.*

And yet there was a simple problem in agriculture. It was the problem of pricing the product. There was a problem in the economy. It was the problem of maintaining balance between the income and the outgo of the economy. To handle either problem economists were forced to deal with the creation of money, and this seems to be a "no-no" subject for too many, Clawson included.

A great many monetary experts subscribe to the idea that banks create the real money by making new loans, and are limited in this function by their pragmatic judgment of whether they will be paid back or not. Yet a mature sense of value suggests that there has to be a limiting factor on the profits earned, ergo the ability to pay, and it has to be tangible in nature. If economists ever accepted this contention then they would have to call for a policy of high, rather than low raw material prices, or at least raw material prices in line with other goods and services, because the monetization of raw material production creates the real money. High raw material prices create the income, even if the alternative is more profitable to a few. And that is the problem. Periodically, we suffocate the economy by choking it with excessive credit on which the interest costs constantly encroach on the standard of living of the consumer to the point of national bankruptcy.

There is a reason why raw material prices are kept low as a matter of public policy. By keeping them low, an economy is forced to borrow in order to consume its own production. (When raw material prices are kept at parity, the consumers in the economy earn enough to buy the production, and many people get in on the action.) Excessive debt, historically, has been used to funnel the wealth of the nation into ever fewer hands. The 1970 welfare roll of 9.5 million people (or a total of 22 million receiv-

---

* On June 3, 1970, I and two farmers—Jack Grimmer of California, and [NFO Vice President] Erhard Pfingston of Iowa—met with Dr. Hendrick Houthakker of the Council of Economic Advisers. Houthakker argued that farm prices had to be kept at a "distress level" in order to remove the excess human resources from agriculture, and to cause farm production to flow rapidly into world markets. Every argument he offered came straight from CED policy. A native of the Netherlands, Houthakker came to the U.S. in 1951. He became a citizen in 1966.

ing less than $3,335 per annum) out of 200 million suggests to what extent people have been shared out.

There is a truth in economics that charges of "fundamentalism" cannot wipe away. A nation that has all its own raw materials can have any level of prosperity it desires at any wage level it likes. Only one requirement has to be met. Raw material prices have to stay in balance with cost factors—with wages and interest.

The policy writers, Clawson included, suggested that there is some way for the economy to function by taking the consumer price level, subtracting transportation costs, wage costs, manufacturing costs, etc., and then giving the raw material producer what is left over, whether it meets his costs in production or not. This rates as nonsense. And the time has come to call it nonsense in no uncertain terms.

## [7] GREAT MYTHS OF ECONOMICS

Even without the details, common sense people answered their own questions about free trade, hence an answering spate of "protectionist myth" editorials in the public prints during Wilken's last year. Hardback codifications took up the battle cry.

"Take the protectionist myth," echoed Don Paarlberg in *Great Myths of Economists*.

"Wouldn't we be in much better shape if we could staunch the surge of imported steel, shoes and autos, protecting profits and jobs of American workers in these industries? The answer lies in a counterquestion: Where would foreigners get the dollars to buy our airliners, movies and computers? It's also demonstrable that foreign know-how and innovation have widened the product choices of American consumers, spurred domestic production of such items as compact cars and lightweight bicycles, and helped keep retail prices from rising even more.

"If trade indeed were a one-way street, then logically one would be led from the proposition of 'Buy American' to 'Buy Pennsylvania' to 'Buy Wilkes-Barre.'

"A witty French economist, Frederick Bastiat, in 1845, with tongue in cheek, carried the protectionists' case somewhat further than they cared to go. Noting that sunlight was free, it thus was an 'unfair' source of illumination. France, he said, would be better off if all houses were built without windows. Great benefits, he argued, would accrue to his 'petitioners—the manufacturers of Candles, Gaslights, Lamps, Candlesticks, Street Lamps, Snuffers, Extinguishers, and the producers of Oil, Tallow, Rosin, Alcohol, and, generally, of everything connected with Lighting.' "

But men like Paarlberg didn't explain the real mechanism behind the two-way street called trade. The rancher in Johnson County, Kansas paid more taxes on a steer than the entire cost of production in New Zealand. This man couldn't become so efficient he could compete. Imports thus entered to break the price structure of the domestic producer. And the two-way street called trade wasn't a two-way street at all, but two one-way streets serving the powers that be each way.

The goods that entered from abroad weren't paid for at half the parity it costs to produce them. The U.S. didn't pay for cheap steel with high priced IBM machines. It paid for cheap steel with cheap wheat and cheap soybeans. Thus the public policy of keeping farm prices cheap had its function, but Paarlberg did not spell out that function. Cheap raw material prices in the U.S. served to keep cheap raw material prices the world over, particularly in underdeveloped nations.

Who, after all, was being protected, when a loincloth producer was permitted to sell production to the U.S. after manufacturing it under conditions that would not have been tolerated here? Who was being protected when the cheese could be handled in wooden buckets abroad, whereas stainless steel tanks were required here?

There was only one solution to this problem, Wilken held, thereby throwing his arm around the economics of Colin Clark. The high market economy had to practice equity of trade. It had to pay its own parity when it imported production, and charge its own parity when it exported. International trade, after all, was stuff for stuff—and gold paid out for stuff was no more than simple barter. That all this clashed with the ground rules for profit via exploitation and international trade condemned the equity of trade principle, Wilken realized. Only one development might make it different—*if the people understood, if Congress understood.*

With a buying public mortgaged up to the hilt, people indeed went to hamburger. The advice of the first five presidents after WWII—Truman, Eisenhower, Kennedy, Johnson and Nixon—has been exactly the same. All five chief executives have been in favor of getting farm prices down to what is called the world level. This policy conforms to Cordell Hull's victory in achieving free trade via the Reciprocal Trade Agreements Act of 1934.

The post WWII effect of this public policy has been to drive farm prices down. As a result, business has lost its markets in rural America. It has lost new capital for expansion and has been forced to turn to borrowed capital. When the going concern of business has to borrow its capital, it has to pay interest. After paying interest and wages, private enterprise paid only about 3% on stocks as dividends by 1967, even less by the end of the decade. As raw materials went down, business lost money for the simple reason that it lost the volume of markets necessary to earn the profit to meet wages and capital costs.

Raw material prices in the United States are subject to constant and devastating price attacks from the rest of the world under a system of low tariffs simply because the United States is the high market. The low cost producer sells to the high market, and the high market buys cheap until the very process pulls down its own standard of living to comply with world standards.

## [8] INTERNATIONAL INVESTMENTS

Looking the world over during his last days, Wilken saw production and consumption with all the earmarks of bookkeeping out of whack. *U.S. News & World Report* had detailed massive pileups of goods, wool in Australia, copper in Zambia, cotton in the Sudan—and nowhere was consumption relieving production, even with goods being loaded back and forth in the international markets.

Reading the daily papers, one almost got the impression that the world's economic chaos has grown out of problems of detail, when in fact every bit of it has been manufactured by indifference to a basic principle.

The basic principles that govern international investments had been ignored, and the world was about to pay the piper. At the grassroots level in America, this situation had been tolerated largely because almost 200 million Americans did not understand how an exchange economy functioned. At the level of high finance, these same principles had been ignored not through ignorance, but to comply with thoroughly informed self-interest.

During a single year in the late 1960s, American companies invested over $10 billion in nations around the world—or a little over 14% of their capital investments left the country. During that decade, capital flowed out of the country at an ever-accelerating rate.

Looking history squarely in the eye, one point stood out. Investments that flow into foreign nations cannot be repaid, not unless the investor nation accepts low priced goods in return. Simple trade, of course, remains stuff for stuff. But this is not the same as when investments have been poured into a foreign nation.

The Britisher, Reginald McKenna, explained this point to the American Bankers Association at a time when the U.S. and the world were building for 1929. "For over two centuries British capital has been lent to other countries. Year by year, England produced more than she either consumed herself or could exchange for the products of other nations, and she could not obtain a market for the surplus unless she gave the purchaser a long credit . . . British factories and workshops were kept in good employment, but it was a condition of their prosperity that a part of their output should be disposed of in this way. British creditors received a good return on their investments, but the ability of the debtors to pay has been dependent . . . on the development of their country being fostered by the receipt of further loans."

In the aggregate, England was caught in the bind that required her to return more in loans than she received in interest each year. Said McKenna: ". . . if the payment of past debts depends necessarily upon the receipt of further loans, debts on balance are not paid at all."

In short, while an individual firm might gain, the nation has to lose as an arithmetical certainty. England dropped the lead in this game because of WWI. And that nation cannot be said to have recovered from two centuries of capital exportation to this day.

After WWII, the U.S. became the world's big creditor nation. Before 1929, it poured out its capital until the home markets no longer had the purchasing power to consume the American production. Then, as now, agriculture was required to absorb the shock waves as long as possible ahead of the rest of the economy.

Hard on the heels of WWII, the same thing started happening again. To speed the earnings into international channels, the system required imports of cheap goods. As soon as full parity for agriculture was abandoned, imports created surpluses in commodities, and these "surpluses" drove down prices.

That is why capital exportation took on a new dimension the minute farm parity was scaled back from 90% during the first years of the Ezra Taft Benson era. It became the calculated judgment of those in public policy positions that the exportation of capital could continue if the faltering purchasing power was shored up by sinking raw material prices in the U.S. The result became a two decade long decline in farm prices at home, fantastic credit expansion, and an age of inflation.

Agriculture was underpaid by approximately 50% of its proper share during that period.

And what has been the result on the international scene? Almost without exception, agricultural income became scaled downward throughout the world. Except in Common Market countries, the shortage of purchasing power has required country after country to stack up goods, and look for sales in international markets.

In the meantime, the international investment game goes on. Everything else being equal, investments flow to the lowest wage area, just as cheap production seeks the highest markets. Indeed, as automation becomes standard fare around the world, the only differential advantage left for free capital is the price of labor.

Writing in the late 18th century, Adam Smith confidently believed that labor itself would resolve this issue, because people would demand standard wages among the several trading nations. Unhappily, with internationalism reaching into black and yellow countries, this has not proved to be the case. Indeed, a disparity in wages between the U.S. and even developed nations in the European Economic Community persists.

The habit nowadays is to equate human exploitation with efficiency, and therefore the "more efficient" can pour production into a high wage area until it breaks the high market. Allowing goods and commodities to flow to the high market is exactly the same as opening the high wage area to free immigration. Indeed, before the U.S. closed its doors, a million souls a year entered the land of higher wage promise. And unions were powerless until immigration laws became a reality.

Because commodities and cheap manufactured goods are easily substituted for the actual movement of labor, unorganized agriculture has always been the first to suffer from import invasion. Late in the game, the effect of import price destruction visits itself on the industrial sector—and, therefore, it is usually the industrial sector that is the first to scream for higher tariffs.

## [9] THOSE WHO TURN TO TARIFFS

Those who turn to tariffs when they suffer find the sledding rough because without free entry of goods or commodities, foreigners must be allowed to keep as gifts all the investments that have been made. Indeed, it is a basic generalization that as long as the movement of capital is not controlled, a policy of tariffs must fail.

In order to permit free investments abroad, the American public policy for almost two decades running has been to keep American raw materials in line with $35 gold. As a consequence, American farmers have been driven ever downward in their standard of living. Cheap imports, enough of them, and institutional arrangements for doing business, have permitted the exploitation of the American farmer. Farmers, because they do not set their own prices, have been helpless from day No. 1 in this crazy game.

Ironically, those who advocate complete free world trade are doing it in the name of "one world." They are right, in a sense. One world is what the present low raw materials prices the world over will lead to, but it will be one world in which workers everywhere will have to accept the rate of pay accepted by the lowest paid country in world trade.

Wilken consistently pointed out the fact that low raw material prices—cemented into place by international manipulation—made mandatory almost all of the world's poverty. Earned income in any nation is not created by loans, dice hustling, or printing presses. It is created by production of raw materials and the pricing of that production.

The world will continue to have monetary troubles. All of them hark back to the quite simple fact that when raw materials are not paid for, the monetary effect is exactly the same as if those raw materials were destroyed or not produced in the first place. The act of production creates the income to consume that production only if it is properly priced at every stage of the exchange game.

Bookkeeping can't wipe that fact away.

And the strained logic of government "blue-ribbon" commissions can't wipe it away.

# CHAPTER 8: TAPE NO. 4

Q. I understand that you and your associates testified in favor of farm commodity supports in 1942—the Steagall Amendment. Why were the support programs handled by a Banking and Currency Committee, rather than an agricultural committee?

WILKEN. In my research work, I went through the monetary end of this thing from the time we became a nation. I haven't mentioned money too often. I have concentrated on pointing out the 7 times turn of the new farm dollar. And I have illustrated how income shortages develop in the various sectors of the economy. Now why the price supports for farm production? The 90% price support measure was a monetary bill, and that's why it was handled by the currency committee rather than a farm committee. If we'd take 25 basic raw materials—most of them agricultural—and stabilize them at 90% of parity for support, and impose a 110% ceiling, we'd have the money and we'd have the stability. And we can't solve this matter of imbalance, low farm income, and city problems until we put a price on basic raw materials. We can kick out the Federal Reserve, but that isn't going to get us a farm price. Now in the Constitution it says Congress shall issue the money and regulate the value thereof. When you establish parity for basic raw materials, you create the flow of money that you need, and you don't have to worry about financial control. You have the control. So the point that I want to make is that this 7 times trade turn illustrates the loss. If you establish parity on raw materials through a support program, you solve the monetary problem. And until you support those raw materials you're not going to solve it.

Q. Then you're saying failure to pay parity for raw materials makes possible credit creation.

WILKEN. Well, by manipulating the prices on raw materials, they can shut off the earned income and push people to borrow.

Q. So "they" are really the Federal Reserve?

WILKEN. Well, they manipulate this thing. They know the turn. They manipulate it at the top.

Q. Let me restate this proposition. You said that what the 90% of parity bill did was to monetize farm raw materials. This appears to be an economic concept that hasn't been clearly understood since before Adam Smith. And it furnishes a very clear understanding of the nature of money. Why isn't money understood better by Congress? When was the last monetary hearing in the United States?

WILKEN. In 1939. There hasn't been one since then. Let me go through this monetary angle a little more. The international dealers have always had gold and silver as the monetary metals. And they gave them a fixed price. But when you talk about paying a proper price for farm products, people react. Still we've had a constant price on gold since the early 1930s. And before that it hadn't changed in 100 years.

Q. What did the hearing in 1939 bring out?

WILKEN. Manipulation. From 1873 to 1896, the price of silver broke from $1.32 an ounce to 65 cents an ounce. Along with it the price of wheat dropped a cent a bushel for every cent that silver went down. Why? Well, there's an old saying that wheat is the staff of life. And silver was the poor nation's money. South American nations and India and China didn't have gold. The U.S. was fortunate. We uncovered gold deposits in California and in Colorado and then in the Black Hills, in South Dakota. So we've always had some gold production.

Q. The U.S. in effect had its own money store?

WILKEN. That's right. In 1910-14, the price of silver was about 60 cents an ounce. And then World War I broke out. The price of silver moved up to $1.328 in 1919. But gold stayed at $20.67. The increase in the price of silver gave more buying power to the poor nations—and commodity prices moved up in the United States. Wages moved up to 50 cents an hour. Then in 1920 the international financiers decided to pull the strings to bring the commodity prices back in line with the price of $20.67 gold, or 1910-1914 prices. Remember, during World War I the Eastern banks loaned money to the rural banks so that the people could buy bonds to finance the war. When they called those loans, bonds dropped as low as something like 80 cents on the dollar. We lost 25% of our national income in one year—1919-1920. Then we elected a new administration. The business community realized that it could not have workers to continue the production of industrial America unless they earned good money. Industry wanted to continue the 50 cent an hour wage, but this was impossible as imports could break domestic prices. They wanted price supports. So we had the Fordney-McCumber Tariff Bill. This was to protect manufactured products, and it did. And in the 1925-1929 period, we averaged 55 cents an hour for wages.

Q. How do the monetary metals figure in accomplishing this down, down, down movement on commodities? Gold and silver, for instance?

WILKEN. Going back to 1800, we had bi-metalism. You had $20.67 gold and $1.29 silver. In our country it was on a ratio of 16 to 1. In 1873, we had a big discovery of silver—the Comstock lode in Nevada—and the international financiers decided they weren't going to maintain the price of silver. They just made a commodity out of it. That cut your basic metal for money in half, because silver and gold were equal on that differential in price. When you did that you wrecked the economies of South America, Mexico, and India and China, because they had no gold. Their money was based on silver. At that time it didn't hurt us so much because we had developed gold production in the U.S. So we had the gold production to take care of our international balances. After World War I the price of silver moved back up to $1.38 from about 60 cents in the 1910-'14 period. That of course, increased world commodity prices, because all the foreign nations on silver money had more money. And we moved up from $31 billion of income in 1910 to $79 billion in 1919. Then the international financiers wanted to get this commodity price level back to balance with $20.67 gold. (Gold hadn't been increased in price.) To bring that about they broke the price of silver in the world market from $1.38 to 65 cents an ounce in about six months.

Q. You said they "broke" the price. Who are "they" and how did "they" do this?

WILKEN. "They" are the international money in London and New York. In other words your big banking houses. They wanted to get the commodity prices down to balance with $20.67 gold.

Q. And they had enough of a stockpile to dump on the market to reduce this price of silver that much?

WILKEN. They didn't really have to have a stockpile. All they had to do was sell paper silver. Just sell silver down, down, down. As a result of that, India and China with silver as a monetary metal were bankrupt. Then, as a result of that, we had the Depression because it broke our farm prices—we lost 54% of our national income from 1929 to 1933.

Q. Now when our farm prices started going down prior to 1929, this was also accompanied by quite an expansion of credit in the U.S., was it not?

WILKEN. It was in 1929. You had started out the installment credit thing, and I think the installment credit was up a lot and you had a lot of stocks bought on margins, but in the case of real estate loans you had to pay the interest. But in your mortgages nowadays, you not only have to pay the interest but you have to pay part of the principal each year, so that home mortgage is heavier to carry today than it was back in 1929. In 1929 you had only to pay the interest.

Q. Did the drop in farm prices really cause a national income slump?

WILKEN. To illustrate this thing, our national income dropped to 54% between 1929 and 1933. It always follows the year after agriculture because agriculture is a year ahead. We didn't get back to the 1929 level of national income until 1941.

Q. Did we get to that level in 1941?

WILKEN. Yes, nationally. Seven of the 12 Midwestern states got back to the 1929 income level in 1941, but all 12 of them didn't get back until 1942.

Q. How about the nation as a whole?

WILKEN. Well, it got back too. They had $104 billion income in 1941. And it was $81.6 billion in 1940.

Q. What was the big meeting in London in 1925 on silver?

WILKEN. That was a discussion about bringing silver back into the picture and doubling the monetary metal. The gold supply—at the $20.67 price—wasn't enough to take care of the money needs of the United States since income had moved from $33 billion in 1910-1914 to $82 billion in 1925-1929.

Q. Why couldn't they just revalue gold?

WILKEN. They could have, but they didn't. Instead, they revalued commodities down. This was the decision.

Q. Why couldn't international financiers break commodity prices by reducing the price of silver in 1949?

WILKEN. They couldn't do that because silver was monetized at 50 cents an ounce. That's why there was a fight to knock out 90% parity. I've related how the 1948 bill for 60-90% sliding scale was passed. The purpose was to reduce farm prices down to balance with gold at $35, which is the price Roosevelt put on it.

Q. Now you said that in the five years after British devaluation we shipped in $6 billion more in farm production than we exported. What kind of farm products were those?

WILKEN. Everything. And that's how we accumulated some of our surplus. To illustrate it, in 1951 we imported $1.7 million more farm products than we exported. In spite of that, the price was moving up. We had a ceiling at that time. Now there have been different methods for judging what the value of gold ought to be. I always use the consumer price level as the guide stick because the consumer price level really reflects average costs, labor, materials, etc. So if I were to adjust the price of gold, I'd adjust it in ratio with the consumer price level. That would bring it up to about $70. Now if you wanted to bring silver back in you could.

Q. Why would you support non-farm raw materials with 90% parity?

WILKEN. They add to stability when supported. In the case of copper, lead and zinc, all you would need to do to support those prices would be a tariff at the parity level. We are only producing about half of the copper, lead and zinc that we use.

Q. In other words, you would put in a variable levy system?

WILKEN. That's right. If the world prices are at our parity level, we wouldn't need a levy. To bring about equity of trade, suppose we bought some copper in addition to what we produce and we collect the 30 cent foreign duty on it. We credit the nation we bought the copper from and then we apply that amount as payment for American goods at the American price level. This would give equity of trade.

Q. This sounds very much like what they're trying to do in the European Economic Community. Sort of a McNary-Haugen approach, isn't it?

WILKEN. The old McNary-Haugen Bill was decided on to protect the American price level, and if it hadn't been vetoed it would have worked. This was the same idea I used in the bill for Senator Gillette and Congressman Harrington with 75% price support and a tariff at the parity level in the late 1930s. That would have worked. Here's my contention. Here we are from 1929 through the Depression, on through World War II and then to 1952—we've got a ten-year record showing that it is not only possible to keep prices in balance, but that it can be done without any cost. Why don't we go back to it? Why don't we use something that we know works? Instead, we're doing these fool things like mortgaging the future to the hilt year after year.

Q. There is the thinking that if the debt gets too heavy then it can be repudiated. And there are those who talk socialism if the economy should crack up. What would happen to production and consumption?

WILKEN. If you have to repudiate your debt you'll have so much surplus stuff lying around you won't know what to do with it. You'll have all the repossessions dumped on you as a result of debt repudiation. You'll lose your production.

Q. You can visualize almost complete chaos?

WILKEN. There's no question about that.

Q. Why then, don't we join the Common Market countries to make the American parity price the world price?

WILKEN. I can't understand why we don't. We now have this interesting situation where the Common Market countries have adopted the American system—whereas we—the Americans—have thrown our system overboard and adopted a combination of the international system and the Keynesian theory of socialism. You'll have to admit that someone's done an awfully good job of selling the American people a bill of goods. When I served with Homer Capehart's committee we found that 40% of the profits of the four biggest New York banks came from international transactions rather than domestic transactions. They made their profits on international trade and differences in exchange. It comes down to this. We have this static gold price—or international money. And then we have banks creating debts and turning them into money. The minute you borrow you get authority to coin money by writing a check. You in effect become a mint to the extent that the bank gives you a ledger entry, or loan. As long as there was hard money, gold or silver, exchange of goods for gold was no more than barter, domestically or internationally. We still have gold to settle balances between countries simply because they can't trust each other. I suppose you understand how money is expanded under the Fed. The Fed buys government bonds. It simply issues a check to the seller, and the seller deposits the check back with the bank. Banks deposit with the Federal Reserve. So this makes up the cash reserve, and with our fractional reserve system one bank is entitled to loan out 6 to 25 times more money than they have based on whether deposits are time or demand deposits. But to loan out money, there have to be borrowers. This failure of raw material production to get a price in line with wages and interest has made it possible for banking to run away with the show. So you have them issuing currency for a profit and destroying currency when they feel they have to pull in the string.

Q. How much by way of imports does it take to break prices?

WILKEN. In my book on boom and bust I made the point that when our imports reach 4% of the national income in dollar volume, they knock us down to the world level. It doesn't take a lot of imports.

Q. Why do you think an equity of trade policy is a solution?

WILKEN. The only way you can get the American economy back in balance with the world is for the American economy to either bring the world up or for the U.S. to go down to the world level. International trade is used to bring about imbalance here because it pleases the money lenders. When all the sectors of the economy are in balance, people have profits. They are their own bankers. Without new earned income entering the economy, we have to increase debt or suffer depression. And debt created this way cannot be reduced. It has to grow or it can't be serviced. There isn't any way around the arithmetic of compound interest.

# CHAPTER 9: THE MONEY CREATION PROCESS

*There isn't any way around the arithmetic of compound interest.*
Still nations keep on trying.

It was the French economist, Jacques Rueff, who pointed out that Germany gave the world its greatest economist—Goethe. Goethe, of course, was no economist, yet in *Faust* (Part II)* he clearly proved beyond a shadow of doubt that inflation and government deceit were an invention of the devil. In the poem, Mephistopheles is disguised as the king's jester, in which role he prompts Lord Chancellor to unload these lines:

*To whom it may concern, this note of hand*
Is worth a thousand ducats on demand,
The pledge whereof and guarantee is found
*In treasure buried in the Emperor's ground.*

The government, however, pursues wild credit (in the poem) and experiences monetary depreciation, inflation, and is able to point to prosperity. But alas, with great prosperity His Majesty has

*. . . the charming mob all grabbing rush,*
They almost maul the donor in the crush.
The gems he flicks around as in a dream,
And snatchers fill the hall in greedy stream.
But lo, a trick quite new to me:
The thing each seizes eagerly
Rewards him with a scurvy pay,
The gift dissolves and floats away.
The rascal offers wealth untold,
*But gives the glitter, not the gold.*

Sooner or later people discover the glitter, not the gold, and the social consequences are such that government ever after has a hard time of it. Thus it becomes necessary to disguise the consequences of public policy as long as possible.

---

* From Philip Wayne's translation of Goethe's *Faust* (Part II), Penguin Books, Ltd., London, 1959.

# [1] THE WORLD'S GREATEST INVENTOR

Wilfrid C. Krug of Windsor, Ontario thinks Thomas Edison was right when he said, "I guess the world's greatest inventor was the chap who invented 6% compound interest." He was, perhaps, even greater than the fellow who invented credit in the first place. Without credit there could be no consuming interest lug, and without interest there could be no astounding boom or bust requirement in the capital system—perhaps!

Obviously, money is of very ancient origin. Any large economic library has hundreds of texts on the subject, yet the publication that explains the transition from barter to money best may well be a comic book, *The Further Adventures of Robinson Crusoe.*\* A shipwreck brings unexpected new population to Crusoe's island (see pages 119 and 120).

The transition from barter to money was a bit more complicated, of course. Early attempts at expanding the money supply were made by thieves, both those who counterfeited and those who ruled. The only safeguard against the Prince who shaved coins and the rascal who counterfeited them was the precious metal. Frederick Soddy's comments on the strong penchant for preserving precious metals in money is not without maximum interest.

"The principle underlying it was perfectly correct to the principles of modern physical science. Since wealth cannot be created out of nothing, but is a product of human effort expended on raw material and sources of energy of the globe, no individual should be able to manufacture a new money to wealth out of nothing and the purchaser should give up something equal in value to (as difficult to come by as) that which he so acquires. It is in this initial point that the modern methods of multiplying claims to wealth fail.

"But even more fatal to democracy has been its failure to provide any proper authority and mechanism for the making and issue of money, as and when it is required, to keep pace with the growth of wealth. National money—whatever it is made of—does not bear, and never has borne, interest, which is the *raison d'etre* for the issue of most modern money. Whatever ends it may be supposed to subserve, bank money is created primarily for that end, and what is worse, then decreated again when the end is served. But a sovereign issued in the reign of George III is now worth no more than when it was issued, and obeys the ordinary law of the conservation of matter. It does not mysteriously

---

\* Pages 6 and 7 of *The Further Adventures of Robinson Crusoe* are reproduced on pages 115-116 with the permission of Grosvenor Associates, 4/5 Copthall Court, Throgmorton Street, London E.C. 2, England, who hold the copyright and keep the booklet in print and available for sale at all times.

appear and as mysteriously disappear like bank money."

In short the first one to put money into circulation gets something for nothing unless it has value in itself, such as gold, or a warehouse receipt. Money always has been and always will be a lodestone for rascals. In an earlier era, when mass men still had sense enough to distrust those who created money, precious metals in coins insured circulation, and gave to the holder of money the wherewithal to make good his claim for a fair share of the community's production. Gold, it turned out, had attributes unavailable in cowry shells, caribou teeth or tobacco.

## [2] GOLD

Gold is found in almost every nation, albeit in niggardly amounts. As Wilfrid Krug wrote, it is "one of the most beautiful of all the elements and one of the heaviest metals known to science. It is the only metal that is yellow in color in its natural state. It does not tarnish when exposed to air and does not rust when buried in the ground. It always retains its particular beauty, color and lustre. It is the most ductible and malleable of the metals. A troy ounce can be drawn into fine wire 59 miles long or it can be beaten into a thin film which will cover 100 square feet—over a thousand times thinner than normal paper. Gold is virtually insoluble and proof against nature's reagents. It is inert to most acids and bases. Its refusal to disintegrate, rust or tarnish has resulted in its being regarded as something that can be counted on to look the same and feel the same a century or five centuries ahead."

Gold is more, many pages more, as detailed by William L. Graham in *The Coming Gold Crisis,* but one thing it is not—"the barbarous relic" defined by John Maynard Keynes.

Permanent money is considered barbarous simply because it bears no interest. Credit money deserves that title because it requires a subtle form of slavery. And until governments learn to create interest-free money, gold deserves a nonpareil rating.

History has shown that when silver and gold supplies increased, economic activities got a shot in the arm. Romance of the metals may have accounted for some of this, but more than likely Wilken was right when he said people "had more money." The importance of a permanent money supply can be detailed with alarming brevity. Egypt and Babylon rose to great heights when they had gold and silver, interest free, and fell when conquest and invasions took it away. When Rome moved the permanent money into Europe it attained fantastic vigor, and when the hordes from the North looted cities and the exchange medium, civilization seemed to melt into history. The Dark Ages have been seen as a time when a crude system of barter became re-established. Without a readily acceptable money, trade and industry came to a standstill. At the time Columbus sailed, the only source of monetary metals was European mines, which yielded about $500,000 annually.

After the discovery of gold in Mexico and Peru, the yellow metal flowed to Spain in an ever-swelling tide. Spain became the most powerful nation in the world, and the effect of gold as a powerful stimulus touched the whole of civilization. And when the influx of permanent money slowed, the effect was felt across all of Europe. In 1800, the yearly supply came to $7 million in terms of a $4.86 pound. By 1812 world production had been cut in half, and by 1816 it had fallen to $2.5 million by the time Andrew Jackson had achieved his reputation as a border captain, world production of gold had fallen to below $1 million per annum.

It has been written in lines like these that between 1800 and 1848, the whole of civilization reflected discontent and poverty. Great Britain's trade was no greater in 1841 than in 1815. In the year 1848, every ninth person was a pauper. Then everything changed. A man named James W. Marshall discovered gold on the American River in California. A few years later, in 1851, more gold was discovered in Australia. Almost overnight, prices and wages improved, and a two-decade long advance in world commerce became the outcome. As a result of the find in California, more gold came into circulation between 1850 and 1870 than had entered the stream of commerce during the previous 250 years.

## [3] PERMANENT MONEY

As the permanent money came closer to matching production of goods and services, interest rates fell. By 1873 newly mined gold was still coming, but at a slower rate. Hard times followed. And then a repeat performance—the Klondike gold rush—and proof that historical happenstance could bring on a permanent money supply at a rate in tune with the production of other raw materials and wealth.

Gold, from pre-history until about 1800, became the international money, the wherewithal to settle debts in trade between nations. The system, or lack thereof, for accomplishing the chore, was far from smooth. Money-changers clogged the ports of the world, shuffling coins and currency, and finding the proper specie for this merchant interested in a transaction with that nation. By 1900, Great Britain had become the world's clearing house, and the arrangement for doing business became the gold standard. Gold expressed the worth of Britain's money, with the central bank fixing a floor for the price of the yellow stuff.

The gold standard *per se* went down the drain with WWI. For one thing, foreign deposits were blocked, and other sticky situations came into being, such as those designed to keep the enemy from enjoying trade benefits. By the time it was all over, the gold-exchange standard had become a reality. Not only gold, but certain reserve currencies could be used in paying off trade debts. At that time the idea seemed conceived in sheer genius, but by the end of the 1920s the whole thing fell for reasons best explained by Carl Wilken, and since then the Bretton Woods Agreement (with drawing rights) has done nothing to safeguard against a repeat performance.*

## [4] TO CREATE MONEY

A permanent, non-interest bearing money no longer figures. The law nowadays proceeds with vengeance against a counterfeiter, but permits banks to create money by wholesale lots and lend it at interest. A recent issue of *The Wall Street Journal* best described the process.

"The process is simplest when the open market staff at the Fed's New York district bank buys, for instance, $1 million of securities from a big commercial bank in New York. To pay for them, the Federal men simply add $1 million to the 'reserve account' that commercial bank has at the Federal Bank; or when the $1 million check is deposited by a dealer in his bank account, that bank also gets the $1 million addition to its reserve account as it sends the check back to the Federal Bank.

"This sets the stage for the multiplication of money. It comes about because the Federal regulations require commercial banks to keep idle as reserves only a fraction of the customer's deposits they receive. Assuming that the reserve requirement is 15%, a bank receiving a check for $1 million needs to keep only $150,000 of reserves behind the deposit. So, it suddenly has $850,000 of 'excess reserves' that the profit motive usually impels it to lend. Here's where the money creation process begins in earnest.

"The bank lends $850,000 by adding that sum to the borrower's checking account on its books. When the borrower spends this money, the check he writes soon winds up in another bank, giving that bank new ability to lend all but the 15% it must keep as reserves. As the process progresses, Federal theoreticians say, the initial $1 million of new reserves evidently supports an extra $6.7 million of checking-account deposits."

*Gold is barbaric because it bears no interest.*

---

* Under the IMF, drawing rights were restricted to 200% of a nation's gold quota. Special drawing rights (paper gold) were set up to buy time and cloud "fundamental disequilibriums." Special drawing rights call for interest, which is why they are not considered barbaric.

Worsening raw material prices bring on borrowing, and borrowing brings on credit creation, or a bigger interest-bearing money supply. As defined by the Federal Reserve Bank of St. Louis, the money stock toward late 1970 was $207.1 billion, $55 billion of which was currency. The billions in CDs weren't counted, nor were the billions in saving deposits, although a mature sense of values would seem to insist that savings and short-term bonds are money in circulation, even though men like Milton Friedman (in *A Monetary History of the United States*) compromise the issue.

## [5] THE FIRST BITE

Interest sits down at the table and eats three meals a day, seven days a week, taking the first bite. Compound interest ultimately brings on a clash between the insatiable appetites of those with money and physical possibility for reasons best explained by allegory.

Plants and animals, too, attempt to, grow geometrically or in a Fibonacci progression. Nature intervenes, either with auto-intoxication or failure of the food supply. Without this regulatory device, a single bacterium spore could blanket the Earth in half a year. In economics, failure of the food supply and auto-intoxication are both represented by bankruptcy. Still the game goes on.* According to the March 11, 1943 issue of the *Congressional Record* (page A 1220) the state of California gifted a hunk of gold quartz to the nation for inclusion in the Washington monument. The quartz was financed by a $975 note due in 1850. In 1851 the note was retired and a bond issue put in its place. By March 1943 California had paid $136,000 interest on this small debt and still owed $2,227,500. Compound interest on that chunk of quartz, given enough time, could have brought not only California, but the United States to its knees. The debt was finally paid in the late 1960s.

## [6] AN HISTORICAL STINK

The term usury has an historical stink about it. The medieval world condemned it, and the Roman Church only recently lifted its prohibition, a move possibly made necessary by the investment successes detailed by Nino Lo Bello in *The Vatican Empire*. Looking back, however, there seems little reason to suspect interest charges as such half as much as the pro-

---

* "God is still reigning in His heaven," wrote Roger W. Babson, "the trees are budding as they have every spring and compound interest is going on just the same every day including Sundays and holidays. . . . The great majority get on at the top and fall at the bottom. . . ."

cess of compound interest, the mathematical device that makes monopoly of the currency metals an easy accomplishment. Commercial expansion has always demanded an increased supply of currency, but whose job was it to see to it that gold was forthcoming? "Get your man into your debt for what he has not got and cannot get, and you may take the skin off him," was the financial aphorism Soddy recited. Debt that could not be paid made slaves as surely as did other forms of legal bondage. Debt substituted for farm earnings, circa 1950 and beyond, kept production coming under conditions little better than subtle slavery. The nation's choice over whether to monetize debt or raw materials made it so.

## [7] ENOUGH DONKEYS

Wilfrid C. Krug, writing in his splendid little book, *What's Happening to our Money?*, sums up both the reason and the explanation as to why people should be entitled to hold gold. He quotes Canadian Senator G.G. McGeer, K.C., who in effect said, *you can't trust your government any more than one country can trust the next*. And a government that delegates its money creation function can't be trusted at all.

Wrote Senator McGeer:

"Government possessing the power to create and issue currency and credit as money and enjoying the right to withdraw both currency and credit from circulation by taxation and otherwise, need not and should not borrow capital at interest as a means of financing governmental work and public enterprise. The government should create, issue and circulate all the currency and credit needed to satisfy the spending power of government and the buying power of consumers. The privilege of creating and issuing money is not only the supreme prerogative of government but it is the government's greatest creative opportunity. By the adoption of these principles, the long-felt need for a uniform medium will be satisfied. The taxpayers will be saved immense sums of interest, discounts and exchange. The financing of all public enterprises, the maintenance of stable government and ordered progress and the conduct of the treasury will become matters of practical administration. The people can and will be furnished with a currency as safe as their own government. Money will cease to be master and become the servant of humanity. . . ."

Only the City of Paderborn, Germany ever stated this principle of distrust for money creators openly.*

---

* Translation of the language on the note shown on page 126: "In Paderborn we haven't got a donkey who can defecate gold. However there are enough donkeys [fools] in the world who take our money as real."

Anyone who proposes an outright issue of money to finance government runs smack into an inventory of invective kept on hand by the super banking fraternity. Witness the case of Henry Ford and Thomas A. Edison recommending that the big Muscle Shoals project be developed with the issuance of $30 million in currency.

"Under the old way" Edison said, "any time we wish to add to the national wealth we are compelled to add to the national debt. Now, that is what Henry Ford wants to prevent. He thinks it is stupid and so do I, that, for the loan of $30 million of their own money, the people of the United States should be compelled to pay $66 million—that is what it amounts to—with interest. People who will not turn a shovelful of dirt nor contribute a pound of material will collect more money from the United States than will the people who supply the material and do the work. That is the terrible thing about interest. In all our great bond issues, the interest is always greater than the principal. All of the great public works cost more than twice the actual cost on that account. Under the present system of doing business we simply add 120 to 150 percent to the stated cost.

"If our nation can issue a dollar bond it can issue a dollar bill. The element that makes the bond good, makes the bill good also. The difference between the bond and the bill is that the bond lets the money brokers collect twice the amount of the bond whereas the currency pays nobody but those who directly contribute to Muscle Shoals in some useful way."

American Bankers Association members came up fighting from their chairs on that one. "We must combat this most damnable propaganda which threatens to disrupt the stability of our currency system," became the outcry. Financial "experts" ridiculed the plan, stating that Edison "lacked instruction in the elementary principle of economics and money."

## [8] COIN AND MONEY

The position that epithets put Edison in was the same one under which Carl Wilken suffered most of his adult life. "The experts," said the *New York Times*, "and the bankers who conduct finance in Wall Street and writers who report finance in the newspapers all were at one opinion about Edison. It was the only thing about which they could agree perfectly, namely that he hadn't the remotest idea of what he was talking about." And yet Edison was right.

The danger passed—and those in the saddle could sigh audibly. People could be made to swallow inflation, imbalance, rural poverty, urban ghettos, wars, all because a bought and paid for education machine somehow managed to school children universally without more than a handful learning something about the nature of coin and money.

First graders nowadays learn that two and two are four.

They should be learning also that compound interest is impossible, that borrowed money is no substitute for earned money, and that the system of credit on which money issuance is based is at best a fraud, at worst a fantastic capital crime.

"The only sound way to get newly earned money into the picture is through the production of new wealth times the price per unit," Wilken added in one of the many postscripts he issued. "Such money does not have to be repaid. The consistent way of developing income is through production of food and fiber. You have broad distribution there, and you have production that enters quickly into the consumption cycle. If you monetize raw materials at full parity, it doesn't matter whether the Fed can create credit—there won't be a need."

In foreign exchange, Wilken called wheat the real gold of the world because it was the staff of life. Wheat should be treated like gold, Wilken said. Base your monetary income on storable commodities. Wilken recalled the great gold finds. "It didn't change the price of gold one iota. What did we do with the gold? We piled it up."

And therein lived the bugbear that earned for Wilken catcalls from the same experts who had pooh-poohed Thomas A. Edison. *We'd be swimming in storable commodities!* has been the reply.

Would we? Wilken proved with facts and figures that since 1910, with the exception of seasonal situations, production of farm commodities had never outrun population, and that surplus crops had been imported, either directly as crop production, or indirectly as a by-product of displacement.

Those who created and extinguished money knew the name of the game, Wilken asserted. Well-informed self interest, not historic ignorance, accounted for the breakdown of domestic buying power, imports, imbalance between the several sectors of the economy, and finally depression. And only Congress could upset the ploys being used by the big boys. "People get the kind of government they deserve. That's why the trade turn principle—this approximate ratio of 1 to 7—should be understood by the man on the street." For only the man on the street can guard it, keep it honest, as he does the fact that two and two are four.

# CHAPTER 10: TAPE NO. 5

Q. Mr. Wilken, to summarize some of the things you've said, can you supply an answer to this riddle? Doesn't India have the classical position that supply and demand economists seek—short supply, lots of people, people starving in fact! Why isn't the farmer in India rich?

WILKEN. The farmer has never had a price in India. Without a price he can't develop production. Without a price, he would lose production, even if he had it. It really makes no difference whether you have a $10 an hour wage rate or a $3 an hour rate—you can have as good a life with one as with the other, if the entire economy is operated in balance. That's why parity for raw materials creates the money, something you can't do with a printing press. Dollars do not constitute money. Buying power does.

Q. Earlier you said parity also creates profits. Can an economy operate without profits as suggested by some of the socialists?

WILKEN. That's the idea of production for use, not profits. The concept itself is based on the idea that a state can take over the productive system, and make the classless society a reality by socializing profits. They beg the question on this, but socialists know there has to be a profit. This was expounded by Karl Marx. I have a copy of a speech made by Karl Marx in Brussels, Belgium in January 1848. The subject was free trade. You see, Great Britain in the early part of the 19th century had corn laws which protected the prices of farm products. Under the doctrine of free trade the British economists of that period told the workers they could buy cheap food from the colonies if Parliament would only do away with the corn laws, and that by spending less for food the workers would have more money to buy other consumer goods. That bill of goods was sold for several reasons, some of which were institutional in nature within Britain itself—a landlord's monopoly. Finally, leaning on the economics of Adam Smith, Great Britain got free trade. Karl Marx analyzed it, and the point he made was very important. He said that if a nation buys cheap raw materials from its colonies, it thereby establishes a cheap market. As a result of that cheap market, the economy is required to reduce wages, because industry is not able to pay labor and still sell its products in a competitive market.

The significant point made in that speech came near the end. Karl Marx said the protective system was conservative and that free trade was destructive—and for that reason and that reason alone he was for free trade. It would hasten the day of the social revolution. One hundred years later Great Britain elected a socialist government.

Q. Now we find that Russia is not a complete success as an economy, and we find China duplicating some of Russia's mistakes. In the background, is inadequate agriculture the real base problem?

WILKEN. I'll tell you what the weakness is in Russia, and what our strength is, although we don't realize it. It's the livestock industry. Our livestock industry processes raw materials. It processes more tonnage of raw material than all American industry put together, if you include water. We have some 580 million acres of grazing lands. On these western ranches, livestock does all the labor in processing that crop. Suppose you have 200 acres in pasture with creeks running through it. Livestock gathers all of that raw material and does the processing. And you've got your corn—as much as 88% of your corn crop is processed by the livestock industry. At least 70 million acres of hay are processed by the livestock industry. Russia and China have no well-developed livestock industry.

Q. Let's say you were in an African country, and you're in charge. It is up to you to see how you can pay for the development of this country. Are you saying that the last thing you'd do is float a loan for getting a refinery, or capital?

WILKEN. The first thing you'd have to do is teach them how to grow food and then develop separate production of food. But if you take it away from agriculture, how can you raise enough stuff for your people to eat? That's why China is in trouble. That is the problem in Russia. When the Communists took over, the farmers found the only thing that they could do away with was their livestock. They butchered their livestock. So Russia lost its livestock farmers. And that's what's been the weakness there ever since. Now in India you have a religious situation. They have, perhaps, 60 million head of cattle trampling crops and eating grain. They won't use these meat animals because of a religious scruple. That's India's big problem. Outside capital can help develop a country, but outside capital wants its return—and in the final analysis no country can afford to let profit leave.

Q. How does the fact of cheap world raw material prices figure in India's problem?

WILKEN. Well, we have oil companies, for instance, out there buying oil at a fraction of what it costs in Oklahoma. Without a price for the oil, India can't pay for our wheat. If we paid them our parity for what we bought, they would be able to pay us parity for wheat, and buy a great deal more than they do now.

Q. Do you subscribe to the idea that a low world raw materials price level leads to war?

WILKEN. In a way. We try to protect capital investments in different countries against expropriation. Let me illustrate what happened in Africa. We gave those people their freedom and those people are uneducated. They just assumed when they had their freedom that they could take over all of this property European people had built up over there. If you go back to 1939, you have a good illustration of that in Mexico. Mexico took over all our oil investments in Mexico. We didn't like it, but we didn't go to war over it. Today American capital can't invest in Mexico unless Mexican nationals control 51% of the corporation.

Q. The nut of the national economic problem—and the nut of the international economic problem—then, is agriculture?

WILKEN. Certainly. And that's the reason agriculture is listed separately in the *Economic Report of the President*. It is the largest industry in the world. There is nothing that can compare to agriculture. Just to give you an idea—if you fly from coast to coast, from the Canadian border to the Gulf of Mexico, all you'll see is land. Not mortgages, bonds, paper certificates, but land, grazing land, crop land, and a village here and there, and once in a while a big city. Agriculture is at least as big as 60% of the value assigned to the nation's corporations. In terms of production, agriculture is so big it accounts for 70% of all the resources used in operating the economy each year. I've covered how the six basic segments of the economy operate. But I want you to remember one important point: corporations, small business, rentals and agriculture (the private enterprise sector) have one thing in common. They are all compelled to invest capital in order to operate. They save or assemble savings, and invest the capital that creates every job and every dollar of income in the United States economy. And I have called attention to the wages and interest segments as the cost sector in operating the national economy. Wages and the cost of capital—they have to be borne by the private enterprise sector. Now we have confusion about this because we have several political systems, and we like to call them economic systems. They aren't, of course. There is only one economic system—the capital system. One of the political systems is communism, such as they have in Russia and China. Another is the socialist system. There is fascism. And here in the U.S. we have private enterprise, or individual capitalism. These systems have one thing in common, contrary to the thinking of many people. The standard of living contained under any system is simply the result of production of goods and services. Nothing else. Many people have the idea that socialism or communism has an advantage because the government can crank up the printing presses and turn out money. And they think socialism can create capital that way, do things and have a Utopian society. They can't because they still have to invest, and investment has to come from profit. So keep this private enterprise mechanism in mind. It is a gushing well. It keeps the private enterprise system moving. And the only way you can analyze the system is to look at the well, not at government. The well or boilerhouse or generator that keeps our economy moving is private enterprise, agriculture included. So elimination of private enterprise won't change anything. Can the government operate without a profit? Russia and China and India and even England have proved differently. Regardless of who runs or controls the system, you still have to earn a profit or you won't have the capital to expand. And when you talk about profit, you go right back to agriculture and other raw materials.

Q. Do we have to have farms running into thousands of acres to find a profit?

WILKEN. You don't. You can take a five-acre plot in Iowa and a family to work that plot. That's five acres—not much—yet it can produce enough to feed the family and still have enough to sell to have a good business. You don't need 700 or 800 acres. In Japan you have farmers living off a quarter of an acre.

Q. But we do have the climate of opinion that holds that unless a farmer can have several hundred acres he shouldn't be in business.

WILKEN. Well, that's true, but you still have the people. And somebody is going to have to pay the taxes to take care of them to keep them from starving. My contention is that a family with a little plot of ground to work can raise food, plant grain, and in the long haul be better off than living in the slums of the cities without a job—and on relief. I think there is a weakness in our whole attempt to field a relief system. We should require the individual who gets the relief check to perform a certain number of hours of work in the public interest for that check—cleaning up streets, cleaning up alleys, and so on, instead of just drawing a check and doing nothing. We're teaching our relief clients not to work.

Q. Are we putting a penalty on working?

WILKEN. Well, the relief client is getting a check of, say, $125 so why should he take a job for $150 and lose the $125? Livestock—as I mentioned—takes a lot of personal care. The pressures are subtle, but in the final analysis people are going to give up seven days of work a week, and long days, unless they are paid. They just won't do it for nothing.

Q. But they are doing it temporarily. It has reached fantastic proportions. Up in Pennsylvania, I made a calculation on one farmer. He keeps a hundred head of dairy cattle, that is, he keeps a hundred on the line. He has another 50 head around. Calculated in terms of a 3,000 hour year, this farmer makes 72 cents an hour. Even so, he exploits a lot of free labor from his children and from his wife in the dairy operation. A lot of these things are hard to calculate. No one would believe it, but a really refined audit sometimes reveals that dairy farmers make hardly two bits an hour.

WILKEN. Nevertheless, farmers are leaving the farm, and there are consequences. Let me take something simple. A lot of time something simple is better to understand. Suppose you go out to one of those rural communities and look at an implement dealer. He has a supply of farm machinery, tractors, and the like. Who is his customer? The farmer. Well, the farmer at the end of a feeding operation sells a carload of cattle. So he comes to the dealer and buys a piece of farm machinery. This implement dealer doesn't get one penny from the manufacturer. His income has to come out of the money the farmer pays for this tractor. The minute the farmer buys a tractor, the implement dealer has money to pay his labor bill. They, in turn, have money to buy groceries from the stores, drugs, entertainment, and pay their medical bills. The implement dealer has money to order another piece of machinery from the factory. Then, after the factory gets the order, it can send out an order for steel and prefabricated parts to make that machinery. And you have the material rolling over your transportation system and then back out to the farmer in due time. And the thing these small businessmen must understand is that the income of the community is tied up in little farm factories around the various communities. They have no other source of income. Take agriculture away, and the town is dead. Take away small business and democracy is dead. And we go to fascism or socialism.

Q. Why don't business people in small towns understand?

WILKEN. They have been brainwashed by the newspapers. This farmer for some reason just seems to get money from nowhere. They therefore haven't any interest in the prices of farm products.

Q. When did the Farm Bureau get into the picture?

WILKEN. It was brought in back in the 1914-1915 era to bring about an increase in farm production. In other words, the philosophy went back to Swift's saying about the two blades of grass. So the Bureau was tied up from the start with the Extension Department. Your Extension people did a good job experimenting with seeds—but you have to remember that the farmer in the final analysis has to provide the practical knowledge necessary to make new technology work after it arrives on the farm.

Q. In other words, the Bureau was organized to see if new forces could be put into motion to make production outrun spot demand.

WILKEN. Well, it was done with the purpose of getting cheaper raw materials. And the Farm Bureau in all of its history has never been in favor of a price. And they aren't today.

Q. How is the Farm Bureau able to sell the farmer on this proposition?

WILKEN. They do it by setting up co-ops, cooperative insurance programs, and so on. And they save farmers enough money on that to keep the dues coming in. And then they hijacked bankers and businessmen in towns to take out a membership for goodwill. In this process, they got into the organizations.

Q. Was Farm Bureau spawned by industrialists?

WILKEN. I heard Allan Kline, a president of Farm Bureau, one time. When he became president they made him a member of the Board of Directors of the Federal Reserve Board of Chicago. It all fits together. In testimony before a Congressional Committee it developed that the Federal Reserve System had control of the supply of money, credit, and so on. They could therefore determine the prices of farm products. After that meeting was over I said to Senator Capehart: "There's one weakness in this whole proposition. The Federal Reserve Board can pull the string and shut off credit and the money supply, but when prices go down the Fed can't push on the string. They can't turn it back on because there's no equity to make the loan."

Q. What did Senator Capehart have to say to that?

WILKEN. "In my experience," he said, "I find that you can't sell something to a man who hasn't any money."

Q. In all these questions and answers you've consistently called attention to the fact that a price level in line with $35 gold is liquidating the farms. *Kiplinger* put the average age of farmers at 53 or thereabouts. And there are practically no young people getting into agriculture.

WILKEN. What chance do young people have in agriculture? But that isn't the thing I'm concerned about. There's always going to be an agriculture. But what's going to happen to the rural communities? What's going to happen to the businessmen, the banks, the churches, the schools? The government has big plans to run a big area—10 to 15 counties—under one government. There's talk of taking away the states. There's talk of world police districts.

Q. This is in line with the CED policy paper on local government. Is it reasonable to assume that rural states will be allowed to keep two Senators under such a structure?

WILKEN. Taking away Senators from the farm states will be next. So to get this thing headed off you're going to have to get it done through the Senate while there is a Constitutional Senate. The Congressional vote is already all tied up. You've had some interesting court decisions on all this. I'm not an attorney, but to me what's happened is unconstitutional and against the concepts that our forefathers had when they drafted the Constitution. So here's what's got to be done. Instead of talking about a farm problem, you've got to talk about private enterprise. And this is not being done.

Q. But those in private enterprise do not know anything is wrong, do they?

WILKEN. Well, the corporations don't know what's going on. Just to illustrate—in 1950 corporation profits after taxes was $22.8 billion out of a national income of $241 billion. Then by 1964 we had moved up to $510 billion of income. And in those 14 years the corporate profits after taxes amounted to $22.2 billion, or $600 million less per year than in 1950. And I can take the *Economic Report of the President* and prove to you that corporate profits in 1966 before taxes were $27.6 billion less than they should have been to stay in balance with 1966 wages and interest. And it isn't going to be any different by 1970 and beyond.

Q. Have you made any attempt to call this to the attention of any of the leading corporations?

WILKEN. I did. A neighbor of mine is quite afraid of communism and happens to be quite well off. I pointed out to him that if we don't get this economy straightened out, I didn't see how you're going to head off a social revolution in the United States. I followed up with a letter to him and he sent it to 50 corporation presidents, companies in which this gentleman is a stockholder in the main. In this letter he re-sent, I pointed out what has happened.

Q. Specifically, what did you point out?

WILKEN. In 1947 the experts changed the method of computing national income. Prior to 1947 they computed the national income in terms of profits after taxes, but in 1947 they changed it to corporate profits before taxes. And the labor organizations used that to point to the tremendous increase in profits, failing to mention that from 1929 on the corporate taxes had gone up from 15 to 50%. And if you take corporate profits after taxes, they were in approximate balance with increased wages and interest. Then I pointed out that they had made the change in 1966 when they added $7.5 billion in corporate profits in 1964 with a lead pencil just by shifting interest totals over to corporation profits. Well, Roger Blough of U.S. Steel called their Washington office and talked to this man, and then Blough made a speech at some Eastern college. He used the facts that I had given to him, and this means he must have had his men check to find out that corporate profits hadn't increased faster than wages and interest. After that, I had a two-hour conference with a manager from Republic Steel. I went through this thing with him. Everything was fine until the question came up what do we do about it. I said, "You're not going to be able to restore profitable operation to your corporations until you restore farm prices." "Well," he said, "how do you do it?" I said, "just like we did it for ten years from 1943 to 1952." That was something completely new to him.

Q. What happened after that?

WILKEN. I followed up with a second letter listing the profits year by year after taxes. These were short—I believe—some $197 billion after taxes in 15 years as compared to balancing with wages and interest. And, if you'll recall my balance sheet using 1948-1950 as 100, the shortage of profits was quite comparable to the shortage of net farm income. In other words, they're tied to this correlation. The 14 years 1951-1964 [using a 1965 *Economic Report of the President*] showed corporations with roughly 59 cents profit for every dollar of gross farm income. Now, not having a profit, what did they do? Well, they borrowed the money. They've added $365 billion to their gross corporate debt. Well, they had to pay interest on this debt. They've had to pay the increase in wages. So they've lost the net profits. And here's where it shows up. The dividends based on market value in 1950 were $6.57 per $100 stock value. This moved down to 3% by 1965, and is going lower.

Q. Just about half?

WILKEN. In other words, they are taking it away from the stockholder in the same degree the farmer is losing his.

Q. Is this the reason the government is trying to take away the parity equation? To hide what income should be?

WILKEN. That's right. Senator George McGovern introduced a resolution with 42 Senators asking for an investigation of parity income and parity prices. That's been sidetracked.

Q. So that farmers won't know what they should have?

WILKEN. That's right. But the figures are available. Still the average Congressman never looks at the *Economic Report of the President*. But this *Report* is what has made it possible for me to do this as a one man job. All of that material is assembled. Here they've got the whole economy boiled down to sections. And those six sections have to be kept in balance or you can't have a national income to operate a solvent economy. Now let's assume we restore the 90% price support. Let's suppose the farmer increased his production 5%. Then you'd maintain the price on it. It will increase the income of rural America 5%, creating a 5% larger market for goods from industrial America. And producing those goods, in moving them back and forth, we'll increase the national income 5% and we'll utilize the 5% production.

Q. What about surpluses?

WILKEN. That's mostly misrepresentation. If you take the *Economic Report of the President* and take the production record for agriculture from 1929 to 1942 and then from 1942 to 1965, you'll find we increased our farm production more per year from 1929 to 1942 despite two droughts than we did from 1942 to 1965. We've had a constant increase of 1.7%

farm production from 1910 on. That's about what it was from 1942 to 1966. Sure, we've had a tremendous increase in the acreage output. But the increase was not from increased acreage production. They got it through machinery and through fertilizer. But those two things cost money. And they had to come out of the price the farmer received if he's going to stay in business. Now the other side of the equation is from 1942 to 1966 we've had about 37% increase in population. Now, suddenly, there is some awakening to the fact that we're going to have starvation in the world. And we will have if society doesn't start to pay for this agricultural production.

Q. They *have got* starvation in the world?

WILKEN. Yes, but we'll have some starvation right here in the United States. We're building to the point where we can't feed our own people. Not with the standard of living that we're used to.

Q. What's going to bring this to a head?

WILKEN. You're going to have a surplus of industrial goods because you've industrialized the United States far in excess of the development of the rest of the country. Western Europe is producing and looking for markets in eastern Europe. Japan has industrialized. But when you get all through, you've got several billion people with only $100 per capita income per year. They're not going to buy any automobiles, television sets or $10,000 tractors. So where are you going to sell this production? That's when the thing breaks down. Now here's your increase in credit. Increase in credit has indirectly subsidized the automobile industry. Subsidized the steel industry. Subsidized the production of homes. All at the expense of rural America. In other words, cheap food has created the income to make the down payment and the rest of the money has been placed in a mortgage against their children and great-grandchildren.

Q. What's the trigger mechanism?

WILKEN. When they pan't pay. It's a certain peak of inability to pay. Now for example: you've had a cut in automobile production and housing. Now taking the picture as a whole, you have to add billions to the gross debt to operate the economy each year.

Q. When can you foresee an economic downturn?

WILKEN. It could start any time. For example, you have an economy depending on over $115 billion or more debt expansion per annum. Supposing people say, "No, no more borrowing." For every $1 billion cut in debt expansion you wipe out $2.5 billion unearned income that's supporting the economy. I doubt whether this country can go through a depression without wiping out private enterprise.

# CHAPTER 11: THE DEATH OF PRIVATE ENTERPRISE

"I doubt whether this country can go through a depression without wiping out private enterprise," said Carl Wilken, and with that many hours of taped interviews came to an end. And I had no doubt he concluded that way because the first fact of economic life is people, and a satisfactory way of life for people. That this cannot ever be accomplished with cheap raw materials, Wilken claimed, has escaped all except a handful of those in charge of public policy the world over. Free international trade, Wilken offered again and again in the interview, is a damnable doctrine, a spawning ground for bankruptcy and war.

One thing that is both understood and forgotten until too late, is the fact that the world is organized by countries. These countries are sovereign, and conduct themselves accordingly. The going concern of the nation can imprison people, but it has never imprisoned money. Smart money, seeing that the float of events is destroying purchasing power, abandons such an economy and heads for more favorable sanctums. Whatever the basic reason, whenever the going concern of the nation finds itself failing to earn the capital needed for expansion commensurate with the expanding populations, the symptom of this dislocation can be seen in the "flight of money" from such an economy. Politicians and pundits talk of one world, even of one economic world, but the facts of life are quite different. Certainly, nations are influenced mightily by what other nations do, but in the end major collapse is brought on when a nation refuses to accept the economic fact that it is not earning its way while standing on its own feet, and lives beyond its means long enough. If a nation does not earn the income necessary to engage itself in the program of its desires— wars, wet-nursing the world, social programs beyond the scope of sound operation—then these programs must be fed by embezzling the earnings of the future generations.

The history of almost all civilizations also reveals that when an economy is operated with excessive debt, this debt forces inflation to liquidate that debt. There are only two ways of getting rid of debt—by paying it off, or by repudiating it. Inflation is repudiation and so is deflation. Excessive debt cannot be paid. Nor can it be serviced.

## [1] A MORAL DEVICE

"Bankruptcy is not merely a moral device or a way to achieve equity; it is primarily the especial condition for the efficiency of the price mechanism of the economic system which is usually called capitalism. The system would collapse without it, deprived of the sole compulsion which obliges the individual to bring his otherwise unimpeded activities into conformity with the conditions necessary for the survival of the system," So wrote Jacques Rueff in *The Age of Inflation*.

When Rueff wrote those words in 1948, the Employment Act of 1946 in the United States was already two years old. It required the President to maintain full employment in industrial America as a matter of public policy. Those who remember the debates that attended the full-employment sessions sometimes recall how "boom and bust" were accepted as standard economic procedure. The trick was to stretch out periods of prosperity. Those who really understood the foundation ideas behind the program realized that agriculture was the only unorganized segment, and could therefore be regulated by the economic planners. As long as agriculture could be drained, full employment could be maintained at a level of prosperity not otherwise available. Considering the size of the American agricultural plant, and the stretch-out effect of inflation, this put collapse well beyond the lifetime of anyone in Washington in 1946—maybe!

During the years that followed, it became round-robin stuff to rupture the farm commodity price structure with imports, and key-currency nations such as the United States were insulated from balance of payment problems, courtesy of the International Monetary Fund. "Future students of history will be shocked and angered," opined Reuff, "by the fact that in 1945 the same monetary system that had driven the world to despair and disaster, and had almost destroyed the civilization it was supposed to stand for, was revived on a much wider scope. . . . Since 1945 we have again been setting up the mechanism that, unquestionably, triggered the disaster of 1929-1933. We are now watching the consequences, as they follow in their ineluctable course."

The first symptoms of that course became evident as government moved to shore up home industrial markets by exporting "aid," and by going into the business of having 6% of the globe's population take care of the rest of the world. By inches and miles the effects traveled toward the ultimate economic killing grounds. During the last full year before Kennedy was assassinated, before the *Economic Report of the President* became thoroughly rigged, the, American International Balance Sheet read as follows:

| | |
|---|---|
| CREDITS | $7.6 billion |
| Trade | $4.3 |
| Investment Income | $3.3 |
| DEBITS | $9.9 |
| Military spending | $2.4 |
| Economic Aid | $3.5 |
| Private Investment | $2.5 |
| Short-Term Funds | $0.6 |
| Tourist Spending | $0.9 |
| DEFICIT | $2.3 |

It was moving fast, this international deficit, as was the domestic shortage of income brought on by low raw material prices. The end results, history has warned time after time, will be an era of inflation followed by rationing, wage and price control, socialization of the means of production (labor and farming included), import restrictions, and an end to foreign travel. Freedom itself could become a victim to the reckless policies of the self-serving.

## [2] A LONELY BUSINESS

"It becomes a lonely business," was the way Carl Wilken discussed inflation, "this being right. You can't predict the exact time an economy collapses because you can't tell how much inflation a people can stand. And you can't know how many palliatives the government will use to put off that inevitable day."

There was plenty of reason why inflation became a siren's song. Wage earners would find themselves with more currency, and a tantalizing view of the living standard that had always escaped them. But always, rising prices would cut down the mirage before it could be realized. Most devilish of all, inflation would cut down the hopes and dreams of those who had worked hardest. Savings would evaporate. Annuities, insurance policies would be stolen away. And in the end, inflation would divide people into three classes—those who suffer, those who benefit, and those who escape clean as a whistle. Those who suffer, historically, would count up as the clear majority, and their resentment would be multiplied by their numbers until they would be strong enough to bring down the social arrangements.

"Inflation does more than complicate the work of parliaments; it makes them a laughing-stock and discredits them," wrote Rueff.

If inflation causes parliaments to sacrifice freedom, palliatives to soothe indigestion caused by trade imbalance already have a head start. A running inventory of techniques used to answer the "cause" tells some part of the story.

The first effect of a new low raw materials price policy in the United States, predictably, was a shrunken market, one that required producers to look the world over for a place to sell. In October 1959 the Development Loan Fund started giving an assist to this end—financial help in exporting U.S. products to *needy* countries. This helped a favored few at home, but worsened the trade balance immediately—hence, in 1960, a November edict from the Defense Department that reduced family dependents of military and Defense Department personnel abroad; stepped up financing of American goods going abroad; and the placebo of scaling back State Department stores and PX purchases abroad.

As late as 1960 the world hadn't gotten used to big foreign exchange deficits yet, although low raw material prices were already well into the work of wrecking the country. Out-bound traffic hid the effects, especially when routed through the Pentagon's ledger entries.

A year later, 1961, the word became "buy American," and during the year after President Kennedy passed from the scene it became *discontinuance of overseas hospitals and other sundry installations*. After that, the palliative game never omitted Defense Department traffic, and never permitted the left hand to know what the right hand was doing. On the one hand overseas military construction became a "no-no," emphasis being on a cut-back because the gold was disappearing and foreigners were not buying the production of industrial America—chiefly war goodies—fast enough. At the same time, industrialists were setting up calculator plants overseas, desperately trying to cut production costs on goods sold in the U.S.

Gold movement, in the final analysis, left tell-tale signs. In August 1961 the official policy became "borrow" U.S. dollars from abroad so that they cannot be used to buy gold. And if foreigners allowed dollars to stay in U.S. banks, then they were exempt from limitations on interest. Dollars belonging to Americans thus had two strikes against them. They were not convertible to gold, and they couldn't earn as much interest. The same dollars—in the hands of a foreign owner—were both good as gold and high interest earning items.

In September 1964, another clamp was imposed—an "interest equalization tax" on foreign securities purchased by Americans. Americans are possibly the most ignorant people in the world when it comes to understanding money. However, since a few weren't oblivious, the short-term gold traffic required a cover-up, first by having the Exchange Stabilization Fund rather than the Treasury handle gold transactions, second by covering Federal Reserve gold traffic the same way.

As the crazy game continued, gimmicks continued to buy time—a day at a time if necessary. The heat was put on foreign governments to step up payments of debts. IMF was hit up for loans. Currency swaps became workaday stuff, and the President himself got into the "see America" business because tourism was conceived to pick up some of the tab caused by farmers being paid for less than they produce.

Even the bottle of whiskey brought into the country tax-free did not escape attention. But the big trick was still to come, the one that opened the vault doors and erased for all time a conduit of escape from the consequence of the consequences.

First the 25% gold reserve requirement behind Fed deposits went down the drain. By 1968 the 25% gold cover for the folding money was lifted also, and with that act went the last available warning system. The rest would come, in the fullness of time—rationing, controls, socialism and the loss of freedom itself.

## [3] FANTASTIC ADJUSTMENTS

There was one point with which Wilken explained both the "whys" of balanced expansion and expansion with inflation. The word was abstinence. Productive facilities could not be expanded without inflation except through abstinence. When money was created without abstinence, that very act created inflation because paper capital creation became tantamount to emptying the pipeline. Obviously, new money before new stocks of wealth meant more media, rising prices, classical inflation. The process since WWII had been to over-industrialize, to accumulate permanent capital, but the debts, Wilken argued, could not be paid, not this year or this century, and would have to be repudiated. This, of course, could not be accomplished without fantastic adjustments in the economic and institutional arrangements of the nation.

## [4] THE INFLATIONARY ROUTE

The key to the problem of economic balance has been seen by many, and overlooked by even more. In the popularizations of John Maynard Keynes, the Englishman's work is usually wrapped up in the catch phrase, "deficit finance." Yet Keynes was never as simple as friends and critics have implied.

Of particular significance is what Keynes had to say about inflation, and the implications his theory contained for underdeveloped countries. His observations on the generating power of agriculture are a case in point. Keynes noted that on food produced by the farmer, the price paid for it becomes the income of those in the business, and thus increase their expenditures. A higher living cost creates pressure for higher wage costs. Thus prices rise all around and the inflationary spiral sets in.

This could be avoided, of course, simply by not having any development. Therefore, held Keynes, if there was to be development, investment had to increase relative to consumption. Thus the price paid out at the farm raw materials level increased effective demand and created a trend to inflation. How to keep it in tow emerged as the problem.

Keynes thus arrived at and ignored the solution being proposed by Wilken. Non-inflationary development could be achieved only when quick-yielding investment was made in the consumer goods sector, principally agriculture, because agriculture generated enough of a surplus to support the hydroelectric plants, community centers, and stadium developments that took a long time to pay off. The earned income was determined at the raw material level, not at the industrial plant level, because the income had first to be earned for capital expansion or there could be no hydroelectric plant.

The alternative was to go the inflationary route, to create credit and subject the economy to all the evils that credit and inflation would visit upon it. Progress was more dramatic that way. Gross National Product (no GDP, Gross Domestic Product) could dance a dizzy tune on its way up—but in the end the cause of the cause would have its effect.

By 1948, when Jacques Rueff wrote his book, America decided to go the dramatic route. There was at that time an $8 billion surplus in the federal, state and local budgets, and reconversion from a war economy had accounted for hardly $16 billion in debt expansion.

Farm income had returned to the 1929 level hardly a year after the beginning of WWII. The general level had been balanced since 1942 by commodity price supports on the one hand, and—during the war—by OPA controls on the other. During the early months of the great war, the House Banking and Currency Committee had in effect monetized basic farm raw materials. The Committee was calling wheat, corn—the basic crops—by their correct name. The U.S. Constitution had given Congress the power to create the money and regulate the value thereof. In the middle of the war, no one doubted that unless the government regulated the value of basic raw materials, it could not regulate the value of money, and therefore couldn't maintain economic stability.

But—to repeat—by 1948 America decided to go the dramatic route. First the Senate led the way in scaling down farm price supports, and the minute 60-90% parity moved to the fore farm prices started to slide. As commodity prices hit the skids, national income declined with them on a multiplier of approximately 7. When the Korean War broke out a little later, a few in Congress wanted to go the WWII route again. They wanted to monetize raw materials again, and keep a balance, but the move was blocked because traders sensed great profits ahead if free international trade could be maintained during a war.

Therefore it became the judgment of the economic advisers that raw material prices should be scaled down in homage to international trade, war or no war. Thus there was only one way to operate. More debt had to be created, $40 billion of it a year to fight the Korean War.

When the war ended, debt creation was scaled back to $30 billion, which immediately canceled out $25 billion "unearned income" that debt expansion had accounted for. The 1954 recession followed.

Full employment could not be maintained without either parity raw materials, or more debt expansion. To keep from feeling the full weight of unjustified debt expansion, raw materials were pressured downward.

In 1955, $72 billion of credit was injected into the economy. President Eisenhower was promising the nation a $500 billion national income. On the basis of $300 billion of national income, $72 billion debt creation represented twice as much money as the nation had a right to borrow based on profits and savings. Savings started running out in 1957, and debt expansion fell down to $35 billion, or half the rate of 1935. The 1958 depression followed.

By this time the mandate for debt expansion became clear to those who wanted to go the whole route. The small confederation of Cassandras supporting sound economic procedures failed to carry the day in the general's tent.

In 1959, $69 billion debt was created to shore up the faltering economy, whereas farm prices were pressured downward. But by 1959, the operating loss of the economy had increased to a point where $69 billion was barely enough to keep the momentum. A year later, 1960, the presidential campaign was fought against a background of "we've got to get the country moving again."

President Kennedy did that. He duplicated Ike's tactic simply because he was taking advice from the same school of economists. By year, Wilken calculated the public and private debt injection as follows:

| | |
|---|---|
| 1960 | $ 61 billion |
| 1961 | 79 billion |
| 1962 | 80 billion |
| 1963 | 84 billion |
| President Johnson took over and— | |
| 1964 | 94 billion |
| 1965 | 104 billion |
| 1966 | Wilken's estimate, 115 billion |

With each shot of credit, raw material prices continued a downward trend. Rural America and finally the American democracy were being put on the line. Such a massive shift in the economic body could not be accomplished without a real sales job. Thus the string of policy papers, the CED report, Michigan's Project 80 report, the endless articles out of the land grant colleges, and finally the Food and Fiber Commission Report, all furnishing "laws" that demanded liquidation of the family farm.

The latest important entry before Wilken passed away was the Food and Fiber Commission Report, a remarkable manifesto which stated its case in one whiplash line—"Finally, our central guideline for agricultural policy—the historical concept of parity prices—is inconsistent with the structure of modern agriculture and should be replaced with a better standard of comparison between farm and non-farm incomes."

President Lyndon Johnson's "blue ribbon," 29-man commission on Food and Fiber was headed by Dr. Sherwood O. Berg of the University of Minnesota. Although the commission split 16 to 13 on phasing out farm programs completely, the 29 members translated 18 months of study into general agreement on the following inventory of recommendations:

1. Price supports to be set modestly below a moving average of world market prices to permit U.S. farm products to compete for world markets.

2. The government to rely more on subsidy payments in protecting farm income on grounds that the approach didn't offend the world market.

3. Acreage allotments and marketing quotas to be transferable so as to facilitate production in the most efficient area.

4. A parity of income concept to supplant the parity price index.

5. Phase-out of reclamation, irrigation and land development projects.

6. Establishment of a security food reserve adequate to meet emergency and foreign food aid requirements.

7. Liberalization of world trade, especially in farm products.

8. Elimination of export subsidies and import quotas.

9. The U.S. to trade freely with the Soviet Union and Eastern Europe in non-strategic foods, including food and fiber, eliminating the requirement

that 50% of the wheat shipments to Russia be carried by high-cost U.S. vessels.

Parity offended each article of the Food and Fiber Commission's conjectural economics, and therefore parity had to go.

Not for ten words running did the Report tell why this was so. All it offered was the judgment that in a hungry world and a hungry nation, there was an over-capacity to produce, when in fact the U.S. was not even self-sufficient in meat or dairy.

"The Commission recommends that price supports be set modestly below a moving average of world market prices," stated the Report. Thus a Kansas wheat producer lived in the world's highest cost of production area, and was being programmed into the world's lowest price structure, one that would not pay for the very technology required to continue production.

All these reports and papers touting these strange economic findings did not precede the fact of agriculture's debauchery, but followed at various intervals. They followed because those who wrote them sensed correctly the desires and needs of the economic advisers who wanted to stretch out prosperity at the expense of the foundation segment in the economy, hang the consequences.

Looking history squarely in the eye, many farmers had still to realize that they had been shared out in the first year of this crazy game.

Looking the Employment Act of 1946 squarely in the eye, Wilken pointed out that it was "unconstitutional" to start with because it provided a superb parity for labor and interest collectors, largely at the expense of agriculture. That was what the law was intended to do, and that's what it did.

In a letter that I received from Wilken during mid-1968, he called my attention to the first hint that he was no longer alone in his thinking. In the economic journals and in the better news magazines, words like "overkill," "stabilization crisis," and "unacceptable solutions" started to appear. Writing in the July 8, 1968 issue of *Newsweek*, Henry C. Wallich went a step further. He first implied, then stated the fact that the New Economics was a failure. Wallich arrived at this conclusion because it now appeared that inflation would not bow to stability without economic "fine-tuning," something this many-powered government was incapable of.

"These difficult, perhaps insoluble problems will be the heritage of the New Economics to its successors, whoever they may be," wrote Wallich. "No doubt the newcomers will make their own quota of mistakes. But there should be no doubt that whatever calamities befall hereafter will have their roots in the mistakes made heretofore."

# CHAPTER 12: RAW MATERIALS

One of the great mysteries of World War I involved the naval collier *Cyclops*. For that ship, with some 15 officers, 211 sailors and 57 passengers, and a cargo of manganese ore, disappeared without a trace. The ship had been routed into the South American seas in order to obtain no more than 15,000 tons of manganese ore for a nation that ordinarily required 800,000 tons a year.

## [1] THE STARCH IN STEEL

Manganese is manganese, just as gold is gold, regardless of the grade of ore in which it first appears. Manganese became strategic mineral No. 1 in 1914 because of the war, and has always been at the top of the list of military emergency procurement requirements. "Manganese is the starch in steel. Without manganese there can be no satisfactory steel product. There is no known substitute for manganese. It stands in a category all its own," according to testimony by mining engineer J. Carson Adkerson before the House Subcommittee on Mines and Mining of the Committee on Public Lands, 1948. Or, as Colonel C.T. Harris, Director of the Planning Branch Office of the Assistant Secretary of War told the Military Affairs Committee of the House in 1937, "I place manganese at the top of the list, chromium next, and the minerals more or less at the top of the list. Rubber would have a high priority, also. . . ." Why? "There is not a substitute for manganese."

Modern war and modern industrial life is impossible without manganese, just as life is impossible without food. There is a tenuous connection between the loss of the *Cyclops* and the price of wheat in Kansas, and because of it the Raw Materials National Council was born in Sioux City, Iowa.

J. Carson Adkerson believed he could bring on manganese production in the United States by the simple process of calling attention to existing deposits and causing lawmakers to write the appropriate ground rules. Existence of deposits was common knowledge among mining engineers.

University, state mining bureaus and United States geological surveys indicated the existence of deposits in Arizona, Arkansas, California, Colorado, Georgia, Nevada, Tennessee, Virginia, Idaho, Montana, Utah, Oregon, South Dakota. These were technical bulletins with long running titles (*Manganese-Bearing Deposits Near Lake Crescent and Humptulips, Washington* to mention one) that described the properties and ore characteristics.* And yet there was little or no manganese production in the United States.

Deposits in Russia and India were reputed to be rich, yet testimony before House Committees and data from the *Bureau of Mines Yearbooks* indicated that ore-wise, foreign suppliers had no advantage over American properties.

Adkerson found that, in fact, manganese ores were never high grade. In India native labor hand-selected lumps of ore for 1 cent an hour. In

---

* The "yes-we-do" and "no-we-don't" have manganese question runs like a jagged scar through Congressional hearings. This is an extract from the testimony of Francis P. Garvan, president, Chemical Foundation, February 12, 1937, in hearings before the Finance Committee of the Senate on extending the Reciprocal Trade Agreement Act.

SENATOR BARKLEY. Don't you know, Mr. Garvan, that in 1929 and 1930 the large steel manufacturers protested to this committee and to the committee of the House against the imposition of the tariff which the bill carried on manganese, making the statement that they could not obtain or develop enough manganese in this country to supply the needs of the steel industry, and that in spite of the fact that the tariff went on in behalf of these low-grade ores and in behalf of their development, that they never were able to produce and have never been able to produce enough manganese to supply the steel industry in this country; that, regardless of any trade agreements, they have not done it and cannot do it?

MR. GARVAN. Just a moment. I agree with you absolutely that that was a brutal and selfish money proposition of the steel companies and a desperately stupid one, and if you call them here today they will repudiate it.

SENATOR CLARK. Were they any more stupid than they are now, when you say their faces were so white? [This referred to an earlier exchange in which faces were characterized as "white."]

MR. GARVAN. I think now they are more enlightened.

SENATOR CLARK. They were not any more enlightened when they testified last year before the Munitions Committee?

MR. GARVAN. They have found they have not got any manganese in case of war; that it can be cut off by an airplane or shipping war. Testifying before the House Committee on Military Affairs, May 25, 1937, J. Carson Adkerson read off the names of technical reports on deposits of manganese: *Manganese Ore Deposits in Arizona*, published by the University of Arizona; *Manganese Deposits of the Caddo Gap and The Queen Quadrangles, Arkansas*, published by the U.S. Geological Survey; *Manganese and Chromium in California*, published by the California State Mining Bureau; *Manganese Deposits in Colorado*, published by the Colorado Geological Survey; *Preliminary Report on the Manganese Deposits of Georgia*, published by the Geological Survey of Georgia; *Bedded Deposits of Manganese Oxides Near Las Vegas, Nevada*, published by the University of Nevada; *Manganese Deposits of East Tennessee*, published by the U.S. Geological Survey; *Manganese Deposits of the*

Russia, W.A. Harriman & Company* control of Caucasian deposits and cheap labor similarly controlled world prices, a task the Communists took over in the late 1920s when they expropriated Harriman properties.

## [2] COMMERCIAL PRESSURE ON THESE COUNTRIES

In 1922, Congress imposed a tariff of 1 cent a pound on manganese ore, a move that ran counter to the wishes of the steel industry. Since there were no more than three buyers of manganese ore—that is, no more than three firms did all the smelting of raw production into ferromanganese—it became no difficult matter for steel companies to bring about price collusion and a meeting of the minds. That "meeting" in fact surfaced in the form of a policy paper—*International Control of Minerals*—which was published in 1925 by the American Institute of Mining and Metallurgical Engineers and the Mining and Metallurgical Society of America. This book called for freedom of exploration in backward countries. The general thesis recognized that "Political and commercial pressure on these countries, therefore, seems inevitable."

The steel industry wanted cheap manganese, and the steel industry had already made an end run around the Sherman Anti-trust laws with the *holding company* idea. The holding company concept was born—not without umbilical cord—in the Wall Street offices of James B. Dill at the start of Century 21. J.P. Morgan and his associates wanted to eliminate Andrew Carnegie from the growing steel business. It was Dill who invented the holding company and secured its legalization by the state of New Jersey. The idea was a natural. Firms had heretofore invested surplus savings in other corporations. A slight expansion of the idea enabled them to do the same for the purpose of controlling competing corpora-

---

*West Foot of the Blue Ridge, Virginia*, published by the Virginia Geological Survey; *Possibilities for Manganese Ore on Certain Undeveloped Tracts in Shenandoah Valley, Virginia*, published by the U.S. Geological Survey; *Manganese Deposits of Western Virginia*, published by the Virginia Geological Survey; *A Manganese Deposit of Pleistocene Age in Bannock County, Idaho*, published by the U.S. Geological Survey; *Reserves of Lake Superior Manganiferous Iron Ores*, published by the American Institute of Mining and Metallurgical Engineers; *Manganese-Iron Carbonate Near Chamberlain, South Dakota*, published by the U.S. Department of Interior; and *Deposits of Manganese Ore in Montana, Utah, Oregon and Washington*, published by the U.S. Geological Survey.

There was other literature on the existence of high grade ore—metallic manganese in one instance—and yet the steel industry appeared regularly before Congressional Committees to testify that there was no ore, or that it was low grade, when the fact was that ore produced abroad with wages as low as 1 cent an hour was the source of their intelligence and their rationale for the big lie.

* The same Harriman who became Secretary of Commerce during the Truman Administration.

tions. Thus the holding company became the so-called financial company with all the benefits that limited liability could account for. Dill's idea was not unlike the one used by Distillers Company, Ltd., the British holding company that brought competing Scotch whisky producers under a parent firm.

By creating shares and trading these for shares of the several industrial firms, the Morgan holding operation in effect printed its own money and gathered together the competitors of Carnegie. Carnegie's price for getting out is reputed to have been three times the replacement value of his steel enterprises.

Such control over the industry as a whole legalized a cartel, a cartel that could maintain steel prices and be politically powerful enough to control prices of raw materials. It was this type of capitalism that brought on 1929, a point John R. Commons made when he characterized the period of 1900 to 1929 as the "peak of capitalism in the United States."

To cope with such power, a struggling industry had only one avenue of appeal—the Congress of the United States, the halls of justice, and an abiding faith in the Constitution of the United States.

By December of 1935, American raw materials producers had been assured of "early consummation of pending trade agreements with the Netherlands and Honduras, and subsequent ratification in the American duty on quicksilver." J. Carson Adkerson, an engineer and president of the American Manganese Association, had been a tireless Hill worker, first to protect his own group, second to save the nation from what he considered a terrible strategic blunder. In an interview with the Washington Bureau of the *Journal of Commerce* that year, he unloaded this general statement:

"Manufacturers and consumers want raw materials as cheaply as possible. Through reciprocal trade treaties tariffs, on American raw materials are being traded away and advantages given to manufactured products. Continuation of this policy will mean that products of the ground, produced largely by unskilled labor, will come increasingly from foreign countries and products of our factories will be exported. It will mean curtailment or destruction of many raw material and agricultural industries in the United States. Pursuant to this policy, tariff reductions have been granted on lumber, limestone, cement, manganese, ferromanganese, ferro silicon, feldspar, talc, firebrick, glass sand, fish, dairy products, furs, poultry, hay, cattle, potatoes, fruits, and many other raw material products of American forests, farms and mines."

It was through manganese that the parity idea was introduced to O.L. Brownlee, editor of the *Sioux City Tribune*. "It came about," wrote J. Carson Adkerson, "through research I carried on and disclosure of the amount of subsidy given the steel industry through tariffs."

Adkerson gave the detailed figures to Senator Tasker C. Oddie of Nevada in 1929. Oddie had them confirmed by the Tariff Commission, where Dr. John Lee Coulter was chief economist. He used the data on the Senate floor in the tariff debates that year—and manganese won a measure of tariff protection. At approximately the same time, McNary-Haugen also won in Congress, but farmers lost out when President Calvin Coolidge vetoed the measure. During the late 1930s, Adkerson had his figures brought up to date and confirmed through the Tariff Commission on request of Congressman Andrew Jackson May of Kentucky, then chairman of the Committee of Military Affairs. Congressman Francis H. Case of South Dakota in turn used the data to show that steel had been protected to the tune of $8,468,961,511 between 1922 and 1937.

In the meantime, before 1935, the farm situation had reached crisis proportions. The focal point of discontent became Woodbury County, Iowa—indeed, the entire tier of counties along the western border of the state. At one point Milo Reno's militants disputed highway space with deputies and their tear gas. Some 43 farmers were taken to Council Bluffs and jailed. In short order, a sullen mob of perhaps 500 farmers arrived with threats to take the Courthouse apart, stone by stone. Law enforcement officials, with busses gassed and ready to go, waited in Des Moines, some 150 miles away. A word from Governor Dan Turner and they would have been on their way. At the last minute, tragedy was averted. A farmer entered the building under a flag of truce to offer some unencumbered property as bail. The weary lawmen grasped the straw.

There had been other incidents—stoning of vehicles, deputies humbled, and Andersonville-style stockades for the errant farmers.

Looking back on that era some 35 years later, Adkerson recalled, "Whenever I went into the Senate gallery, it seemed some Senator from a steel state was on the floor calling attention to the huge sum appropriated to the Commodity Credit Corporation. . . ." Adkerson realized how small it was compared to the amounts the steel people were getting. Adkerson knew no one in Sioux City, but through newspaper accounts he turned up the name of O.L. Brownlee of the *Sioux City Tribune*, who seemed to be a spokesman for the farmers. Adkerson wrote Brownlee a one paragraph letter to tell him that he had a solution to the farm problem. Almost immediately, Brownlee left for Washington. For several days the two men exchanged facts. Adkerson called Brownlee's attention to steel industry protection figures, and handed him a tract entitled *Parity for the Farmer*.

On January 20, 1936, Adkerson announced the formation of a "committee of four" to direct a fight against the New Deal's reciprocal trade agreements. The committee, *The Journal of Commerce* announced, would be known as the Raw Materials National Council. Adkerson represented the American Manganese Producers Association. O.L. Brownlee represented the League for Economic Equality, and was named secretary of the group. J.J. Underwood, Seattle, Washington, represented Western Forest Products, and became treasurer. And Clarence C. Dill, former Senator from Washington, was named general counsel.

## [3] I'VE ALWAYS LIKED FARMING

Carl H. Wilken was born on a farm not too far from Wall Lake, Iowa, and he grew up on a farm, and in the fullness of his years he came to wear the marks of a farmer, marks that included *resourcefulness* and *unillusioned self-sufficiency*. During his first eight years of formal education, Wilken walked a mile and a half each way to and from school. Later, when he came to attend high school in Odebolt, "I sometimes rode on horseback for five miles each way." The term *affluent society* hadn't been invented yet, and so it was not until a couple of years had gone by (one of which was spent in religious training) that Wilken entered the University of Iowa.

There was little of the meteoric in the career of Carl Wilken. He attended officer's training school after war broke out in 1917, and in due time he emerged as a "90 day wonder." As a lieutenant he was stationed at Fort Snelling for some eight months inducting draftees, and then in August 1918 he was transferred to the University of Louisiana, and still later to the Southern College in Florida, where he took charge of students in a training camp.

There was something quite typical about all this. The young farm boy off to service, a war-time marriage, and the hard decision of whether to make the service a career or return to the soil and the life so many farm boys loved because of its natural rewards, yet hated for reasons that ever escaped them. After November 11, Wilken handled these thoughts amid the *repple-depple* atmosphere of men going home, rifles and equipment being cosmolined for days still unborn. "I've always liked farming," Wilken told me in 1967. "And there's no place I would rather be today than operating a farm. I decided to go back to the farm."

The farm, after all, was the great teacher of Carl H. Wilken. Home, "I had to pay $1.54 a bushel for 500 bushels of corn I needed for brood sows and their offspring. In 1920 corn was selling for $2 a bushel in Iowa on July 1, and it fell off 75 cents a bushel in three days." It was young Wilken's first big lesson concerning the fact that markets are rigged. The following spring, corn had dropped to 27 cents a bushel. "That kind of a drop couldn't have happened if there had been anything to the law of supply and demand." It was something to mull over, to fill the thinking spells during those long, cold Iowa nights.

Somehow Wilken weathered that storm, and looking back some 45 years later he figured 1922 through 1929 prices pretty good, after all. The Depression came, of course, and by 1932 Iowa farmers were selling corn for 10 cents a bushel. Economic distress became so acute it brought on a Corn Belt rebellion replete with judges being beaten and penny auctions,* and put to the fore once again the leader of the Iowa cow war, Milo Reno. And Reno's Farmers Holiday Association became one of those many unfathomable impulses that caused the New Deal to answer unrest with NRA, NLB, WPA, CCC—"With all these letters I got their goat, and still I crammed it down their throats," a Depression jingle about Roosevelt reminded—and an AAA for agriculture.

## [4] NEW AND DARING IDEAS

A few in Congress wanted new and daring ideas, not more of the conjectural economics that had brought on disaster in the first place. Explosive frustration among the people didn't give a hoot about Marshallian models, or any of the *laissez faire* stuff some of the holdovers and some of the new people in Washington were spouting. And though the nostrum came on in platoons, one stood out. Congress, during the '30s passed legislation that provided for 45 cent corn. Corn was selling for 14 cents a bushel at the time, and therefore a jump in price to 45 cents represented a fantastic overnight gain, though not a movement as fantastic as the price drop in the first place.

Almost everyone believed that a short supply would deliver upward price pressure. Accordingly, the new law was geared to one proposition—taking acres out of production! Under AAA, those who measured the acres to be retired were elected by farmers, first in the township, then in the county. Wilken got the job, and in 1933, he later recalled, he made the biggest corn loan under the program for the entire state. One farmer had some 335,000 bushels of corn on one of his farms. Wilken measured the corn, "and I drove to Omaha on a Saturday morning. And by Saturday noon he had a check from the government for the 45 cents a bushel for his corn. I'll never forget a remark that he made on the way back," Wilk-

---

* In 1968 I coauthored a book with George J. Walters entitled *A Farmer's Guide to Homestead Rights*, and sent a copy to Carl H. Wilken. His response came essentially as expected. He saw no solution to anything in penny auctions, moratorium laws, or, in the individual shelter bankrupt farmers might find behind each state's homestead laws, and therefore didn't believe the book worth publishing. He did not appreciate proposals for saving a few individuals at a time.

en recalled. "He was a millionaire and he said, 'I didn't need the money, but I thought it was a good sale.' "

Acres were taken out of production, but still the equation did not work out. In 1934 corn production was cut more than a billion bushels under the 1925-1929 average. "Then instead of having a surplus lying around we didn't have enough to feed our cattle, and we shot cattle in northwestern Iowa, South Dakota, the Plains and Texas and dumped them into trenches and buried them. We didn't have the feed to keep them from starving."

During that same period, the nation had some 12 million people out of work, people so poor they couldn't turn up a nickel for a sandwich. The starving would have been happy to buy beef, but somehow the system failed to deliver the purchasing power.

In 1934 corn moved up to a dollar a bushel—a bit above parity—but by 1935 the equation was thrown out of whack again. Dust bowl days notwithstanding, the 1935 crop came in at approximately 80% of the 1925-1929 average. Immediately, as if hit in the head with a sledgehammer, the price of corn fell to the support level—or to 45 cents a bushel. And it remained there until early July 1936. In other words, 80% of a full crop failed to maintain parity for corn under the existing institutional arrangements. Wilken came to know corn and its relationship to other commodities to a subtle degree. He saw speculators run prices up to $1.20, and he watched every normal crop break prices rapidly to the 45 cent support level. And farmers who didn't go into the support program—they ended up selling corn at 35 cents a bushel in 1937.

## [5] WHAT BROUGHT IT ALL ABOUT

"I decided that I was going to find out just what brought it all about," Wilken said.

With that Wilken signed the articles of incorporation for the Raw Materials National Council with O.L. Brownlee, editor of the *Sioux City Tribune*,* and Garrett E. Roelfs, a Senator in the Iowa State Legislature. It was simply an organizational tool under the auspices of which funds could be pulled in to keep research alive. "We never had a board meeting," Wilken told me. "We just incorporated the thing in Woodbury County, Iowa. The purpose of it was to make a study of the economic record and to find out why we had this Depression in 1929 when the experts said that we were never going to have another depression." A kickoff meeting of sorts was held in 1936.

---

* Later merged to become the *Sioux City Journal-Tribune,* and now known as the *Sioux City Journal.*

"Brownlee called a meeting of farmers in Sioux City to discuss farm problems and further explore the subject," Adkerson explained in a letter dated August 2, 1970. "At Brownlee's request I attended this meeting as observer only—stayed in the background—had nothing to say, wanted only to see and get the feeling of the farmers. Parity was not then introduced. We wanted more research and plans as to how to handle [things]. Brownlee was chief spokesman at the meeting. Hundreds were there from several states. Wilken was there, but did not speak or take part in the meeting. I did not meet him then," but he was pointed out as head of the Progressive Farmers of Iowa. This meeting was widely publicized. An application for the Charter of Raw Materials National Council followed. One of the first letterheads included, in addition to Adkerson, Brownlee, Dill, Underwood and Wilken, business leaders such as Irving Paris of New York City (real estate), H.A. Pumpelly of Owego, New York (mine and land operator), Karl M. Leute, Minneapolis, Minnesota (mining interests), Jes Briegel, New York (investments).

## [6] DR. JOHN LEE COULTER AND CHARLES B. RAY

The small group solicited funds. Wilken lined up some 25 Sioux City businessmen as an Advisory Committee, both because they were interested in answers, and because they had no intellectual commitments. General Wood of Sears Roebuck sent over $2,500 at one time, and a check for $4,500 another—and more important, the firm helped research direction by introducing Wilken to Charles B. Ray. Another important leader soon arrived—Dr. John Lee Coulter.

"He was my teacher," Wilken said, referring to Coulter, an impressive scholar, and lineal descendant of John R. Commons era Wisconsin institutional economists. Much as Wilken, Coulter had grown up with agriculture. His doctor's thesis at the University of Wisconsin was entitled *Industrial History of the Valley of the Red River of the North*, and dealt with the bonanza farms. Later, as President of North Dakota A&M, Fargo, he reasoned out many of the fundamentals on which Wilken's research would hinge.* The growth of technology and what it meant to world trade did not escape him. "In 1875," he wrote in his *Industrial History*, "the flail was more common than any machine in Massachusetts and Connecticut. . . . In 1876 an average of 600 threshing machines were placed in the field in

---

* By any standard, John Lee Coulter rated recognition as a professional economist. He took his A.B., A.M. and LL.D. from the University of North Dakota before achieving his Ph.D. at Wisconsin. He also studied at the University of Minnesota and Iowa State College. North Dakota A&M awarded him an honorary Doctor of Science degree in 1950. Throughout a long career he taught at schools such as Iowa State, the University of

Minnesota at an average cost of $650," *sans* engine or horse power. Even then the world endured a cry of get efficient, get bigger or get out, because markets were perceived to be "out there," and production was all that counted. Speaking at a commencement address at Fargo in mid-1928, Coulter warned: "Taking the world as a whole . . . the United States of America with its 6% of the total population has on the average about 60% of all the evidences of the new 20th century civilization. About 4% of the world's population scattered here and there over the rest of the earth have most of the other 40%."

Before he departed the Dakota scene to join the United States Tariff Commission, Coulter warned farmers: "It is wrong to live in a state like this with such wonderful soil, such moderate temperature and with so nearly the right amount of rainfall and not take up more diversified farming."

Diversified farming! Yes, the real economics of agriculture's role was best preserved by the diversified farm and the family farm. Removal of families from farms because they weren't needed to farm so they could go to cities where they weren't needed to make widgets was tantamount to telling people they weren't needed—the first big step toward despotism!

Coulter served as chief economist and Advisory Board Chairman of the U.S. Tariff Commission for 1929, and stayed on as a Commission member from 1930 to 1934. It was under Coulter's direction that J. Carson Adkerson first confirmed his manganese data. Coulter wrote *Cooperation Among Farmers* in 1911, and more or less closed out the active part of his career with the publication of *Postwar Fiscal Problems and Policies* in 1945.

In the main support money for the Raw Materials National Council came in $100 and $200 amounts. The Council's office was simply a one room affair with at least enough space for Wilken and a secretary. Corn was still first among many of the things Wilken hoped to consider. The academic world and those who believed it had been filled to the ears with the proposition that surpluses were accounting for low farm prices. And yet Wilken's first pass through available statistics revealed that Depression crops were categorically smaller than crops in the 1920s. The equation seemed to hold for feed grain as well as red meat. In fact, a thorough run-through revealed that there had not been a surplus in terms of population expansion from 1910 onward.

---

Wisconsin, the University of Minnesota, Knapp School of Country Life at Nashville, West Virginia College of Agriculture (where he was Dean), plus North Dakota A&M, where he was President. Coulter also taught occasional classes at other schools. He served on the editorial staff of the *Quarterly Journal of American Statistics Association* and the *American Economic Review*.

Wilken next checked the import-export situation. In 1929 exports represented about 52% of the total income. By subtracting like imports from exports, he discovered that 98% of domestic production was consumed in the United States. And it hardly seemed possible that the 2% affected by tariffs could break apart the going economy of a nation.

All this might seem mundane to a trained economist, but to Wilken it was a revelation, and he refused to pass over it and go to more heady subjects. It was at this point that his real education began. There was next to nothing by way of economic theory and empirical evidence that could be used for guidance, except some of the precepts Coulter unfolded. The learned ones Karl Marx called "classical economists" had been proved so wrong it became a test of human endurance to read their tomes for the bare spark of reality they contained.

"If you write this up—this information that I'm giving you, for heavens sake don't call it the Wilken theory," Wilken cautioned me. "Point out that it is a factual analysis of the economic record of the United States—the balance sheet." Wilken did not like to be called an economist. His letters and articles were usually signed, "Economic Analyst." He rejected "all those fancy theories." Wilken, of course, didn't wear well the trappings of formal scholarship, and made no claim to the standing that credentials implied. What he knew, he knew, and it had to stand on its own feet.

Still, a procedure requires a theory. And I believe much of Wilken's system of analysis came straight from Charles B. Ray, an engineer at Sears, Roebuck, an obvious student of Frederick Soddy, and a scientist who realized that economics had to work according to and not against the principles of physical science. During all my interviews I found Carl Wilken to be completely honest, and therefore I can call up no logical reason to question his statement before the 26th annual meeting of the National Association of Commissioners, Secretaries and Directors of Agriculture. "Mr. [Charles] Ray had devoted ten years to just what he has given you today," Wilken told the officials, and Ray had just unloaded the trade turn idea.

This would put the origin of Ray's methodology well into the early 1930s, since Sears, Roebuck at that time was constantly giving public expression to "ideas" needed to cope with the Depression. In any case, Wilken, Ray and Coulter were talking the same language.

As an industrial engineer turned economist in the employ of Sears, Ray concerned himself mightily with the chore of predicting economic behavior. The economic principle involved in Ray's work was the mechanical "law of the lever." "This economic equation was first stated by the French Physiocrats in the middle of the 18th century," said Ray, "and was adopted later as the basic principle in the rule of economics by Adam Smith in his renowned work, *The Wealth of Nations*." Explaining his technique during WWII, Charles Ray pointed out that "The farmer was and will be in all time the first laborer and capitalist, and as such hires and pays himself more than is true of any other form of labor. In 1700 to 1800 our nation's farmer-pioneers were creating the first basic capital in the wealth of this nation (as in any other) by raw labor out of the soil. Ninety percent of our nation's population was in very small rural areas. Manufacturing and service, as we know them, were insignificant.

"We had a one-wheel national economy—agriculture. Sometime later on, we had a two-wheel national economy—(because of division of labor and technological improvement). By 1912 we had a three-wheel national economy. By 1927, a four-wheel national economy . . .

"Simply stated in another way, in 1800 a farmer through his basic labor and capital and production hired only himself and a fraction of another worker. In 1912 a composite farmer and miner hired himself and two other workers. In 1927 a composite farmer and miner hired himself and three other workers, and in 1947 will hire himself and four other workers providing only that the farmer and miner are paid 100%, annual raw material price parity which represents the real value of their labor and capital economically.

"Being such an individual the farmer may, therefore, be properly said to hire all other labor in society in accordance with an immutable economic law requiring equitable labor wage (price) exchange for our national economy to properly function at 'full capacity.' To the degree that we economically disfranchise both the labor and capital of agriculture in vicious, fluctuating, speculative, future commodity markets (which should be abolished as illegal) the result of the operation of an immutable economic law of compensation is deprivation of national and world economy in the same ratio. This causes poverty, insecurity, revolution and wars. Abraham Lincoln stated this economic principle empirically but clearly and simply—'Labor is prior to and creates all capital.' "

According to Ray, farm prices in 1929 were at a perfectly normal level, but were collapsed through manipulation and panic in the wake of the stock market crash. Two of England's and one of France's foremost banker-economists—Stamp, Vickers and Reynaud—pointed out the quite simple fact that the collapse of the raw commodity markets and stock markets in the U.S. brought on the collapse of the world raw commodity markets and world trade.

The few dollars that Sears donated to Raw Materials National Council were welcomed enough. More welcomed were the many discussions Wilken enjoyed with Charles B. Ray.

# [7] THE BREAKDOWN OF MONEY

Wilken's first important text for study was *The Breakdown of Money*, by Christopher Hollis. Thirty years later Wilken could recite passages from a chapter entitled, "The American Slump," and recite them so accurately that tape transcriptions matched perfectly with the book itself, except for a stray "and" or "but!" The two opening paragraphs were enough:

"There is no reason, other than a monetary reason, why there should have been an American slump.

"That is to say, there is no invention which was known to men in 1928 and which has since been forgotten. There has been no failure of a harvest nor natural calamity. The United States are only dependent for their standard of living to the extent of 2% on foreign goods. The only raw material of importance in which she is not self-supporting is rubber. There has been no failure of the world's rubber crop; rather has its production been artificially restricted. There it is clear that America is in a position to offer to the rubber-growers of the East their choice of almost any other commodity that they wish to exchange against their rubber and the rubber-growers are only too anxious to sell for any price at all that they can get. So, too, are the producers of tin, jute and manganese, her next most important imports. Her calamities cannot then be ascribed to a failure of foreign supplies. We are told that the depression [*sic*] has taught the Americans that they cannot hope to sell abroad unless they are willing to buy from abroad. But why should they wish to sell abroad if they can produce for themselves almost everything that they either need or want?"

The figures Hollis offered on foreign trade matched those Wilken developed. "The minute I read that, I started to look at income records." And it can be stated fairly that Wilken looked at income records to the end of his days. The opening observation by Hollis had been revealing enough. It was further explained when Wilken sent to London for a book entitled *Economic Tribulation*, by Vincent C. Vickers.

# [8] THE DRONES

An Eaton and Oxford educated Britisher, Vickers had been a Deputy Lieutenant of the City of London, a director of Vickers, Ltd., and for 22 years a director of London Assurance. In 1910 he became a Governor of the Bank of England. Speaking from the chair of experience, Vickers handed out observations Wilken could appreciate, understand and build upon. "When a productive industry is unable to meet its commitments, it fails and goes into bankruptcy," Vickers wrote. "When the money industry fails, the whole country is forced to make sacrifices in order to save the financial interests."

That much had come clear during the months of bank closures and acute money distress. But what Vickers said next seemed even more important. "If productive industry could cut out the intervening profit of the middleman and trade direct with the individual consumers of their products, there would follow an immediate demand throughout the country for a much greater production, necessitating an increased employment of labour and therefore an eventual reduction of taxation." Vickers went on to point out that this was impossible, but he cautioned all who would read and learn that "These middlemen, these agents, these brokers and jobbers, money and metal exchange operators, moneylenders, issuing houses, banks and insurance companies—these *entrepreneurs* create nothing at all. They are the drones of the national beehive and live and are dependent upon the honey that others collect. Like the unemployed, they are supported at the cost of the nation."

And what about the drones? They grow rich with the ups and downs of trade, whereas the "productive industry grows rich upon stable markets, a constant price level, and the absence of violent economic fluctuations." Thus the name of the international game—playing off one nation against the other—involving them in an "economic gamble at which none can win!"

Vickers knew whereof he wrote. His trenchant lines are as valid today as they were when Raw Materials National Council worker Carl Wilken first read them.

"The first consideration of a nation is, or should be, the protection of its own nationals and its own industries. It will never allow, in principle, a foreign importation to ruin its own producers of that same commodity. In other words, no one will buy a pair of boots for a sovereign if he can get them for less. And so, gradually, it dawns upon us that the whole question of International Trade, and of greater freedom in exchanging goods with one another, is not a question of the real value of the exports themselves but of the *price* of those exports—that is to say, the money value. The problem is therefore essentially a money problem. The value of a ton of butter may be the same everywhere, but its price when delivered to this country or that may be very cheap in one market and prohibitive in another. Why? Because we do not possess, and have never possessed, a true and honest measure of value. Those 'umbrellas,' those trade restrictions, came into being solely because money in one country buys much more, or much less, than it does in some other country."

Vickers argued that free international trade was not dependent on elimination of trade restrictions. It depended, he said, on a better money system—one based on an index of goods and commodities.

The economic drones saw it differently. Imported agricultural production was good for the trade, but bad for the farmer. And the farmer had to be kept down because his prosperity might damage the welfare of the drones. And dronedom the world over had enlisted public policy in order to become a sector of any economy that could always profit at the expense of others.

Again and again Vickers scored "This national and mainly international dictatorship of money, which plays off one country against another and which, through the ownership of a large portion of the Press, converts the advertisement of its own private opinion into the semblance of general public opinion. . . ." This was no cornpone rustic speaking, but an ex-Governor of the Bank of England, a man who knew exactly what he said and why economic theory and empirical studies seemed to lead to nowhere.

Wilken continued to absorb economics pragmatically. In the end he fell back on Hollis and Vickers and the realization that most theories had become mere euphemisms for obfuscation, and that in the main the truth of the riddle would have to flow from the facts. And the facts started with two items: corn was chiefly water and sunshine, and that price was something the drones put on it because the producers were too busy producing to ride the back of others.

Here, after all, at the primary production level, could be found the key to the creation of real money as opposed to legal tender. Beyond that, simple bookkeeping would have to account for profit by defining the difference between those who added to the product and those who merely added to the price.

# [9] ON A RATIO OF SEVEN

Wilken learned that the value of farm production had a striking correlation with the factory payrolls from 1928 to 1932. He also learned that for every dollar that national payrolls fell off, national income fell off on a ratio of approximately 7. The columnar sheets were piled high in Wilken's office. Dovetailed toward a conclusion almost anyone could understand, they argued briefly and succinctly that 75% of parity was better than 52% of parity, and in 1947, 45 cent corn meant that farmers were getting 52% as much as their corn was worth. Having studied Christopher Hollis plus many economists Hollis had summoned as citations—Frederick Soddy, included—Wilken could show that 45 cent corn (or 52% of parity) had been arrived at because it represented the average world price and conformed with the traditional concepts then being pushed forward—free trade and a free world market. And, of course, 45 cent corn put that basic commodity squarely in line with $20.67 gold. (Although the price of gold had been raised to $35, statisticians and traders still calculated corn in terms of $20.67 gold.)

By any standard, work at the Raw Materials National Council proceeded rapidly. By January 1937 preliminary codifications had become definitive enough to form the basis of a farm bill—one introduced in Congress by Senator Guy Gillette and Representative Vincent Harrington. The measure called for 75% of parity and proposed a tariff on all farm products processed in bulk. Economically, it did not differ greatly from the McNary-Haugen bills of the 1920s. "The general concept was pretty much the same," Wilken agreed. "In other words, it was designed to protect the American price against the competition of the chief products of the rest of the world."

In any case, the Gillette-Harrington probe was more or less perfunctory. A new farm bill was being proposed. Styled Pope-McGill, it commanded the lion's share of attention in late 1937, and it was through hearings on Pope-McGill that Wilken's research first achieved widespread publication.

# INTERLUDE

# CHAPTER 13: THE NAME OF PROOF

The raw materials exchange equation invites detailed proof. Engineers who compute the weight of water behind a dam, or the nautical requirements for keeping a ship afloat, can have confidence in the rules of calculus and mathematics. The chemistry of a material and the stress factors computed in the structure, after all, are based on physical laws, and not on abstractions such as the dollars conjured into existence by a banker on the basis of collateral already on hand.

This is the reason I have included Table 1 on page 170. There is no reason to shun a table, chart or graph. In a way, these devices communicate more clearly than narrative, and leave no room to squirm for those who reject the premises of the earlier chapters. Nevertheless, it must be pointed out that the several columns presented have been codified from more detailed statistical arrays. For instance, the column styled METALLIC includes totals for copper, zinc, lead, manganese, tungsten, gold, silver, iron and scrap iron production.

The column for FUELS includes crude oil, natural gas, bituminous and anthracite coal while the column labeled OTHERS includes bauxite, uranium, quarried stone, sand and gravel, cement materials, ag lime, phosphates and potash. These two columns are the NONMETALLIC minerals. Principal raw materials that govern the earned income of the world, and in turn the income and savings of nations and their appropriate weighted importance are charted on page 168.

Note that during the 25-year period from 1929 to 1953, fully 70% of the raw materials input used to operate the economy was of farm origin. We will consider this 25-year time frame as a model, for it will be noted that after 1952-1953, the nation's managers presumed to repeal the laws of physics, and then injected debt no longer justified by profits and savings as a substitute for earnings.

Note that in Table 2 on page 173 full use has been made of the preliminary data assembled in Table 1. The last column of Table 1 has become the second column of Table 2. Here again, attention is directed to the time frame1929-1953, with commentary on later years deferred for down-

## The Raw Materials Base That Governs National Income

| 20 | 19 | 9 | 12 | 11 | 11 | 18 |
|---|---|---|---|---|---|---|
| Wheat | Cattle | Cottonseed oil | Cotton | Platinum | Coal | Hides |
| Corn | Sheep | Olive oil | Wool | Gold | Coke | Newsprint |
| Oats | Hogs | Coffee | Silk | Silver | Natural gas | Lumber |
| Soybeand | Poultry | Cocoa | Hamp | Titanium | Petroleum | Turpentine |
| Barley | Lard | Tea | Jute | Magnesium | | Linseed oil |
| Rye | Butter | Sugar | | Bauxite | | Phosphates |
| Rice | | | | Cobalt | | Potash |
| | | | | Nickel | | Nitrate of soda |
| | | | | Chrome | | Rubber |
| | | | | Manganese | | Linseed meal |
| | | | | Uranium | | |
| | | | | Scrap iron | | |
| | | | | Pig iron | | |
| | | | | Zinc | | |
| | | | | Tin | | |
| | | | | Lead | | |
| | | | | Copper | | |

*This list could be fleshed out to include spices, fish, opium, tobacco and precious stones. The last raw material of significance to be added to the international trades has been blood, and—with the advent of abortions worldwide—human fetuses.*

track analysis. Data for years between 1953 and 2002 have extended several columns, it being understood that numbers are usually tardy in arriving for the most recent year. A glance at Table 1 will reveal that realized gross farm income now resurfaces as column 2 in Table 2. The total of the minerals in Table 1 is now column 3 in Table 2. Gross farm income and gross mineral income are added together to become column 4, which serves up the total for mineral and farm income.

To get gross farm production as a percent of national income, divide national income into gross farm income. The total of the 25 years national income 1929-1953 so divided into farm income yield a rounded 14.1%. Taking that 25-year period, here is the arithmetic.

$$3.4883 \, \overline{\smash{\big)}\, .493464} \quad .1414626$$

The quotient is .1414626 × 100%, or 14.1% rounded off.

To get gross mineral production as a percentage of national income, divide national income into gross mineral production. Again the 25-year period divided into national income delivers the figure to be 6.00% of national income.

The combined total of raw materials production—farm and mineral—divided into national income provides an answer of 20.15079%, which rounds off to 20.2%. That is where we get the equation that says gross national income will be five times more than the gross of the raw materials input under conditions of parity prices and full employment. Only a change in the state of the arts which advances agriculture beyond its 25-year relationship with the industrial sector could upset that natural formula.

$$3.4883 \overline{\smash{\big)}\ .70292} \quad .2015079$$

The raw materials exchange equation that rachets national income to a level five-fold higher than raw materials income is also based on the proposition that without debt injection to alter the equation—fully 70% of all economic activity is geared to answering the wants of the population—food, clothing, and household comforts. The statistical support for this finding follows on page 175 as Table 3.

It is necessary to reflect on what these data are telling us, and we are required to permit the results to be developed from the evidence. So-called common sense and/or theories will not serve us in this endeavor simply because too few laymen will invoke the proper level of abstraction, and too many professionals will attempt their task with unclean hands. The idol called science has become the servant of vested interests. A military-industrial-university complex has enlisted at least 70% of all scientists for the purpose of developing more sophisticated killing machines. On the basis of debt this complex has lifted apparent gross national income to dizzy heights. Highways and cities, baseball and football stadiums—usually constructed on the basis of debt—dazzle the populace, and opulence created by transferring wealth from one sector to the next has conspired to deny the prime mover status of the raw materials on which all industrial development is based.

The destruction of the raw materials ratio based on defective logic has been hailed as a triumph by academia. But as Yogi Berra put it, "The game isn't over until its over." The scorecard has to be enlarged to calculate the turn of the debt dollar.

A codification of mineral income compared to gross farm income is presented in the table now made part of this narrative. These data were mined from the *Economic Report of the President* and the *Survey of Current Business* by Carl Wilken and published in *All New Wealth Comes From the Soil*. Since these data have been revised by government agen-

cies during the past several decades, slight variations may be revealed
when compared to recent publications containing data for the same years.

### TABLE 1
### VALUE OF MINERAL PRODUCTION IN THE UNITED STATES
#### *(Billions of Dollars)*

| YEAR | METALLIC | NONMETALLIC FUELS | OTHER | TOTAL | GROSS FARM INC. |
|------|----------|-------|-------|-------|-----------------|
| 1929 | 1.5 | 3.2 | 1.2 | 5.9 | 13.8 |
| 1930 | 1.0 | 2.8 | 1.0 | 4.8 | 11.4 |
| 1931 | 0.6 | 1.9 | 0.7 | 3.2 | 8.4 |
| 1932 | 0.3 | 1.7 | 0.4 | 2.5 | 6.4 |
| 1933 | 0.4 | 1.7 | 0.5 | 2.6 | 7.1 |
| 1934 | 0.5 | 2.2 | 0.5 | 3.3 | 8.5 |
| 1935 | 0.7 | 2.3 | 0.6 | 3.7 | 9.6 |
| 1936 | 1.1 | 2.8 | 0.7 | 4.6 | 10.6 |
| 1937 | 1.5 | 3.2 | 0.7 | 5.4 | 11.2 |
| 1938 | 0.9 | 2.8 | 0.7 | 4.4 | 10.0 |
| 1939 | 1.3 | 2.8 | 0.8 | 4.9 | 10.4 |
| 1940 | 1.7 | 3.1 | 0.8 | 5.6 | 10.9 |
| 1941 | 2.1 | 3.7 | 1.0 | 6.9 | 13.7 |
| 1942 | 2.4 | 4.1 | 1.1 | 7.6 | 18.6 |
| 1943 | 2.5 | 4.6 | 1.0 | 8.1 | 22.9 |
| 1944 | 2.3 | 5.2 | 0.9 | 8.4 | 24.1 |
| 1945 | 2.0 | 5.2 | 1.0 | 8.1 | 25.3 |
| 1946 | 1.8 | 5.8 | 1.3 | 8.9 | 29.0 |
| 1947 | 2.9 | 7.9 | 1.6 | 12.5 | 34.0 |
| 1948 | 3.5 | 10.4 | 1.9 | 15.8 | 34.5 |
| 1949 | 3.1 | 8.7 | 1.9 | 13.6 | 31.8 |
| 1950 | 3.7 | 9.5 | 2.2 | 15.4 | 32.1 |
| 1951 | 4.4 | 10.7 | 2.5 | 17.6 | 36.9 |
| 1952 | 4.2 | 10.4 | 2.6 | 17.3 | 36.8 |
| 1953 | 4.7 | 11.0 | 3.0 | 18.7 | 35.4 |

Starting in 1953, data presented in Table 1 include governemnt payments. The statistical series reported from 1954 forward have been re-
peatedly revised or adjusted in the records of U.S. Bureau of Mines, Department of Interior, and Natural Agricultural Statistics Service, USDA.

As noted elsewhere in this book, the Eisenhower administration joined
the Republican to the Democratic Party as far as farm policy was concerned, reducing farm income to a world level. The implementation of
the Aiken Bill (sliding farm parity) deprived farm income, then national

income of the support and earned income stability the American system had always accounted for. The first great debt injection was twice as large as prudence should have allowed based on profits and savings. The rest of the story can be observed in the apparent disintegration of the traditional ratio, 1 to 5, between raw materials and national income. The numbers that follow were assembled by the National Organization for Raw Materials, the successor to the old Raw Materials National Council.

**TABLE 1**

*(continued)*

| YEAR | METALLIC | NONMETALLIC FUELS | OTHER | TOTAL | GROSS FARM INC. |
|---|---|---|---|---|---|
| 1954 | 1.5 | 9.9 | 2.6 | 14.1 | 30.0 |
| 1955 | 2.1 | 10.8 | 3.0 | 15.8 | 29.6 |
| 1956 | 2.4 | 11.7 | 3.3 | 17.4 | 30.6 |
| 1957 | 2.1 | 12.7 | 3.3 | 18.1 | 29.8 |
| 1958 | 1.6 | 11.6 | 3.3 | 16.5 | 33.4 |
| 1959 | 1.6 | 12.0 | 3.7 | 17.2 | 33.5 |
| 1960 | 2.0 | 12.1 | 3.9 | 18.0 | 34.0 |
| 1961 | 1.9 | 12.4 | 3.9 | 18.2 | 35.2 |
| 1962 | 1.9 | 12.8 | 4.1 | 18.8 | 36.5 |
| 1963 | 2.0 | 13.3 | 4.3 | 19.6 | 37.5 |
| 1964 | 2.3 | 13.6 | 4.6 | 20.5 | 37.3 |
| 1965 | 2.5 | 14.0 | 4.9 | 21.5 | 39.4 |
| 1966 | 2.7 | 15.1 | 5.2 | 23.0 | 43.4 |
| 1967 | 2.3 | 16.2 | 5.2 | 23.7 | 42.8 |
| 1968 | 2.7 | 16.8 | 5.4 | 25.0 | 44.2 |
| 1969 | 3.3 | 18.0 | 5.6 | 26.9 | 48.2 |
| 1970 | 3.9 | 20.2 | 5.7 | 29.8 | 50.5 |
| 1971 | 3.4 | 21.3 | 6.1 | 30.7 | 52.7 |
| 1972 | 3.6 | 22.1 | 6.5 | 32.2 | 61.1 |
| 1973 | 4.4 | 25.0 | 7.4 | 36.8 | 86.9 |
| 1974 | 5.6 | 40.9 | 8.6 | 55.1 | 92.4 |
| 1975 | 5.2 | 47.6 | 9.5 | 62.3 | 88.9 |
| 1976 | 6.1 | 52.5 | 10.6 | 69.2 | 95.4 |
| 1977 | 5.8 | 59.6 | 11.7 | 77.1 | 96.2 |
| 1978 | 6.3 | 61.4 | 13.5 | 81.3 | 112.4 |
| 1979 | 8.5 | 82.2 | 15.4 | 106.1 | 131.5 |
| 1980 | 8.9 | 120.5 | 16.2 | 145.6 | 139.7 |
| 1981 | 8.8 | 160.7 | 16.4 | 185.9 | 141.6 |
| 1982 | 5.5 | 158.6 | 14.2 | 178.3 | 142.6 |
| 1983 | 5.9 | 147.1 | 15.3 | 168.2 | 136.8 |

**TABLE 1**

*(continued)*

| YEAR | METALLIC | NONMETALLIC FUELS | OTHER | TOTAL | GROSS FARM INC. |
|------|----------|-------|-------|-------|-----------------|
| 1984 | 6.0 | 155.7 | 17.2 | 178.9 | 142.8 |
| 1985 | 5.6 | 144.5 | 17.7 | 167.8 | 144.1 |
| 1986 | 5.8 | 93.5 | 17.6 | 117.0 | 135.4 |
| 1987 | 7.4 | 97.2 | 18.9 | 123.6 | 141.8 |
| 1988 | 10.2 | 88.7 | 19.8 | 118.8 | 151.2 |
| 1989 | 11.9 | 96.1 | 20.4 | 128.4 | 160.8 |
| 1990 | 12.4 | 108.0 | 21.0 | 141.4 | 169.5 |
| 1991 | 11.0 | 96.6 | 20.0 | 127.6 | 167.9 |
| 1992 | 11.5 | 95.5 | 20.5 | 127.5 | 171.4 |
| 1993 | 10.8 | 93.1 | 21.2 | 125.1 | 178.2 |
| 1994 | 11.9 | 88.6 | 23.1 | 123.6 | 181.3 |
| 1995 | 14.0 | 84.7 | 24.6 | 123.3 | 188.0 |
| 1996 | 13.0 | 106.4 | 25.8 | 145.2 | 199.3 |
| 1997 | 13.1 | 106.4 | 27.3 | 146.8 | 207.6 |
| 1998 | 11.1 | 83.0 | 28.2 | 122.3 | 195.8 |
| 1999 | 9.8 | 94.4 | 29.3 | 133.5 | 188.1 |
| 2000 | 10.1 | 147.6 | 29.2 | 186.9 | 193.6 |

*Sources:* All New Wealth Comes From the Soil, *Table I;* Mineral Yearbook, *U.S. Bureau of Mines;* Economic Report of the President; *National Agricultural Statistics Service, USDA*

Since 1954, national income has represented little more than the reverse multiplier of debt escalated to national income, farm income being reduced to hardly more than half a percent of national income.

Inflation is usually a consequence of reckless debt injection. The debt tornado has been called a foundation for national income when in fact it is both an economic incubus and succubus.

During the scenario presented as the last part of Table 1, public and private debt grew exponentially from less than $1 trillion to over $18 trillion, circa 2000.

The statistical narration continues with Table 2. The last column above becomes the second column in Table 2.

## TABLE 2
## TOTAL VALUE OF RAW MATERIAL PRODUCTION
## AND PERCENTAGE OF NATIONAL INCOME
### (Billions of Dollars)

| YEAR | NATIONAL INCOME | GROSS FARM | GROSS MINERAL | TOTAL MINERAL & FARM |
|------|------|------|------|------|
| 1929 | 87.8 | 13.8 | 5.9 | 19.7 |
| 1930 | 75.7 | 11.4 | 4.8 | 16.2 |
| 1931 | 59.7 | 8.4 | 3.2 | 11.5 |
| 1932 | 42.5 | 6.4 | 2.5 | 8.9 |
| 1933 | 40.2 | 7.1 | 2.6 | 9.6 |
| 1934 | 49.0 | 8.5 | 3.3 | 11.8 |
| 1935 | 57.1 | 9.6 | 3.7 | 13.2 |
| 1936 | 64.9 | 10.6 | 4.6 | 15.2 |
| 1937 | 73.6 | 11.2 | 5.4 | 16.6 |
| 1938 | 67.6 | 10.0 | 4.4 | 14.4 |
| 1939 | 72.8 | 10.4 | 4.9 | 15.3 |
| 1940 | 81.6 | 10.9 | 5.6 | 16.5 |
| 1941 | 104.7 | 13.7 | 6.9 | 20.6 |
| 1942 | 137.7 | 18.6 | 7.6 | 26.2 |
| 1943 | 170.3 | 22.9 | 8.1 | 30.9 |
| 1944 | 182.6 | 24.1 | 8.4 | 32.5 |
| 1945 | 181.2 | 25.3 | 8.1 | 33.5 |
| 1946 | 180.9 | 29.0 | 8.9 | 37.9 |
| 1947 | 198.2 | 34.0 | 12.5 | 46.5 |
| 1948 | 223.5 | 34.5 | 15.8 | 50.3 |
| 1949 | 217.7 | 31.8 | 13.6 | 45.4 |
| 1950 | 241.9 | 32.1 | 15.4 | 47.5 |
| 1951 | 279.3 | 36.9 | 17.6 | 54.5 |
| 1952 | 292.2 | 36.8 | 17.3 | 54.1 |
| 1953 | 305.6 | 35.4 | 18.7 | 54.1 |
| 1954 | 301.8 | 30.0 | 14.1 | 44.1 |
| 1955 | 330.3 | 29.6 | 15.8 | 45.4 |
| 1956 | 350.8 | 30.6 | 17.4 | 48.0 |
| 1957 | 367.0 | 29.8 | 18.1 | 47.9 |
| 1958 | 367.3 | 33.4 | 16.5 | 49.9 |
| 1959 | 400.7 | 33.5 | 17.2 | 50.7 |
| 1960 | 414.5 | 34.0 | 18.0 | 52.0 |
| 1961 | 434.0 | 35.2 | 18.2 | 53.4 |
| 1962 | 463.8 | 36.5 | 18.8 | 55.3 |
| 1963 | 487.3 | 37.5 | 19.6 | 57.1 |
| 1964 | 522.1 | 37.3 | 20.5 | 57.8 |

**TABLE 2**

*(continued)*

| YEAR | NATIONAL INCOME | GROSS FARM | GROSS MINERAL | TOTAL MINERAL & FARM |
|------|------|------|------|------|
| 1965 | 589.9 | 39.4 | 21.5 | 60.9 |
| 1966 | 644.1 | 43.4 | 23.0 | 66.4 |
| 1967 | 679.2 | 42.8 | 23.7 | 66.5 |
| 1968 | 743.6 | 44.2 | 25.0 | 69.2 |
| 1969 | 805.3 | 48.2 | 26.9 | 75.1 |
| 1970 | 842.0 | 50.5 | 29.8 | 80.3 |
| 1971 | 907.6 | 52.7 | 30.7 | 83.5 |
| 1972 | 1,005.7 | 61.1 | 32.2 | 93.3 |
| 1973 | 1,146.5 | 86.9 | 36.8 | 123.7 |
| 1974 | 1,255.5 | 92.4 | 55.1 | 147.5 |
| 1975 | 1,327.7 | 88.9 | 62.3 | 151.2 |
| 1976 | 1,489.9 | 95.4 | 69.2 | 164.5 |
| 1977 | 1,671.6 | 96.2 | 77.1 | 173.3 |
| 1978 | 1,909.1 | 112.4 | 81.3 | 193.6 |
| 1979 | 2,149.0 | 131.5 | 106.1 | 237.7 |
| 1980 | 2,326.6 | 139.7 | 145.6 | 285.3 |
| 1981 | 2,553.7 | 141.6 | 185.9 | 327.6 |
| 1982 | 2,634.6 | 142.6 | 178.3 | 320.8 |
| 1983 | 2,811.5 | 136.8 | 168.2 | 305.0 |
| 1984 | 3,156.4 | 142.8 | 178.9 | 321.7 |
| 1985 | 3,352.6 | 144.1 | 167.8 | 311.9 |
| 1986 | 3,508.1 | 135.4 | 117.0 | 252.4 |
| 1987 | 3,812.3 | 141.8 | 123.6 | 265.4 |
| 1988 | 4,170.8 | 151.2 | 118.8 | 270.0 |
| 1989 | 4,420.6 | 160.8 | 128.4 | 289.2 |
| 1990 | 4,681.2 | 169.5 | 141.4 | 310.9 |
| 1991 | 4,789.0 | 167.9 | 127.6 | 295.5 |
| 1992 | 5,049.9 | 171.4 | 127.5 | 298.9 |
| 1993 | 5,302.6 | 178.2 | 125.1 | 303.3 |
| 1994 | 5,612.4 | 181.3 | 123.6 | 304.9 |
| 1995 | 5,931.9 | 188.0 | 123.3 | 311.3 |
| 1996 | 6,238.2 | 199.3 | 145.2 | 344.4 |
| 1997 | 6,634.9 | 207.6 | 146.8 | 354.5 |
| 1998 | 7,041.0 | 195.8 | 122.3 | 318.1 |
| 1999 | 7,501.1 | 188.1 | 133.5 | 321.6 |
| 2000 | 7,949.9 | 193.6 | 186.9 | 380.5 |
| Totals | 124,573.9 | 5,424.4 | 4,120.0 | 9,544.5 |

*These data—from 1929 through 1953—gave the Raw Materials National Council its one to five ratio, meaning $1 of raw materials times the trade turn multiplier delivered $5 national income on an earned basis. See note under Table 1 regarding revisions of the historic records.*

No attempt has been made to split the Table at year 1953-1954. The sudden change in statistical arrays has the same foundation reasons for being.

In any operating society, there is always some new wealth creation, some of it a gift of nature with no demands on human energy. Yet profits and savings at national earnings levels are achieved only when the gift of nature is monetized, that is, turned into money via the agency of production units times price. Units of debt times price yield a phantom profit, as ephemerial as the smoke from a lantern powered magically by mythology.

During any classical period in which parity is achieved for business, labor and agriculture, household maintenance accounts for fully 70% of national expenditures. Table 3 details the drift during depression, prosperity, stability and inflation.

### TABLE 3
### COMPARISON OF CONSUMER EXPENDITURES FOR FOOD, CLOTHING, BEVERAGES AND TOBACCO TO TOTAL CONSUMER GOODS EXPENDITURES
(Billions of Dollars)

| YEAR | I CONSUMER GOODS EXPENDITURES | II FOOD, BEVERAGE, TOBACCO | III CLOTHING | IV COLUMNS II & III | V PERCENTAGE OF COLUMN IV TO COLUMN I |
|------|------|------|------|------|------|
| 1929 | 46.9 | 21.2 | 11.2 | 33.4 | 70.0 |
| 1930 | 41.2 | 19.4 | 9.7 | 29.1 | 70.0 |
| 1931 | 34.4 | 16.2 | 8.2 | 24.4 | 71.0 |
| 1932 | 26.4 | 12.7 | 6.0 | 18.7 | 71.0 |
| 1933 | 25.7 | 12.8 | 5.4 | 18.1 | 70.0 |
| 1934 | 30.9 | 15.5 | 6.6 | 22.1 | 71.0 |
| 1935 | 34.4 | 17.6 | 7.0 | 24.6 | 71.0 |
| 1936 | 39.1 | 20.0 | 7.7 | 27.6 | 70.0 |
| 1937 | 42.1 | 21.6 | 8.1 | 29.6 | 70.0 |
| 1938 | 39.7 | 20.6 | 8.0 | 28.7 | 72.0 |
| 1939 | 41.8 | 20.9 | 8.4 | 29.3 | 70.0 |
| 1940 | 45.0 | 22.2 | 8.9 | 31.1 | 70.0 |
| 1941 | 52.9 | 25.7 | 10.5 | 36.3 | 69.0 |
| 1942 | 58.3 | 31.2 | 13.1 | 44.2 | 76.0 |
| 1943 | 65.8 | 36.4 | 16.0 | 52.4 | 80.0 |

## TABLE 3
### (continued)

| YEAR | I CONSUMER GOODS EXPENDITURES | II FOOD, BEVERAGE, TOBACCO | III CLOTHING | IV COLUMNS II & III | V PERCENTAGE OF COLUMN IV TO COLUMN I |
|------|------|------|------|------|------|
| 1944 | 72.1 | 40.1 | 17.5 | 57.6 | 80.0 |
| 1945 | 81.2 | 44.6 | 19.7 | 64.3 | 80.0 |
| 1946 | 100.4 | 52.3 | 22.2 | 74.5 | 74.0 |
| 1947 | 113.7 | 58.0 | 23.0 | 81.0 | 72.0 |
| 1948 | 120.9 | 61.4 | 23.9 | 85.3 | 71.0 |
| 1949 | 120.4 | 60.7 | 22.7 | 83.4 | 70.0 |
| 1950 | 129.0 | 63.2 | 22.7 | 85.9 | 67.3 |
| 1951 | 138.2 | 71.2 | 24.2 | 95.5 | 70.0 |
| 1952 | 142.8 | 75.1 | 24.8 | 99.9 | 70.0 |
| 1953 | 148.7 | 77.2 | 24.6 | 101.7 | 68.4 |
| 1954 | 150.2 | 78.4 | 24.5 | 102.9 | 68.5 |
| 1955 | 161.8 | 81.4 | 25.6 | 107.0 | 66.1 |
| 1956 | 168.9 | 76.7 | 24.4 | 101.1 | 59.9 |
| 1957 | 177.1 | 80.8 | 25.4 | 106.2 | 60.0 |
| 1958 | 179.1 | 83.9 | 24.9 | 108.8 | 60.7 |
| 1959 | 191.2 | 87.3 | 26.4 | 113.7 | 59.5 |
| 1960 | 196.2 | 89.2 | 27.0 | 116.2 | 59.2 |
| 1961 | 198.4 | 91.1 | 27.6 | 118.7 | 59.8 |
| 1962 | 209.7 | 93.3 | 29.0 | 122.3 | 58.3 |
| 1963 | 219.8 | 95.8 | 29.8 | 125.6 | 57.1 |
| 1964 | 235.4 | 101.2 | 32.4 | 133.6 | 56.8 |
| 1965 | 254.9 | 108.8 | 34.1 | 142.9 | 56.1 |
| 1966 | 277.1 | 117.8 | 37.4 | 155.2 | 56.0 |
| 1967 | 287.5 | 121.4 | 39.2 | 160.6 | 55.9 |
| 1968 | 316.5 | 131.6 | 43.2 | 174.8 | 55.2 |
| 1969 | 339.1 | 141.3 | 46.5 | 187.8 | 55.4 |
| 1970 | 357.0 | 154.6 | 47.8 | 202.4 | 56.7 |
| 1971 | 382.4 | 161.0 | 51.7 | 212.7 | 55.6 |
| 1972 | 418.4 | 173.6 | 56.4 | 230.0 | 55.0 |
| 1973 | 466.6 | 192.8 | 62.5 | 255.3 | 54.7 |
| 1974 | 506.8 | 215.9 | 66.0 | 281.9 | 55.6 |
| 1975 | 554.2 | 238.3 | 70.8 | 309.1 | 55.8 |
| 1976 | 617.2 | 259.3 | 76.6 | 335.9 | 54.4 |
| 1977 | 678.4 | 279.7 | 84.1 | 363.8 | 53.6 |
| 1978 | 751.9 | 307.9 | 94.3 | 402.2 | 53.5 |
| 1979 | 838.8 | 343.9 | 101.2 | 445.1 | 53.1 |

TABLE 3
(*continued*)

| YEAR | I CONSUMER GOODS EXPENDITURES | II FOOD, BEVERAGE, TOBACCO | III CLOTHING | IV COLUMNS II & III | V PERCENTAGE OF COLUMN IV TO COLUMN I |
|---|---|---|---|---|---|
| 1980 | 910.3 | 376.9 | 107.3 | 484.2 | 53.2 |
| 1981 | 990.2 | 406.3 | 117.2 | 523.5 | 52.9 |
| 1982 | 1,027.8 | 427.7 | 120.5 | 548.2 | 53.3 |
| 1983 | 1,112.4 | 451.3 | 130.9 | 582.2 | 52.3 |
| 1984 | 1,211.6 | 476.6 | 142.5 | 619.1 | 51.1 |
| 1985 | 1,292.1 | 498.4 | 152.1 | 650.5 | 50.3 |
| 1986 | 1,359.8 | 524.2 | 163.1 | 687.3 | 50.5 |
| 1987 | 1,435.0 | 549.8 | 174.4 | 724.2 | 50.5 |
| 1988 | 1,533.1 | 588.2 | 185.5 | 773.7 | 50.5 |
| 1989 | 1,633.2 | 630.5 | 198.9 | 829.4 | 50.8 |
| 1990 | 1,713.7 | 677.9 | 204.1 | 882.0 | 51.5 |
| 1991 | 1,721.8 | 700.0 | 208.7 | 908.7 | 52.8 |
| 1992 | 1,793.7 | 717.3 | 221.9 | 939.2 | 52.4 |
| 1993 | 1,888.6 | 742.8 | 231.1 | 973.9 | 51.6 |
| 1994 | 1,998.8 | 773.6 | 240.7 | 1,014.3 | 50.7 |
| 1995 | 2,087.0 | 802.5 | 247.8 | 1,050.3 | 50.3 |
| 1996 | 2,190.6 | 834.2 | 258.6 | 1,092.8 | 49.9 |
| 1997 | 2,284.1 | 862.0 | 271.7 | 1,133.7 | 49.6 |
| 1998 | 2,401.7 | 900.2 | 284.8 | 1,185.0 | 49.3 |
| 1999 | 2,592.2 | 963.5 | 300.9 | 1,264.4 | 48.8 |
| 2000 | 2,809.2 | 1,029.6 | 319.1 | 1,348.7 | 48.0 |

*Source of Data—U.S. Department of Commerce.*
*These data—for the 25-year classic period (1929-1953)—reveal that 70% of all consumer expenditures have to do with household and family maintenance.*

The above data tells some parts of the story—but not all of it. Obviously, the ratio between farm and raw materials income and national income becomes meaningless once excessive debt enters the equation. Moreover, with farm income not even half a percent of national income, and with the trade turn multiplier raised to a new state-of-the-arts level of 10.4, the earned income factor retains hardly any relationship to national income. It—with all other raw materials added—explains why savings have all but disappeared for the American economy.

Debt spawns more debt and only pretends to deliver national income.

# FOUR ENGINEER-ECONOMISTS

# CHAPTER 14: PARECONOMY

"Parity," intoned Congressman Vincent F. Harrington of Iowa, is "derived from the Latin *paritas*, meaning equal. *Webster's Dictionary* defines it as 'the quality of being equal or equivalent, a like state or degree; equality'—and, again—'equality in purchasing power.'" Harrington was defending the parity bill he had introduced in the House, one he had pushed with utmost zeal ever since Carl Wilken first explained the name of the game. As a matter of fact, Wilken had written the bill, and though other measures came to command the spotlight—notably the Pope-McGill bill of the late 1930s—the earliest parity bill by Harrington announced to Congress that depression would go on and on until farmers had achieved full parity at the marketplace.

"Briefly," Harrington told his colleagues, "the bill assures producers of basic crops parity prices for their product without *acreage restriction*. Crops included are wheat, corn, oats, cotton, sugar, and tobacco, with a provision for inclusion of rye, barley, and rice at the discretion of the Secretary of Agriculture."

The Secretary of Agriculture, according to the Harrington bill, would be authorized to make loans of not less than 75% of parity price of crops covered, based on an index 1922-1929 = 100.

Then and ever since, the words *"without acreage restriction"* stuck in the craw of those who had been nourished on a steady diet of free trade economics. Being told to let go of the supply and demand maxim was like telling a 4th century sailor that the Earth wasn't flat.

Yet there was another equally important point in Wilken's thinking.

"Mr. Speaker, I am asking that the farmer be given back his American market. I am asking that we repeal oppressive laws and allow industry to operate to the end that all men have jobs in private employment at reasonable wages," said Harrington. Why this McNary-Haugen approach as late as 1937?

"The imports of farm products and the constant threat of even larger imports has forced the dairy and farm market to the bottom and is going to keep it there. The farmer in his desperation to make ends meet is going to come to the Congress and ask for large appropriations. He is going to demand payments, subsidies, and other payments in a desperate effort to keep out of bankruptcy. Whatever this Congress may do to aid the farmers' price structure will only be met by a further flood of imports . . . To restore agricultural conditions, not only in my state but in the nation, I believe it absolutely necessary that we first repeal the trade agreements and restore former duties on farm products. The American farmer must be given back that which up to now he has always had—the American market."

Canned corned beef, chilled pork cuts, and everything from beef livers to bacon was coming into the country from Argentina, Brazil and Canada, as were cooked hams from Denmark, meat paste in jars from England, tinned pork butts from Estonia, smoked sausage from Germany, cooked picnics from Holland, pork loins from Hungary, smoked bacon from the Irish Free State, and products that filled pages in the National Provisioner each day, loads in terms of tons from Switzerland, Romania, Poland, Paraguay, Lithuania and Italy, until the country imported enough production to break the American market price, and bring it into line with the world average. And all the while it remained almost impossible to find someone who didn't think that farmers were producing too much, hence low prices.

# [1] MY NAME IS CARL H. WILKEN

"My name is Carl H. Wilken. My home address is Wall Lake, Iowa. I am at present living in Sioux City, acting as president of the Progressive Farmers of Iowa, a farm organization."*

The occasion was a hearing on corn before the Senate Committee on Agriculture and Forestry, 75th Congress, 2nd session. Carl H. Wilken had come to tell the Senators a little more than how the hogs ate the chickens. The Raw Materials National Council had been incorporated a year earlier, and the first of Wilken research results had been used to structure a farm

---

* On July 6, 1932 Carl Wilken called a meeting at the Jackson Hotel in Sioux City, Iowa for the purpose of breaking Milo Reno's "strangle hold" on the Farmers Union. The words are Wilken's. John L. Shover does not cover this development with much satisfaction in *Cornbelt Rebellion*, and Milo Reno [a memorial volume by Farmers Union] ignores it for all practical purposes. Hans Wilken, Carl Wilken's brother, wrote me that farmers believed money was being squandered. The Sioux City meetings and others across Iowa split the Farmers Union. Co-op properties were taken over by insurgents, usually through bankruptcy proceedings. A few of the resolutions carried at the July 6 meeting tell something about the tone of the times:

"No Secrecy.

"Dues $2.50 and no initiation fee.

"The State to be divided in districts, each district to elect its own director to the Fraternal Board, Oil Board, Service Board and Farmers Union Life Stock Commission Board.

"No connection with the Federal Farm Board of subsidy from any Government source.

"No Nepotism."

The Wilken-Reno battle became lost as a bigger story took shape—Reno's Farmers' Holiday Movement, the Depression, and also the formation of the Raw Materials National Council.

bill by Congressman Harrington and Senator Gillette, one that called for 75% of parity for basic farm crops. The Senators had listened briefly to another Raw Materials National Council spokesman, O.L. Brownlee, who was editor of the *The Sioux City Tribune*. They wanted to be polite, Senator McGill said, but "We are trying to get this over," and "If you are going to read all you have got there in your hand we will not have time for it." Brownlee got about five minutes. He could be dismissed because he was an editor. But Wilken was a farmer and furthermore he represented farmers, some 7,000 of them Senator Pope was quick to find out. This single fact was worth valuable minutes.

## [2] APPROXIMATELY WORLD PRICES

There were several reasons Wilken and his associates opposed the Pope-McGill bill. "The system of commodity credits it proposes," Wilken testified, "ranging from 85 to 52% of parity, would automatically fix the ceiling price of the basic commodities at levels approximating world prices. The so-called parity payments it provides would constitute a raid on the United States Treasury and cannot properly be figured as a part of the market price."

The Pope-McGill bill had other faults. It contemplated no more than controlled scarcity, and therefore made no provision for a reserve or inventory. It failed to consider a surplus, and therefore made no provision for surplus disposal. Worst of all, the Pope-McGill bill did nothing to protect the farmer in what was rightfully his—the American market. One at a time Wilken scored points.

"The bill makes a gesture at developing new uses by appropriating $10 million, but fails to specify how or for what purposes it shall be used. The land-use policies this bill proposes contemplates curtailment of production of basic crops instead of diverting land to nonfood crops or the supplying of products which we now import." Wilken objected to the regimentation of land and men, and he objected to the bureaucratic controls. "The Pope-McGill bill would delude consumers into believing they were obtaining cheap food while penalizing them with taxes, to make up the so-called parity payments to farmers and unnecessary expenses incident to administration . . ." In summary form, Wilken drove home his chief point with one sledgehammer line. "The bill, Senator," he answered Senator Pope, "can be made all right. Its objective is fine, but it is not written so that it can possibly obtain the objectives."

When a witness disagrees with the inquisitors during a Congressional hearing, the procedure of choice is to invoke ridicule, levity, and sarcasm, and when possible to lure a witness into a contradiction, the intellectual signal of defeat.

SENATOR POPE. I take it that you did not participate in either the Agricultural Adjustment or the Soil Conservation Act as a farmer?

MR. WILKEN. I did participate; yes, sir.

SENATOR POPE. You did?

MR. WILKEN. Absolutely.

SENATOR POPE. And why?

MR. WILKEN. Because of the check I could get [Laughter and applause.]

SENATOR POPE. That looked rather attractive to you—the check that you would get under the bill. Now, is that the only reason you participated? Did you have an interest in conserving your soil?

MR. WILKEN. I have always conserved my soil. The principal reason that I took this benefit payment was that I knew it would end up in a national deficit, which I would some day have to pay, so I wanted to be sure to get my money to be able to pay it. [Applause.]

SENATOR POPE. And you participated in the Agricultural Adjustment Act?

MR. WILKEN. Yes, Sir.

SENATOR POPE. To get a check?

MR. WILKEN. Yes, Sir.

SENATOR POPE. You did not have any interest in controlling the surplus or keeping down the production so as to increase the price of the products the farmers generally have to sell?

MR. WILKEN. If you read brief No. 1 you will find analyzed in there the fact that production does not have anything to do with price.

Wilken filed his two briefs with the Committee that day, but they were not made part of the record. Some 30 years later, the files from that hearing had either been published or warehoused, and the inquiry that I made gained me the information that such papers were not always kept. Perhaps they weren't read either, judging from the dour results legislation managed to achieve up to and well into World War II.

Brief 1 and brief 2, however, had been printed into a brochure, Wilken told me, and the text was still available somewhere. It was titled, *Pareconomy—The Way to Prosperity*, he said. Wilken usually wrote and rewrote, edited and re-edited his papers. Still the slightly updated text of *Pareconomy* as inserted into the *Congressional Record* on May 4, 1939 by Congressman Harrington remained very close to the original submitted to the Senate Committee, and another version was published as transcript proceedings of the First Congress on Industry and Raw Materials, November 14-16, 1938. As abstracted in depth below, the paper reveals the refinement of thinking Wilken had attained as early as 1937—a mode of thought and habit of expression he was to improve upon until his last hours.

# PARECONOMY–THE WAY TO PROSPERITY

Ten million people are out of work, one-third of our population is underfed, underhoused, and underclothed, and the other two-thirds are doing without the things that they would like to have to increase their general welfare and happiness.

All because of the fact that we have too much of everything. Our people are hungry because we have too much food; our people are living in hovels because we have too much building material; and so on down the list. It does not make sense. The quotation, "What poor fools these mortals be," still holds true.

The problem of an organized society is how to bring enough money into circulation each year to enable the people to buy the wealth they can produce in order that all may live on an American standard, provide for the needs of government and have something for a savings account as a foundation for security and growth.

There are just three ways to bring money into circulation, *viz.*:

1. By the production and sale of the raw materials—products of the ground. That is the dollar we earn.

2. By direct issue by the Government as provided in the Constitution. The issue of money leads to inflation.

3. By taxation or some form of credit device. That is the method we have been following, and it leads to bankruptcy, because it dissipates the savings and future earnings of our people.

## PRODUCTION AND PRICE

The process of creating wealth starts with the production of raw materials—the products of the ground. Manufacturing, transportation, and other functions of business and capital represent only services which could not be performed at all if the raw materials were not first produced.

The amount of real wealth brought into existence is measured by the number of units of raw materials produced. Society has invented measures of weight, length, and volume which never fluctuate and remain constant year after year, but our measure of value resembles a modern jitterbug.

The amount of goods and services such units of new wealth will buy is measured by the price per unit received by the producer of such new wealth. Therefore, the number of units of raw materials produced times the price received equals the new dollar income created during each production cycle or year; the turnover of these dollars in the channels of trade determines the wages of labor and the collective income of the nation.

For example, the sale of 1,000 bushels of wheat at $1 per bushel draws upon our capital structure for $1,000 and starts $1,000 on the way into our trade channels. One thousand bushels of wheat at 50 cents per bushel draw out only $500 and reduce the primary flow of money accordingly.

It is the bushels of wheat, tons of coal, pounds of meat, etc., that the people trade. The dollar measures the relationship of the commodities exchanged. When the producer spends the dollar received for his product he passes the purchasing power to the next man and the next.

The units of raw materials—new wealth—are transformed by industry into other forms of wealth and become permanent assets of society. That is not true of either the dollar of issue or the credit dollar.

Thus the dollar brought into circulation by the production and sale of raw materials—new wealth—is the only dollar which represents real wealth. It naturally follows that our national income is based on the amount and value of the new wealth produced. This leads us to the following formula: The sale of the annual production of new wealth must bring into circulation enough money so that, when turned over in the channels of business, it will provide a national income sufficient to operate the nation as a solvent business institution.

## RELATIONSHIP OF GROSS FARM INCOME TO NATIONAL INCOME

Since the gross agricultural income represents roughly 80% * of all new wealth income and largely gauges the industrial demand for other products of new wealth, the relationship of agricultural income to national income becomes the governing factor in our economy.

The relationship of agricultural income to factory payrolls (the best index to the state of industry) and national income averages for all practical purposes 1-1-7 meaning that each $1 of gross farm income creates $1 of factory payrolls and $7 of national income or business in the United States.

That formula or relationship is the most important discovery since the signing of the Declaration of Independence and the writing of the Constitution of the United States, because it is the key to an economic democracy. Let us examine it briefly in order that we may realize its importance.

With that definite relationship holding true it makes it possible for a few men who control the speculative markets of the world to bring depression upon a nation of 130 million people and force them to exist by borrowing from their savings and by placing a mortgage on their future income, and in addition to that, take away their equity in their homes and other real estate.

---

* A rough percentage refined in later presentations.

In July 1937, for example, the wheat market was in a strong position and our domestic grain buyers bought wheat for $1.14 and $1.15 per bushel as fast as it came to the market. But, a few weeks later the men in control of the grain markets of the world forced the price of wheat downward about 30 cents per bushel. For every 30 cents taken off the price of a bushel of wheat they deprived the man on the factory payroll of 30 cents and they deprived the American people of $2.10 in collective income.

On the other hand, the formula means that whenever this nation will use its good common sense and stabilize farm prices in direct proportion to the national income needed for prosperity our depression will be over. And it also means that the farm problem and the question of a price for raw materials is the number 1 problem of every farmer, laborer, and businessman in the United States.

One of the most interesting examples of the loss we have suffered as a nation because we didn't mark the price of our new wealth properly is a comparison of the years 1928 and 1932, the former a year of prosperity and the latter a year of depression.

The *Agricultural Yearbook* for 1935 shows that in 1928 our total production of corn, oats, wheat, barley, rye, and flax was 5,333,000,000 bushels. In 1932 our production of the same crops was a little over 1% less and totaled 5,253,000,000 bushels. In 1928 the production of our principal meats, pork, beef, mutton, and veal, totaled 17,007,000,000 pounds. In 1932 our production of the same meats was 16,800,000,000 pounds.

The record shows further that in spite of the fact that over 10 million people were unemployed in 1932 we consumed within the United States all but 148,000,000 pounds of this meat, or a little over 1 pound per capita. And we allowed that surplus to reduce the income of the United States $45 billion, an amount equal to the total value of all the farm products produced in the 4-year period 1923-'26, inclusive. Yet we claim to be an intelligent people.

If the price for corn and other products had been the same in 1932 as in 1928 it would have been impossible to have a depression, unemployment, and hunger. We had the wealth, but allowed someone else to fix the price of that wealth.

## CONSEQUENCE OF FAILING TO STABILIZE FARM PRICES

Failure to stabilize farm prices at the 1926 level, when parity or an equal exchange value prevailed for agriculture, industry, and labor, has deprived this nation of $233 billion of national income in the 82 years beginning January 1, 1930, and ending July 31, 1938, and will cost us an additional loss of $16 billion in the last 6 months of 1938.

Failure to stabilize farm new wealth prices at the level which existed in 1926, when parity or equal exchange value prevailed for agriculture, industry, and labor, has cost this nation in 82 years (January 1, 1930, to July 1, 1938, inclusive) approximately $233 billion of national income which the people might have had as shown by the following table:

| Year | Gross income from farm production | Deficiency from 1926 level (1930-37) | Labor income | Deficiency from 1926 level (1930-37) | National income (gross) | Deficiency from 1926 level (1930-37) |
|---|---|---|---|---|---|---|
| 1921[1] | 8,927 | .... | 8,300 | .... | ..... | ..... |
| 1922 | 9,944 | .... | 9,000 | .... | ..... | ..... |
| 1923 | 11,041 | .... | 11,000 | .... | ..... | ..... |
| 1924 | 11,337 | .... | 10,100 | .... | ..... | ..... |
| 1925 | 11,968 | .... | 11,000 | .... | ..... | ..... |
| 1926 | 11,480 | .... | 11,400 | .... | 80,360 | ..... |
| 1927 | 11,616 | .... | 11,200 | .... | 81,312 | ..... |
| 1928 | 11,741 | .... | 11,300 | .... | 82,187 | ..... |
| 1929 | 11,941 | .... | 11,700 | .... | 83,587 | ..... |
| 1930 | 9,454 | 2,026 | 9,600 | 2,026 | 66,178 | 14,182 |
| 1931 | 6,986 | 4,512 | 7,000 | 4,512 | 48,776 | 31,584 |
| 1932 | 5,331 | 6,149 | 5,200 | 6,149 | 37,317 | 43,043 |
| 1933 | 6,256 | 5,224 | 5,500 | 5,244 | 43,792 | 36,568 |
| 1934 | 7,000 | 4,480 | 6,800 | 4,480 | 49,000 | 31,360 |
| 1935 | 8,100 | 3,380 | 7,600 | 3,380 | 56,700 | 23,660 |
| 1936 | 8,600 | 2,880 | 8,800 | 2,880 | 60,200 | 20,160 |
| 1937 | 9,000 | 2,480 | 9,000 | 2,480 | 63,000 | 17,360 |
| 1938 | 3,500 | 2,240 | 3,400 | 2,300 | 24,500 | 15,680 |
| Total | | 33,371 | | 33,431 | | 233,597 |

[1] 1921-33 *Agricultural Yearbook*, 1935.

Agricultural income must be brought up to $15 billion per year, which is entirely possible without resort to subsidies or conflict with any principle of constitutional law.

When we first discovered this formula, 1-1-7 and applied it to our economy the apparent loss was so enormous that we doubted our findings. I imagine that some of the people who have heard us explain this loss have felt that there was a question as to our sanity.

There is an old saying, however, that after you have made sure you are right, fight toward the goal. For the past one and one-half years we have been contacting different groups of people in the United States and have challenged them to break down or disprove the 1-1-7 relationship. They have been unable to do so.

It seems that we have even been able to get the facts to our brain trusters. On November 3, 1938, Dr. Louis H. Bean, economic adviser to the Department of Agriculture, in a speech at Lexington, Kentucky, pointed out to an audience that the gross farm income is approximately 14% of the national income rather than 1 to 7. But 7 times 14 almost equals 100%, so we must admit that Dr. Bean is catching on.

Dr. Bean, however, out-billions our figures and I will quote from his address. "The accumulated losses in our money income, national and farm, contrasted with what our incomes might have been, are enormous. In 1930 our national income fell $14 billion below the standard I have suggested. In 1932 it was $46 billion below; in 1937, $23 billion; and in 1938, $36 billion—a total accumulated loss for the years 1930-38 of around $295 billion."

The difference in total figures is due to the fact that Dr. Bean uses the year 1929, which was approximately 104% of parity, as a base, and we have used the year 1926, which was actually a period of parity exchange relationship, or a period when our dollar in its relationship to commodities was 100 cents.

I notice also that Dr. Bean, in his address, stresses the fact that the farm income depends on the national income when the reverse is true. Dr. Bean should try pumping water out of a well that has no spring flowing into it. Then he would realize that we must have the spring or flow of new wealth before we can have any national income.

[As additional proof of our contention, I would like to quote from Report No. 1295, prepared by the Senate Agricultural Committee to accompany the Pope-McGill Bill, our Nation's last abortive attempt at farm legislation. On page 14 of this report the committee shows that 1926 was the only year since 1800 that we had a 100-cent dollar in its exchange for the products of different groups. On page 17 of the same report the committee states as follows: "Agriculture demands that the farmer should have a 100-cent dollar: that the purchasing power of the dollar should be fixed and established at that point to serve the best interests of the people, trade, commerce, and industry, and that when that value is once fixed it should be stabilized at such value."]*

Their intentions seem to have been good, but the result was the passage of a bill which, if carried out as written, will stabilize the farm income at 52% instead of 100% of parity and will mean a perpetual de-

---

* Passage added in *Congressional Record* version of *Pareconomy*, and also in the "Proceedings" version.

pression and forced bankruptcy for the United States.

We suggest to the committee that in their next attempt they carry out their intention of giving the farmer a full parity price or a 100 cent dollar.

The cure for depression is to establish a parity relationship for all new wealth produced. Such legislation has been the apparent aim of Congress, but their thinking has been so confused with the many complexes of surplus, foreign trade, the Supreme Court, etc., that I feel it might be well to discuss some of them.

## SURPLUS

The surplus problem is the biggest bogeyman of them all and the least understood. Surpluses are created by unequal production due to the vagaries of nature, and are created by underconsumption due to lower or higher than parity prices. The parity price level is the point of continual maximum consumption.

Under our present system of operation at less than parity prices, we are fighting two surpluses—that of underconsumption and the natural surplus of seasonal production.

Our attempts at production control have been rather futile because the program which we adopted was one of increased production. It is a well-known fact that when a farmer buys a rundown or overcropped farm he seeds it to clover, but not to produce less—to produce more.

Our soil-building program, even though the farmers were led to believe that they were reducing production to obtain a price, will result in greater production. The same result would occur if we had a parity price relationship. The laws of nature would force the farmer to rotate his crops with legumes in order that he might produce more. In years of high prices we find that the acres in cultivation are reduced and that in years of low prices the acres of land in tillable crops are increased.

But, strange as it may seem, the records indicate that we never have had a permanent surplus of farm products. Even with the tremendous underconsumption that prevailed in 1932, the record shows a net import of farm products in that year of $7,000,000.

During the 5-year period 1926-30, when the average exchange value of the dollar approximated parity, the record shows that we imported an average annual net import of $350 million. In other words, we consumed all that we produced in the United States, plus $350 million of foreign farm products each year.

It might be interesting to mention a few of the items that we imported on the average each year during that period. We imported 378,135 head of cattle, 447,000,000 pounds of cheese, 253,000,000 pounds of wool, etc., each year.

## FOREIGN TRADE

The second complex which we must discuss is that of foreign trade. The very fact that we had a net import of farm products would indicate that the world market for farm products depends on the domestic market in the United States.

Our foreign trade depends on what we buy from other nations and not on what they buy from us. For example, if we would increase our farm prices to the parity level so that our national income would be increased to $85 billion, we would require about $5 billion of imports. These imports would create the credits for any exports that we might wish to make.

Tariffs do not materially hinder imports and exports. If we were to protect our American market up to the parity level, the demand for foreign products would actually be increased because of the added purchasing power and consumptive demand in the United States.

We consume within the United States about one-half of the world's production of new wealth, and if 50% of the world's market were restored to our parity level, it would do much to restore world prosperity.

If we established the value of our dollar at parity, with tariff protection up to that point, the rest of the world could revalue its monetary medium up to that level in much the same way that they increased their price of gold when we increased ours.

## THE COST OF A FARM PROGRAM

I will now discuss the question of what a farm program of parity prices will cost the government. If we will realize that the government is none other than ourselves, and use the 1-7 relationship of farm income to national income as a guide, a little arithmetic will show a huge profit.

For example, the parity value of all farm products annually produced is approximately $12 billion. With that as a base for our primary gross farm income, the dollar turn-over will create approximately $85 billion of collective income for the nation.

If we were to tax this collective income for enough to give away 10% of our total production, it would require $1.2 billion leaving a net of $83.8 billion.

Compare this to our national income of about $55 billion for 1938 and a national deficit of about $4 billion annually.

In other words, if we had our price level stabilized at parity we could give 10% of our farm products to China and increase our national income $32 billion at the same time.

Our experience during the World War proves this contention. We gave the Allies about $10 billion worth of goods each year—at least, we haven't been paid for them—and our laboring men were wearing silk shirts while at work and they had the money to pay for them.

## WHAT CAN BE DONE?

We now come to the question of how can we establish parity prices for farm products? Can a program be devised to do the job? Yes, we feel that a very simple program to maintain parity prices can be put into operation.

All we need to do is to pattern our farm program after that of our life-insurance companies. Using the law of averages and a little arithmetic, they establish the cost of insurance per thousand on a 10, 20, or 30-year policy. Reserves are created to take care of unexpected losses, and our state laws require the insurance companies to carry a 40% reserve to protect the policy-holders. Life insurance, up to this time, has been the soundest business in our financial setup.

We have the same condition of natural hazards in the production of farm products that life-insurance companies have in death losses. Let us, then, follow the same procedure.

A normal crop at parity prices is the foundation for our prosperity, or a sufficient income to operate the nation as a solvent business institution. Let us use 100 units of new wealth as a basis for a simple analysis of what should be done.

Our first step should be to provide against droughts and other production hazards. Reserves of at least 35% should be created on every farm so that in years like 1934 and 1936 we will have our 100 units of wealth, and enough feed for our livestock.

If we produce in excess of normal needs after the reserve has been established, we can add to the reserve as insurance companies do and as we have done with gold, or we can dispose of it and pay ourselves an additional dividend.

For example, supposing we had 10% in excess of our reserves and annual requirements. If we could dispose of the excess at parity we would increase our normal prosperity 10%, if we dispose of it at 50% of parity we would increase our normal prosperity 5%. Finally, if we gave it to the Chinese we would still have prosperity because we have the base of 100 units which at parity prices means prosperity.

Legislation providing for handling the farm problem in that way can be, in fact already has been, written and was introduced in Congress as the Harrington Bill.

The bill provides for a loan of 75% of parity on all basic farm crops with the loans callable at parity. Such a loan would have the practical effect of stabilizing grain prices at parity.

At the present time we are using the commodity loan, but the loans have a call date on them such as October 1, and their practical effect is to set the top price and the bottom price under normal conditions. The call date also allows corn processors and millers to use the future market to buy at the low as established by the loan.

The corn trade, on the other hand, is fearful of dumping on the call date and is unwilling to buy because of possible market losses when the loan is called. Under the Harrington Bill loans would not be callable until a 35% reserve had been established or the price had reached parity.

Such a loan would do two things. It would place the farmer in the same position as the merchant and provide for the orderly marketing of the grain at the parity price level. Second, the mandatory loan of 75% would automatically create the credit dollars needed to operate the nation.

With the loan callable at parity it would fix the value of the dollar at the parity price level and, as suggested by the Senate Agricultural Committee, fix the value at 100 cents.

The next step in the bill is to take care of the excess if and when it occurs. In the bill we provide that the Commodity Credit Corporation act collectively for all of us in the disposal of the surplus. The surplus cannot be dumped on the domestic market, thus assuring every dealer that the price is not going to be forced below parity, and it must be sold in the foreign market, to new industries, added to the reserve or by gift to be used as food for the poor, thus avoiding the necessity of community chest funds, etc.

The direct loss on the excess, if any, must be absorbed by society as a whole, which can easily be done because of the gain of about $32 billion in national income resulting from parity prices.

Any products subsidized by sale into new industries, although showing a direct loss, will increase the collective income because of the turnover of the dollar.

For example, a bushel of corn sold at 40 cents to a new industry such as power alcohol would turn over 7 times and create $2.80 in national income.

It might be well to say a few words about alcohol. The alcohol industry for power and other industrial purposes is destined to be one of the largest industries in the United States. Oil companies, of course, will at first react against the use of alcohol as a fuel. But if they can be brought to realize that surplus grains can be used for fuel purposes and in that way help to stabilize prices at parity, the additional volume of business resulting from increased national income will more than offset any loss in gallonage through replacement by alcohol.

A simple bill exempting motor fuel containing 10% of alcohol from payment of the 1 cent federal tax on motor fuel would start that industry off at a fast pace and make it possible for it to pay parity prices for raw materials.

This, of course, is an indirect subsidy, but that is the method we have used for many years to help industry.

Many other new industries can be built to consume our raw materials and to employ our idle labor.

The protective tariff and the turnover of the dollar have been the two contributing factors in making it possible for the 130 million people in the United States to do 50% of the world's business. With the aid of the tariff system we maintain the price of what we produced. We protected the home market for our own people, and the turnover of our money in that market made this a rich nation.

In the words of Abraham Lincoln, "When we trade with ourselves we have both the goods and the money."

## TARIFFS

The tariff problem has been the greatest political football this country has ever known. At the present time we have the so-called free trade party in control, but their record does not make them free traders. They also believe in tariffs.

Through the use of reciprocal trade agreements they reduced the rates on farm products, while at the same time the steel industry enjoyed the benefits of a tariff system which in effect increased the tariff on steel from $8.14 per ton in 1932 to $14.47 in 1937.

If tariff protection is a good thing for the steel industry, why isn't it also a good thing for agriculture?

Our tariff problem must be based on arithmetic rather than on the power of pressure groups. In the Harrington Bill we have devised such tariff protection.

Under the Harrington Bill all importers of farm products or competitive products would be required to pay a license fee equivalent to the difference between the landed cost and the domestic parity price at the point of entry plus freight from the nearest rate-basing point. The amount of the fee, being based on price, would move up and down with the world market and would protect us against manipulation of foreign exchange and foreign markets.

Such a tariff for industry and agriculture would make it possible to trade our surplus with other nations without any loss.

For example, if we traded a bushel of corn in the world market at 45 cents per bushel for a pocket knife at the world price of 45 cents when it entered the United States, we would collect a license fee representing the difference between the world and the domestic parity price and in that way absorb the loss on the corn, and vice versa.

I have given you in brief the essential features of a suggested bill. A bill that would give us an economy of parity price relationship, or, as we say it, "pareconomy." The same objective can be obtained by other methods, but after examining all the farm bills that have been written, I feel that the Harrington Bill is the most simple and democratic approach to the whole problem.

It has one weakness, if it can be called a weakness, and that is its democratic approach. It depends on the basic foundation of every democratic form of government—the intelligent cooperation of society.

Under the bill dealers are not forced to pay parity prices. We feel that if the measure of the 1-1-7 relationship of the farm dollar to national income is understood, that business will police itself. The man who would pay less than parity for farm production would be public enemy No. 1, and every businessman would be on his trail.

But if it must be done by legislation which will force the dealer to pay parity prices, we will offer no objection.

## IN CONCLUSION

In conclusion I would like to impress upon you the importance of the message I have given you. We are losing in daily dollar income about 60 cents per capita, or about $230 per capita for 1938.

This loss of income is resulting in mass poverty, the most fertile soil for the various *isms* that have attacked the world. Even in our own nation we hear charges and countercharges of communism, fascism, etc. Let us act before it is too late.

We must make this problem of parity prices for new wealth our No. 1 problem. Let's take off our coats and roll up our sleeves and get the job done. Our welfare and our happiness and prosperity are at stake.

Let's forget our political differences, because, after all, parity prices will be the same regardless of what political party introduces and passes the required legislation. We should organize public opinion and ask our Congressmen and Senators to make it their No. 1 problem. Finally, let's stop mortgaging our future, and let's insist that our next Congress stop the racketeering in our economy.

The parity price structure for farm products will automatically make it possible to balance our budget within 12 months and make it possible for our nation to operate as a solvent business institution.

I have given you the key that will unlock the door to a prosperity such as this nation has never enjoyed.

## [3] THE OBSERVED FACTS OF THE SITUATION

Carl Wilken scoffed at "theories," and yet his *Pareconomy* gave expression to theory in its purest form. It did more. It explained the real frustration Wilken was to endure as long as he lived, because everything he said and wrote depended on "the intelligent cooperation of society." And society in all ages had prescribed conditions Wilken could not and would not comply with. A Law of Credentials was the first and chief of these.

An economist to be worthy of his salt (in the academic eye) has to have certain credentials. These credentials are not necessarily documents, although college degrees are necessary, but rather professional acceptance born of a willingness to earn one's way under the *old rules* before venturing into uncharted waters. More than one great thinker has been scuttled on grounds that his work contained irrelevant appeals to ethics, to extra-economic considerations, to questions that had been settled, that he didn't obey the rules, in short, and that the treatment of the subject was therefore not scientific. Up to the late 1920s, anyone who violated the Law of Credentials was automatically assigned a membership in the "underworld" of economics. Even today, anyone not entitled to speak can hardly dare do so and hope to have an idea evaluated solely on the merit of the idea.

"It would be laughable, if it were not tragic," wrote Colin Clark in *The Conditions of Economic Progress*, "to watch the stream of books and articles attempting to solve the exceptionally complex problems of present-day economics by theoretical arguments, often without a single reference to the observed facts of the situation."

*The observed facts of the situation!*

This single line by Colin Clark was cast for the benefit of men such as Carl Wilken, objectors who insisted that conclusions had to flow logically from the record, not vice versa.

Always, in every age, on the one hand there have been the ideas, and on the other there had been the social and political forces that made them work or kept them from working. Hardly an economist draws breath these days who has not taken on nourishment from those who have gone before. Very few of the great economic theorists—men of transcendental powers of reasoning—have been all wrong or all right, because none of them proceeded with the observed facts of the situation in tow. They could not. They did not have the tools or the data. They had only vision, but they could hardly check the accuracy of their vision.

If the Greeks and Romans be excepted, one must turn to St. Thomas Aquinas for the first real economic concept—*just price*—which was after all a "cost of production price," a concept later accepted and improved upon by French physiocrats: "The just price of an industrial good should be just as much over and above the cost of materials as the cost of labor." Those early Frenchmen saw clearly what created the wealth of a nation. They saw the necessity for paying the producer of raw materials a fair price, and having modified the findings, Mirabeau thought the *tableau economique* was an invention as important as printing. He believed that the economic law of gravity had been discovered and would become to human reasoning a monument more enduring than brass.

Wilken's concluding remark in the *Pareconomy* paper was much the same: "I have given you the key that will unlock the door to prosperity such as the nation has never enjoyed." To create wealth, Wilken joined the physiocrats in reasoning, a society must bring into being something that had not existed before—in a word, raw materials. The *tableau* recognized that production had to be priced properly at the raw material stage, or new wealth would not flow through the nation's economic arteries without disturbing effects.

It is not without interest that almost all writers still hail the physiocrats for their earnest attempts at a scientific economic system. In that age of faith the theory writers reasoned no one would disobey the Divine Law (once discovered) any more than they would disobey the Law of Gravity. Louis XVI's dismissal of Turgot as finance minister illustrates the difficulty of dealing with recalcitrant special interests by imposing a desired norm.

It was the reasoning of the physiocrats that caused the American colonies to put an end to exploitation by England, despite the fact that Adam Smith's *The Wealth of Nations* was published in 1775. Exploitations of one economy by another, one segment by another, always provided a neck-wringing turn to the goose that laid the golden egg. Slavers who exploited human beings thus got much of the capital that underwrote the industrial revolution in Europe, but left the African land no better off. England's exploitation of the American colonies finally caused old Ben Franklin, the best economic mind in America, and his associates to call for a halt to taxation without representation.

The observed facts of the situation made one thing quite clear to Wilken. Any economy not based on production was indeed a Las Vegas economy and contained the seeds of its own destruction. Changing the rules for the dice hustling did not alter the fact that new money must enter the casino. So far the money managers had contented themselves with borrowing money and injecting this into the economy, and to the unsophisticated the turnover of this borrowed money had erected what little relief there had been from the Depression. Looking at the economic indicators it became all too plain that the nation was spending this unearned money, but the debt was still on the books.

It was obvious to Wilken that manufacturing and industrial interests—national and international—consistently exploited their raw materials producer. This yielded instant profits, but ultimately dried up consumer purchasing power until finally economic collapse brought back balance. America, Wilken argued, could go on wallowing in depression, or name the level of its own prosperity. And the Farm Act of 1938 was not subject to creating very much prosperity.

## [4] THEY HAD TO JUGGLE THE FIGURES

The Farm Act of 1938 came into being, of course, and the formulas that Wilken said couldn't work became law of the land. The commodity loan system made use of a parity equation that George Peek and the McNary-Haugen bills had called for. But the experts still didn't understand the fundamental concepts behind the trade turn. In the final draft of the measure they let stand a calibration that in effect reversed the equation. They provided for a 70% loan if a crop was big enough to be considered 70% of normal. The calculation thus became 70% × 70%, or about 50% of parity if production results were less than disastrous. When I asked Wilken about the result, he answered as follows: "In 1939 there were rumors that they had to juggle the figures to keep the crop report down below 2,900 million bushels so they could continue the 75% of parity loan provision."

# CHAPTER 15: SUPPORTING NATIONAL INCOME

The confusion over whether a lack of buying power triggers a depression, or whether holders of investment funds fail to sense opportunities (as touted by the rate of interest, liquidity preference, and the like) is more manufactured than real. It seems extremely difficult to argue that in a society where tools are developed, factories built, and the state of the arts advanced, that investment leads the way, Carl Wilken pointed out.

Still the assertion that agriculture and other raw materials were the foundation of the economy seemed a hard bite to swallow for Congressmen, largely because their intellectual advisers had become impressed with gadgets, utility creation, and the happy standard of living that an industrial society seemed responsible for. Yet without bountiful agriculture, without efficiency of production preceding the rest of the economy and releasing labor for other pursuits, nations remained undeveloped.

Credit-injection and pump-priming—by making use of the multiplier—could rock an economy off low equilibrium, but unless raw material production was priced at a level of parity with all segments, the economy could starve in the midst of plenty, or be required to tune up the engine of credit expansion until it exploded.

## [1] A GOLDEN ERA

Shortly before 1929 the American people were being told that they had entered a golden era, that there would never be another depression. Yet from 1929 to 1932, international manipulators were able to trigger a 54% drop in farm prices. This 54% reduction in commodity prices was accompanied by a 54% reduction in the national income, or a 1% drop for every 1% that farm prices moved downward.

Did the drop in farm prices encourage consumers with more money to buy more manufactured goods? The record seems to indicate differently. Automobile production and steel production dropped off by 75% and from 1929 to 1933. The 25% of the working population that had become unemployed bought only as much as they could until their savings were exhausted, and then they became recipients of charity handouts. And people hungered in the midst of plenty.

During the 1930-1940 period, farm production was characterized as "surplus" because consumers did not have the money with which to buy. Economic dictionaries define food as having inelastic demand because demand ostensibly "increases or decreases in relatively small volume as prices increase or decrease," but these texts failed to take account of the elasticity of human suffering, and they failed to calculate the scope of improvement in food consumption available even in good times.

Through the decade of the 1930s, the American economy experienced a stabilized depression. In Wilken's words, the economy earned almost no profit. The amount of money injected into the system as public debt was offset by an almost equal amount of liquidated private debt. It was not until 1941-1942, when the pressure of a war economy allowed raw material prices to move up—back to the 1929 level—that the American economy emerged from the decade-long Depression. With the coming of WWII, farm prices moved back to the 1929 level. National income followed.

By 1942 all 12 of the Midwestern farm states were enjoying income at or above the 1929 level, and expanding production by 17%. From 1940 to 1943, according to the Wilken figures, gross farm income increased $12.4 billion. The national income increased approximately seven times this amount and moved up from $81.6 billion in 1930 to $170.3 billion in 1943. With an increase of 112% in national income, and under OPA price ceilings on a 1925-1929 level, surpluses vanished into thin air. People had the money to buy all the food the economy could produce. The stomach proved to be more elastic than anyone had visualized. Even while producing guns and airplanes, the American people enjoyed a higher standard of living than they had experienced during the Depression years of peace.

Very little of the increased farm production was moved overseas because German submarines enforced an embargo, and it was only with difficulty that Americans could feed their own servicemen abroad, men who would have eaten at home in any case, albeit not as well.

The necessity for equitable raw material price levels is not clearly understood by economists because as a class they do not understand either the basic underpinnings of the economy, or the economic reality of a global conflict such as World War II. And, too, many intellectual advisers to the community, sensing the needs of an institutional structure, fear that the principle of inelastic demand for food can turn abundant farm production into even greater economic chaos than that visited through the medium of low farm prices.

Needless to say, if there must be chaos, most institutions wish this chaos off on others. The mentality of the business operator is such that *all gain is not really earned, but achieved at the expense of others*, and that in denying parity at the raw materials level greater gain will be achieved in other sectors. Such thinking, which correctly reflects the common sense of the community, puts into motion institutional imbalance first, general economic imbalance second, and universal chaos in the end.

In the 1920's the Kansas State Board of Agriculture asked Wall Streeter Bernard M. Baruch to examine agriculture and to find a solution to the problem of chronic farm depression. The recorded findings appear in a report entitled, *Putting Farming on a Modern Business Basis*. Baruch in effect found that farming was uneconomic and inefficient because the farmer couldn't adjust his production to meet market conditions the way a factory could, and that the farmer was always at the mercy of nature. But Baruch's big point was that "agriculture's troubles were compounded by its organization, or rather its lack of organization." The individual farmer could not compete with the disposing end of agriculture and every sale the farmer made was a forced sale: he had to take whatever he was offered. His institutional arrangements failed to deliver the necessary countervailing power to effect stability. Baruch did not trouble farmers with a dissertation on international manipulation, and what all this had to do with the price of wheat in Kansas.

## [2] FARM ORGANIZATIONS

In a sense, all farm organizations have been addressed to this problem. Since the Civil War there have been hundreds of farm organizations characterized as "national" that have passed from the mind and memory of man. Without exception they were organized to repair their economic house. They ventured into buying and selling, into cooperative creameries, wool houses, tobacco pools, and they paid the price that goes with mismanagement, and they suffered defeat at the hands of politicians, and institutions that perceived their interests to run counter to interests of farm raw material producers, a view unconsciously shared by farm producers themselves.

"There is still afloat among the rural population a slow-dying tradition of the 'Independent Farmer,'" wrote Thorstein Veblen in *The Engineers and the Price System* (1919), "who is reputed once upon a time to have lived his own life and done his own work as good to him seemed, and who was content to let the world wag. But all that has gone by now as completely as the other things that are told in tales which begin with 'Once upon a time.'" It was a thesis that Veblen repeated again in *Absentee Ownership and Business Enterprise* in 1923, because the farmer's income was being fixed and eroded by "those massive interests that move in the background and find a profit in buying cheap and selling dear."

By buying cheap and selling dear, the "massive interest" traditionally drove farm prices down, drying up basic national income, thus pulling down the house over which greed presided. After 1929, it took World War II to break the spell of low farm and other raw material prices. Government had to construct parity prices for agriculture, ex-farm leader Wilken reasoned, because farmers were a lifetime away from constructing parity for themselves. And the rest of the business community didn't understand why parity raw material prices maintained national income.

## [3] THE FIRST CONGRESS

The Raw Materials National Council hoped to do something about that. When the First Congress of Industry and Raw Materials met in Sioux City November 14-16, 1938, surprising sophistication on the general subject surfaced immediately. J. Carson Adkerson led off. Mining was his forte and it was in connection with mining that Adkerson quoted a paragraph from the *Mining Journal* of Phoenix, Arizona. ". . . there are some who think that ores are natural resources upon which extra taxes should be placed because the wealth of the state is being depleted. The ores of today are created resources; ones which never before existed and which are now available because someone had the capital, vision, nerve, and engineering skill to make them of some value. . . . Mines are not found; they are made. They are created by hard work, capital, tenacity of purpose, research, management, and engineering progress. Such profits as may accrue from any or all of the contributing factors rightfully belong to those whose work made them."

Indeed, who deserved the reward? The creator or money? Or the combination that made wealth spring from the soil? O.L. Brownlee touched a similar theme as he defined the condition of the nation, a condition that "since 1930 has deprived the American people of approximately $235 billion of national or collective income that we could have had if national income had been maintained at the level of the average which existed between the flush years of 1922-1929 inclusive."

Carl Wilken recited his *Pareconomy* paper, of course, and fielded questions—questions about the 1-7 ratio, about soil conservation, about the Sioux City Bill [the Gillette-Harrington farm bill] and the rest of the topics that had to do with farm income or the lack thereof.

Q. What do you think of farm tenancy?

WILKEN. The farm tenancy is a very simple problem. I served on several debt committees and I have served on different boards to adjust differences of the tenant and the landlord, and 98% of those cases I would say grew out of the fact that the tenant couldn't pay his rent. Now, then, the only way to make it possible for the tenant to pay his rent is to put a price on the things he produces. And the same thing is true of ownership. You won't have any question of land ownership because then the farmer can buy a farm. If he is willing to operate it efficiently he can pay for it.

Q. How does the Sioux City Bill compare with the Eicher-Mc-Adoo cost of production bill?

WILKEN. The Eicher-McAdoo Bill and the Gillette-Harrington Bill in theory are the same. They both are striving for price. One is called cost of production and the other a parity price bill. Now then, if the parity price were put into operation and the farmer got parity he would get cost of production plus his share of the annual profit of the nation. He would have cost of production plus profit . . . it is immaterial to me how you do it.

Wilken was at his best when fielding questions. There were others at the podium, but it was to Wilken that most questions were directed because Wilken composed as well on his feet as he did behind the typewriter. Exchanges between Wilken and others on the program for three days running constructed a solid platoon of idea men, men who would sweep the country except for want of support.

There was E.H. Taylor, the associate editor of *Country Gentleman*: "Raw materials represent original wealth—wealth that is turned over many times in the operations of our economic system. . . . We have maintained the raw materials commodity index for eight years, using it along with a number of others to guide us in our business outlook. None of the others has matched it in fore-shadowing the rising and failing conditions of business activity."

There was F.X.A. Eble, Managing Director, Made in America Club, Inc.: "Armour and Company Plead Guilty in Misbranding Case, Admit Selling Siberian Butter as 'Made in U.S.A.' Judge Hulbert, we read, a federal judge of the Southern District Court of New York, imposed a fine of $300 which he felt was totally inadequate, and Mr. Gordon, Assistant United States Attorney, stated that Armour and Company shipped 16,000 pounds of butter to the state of Massachusetts, and that it was able to undersell domestic butter by two cents a pound because it was later discovered that the employees in Armour and Company's establishment in New York had repacked Russian-Siberian butter and labeled it 'Made in U.S.A. from Pasteurized Cream.'"

There was J.C. Mullaney, President, Sioux City Grain Exchange: "It is difficult for us to understand why Polish rye and Polish ham, Argentine beef and Danish bacon must be imported into the United States in order to insure an adequate meat supply for our citizens. We find it hard to believe that it is necessary that our domestic beef market should be invaded by products from Argentina and New Zealand. Our dairy men do not perceive the logic of being compelled to compete for the American butter trade with Lithuania and Finland."

There was M.C. Smithson, President, Southern Ores, Inc. "Years ago the infant industrial East realized that it could not compete with foreign manufacturers, and it is high time that we, the raw material producers, recognize that neither can we compete with the foreign raw materials."

There was Adrian L. Bowers, former Federal Farm Debt Conciliator: "I am not, and am not urging you to be apostles of calamity. I believe in the ultimate saneness and greatness of this country. . . . I believe the nearest approach to wisdom is the sober second thought of our people. Therefore, when this simple truth is presented—that there can be no prosperity for America until American agriculture prospers, then there will be a demand for parity and our voices. . . .will become the voice of the legion and will he heard."

And there was A.M. Loomis, Secretary, National Dairy Union: "One of the forgotten items of American agriculture and political economics has been the production of fats and oils and of oil-bearing materials. . . . The invasion of our domestic markets by this flood of imported fats and oils at the rate of nearly 6 million pounds, nearly 3,000 tons a day, follows three routes. One route is into the paint and varnish and floor covering industry (the drying oils), the second route is into the food industry (cooking oils, shortening, oleomargarine and salad oils), the third route is into the industries (soaps, lubricants, printing inks, and many lesser items). The powerful opponents of any concerted effort toward national sufficiency in fats and oils are the selfish industrialists who prefer to make big profits from cheap jungle fats, rather than pay fair domestic prices for domestic fats."

And there were others, present in fact or in spirit. Dr. Melvin T. Copeland of Harvard Graduate School of Business Administration, had published two important papers on raw material values and their relation to business conditions. Wrote Copeland: "Had it not been for the raw commodity price situation, the Depression which began in 1929 might have been mild and of relatively short duration. But, as raw commodity prices slumped, inventory values fell, losses mounted and more and more hesitation in buying transpired. Fear of further losses deadened initiative. At just that time, furthermore, substantial increases in production appeared in several raw commodity industries—copper, lead, zinc, oil, sugar, wheat, rayon and coffee. These additional supplies added to the demoralization of world markets, not only for these commodities themselves but sympathetically for other commodities as well. An epidemic of bank failures in the United States, which was caused in part by the slump in commodity prices, seriously aggravated a bad situation."

Such thinking was bound to leave its mark.

## [4] NASDA

Following the meeting in Sioux City, Wilken continued his research. He traced the income record of the nation from 1921 to 1940, and cemented into place the 1:7 ratio between farm income and national income. By 1941 he was able to publish his first income equation, or balance sheet, which was presented with a picture on the first page illustrating agriculture as one gear wheel driving the other six segments of the economy. The booklet had as its title, *Prosperity is Within our Grasp*. In due time a copy went out to each of the 48 members of the National Association of Commissioners, Secretaries and Directors of Agriculture, NASDA, because these elected and appointed officials had close ties with the political machinery of each state. "They had the prestige," Wilken pointed out. "So when they came to Washington and sent out invitations to members of Congress from the different states, there was a good turnout."

During 1941 and 1942, there were several meetings which from 100 to 125 members of Congress attended, dinner meetings that filled the lawmakers with food, yet left them hungry for more of the foundation economics that Wilken, Coulter and Ray supplied.

Although the NASDA-fed move was frankly political—to get a fair deal for agriculture—the meetings were nonpolitical party-wise. The NASDA members paid no attention to political sides of the aisle. Yet Commissioners such as R.A. Trovatten of Minnesota, Math Dahl of North Dakota, E.H. Everson of South Dakota (also a former president of the Farmers Union) were more than rank and file party representatives when they hit Washington. Their sophistication and rapport with grass roots thinking swayed Governors, Representatives and Senators—in short, votes! The real strength of NASDA came straight out of the constitutional offices of the old south— where Roy Jones was Commissioner of South Carolina. Tom Linder held office in Georgia, and James McDonald handled the Secretary's chore for Texas. Almost all the important Congressional Committee posts had through the decades become the private property of southern lawmakers. The NASDA leaders used their prestige to fill the halls for Wilken, Ray and Coulter, and they brought the farm groups together into a loose-knit coalition—13 of them at one time—to invite support for what Wilken and his associates were saying.

# [5] AN UNEQUAL PRICE BALANCE

Giving expression to these several principles in a language laymen could understand absorbed Carl Wilken no end. Congressmen and Senators didn't understand Lorenz curves, Sigma, or econometrics. "Keep it simple," Dr. John Lee Coulter warned Wilken. "Keep it simple."

Wilken kept it simple, both when tripping to Washington for conversations with Congressional leaders, and when feeding his findings to the Southern Commissioners of Agriculture, who had a live wire regional association. The rationale of the system had to come first. Here are a few paragraphs Wilken both printed and used orally, as taken from *Prosperity is Within our Grasp* and from a later re-issue called *A Prosperous Post-War Era is Possible*.

"The American people have become a group of specialists and have forgotten that each group is interwoven with every other group in an indivisible economy, with each group a multiple of the complete economy of the United States," Wilken told the Commissioners when they met in small groups and at sectional gatherings. "As special groups gain advantage over each other they immediately find that other elements of our economy, those which furnish the markets, do not keep pace with them in the consumption of goods and they all fall back in what is usually called a depression. *In fact a depression is nothing more than an unequal price balance between groups.*"

Always, Carl Wilken claimed that the real answer to the economic riddle had been obscured by "a lot of theory and political philosophy which never has worked in maintaining a stable price level or sustained prosperity. With an ample supply of raw materials and labor, proper pricing of goods and services should automatically create the income to exchange and consume our production."

The Commissioners had never heard of Say's Law of Markets, or Carl Wilken's modification thereof, so the heady stuff didn't matter, and Wilken could proceed simply and effectively.

"It is a simple fact that the financial measure of our economic welfare, whether individual, corporate or governmental, consists of adding up two columns of figures—income and disbursements. Regardless of what our theories may be, these two totals tell the story of our economic well-being."

Here is an edited abstract of Wilken's foundation concept as he expressed it to Congressmen and Commissioners during the months before WWII:

*Income consists of primary bartering power, which is created by the production and sale of new wealth—things obtained from the earth, farms, mines and seas—and earned income, which is derived from wages, interest and profits.*

*Disbursements include everything on the "outgo" side of the ledger, whether in the accounts of an individual or the government. Even the wages and salaries of those in public service must be regarded as disbursements, since public employees are not producers of wealth.*

*The amount of primary bartering power, or primary income, depends upon two things—the number of units produced and the price received for them by the producer. In the processing industries and professions the amount of income is governed by hours or days of labor times the rate of pay.*

*It is therefore fundamentally necessary that the total annual production of goods and services rendered, times prices, plus wages, interest, fees and profits must create an income large enough to pay for all the costs of operating the nation as a business. The total must pay for the costs of government, pay the cost of producing raw materials and for their processing and distribution.*

The approach was simple enough, too simple for the professionals who chose to barricade themselves behind the formidable complexities of their craft. But it made sense to men who understood agriculture, who frequently lived close to the soil, and reckoned income in the same homely way that Carl Wilken expressed it. Here, after all, was a nation with plenty of raw materials, ample factories, a developed system of transportation and a willing labor force—all the fundamentals of prosperity—and yet people were jobless, hungry, and farmers were going bankrupt with bumper crops in their bins.

Wilken explained why. "Our problem has not been one of production, but of distribution. We have been unable to get the necessary distribution of income, which in turn is ability to buy, into the hands of consumers. Our problem, then, is to put more dollars in the hands of the consuming public. This can be done only by increasing the number of units of production and by maintaining proper prices for the goods produced and of course by maintaining wages, fees, profits, interest rates, all of which supply income and in turn purchasing power."

The problem, Wilken told one group after another, was not money. There was plenty of capital to carry on business. The nation could have any level of prosperity it desired if it only realized that capital was not the creator, but the result of past earnings by labor and production of raw materials. People could live without capital. They could not live without real wealth.

Wilken was starting to get a little abstract at this point in his presentation, and he realized it. His next few lines straightened things out, and got the administrators back to earth again. "Having plenty of money in our capital reservoir reduces our problem to one of drawing the money from the reservoir in proper proportions, allowing it to circulate through the channels of trade and flow back into the reservoir."

How, then, could money be withdrawn from the capital reservoir soundly? There was only one way, Wilken argued. "The sound method of drawing money from the capital reservoir is by the annual production and sale of goods and services. In other words—earning it."

Wilken used a bushel of corn as an example. When the primary producer, the farmer, took the corn to market, the first step in the distribution system became a fact. The elevator operator was equipped with capital that had been created through the years of an expanding economy, and the savings of people. With his capital he helped make up, and in fact was a part of, the reservoir of credit dollars. When the price of corn was 80 cents a bushel, the elevator operator drew 80 cents out of the capital reservoir and paid the farmer for the corn. The farmer had earned the 80 cents by producing the corn, and to him the 80 cents constituted new money, money that offset the bushel of corn now part of the economy. The 80 cents did not have to be repaid by the farmer.

But, said Wilken, when the price of corn was only 40 cents a bushel, the elevator operator drew only 40 cents from the capital reservoir, "and simple arithmetic tells us that the flow of money from the reservoir in that case is just half as large as when the corn is priced at 80 cents."

Wilken took his little example all the way. "Compare this with the resale by the elevator operator. When he gets his check, he must first restore the 80 cents to his capital structure, leaving for him his margin or service charge."

.Now, what about the farmer. "The farmer spends his 80 cents with the grocer and the grocer has 80 cents of income with which to pay his overhead and reorder from the wholesaler, who in turn has income to buy from the manufacturers. This," Wilken concluded, "gives us a picture of how the agricultural dollar, passing from hand to hand, duplicates itself and its purchasing power."

Even as explained in schoolboy language, this message was something laymen could understand. The academic people could disagree, but if they were right why didn't their system work? The observed facts of the situation, Wilken challenged, contained the answer. Falling back on Charles B. Ray's "several wheeled economy" concept, Wilken presented his collected arrays of figures. The correlations proved too striking to be ignored. Each dollar of farm income translated into a dollar of factory payrolls and a grand total for all groups of $7 in national income or purchasing power. Although Wilken's figures covered everything from 1921 through 1938 at that time, the whole story was handed to the Commissioners in three whiplash lines:

|      | Farm | Income<br>Factory | National |
|------|------|-------------------|----------|
| 1928 | $11,700,000,000 | $11,400,000,000 | $82,000,000,000 |
| 1932 | 5,300,000,000 | 5,200,000,000 | *39,000,000,000 |
| Loss | $ 6,400,000,000 | $ 6,200,000,000 | $43,000,000,000 |

* After deducting $9,000,000,000 capital losses.

Here was a record of two years of actual operation in which physical production remained the same. Yet because the institutional arrangements of the market failed to maintain parity prices at the foundation level, at the farmer's tailgate, buying power was curtailed for factory products with resulting unemployment.

Wilken outlined three definite steps that had to be taken immediately:

1. Agricultural prices and industrial prices had to be returned to balance by basing them on a common index—preferably that of 1926.

2. The parity thus established had to be protected by means of tariffs geared to the same index. This was necessary to prevent foreign products from coming into the United States and underselling products of domestic origin, thereby rupturing prices of the home markets.

3. New industries had to be encouraged to consume for non-food and non-fabric purposes any surpluses of agricultural raw materials not required for human consumption, and to absorb industrial labor rendered idle by technological improvements in both farming and industry.

Shortly before the Japanese bombed Pearl Harbor, Wilken and his associates were alone in telling Congressional leaders why the depression continued to be a depression after ten years of nostrums that couldn't work. Agriculture had barely averaged 75% of parity all the while. And because the primary bartering power created by agriculture was only 75% of parity, there was only 75% of a full demand for other raw materials, labor remained only 75% employed, and collectively the American people had only 75% of the national income which they would have had under a full parity economy.

Before small conclaves in Washington, and from the stage of big meetings at Sioux City during the last of the pre-war months, Wilken sharpened his hyperboles and refined his mode of thought. His conclusion remained essentially the same when spoken and when published, as comparison between one of my tapes and this printed version confirmed.

"Under a system of economy whereby prices and tariffs are based on a common index it is possible to draw from the reservoir a supply of money sufficient to provide enough primary bartering power to yield an annual income ample to meet every need of society. When the proper amount of primary bartering power is supplied by the sale of raw materials, the turnover of the capital thus created, as it flows through the channels of commerce, will yield a sum actually seven times greater than the sum drawn from the capital reservoir by the sale of agricultural raw materials.

"It is possible to operate the national economy with a degree of exactitude comparable with the manner in which a life insurance company is operated. When average production can be determined, when the number of times the raw material or new wealth dollars will turn over in commerce is known, and the price point at which the maximum volume of goods will exchange is parity, we have a sound formula upon which to base our collective business operations.

"Under such a formula there can be no mystery about the functioning of money or the operations of credit. Money then would become a true and unvarying measure of value. Credit operations then would be sound because they would be based on known values determined by scientific mathematical calculations."

"Look," Wilken would say during the years after the Employment Act of 1946, GATT, the International Wheat Agreements, the International Monetary Fund, free trade and all the rest had put the skids to full parity and solvency for the economy. "Look, that's why this country was founded. The Revolution was a monetary war," and the nation that came into being as a result embodied in its Constitution complete rejection of free international exploitation. Ben Franklin, writing in *Positions to be Examined Concerning National Wealth*, April 4, 1769, figured there were only three ways a nation could become wealthy. It could make war and take the wealth of another by force. It could trade freely and make a profit by cheating, because the exchange of goods was beneficial only in increasing the variety of stuff a consumer could use, but to make a monetary profit (the real meaning of Franklin's statement) requires a policy of overpricing one product as compared to another. But a nation could profit through agriculture, where by planting the seed we create new wealth as if by a miracle.

That is why, Wilken pointed out, Subsection 5 of Section 8 of the U.S. Constitution authorizes Congress "to coin money, regulate the value thereof, and of foreign coin, and to fix the standards of weights and measures."

"Congress has fixed standards of weights and measures which never vary," Wilken said. "But Congress has failed, especially in recent years, to regulate the value of money in terms of goods as it is empowered to do.

"The third act of the First Congress was a Tariff law, the purpose of which was not to protect infant industries but to prevent cheap foreign goods and debased foreign currencies from determining the value of

American money in terms of goods, commodities, labor, etc.

"Many members of that First Congress had been members of the Constitutional Convention. They understood the purposes of the founding fathers. They knew that the intent of the Constitution was to establish a parity economy. They knew that economic equality and justice was essential to the preservation of political equality and justice."

Wilken almost always scored his points with simple illustrations.

"If two persons engage in a series of ten transactions and one has a 10% advantage [based on the first transaction] over the other each time, the favored party will have all the money or property and the other will be bankrupt after the tenth transaction." How income was recycled, in short, depended on continued stability of national income. Support for farm income therefore became support for national income.

Low farm prices explained why a third of the population lived in a state bordering on beggary on the eve of WWII, and why the great middle class was at the point of being wiped out.

## [6] I ADVISED

Well, what do we do about it? This becomes the inevitable question at each of the meetings. And several decades later I covered the same point by asking Wilken, "Exactly what did you tell them to do?"

"I advised the Commissioners to ask for a 90% support bill for basic farm crops because in my opinion the end results would average near 100%. A lot of people have asked me, 'What about 100%.' Well, as you know, agriculture produces a year ahead of time. In other words the crop from one year will supply the society while the farmer produces the next crop. If the farmer gets 90% at harvest time, remember he doesn't have to pay storage costs or handle the capital investment. In other words, he's really getting 100% of parity because he doesn't have to pay those other charges. And at the other end of the legislation, we didn't want the administration to dispose of any products at less than 105% plus carrying costs. In other words, what we really had during the ten years we operated under the 90% price support bill, we had a 90% floor and 110% ceiling. The 110% ceiling was to protect the consumers, so if the price started going beyond that level crops could be brought out of the stockpile in case of a short crop. One of the things that happened that made it possible to sell the Commissioners and Congressmen was that the records of the 1930s proved that in spite of all the New Deal legislation we had we never got back to the 1929 price level for farm products and gross farm income. Nor did the national income return to the 1929 level. Nor did the 12 Midwestern states—which produce 42% of the farm production—get back to the 1929 level. With the outbreak of war in Europe the competitive situation with imports fell off, and German submarines helped to prevent imports by sinking ships. And they also prevented our exports, so in 1941 our exports fell off $350 million. In 1940 our gross farm income was $11 billion as compared to $13.9 billion in 1929. The national income was $81.6 billion compared to $87.8 billion in 1929. And we still had 8.5 million people out of work. And we still talked about surpluses. From 1940 to 1942 we had an increase—the greatest two-year increase in our history—and by 1943 the value of farm production moved up from $11 billion to $23.4 billion. People were told those were war prices. That's a complete misrepresentation because the wholesale prices in 1943 were almost exactly the same as in 1925-1929. In other words all we had was a recovery back to the price which we should have had the common sense to maintain in the first place."

# CHAPTER 16: THE REAL ISSUES

But we didn't have the common sense to maintain prices for agriculture largely because folklore got in the way. The folklore of "unregulated private business," "the free market," "the market mechanism," and "regulation by competition," like Bram Stoker's undead, all continued to walk the planet despite the fact that death came many decades ago. Business enterprise itself buried the free market when it saw to it that competition could no longer survive. Indeed, many decades before Carl Wilken even thought of putting the pencil to corn prices "to see where the results would take me," super business had learned to administer prices, shade international dealings, and *weight* the advantages for dealings in the domestic economy as well.

## [1] A TROUBLESOME CHECK AND BALANCE DEVICE

John Lee Coulter, as a former Chairman of the United States Tariff Commission, filled in the details for Wilken. In summary form, Coulter told Wilken how Constitutional provisions were being circumvented, and how imports routinely ruptured the domestic price structure. The Constitution, after all, required the President to negotiate treaties and Congress to approve or reject them. As is usually the case at turning points in history, an emergency was perceived to exist. In 1933 and 1934 the President experienced no difficulty in gaining Congress a little side departure clause, one that made an end run around a troublesome check and balance device in the Constitution. An Amendment was adopted to the Tariff Act of 1930 which provided for "trade agreements." Trade agreements, the reasoning had it, were not treaties and therefore they avoided the unhandy business of having the details of international trade printed in a *Congressional Record* and hung out like dirty laundry for the world to see. The emergency that gave rise to the trade agreements ploy has never departed.

Speaking before the American Livestock Association shortly before WWII, Coulter pointed with damning finality to the fact that "Foreign countries are promised all manner of special advantages in the markets of the

United States in return for agreeing to suggestions from the United States as to how these foreign countries should conduct their own affairs."

With and without such political pronouncements, Coulter taught Wilken something about the investigational procedure. He schooled Wilken in the real issues, and showed him how to separate facts from catch phrases.

The backbone of Coulter's thinking was simply that "There are no isolationists in the United States and no free traders" because "90% of us are for something far less than embargo on the one hand, but far more than free trade on the others." The record proves his contention.

A century before World War II, only 5% of the nation's imports were on the free list; 90 years before the great conflict, 15% were on the free list; 65 years before Pearl Harbor, 25% were on the free list. By 1900 approximately 50% of the items imported could enter the nation free, and at the time Coulter instructed Wilken some 60 to 70% of the imported items were on the free list.

"High tariff did not cause depression, and low tariff will not restore prosperity. The tariff acts since the World War (acts of 1921, 1922 and 1930) averaged considerably lower than the average rates of duty in tariff acts for 50 years before the World War," Coulter said. And with the *Statistical Abstract of the United States*, issued May 1, 1939, he could prove that the protective tariffs did not set new high tariff rates, but tariff levels somewhat lower than the average tariff acts maintained for 50 years before World War I.

True, imports decreased fully two-thirds between 1929 and 1933, but this falloff was not caused by tariffs, since two-thirds of the imports were on the free list, and remained on the free list.

A little pencil pushing told Coulter something few of his colleagues even guessed. Imports into 109 countries averaged slightly more than $33 billion annually during the five-year period, 1925-1929. Then world imports dropped (in response to world-wide collapse in prices, especially on raw materials such as rubber, sugar, coffee, milk, tin, and many others). By 1930—before passage of the Smoot-Hawley Tariff Act—world imports had fallen below $29 billion, a decrease of nearly $7 billion. By 1931 imports fell another $8 billion, or to a level of $21 billion. A year later, imports fell another $7 billion, or to less than $14 billion.

"Just as the Tariff Act of 1930 had no measurable relationship to the world-wide decline in imports and exports, so, too," said Coulter, "the so-called Reciprocal Trade Agreements Act had no relationship to recovery."

Certain lessons emerged from all this. Coulter found that "whereas prices in general advanced about 20% between 1934 and 1937, prices of commodities on which tariff reductions were made decreased about 9.9%."

Thus it appeared that the concessions made by the U. S. in effect brought on the following general results.

1. They served to force farm prices down and prevented them from recovering.

2. They displaced farm products in the American market by encouraging an increase in imports.

3. They displaced factory products, thus causing unemployment in the industrial sector, and hurting the farm market by lowering the purchasing power of factory wage earners.

4. They thus became a factor in holding down factory payrolls because of the severe competition from foreign products, thus lowering labor's purchasing power and interfering with development of a profitable market in the United States for the products of the farm.

By 1937, duties on 47% of all dutiable farm raw materials had been lowered in homage to the Reciprocal Trade Agreements. Although the law also permitted increases in tariffs, none were made.

## [2] BRASH THOUGHTS

Super business continued to deal in platitudes, and run-of-the-mill economists continued to deal in mathematical models during the months before WWII, but some members of Congress were thinking new and brash thoughts. In the House and Senate chambers, a few lawmakers spoke of complying with a long-neglected Constitutional mandate, that of regulating the value of the dollar. On March 20, 1939, Senate floor activity took this turn:

MR. THOMAS OF OKLAHOMA [Senator Elmer Thomas]. Mr. President, from the Committee on Agriculture and Forestry I report back favorably, with amendments, Senate bill 1855, to relieve the existing national economic emergency by increasing agricultural purchasing power, to increase the national income, to make possible a balancing of the Budget, and, acting under the power conferred by section 8 of Article I of the Constitution, to regulate the value of the dollar in the interest of general welfare, and for other purposes; and I submit a report (No. 180) thereon. The bill has to do with the agricultural problem, but it involves and relates to monetary affairs; so I ask that the bill and report be referred to the Committee on Banking and Currency for the consideration of that committee.

It was so ordered.

This kind of thinking was a breakthrough for Wilken, because it sold an idea, and repudiated the *political confidence* ideas expressed by Carl Snyder in *Capitalism the Creator*. Wilken knew—if the bankers and super business folk did not, that *capital was really the result of progress, not the cause.*

The value of the dollar could not be regulated, obviously, if institutional business could dice up the country and field organized teams against the unorganized sectors of the economy. The Temporary National Economic Committee of 1940, 1941 had ferreted out some parts of the story. *Holding companies* and the *mature fortunes* were already current coin, placed in circulation by a fawning government with so little knowledge of its own history that it equated free enterprise with free international trade, and *laissez faire* with heads-up monopoly. Less than 15 steel companies dominated the industry, and hardly four produced 75% of the total. Some 20 companies had taken over the petroleum trade, with a half dozen in dominant positions. Hardly four companies dominated all rubber products. A handful ran the grain trade.

Wilken and his associates pointed out that there was something quite unreal about "regulation by competition" under the circumstances. The term *price leadership* had already become a fixture in the economist's lexicon, and still the academic set talked of free markets, and supply and demand for farm products. The converts to Wilken's thinking came on in small groups at first, then in platoons.

"What fixes the prices even under the most innocent circumstances, not to mention monopoly agreements, of such products as gasoline, tobacco, chemicals in a hundred forms, cement, lumber, agricultural implements, beef and pork, and cattle and hogs?" asked Senator Guy M. Gillette of Iowa. He asked it not to thank the question in pure academic form, or to recite how it stimulated activity between the ears, but to find answers. Here was a country in which 44 of 48 states maintained fair trade laws to protect "Swift & Co. and Armour," down to the final consumer, Gillette said, but hell would have no fury compared to what would be raised "if I should introduce a bill enabling the farmer to fix the price of a Poland China hog or a Hereford steer all the way from the farm through the slaughterhouse, to the regional distributor, down to the butcher shop in the sale of the consumer."

Super business had so many methods for control that they became a virtual catalog. There were the patents—"the strangle hold the patent monopolists have upon the products which the farmer buys. This extends all the way from the unending series of patented gadgets on agricultural machinery down through the various patented processes for making gasoline to the patented chicken feed which he feeds the hens. Even the medicine which he gives the children is likely to be patented or controlled by other means which makes it equally expensive," Gillette orated.

Antitrust and monopoly law enforcement had accounted for the Consent Decree in Chicago, but this merely prompted the big packers to scuttle the terminal markets, the free markets that copybook maxim insisted still existed. The rigged yellow sheet, the rigged bids at terminals, the rigged cheese market at Plymouth, Wisconsin, all meant farmers paid the bill and kept what was left over, or went into debt. Such conditions were routinely discussed by lawmakers during the late 1930s.

## [3] DURING THE 1920S

They had been discussed before. During the 1920s, farmers understood the folklore of capitalism better than at any time in history. Because of this understanding, the farm problem stood to the forefront as a political issue. To the farm bloc leaders who accounted for the Capper-Volstead Act, the Fordney-McCumber Tariff Bill, and finally the McNary-Haugen Bills, the free market that economists talked about, and the market price mechanism they touted was the most laughable thing in the world.

Between 1922 and 1928, farm leaders and farm oriented lawmakers not only structured the parity concept, but kept it in focus. George Peek* and all those who fought the McNary-Haugen battles reasoned that tariffs for industry put farm producers at a disadvantage. The free market wasn't free and it wasn't a market. It was an exploitative mechanism. Since the solvency of the national economy was a benefit to all, the McNary-Haugen backers fought for an export-debenture plan that made the cost of stability a national concern, rather than an industry expense. With a strong farm bloc in tow, the McNary-Haugen backers won twice, only to be cancelled out by Presidential veto and a Calvin Coolidge broadside. Coolidge charged that the measure aimed at price fixing, taxed producers, manufactured a bureaucracy, invited profiteering, stimulated over-production and sided foreign competitors.

The McNary-Haugen remedy died, but the problem didn't.

In 1928 the Republican Party promised agriculture the institutional business arrangements that farmers had never grown up with. The promise was fulfilled in the form of the Federal Farm Board, designed, constructed and launched to promote orderly marketing of crops. History has never handed down much of a verdict on this ill-fated effort, chaired and led by former Farm Bureau president, Sam Thompson. In any case, it lacked the broad-spectrum concept a depression situation required. By the time it was abolished in May 1933, it had accomplished little more than toy with the idea of price stabilization, and deliver a hard blow to farm prices in the wake of inept market dumping. It left its legacy—an abiding faith in production restriction, because handling surplus was perceived to be unworkable.

---

* The George Peek story is covered in *George N. Peek and the Fight for Farm Parity*, by Gilbert C. Fite.

# [4] A COMMODITY DOLLAR

Dump, destroy or prevent surplus has almost always been the name of the "protect farm income" game. Here and there a scholar-type has arisen to recall Joseph in the Bible,* or ancient Peru's ever-normal granary, but in the main "conserving the production" has had few advocates.

Slain pigs notwithstanding, most of the New Deal measures tied the "prevent surplus" idea to a concept of "conserving the production." The early support programs worked to the extent that they were subject to working. Carl Wilken, the NASDA chiefs, and all the recent converts argued that less than full parity meant continued exploitation of the farmer and continued depression for the nation.

By 1937 Congress had learned something about what was really the author of economic collapse. As John R. Commons correctly pointed out in *The Economics of Collective Action*, two grades of security owned by the banks had become the trigger mechanism, because in "enforcing those two grades of security, the banks bring on two kinds of business depression, illustrated by the commodity depression of 1920 and the securities depression of 1929."

The commodity depression of 1920 was brought on because businessmen were compelled to unload their inventories for cash in order to make good bank commitments. This, Commons pointed out, was quite different from the 1929 affair, repeated in 1937, both of which were triggered by forced sales of securities.

In 1935, writing in *100% Money*, Irving Fisher published a finding that seemed dazzling in its purity. Fisher proposed 100% reserves for banks, some of which could be cash, some of which would be kept in government bonds. With the knowledge that forced sales of government bonds

---

* The role of Joseph is usually misunderstood, as Emil Ludwig clearly points out in *The Nile*. "Out of the vagaries of the elements, the seven years failure of the Ethiopian rain and the Nile flood, he made the ruler of the country, faced with revolution and overthrow, owner of the whole land . . . [Joseph] calculated his dictatorial power in advance for the time when famine would come and the people would find Pharaoh the sole seller of corn. So they came and offered him first all their cattle, then their bodies, then their lands if he would only give them food."

Goethe touched on the genius of Joseph, who "saved Egypt from starvation by foresight and wisdom, and at the same time put the king into possession of the land by an unprecedented speculation." Goethe had his Mephistopheles, do the opposite—that is create fraudulent inflation for the emperor much as have government economists during the post Korean War period in the United States.

Former Georgia Commissioner of Agriculture, Tom Linder, summed up the "Joseph lesson" in his *Timetable of Bible Prophecy* as follows: "As soon as Joseph moved the people to the cities and he had taken legal title to the land; then he moved the people back to the fields. But they went back as servants of Pharaoh."

is always fatal to stability, the Fisher plan called on government to redeem its bonds at par simply by issuing legal tender. The general idea here was that money would be force issued at precisely the time it was needed to head off depression. Interest-bearing bonds, instead of compounding and strangling the economy, would be exchanged for non-interest bearing legal tender money.

The Fisher thesis prompted a Columbia University professor named Benjamin Graham to develop the idea that in fact became the Coulter-Ray-Wilken parity approach, the monetization of basic raw materials.

In *Storage and Stability* Graham argued for the establishment of a new money, a commodity dollar, that could circulate the same as if it were a silver dollar, Federal Reserve Note, United States Note or National Bank Note. Let Gresham's law decide which money was best, Graham suggested. Under the plan, some 20 basic commodities—everything from steel ingots to wheat—were to be supported by the government. "The only expense connected with instituting and maintaining the Monetary Storage system is the cost of storing the various commodities in the unit," wrote Graham. "The actual acquisition of the commodities does not involve any expense or entail any annual interest charges, for they pay for themselves by qualifying as the backing for currency—in the same way as our gold and silver reserves have always done."

At parity, full monetization of raw materials thus became an interest-free way of creating money, with only the physical storage cost as a deficit. Storing gold and silver had never posed much of a problem. Storing wheat and zinc was only slightly more difficult. In any case, the scheme made money meaningful to people.

People understand physical reality. They do not understand the metaphysical money system under which the nation now operates. Even college graduates do not understand the fact that the money supply is literally a creation that takes place with each credit transaction. Some of those with degrees in business do not know that the banker creates a non-interest bearing debt and exchanges it with the bank customer's debt for a similar amount plus interest with each loan. This is deposit money, a currency created with a transaction and extinguished with another transaction. Coins and folding money, now stripped of any real tie to physics, are equally fiduciary—that is, dependent on confidence, good faith.

How little the present money system can be understood by reasoning from physics is illustrated in this imaginary dialogue between a Socrates from another planet and an economist.*

---

* The conversation between the economist and Socrates first appeared in *Lloyd's Bank Monthly Review*, May 1939. It was reprinted in *The Economics of Collective Action*, by John R. Commons.

SOCRATES. I see that your chief piece of money carries a legend affirming that it is a promise to pay the bearer the sum of one pound. What is this thing, a pound, of which payment is thus promised?

OECONOMIST. A pound is the British unit of account.

SOCRATES. So there is, I suppose, some concrete object which embodies more firmly that abstract unit of account than does this paper promise?

OECONOMIST. There is no such object, O Socrates.

SOCRATES. Indeed? Then what your Bank promises is to give the holder of this promise another promise stamped with a different number in case he regards the number stamped on this promise as in some way ill-omened?

OECONOMIST. It would seem indeed to be promising something of that kind.

SOCRATES. So that in order to be in a position to fulfill its promises all the Bank has to do is keep a store of such promises stamped with all sorts of different numbers?

OECONOMIST. By no means, Socrates—that would make its balance-sheet a subject for mockery, and in the eyes of our people there resides in a balance-sheet a certain awe and holiness. The Bank has to keep a store of Government securities and a store of gold.

SOCRATES. What are Government securities?

OECONOMIST. Promises by the Government to pay certain sums of money at certain dates.

SOCRATES. What are sums of money? Do you mean Bank of England notes?

OECONOMIST. I suppose I do.

SOCRATES. So these promises to pay promises are thought to be in some way solider and more sacred than the promises themselves?

OECONOMIST. They are so thought, as it appears.

SOCRATES. I see. Now tell me about the gold. It has to be a certain weight, I suppose?

OECONOMIST. Not of a certain weight, but of a certain value in terms of the promises.

SOCRATES. So that the less each of its promises is worth, the more promises the Bank can lawfully make?

OECONOMIST. There are complications, Socrates, but it seems to amount to something of that kind.

SOCRATES. Do you find that your monetary system works well?

OECONOMIST. Pretty well, thank you, Socrates, on the whole.

SOCRATES. That would be, I suppose, not because of the rather strange rules of which you have told me, but because it is administered by men of ability and wisdom?

OECONOMIST. It would seem that that must be the reason, rather than the rules themselves, O Socrates.

# [5] MONETIZATION OF RAW MATERIALS

Carl H. Wilken considered the Graham book too heady for instant translation to Congressmen and refused to use the term, *monetization of raw materials* until the year before his death. He and his associates preferred instead to sell the basic principles of the foundation nature of raw materials, the trade turn, and the fact that stable raw materials in fact support the national income. A full 90% of parity law, they reasoned, would accomplish the same thing.

By early 1939, the Wilken concept of full parity had made fantastic inroads. Speaking of the general concept on the radio, Congressman H. Carl Anderson of Minnesota called it "a prosperity measure for every man, woman and child in America. It might just as well be called a business revival bill or reemployment act of 1939." Every Senator voted with the concept at one time or another during the end year of the decade.

Why? Because, in the words of Representative John W. Flannagan Jr. of Virginia, "for every dollar you add to the farm income you add $7 to the national income. . . . There is a direct relationship between the farm income and the national income. As I stated, $1 in farm income produces $7 in national income. Why? Because the farm dollar, like the laboring man's dollar, is not hoarded but goes into circulation. It is the dollar that makes the wheels go round."

And failure to make the wheels go round had a fantastic social cost attached. All of this was pure Carl Wilken economics, with or without footnotes. On the eve of WWII, Carl Wilken handed the first complete set of tabulations over to the National Association of Commissioners, Secretaries and Directors of Agriculture. In no uncertain terms, the state-level farm leaders were told exactly what the 1930s had cost each state because the farmer was being paid for less wealth than he produced.

# [6] HARBINGER

Working with Wilken, Ray and Coulter, the state Commissioners, Secretaries and Directors of agriculture, by 1941, had convinced most of Congress that full parity was a requirement for private enterprise, not just a sop for the hoemen. Only one turn of events remained before Wilken and his small band of Cassandras were to reach an unreachable goal.

A harbinger of that turn of events came to Des Moines in February 1941 to appear before the National Farm Institute. He was John Kenneth Galbraith who spoke as economic adviser to the Agricultural Division of the Advisory Commission to the Council of National Defense. Agriculture had a responsibility, Galbraith said, namely that of furnishing adequate food and fiber materials, and their group aims would therefore have to be subordinated to national policy. But, he admitted, "If the common man can buy beefsteak and pork chops because he has a defense job, surely he can be given a job which will enable him to keep on buying when the world again becomes secure."

# CHAPTER 17: THE STEAGALL AMENDMENT

Did Congress in 1942 really understand that by supporting farm prices at full parity they were supporting the national income?

Carl Wilken said: "Enough of them did."*

Wilken and his associates, NASDA officials included, had testified and taught ever since Wilken's first balance sheet brought the Raw Materials National Council and the agricultural chiefs of the several states together. The little groups met every available afternoon and night, consuming the hours in a manner only intriguing subject matter could account for.

## [1] TWO- OR THREE-MAN MEETINGS

In the one-, two- or three-man meetings, Wilken's comments stayed fairly close to a fundamental outline. Industry, agriculture and labor, in order to pay the taxes would have to earn the income with which to pay them. "Their income is limited by the number of units of goods and services produce times the price per unit," Wilken told the House Ways and Means Committee shortly after the Japanese bombed Pearl Harbor, "As a result, the two fundamental factors which this Committee must take into consideration are production and price, because they determine the income from which you must obtain any taxes that may be levied."

If Congress chose to destroy the purchasing power for goods normally produced and required, then it would also destroy the income derived from this production, Wilken testified. And in so doing Congress would destroy the tax base. National income could not be maintained without full production from agriculture and a full price for that production. The war effort required more, not less income. And there was only one way to increase income—production times price!

"Labor is basic to all production," Wilken testified at one point. "If we

---

* I met with Congressman Wright Patman on June 2, 1970 to discuss this. Patman said the Committees didn't "buy" the principles Wilken was talking about, but that a great many Representatives and Senators did. He agreed that with or without fanfare they incorporated their thinking in their votes. Former Congressman Hoeven confirmed this by letter. Other survivors of that era who knew Wilken have told me essentially the same thing.

were to increase our units of labor 25% and thereby increase the units of raw materials produced 25%, the same average price that prevailed in 1941 would give us an added raw material income for 1942 to the extent of $4.5 billion and increase our retail sales $13.5 billion."

Before committee after committee Wilken recited the raw materials equation—the observed fact that under existing state of the arts national income moves on a direct ratio to farm income. Always, he reminded that Congress had the authority to regulate the value of the dollar until the idea fairly spilled over and inundated both chambers.

The ideas Carl Wilken expounded were many and varied. Wilken updated for the House Ways and Means Committee the import-export observations John Lee Coulter had recited earlier, and with plain arithmetic he put down the conceit that the Smoot-Hawley Tariff had brought on the Depression in the first place.

"The Reciprocal Trade Agreements did not expand exports of farm products," Wilken told the lawmakers "and the overall picture, comparing industry with the farm, is this: In the period from 1934 to 1939, industry exported approximately $10 billion of manufactured goods, and we imported about $3 billion of manufactured goods. The farmer, on the other hand, who was to get the benefit, exported $6 billion of farm products and was faced with an import of $10 billion. In other words, during that period we had a net import of about $670 million per year, which, when translated into American dollars and production, was the equivalent of about 50 million acres annually."

Wilken reminded the lawmakers that out-migration from farms required new industries, and one that was being scuttled by the going concerns in America was the farmers' alcohol industry. As a son of the corn-belt, Wilken had watched with keen interest when Iowa and Nebraska farmers first took their farmers' alcohol idea to Washington, with blessings from the State of Nebraska in tow.

"We were greeted with enthusiasm by the President and all members of the Congress we talked to," wrote Donald Despain, one of the Committee members who had journeyed to Washington in the early 1930s to see if alcohol couldn't be made a required additive for gasoline. "All agreed 'this is the solution to the farm surplus problem. . . .' Then something happened! The petroleum industry . . . launched a $2 million campaign to defeat the Farmer's Alcohol Blend Program," summarized Despain in *The One and Only Solution to the Farm Problem*. Now, with war a grim reality, Wilken reminded the lawmakers of farmers' alcohol, and his testimony helped the program surface again.

During WWII, use of a 50% alcohol additive in aviation gasoline kicked up the speed of American pursuit ships by approximately 50 m.p.h. B-29 bombers also used 100 proof farmers' alcohol. When gasoline was 21 cents a gallon, farmers' alcohol was economical up to a $2.00 per bushel corn price. Alcohol also became the raw material end of synthetic rubber production during the war. Three plants were established by the Defense Plant Corporation, upon recommendation of the Baruch Committee, in grain-production areas—one at Kansas City, Missouri; one at Omaha, Nebraska; and one at Muscatine, Iowa. After WWII, farmers' alcohol plants were discontinued. Senator Gillette investigated farmers' alcohol after the war, but his Committee produced little more than proof that the idea was feasible and that the oil industry wouldn't permit farmers' alcohol in motor vehicles, not if the entire nation choked on pollution. Except for a recent paper by Milton Ericksen at the University of Nebraska in which alcohol figured as a third-degree price discrimination marketing device, the farmers' alcohol idea has just about disappeared from the scene. Circa 1970, the nation's pollution concern might have revived it, but didn't.

## [2] FARM PARITY

But in the main, Wilken talked farm parity, because without parity, production times price would not generate the income necessary to pay for the war. The survival of the establishment required farm parity. Without it, inflation and a brand of fascism would become the heritage for all Americans.

"No other major belligerent has accepted either the alternative of rising prices or that of strangled production," editorialized a booklet prepared by the OPA in 1942. "All have insured full production within the framework of stable prices. They have done this by using subsidies to insulate the cost of living from rising production costs." OPA economists understood how to keep production coming in industrial America. They understood next to nothing about the farm plant.

The Emergency Price Control Act of 1942 came on with startling speed when the war arrived. It put a ceiling on farm prices at 110% of parity, but carried an absolute prohibition against ceiling on wages and salaries. One clause tells how unions made their point at a time when farmers didn't.

"Provided that nothing in this act shall be construed to authorize the regulation of compensation paid by an employer to any of his employees."

The very nature of the "war" problem required parity for every sector, yet somehow the public prints, and those whose opinion on economics was worth at least as much as their opinion on brain surgery, literally pilloried those who wanted full parity for basic farm commodities, and a full income for America in an hour of maximum danger. President Roosevelt himself suggested the frame of reference for the war effort:

"We shall not stop work for a single day. If any dispute arises we shall keep on working while the dispute is solved by mediation, conciliation, or arbitration—until the war is won. . . . We shall not demand special gains or special privileges or advantages for anyone, group or occupation. . . ."

## [3] FARM BLOC

But there was this unique nature of farming to be considered. On the Senate floor, Senator Charles L. McNary recalled for his colleagues the old Marketing Act back in 1929. Vast sums were loaned to the cotton and wheat farmers at that time under the auspices of the Farm Board. "Later it was determined by the Farm Board to throw that accumulated stock on the market, with the result that wheat tumbled in five weeks from 74 to 38 cents a bushel. There is no factor in all the field of agriculture that is so depressing as a surplus owned by the government. I can foresee what would happen to the farmers if this surplus were dumped on the market. The price would eventually go very much below parity."

The 1938 Agricultural Adjustment Act provided a loan rate of not less than 52% of parity on all agricultural commodities except corn. Corn enjoyed a slightly higher rate. But the Department of Agriculture almost invariably fixed the loan rate at the minimum allowable, despite the fact that many Senators and Representatives requested a loan rate nearer the maximum, 75% of parity. Loan rates were fixed at 85% of parity by an Act of Congress on May 26, 1941. The floor set by government tended to become the ceiling simply because farmers had no institutional arrangements for making it any different.

And, in essence, that was what Carl Wilken had iterated and reiterated during countless moonlight seminars. As a result, Farm Bloc lawmakers had held for a 110% parity ceiling and a 90% floor during the opening months of WWII, and it was this concern that caused statesmen such as John H. Bankhead of Alabama, Guy M. Gillette of Iowa, Elmer G. Thomas of Oklahoma, Richard B. Russell of Georgia, and Scott Lucas of Illinois to be labeled traitors to the war cause. "Farm Bloc Hits Again" read the February 12, 1942 editorial headline in the *Boston Herald*, because in the opinion of the paper men were dying with General Douglas MacArthur while "these United States Senators concentrated their efforts on forcing up the price of cotton, wheat corn and other basic farm commodities still further so that some of their constituents might exploit the national emergency more handsomely."

This general attitude persisted, and in 1942 when a parity adjustment measure was under consideration, the cartoon that met Washington readers one morning showed the Farm Bloc sleeping peacefully dreaming of fabulous riches. A clock on the table indicated approaching midnight. Ambassador Grew was saying, "There's a war on, and we are in it for keeps." Price Administrator Nelson was shouting through a trumpet, "We are not winning the battle of production." General Hershey was ringing a bell and crying that every man had to be a soldier. The President was trying to shake the farmer awake. And through all this the Farm Bloc slept. The title of the cartoon said, "It seems to be a case of sleeping sickness."

## [4] THE STEAGALL AMENDMENT

The Steagall Amendment and the support measure that accompanied it simply called for 90% of parity for farm commodities during the war, and for a two-year period after the war. It was this approach to stabilization— an approach few administrators and no editorial cartoonists understood— that brought on the ire of businessman, government expert and newsman alike. During WWII, and ever since, there has existed a lot of confusion regarding the Steagall Amendment. Loosely speaking, the Amendment has been thought of and mentioned as a complete farm price support bill. Actually, the Steagall Amendment applied to non-basic commodities. Steagall commodities were hogs, eggs, poultry, milk and butterfat, dry peas of various varieties, some edible beans, soybeans for oils, peanuts for oil, flaxseed for oil, regular and sweet potatoes, and American-Egyptian cotton. The Steagall measure permitted USDA to support prices "through a commodity loan, purchase or other operation." The price support program at full parity rested on the Agricultural Adjustment Act of 1938 and the Stabilization Act of 1942, as amended, which required the Commodity Credit Corporation to make loans at 90% of parity on corn, wheat, tobacco (with certain exceptions), and rice, and on cotton at 92.5%, for crops harvested through the two-year period beginning with the first day of January immediately following the date on which the President or the Congress declares hostilities to have terminated. Thus the basic commodities actually constituted a second class of agricultural commodities for which price supports were made operative. A third class of farm commodities involved permissible rather than mandatory supports under the CCC, Section 32 funds—*purchase to remove from the market, and discovery of new uses for commodities*. The term Steagall Amendment, however, came to be used by many laymen as a synonym for the full support program.

Through 1942, debate on agriculture rarely faltered. Farm Bloc lawmakers, instructed by Wilken and Coulter, wanted full parity and a permanent basis, but there was the usual burr under the saddle—the American Farm Bureau Federation. How the Farm Bureau stalled and fought a fair deal for farmers emerged July 7 on the Senate floor, when Senator Gillette made public a letter he had received from the Farm Bureau over the signature of Edward A. O'Neal, president.

"I wish to convey to you the position of the American Farm Bureau Federation [on] . . . mandatory loans at 100% of parity prices for corn, wheat, cotton, rice, tobacco and peanuts. I wish to advise that the federation has never asked for government loans at 100% of parity, and that this measure does not have our support." O'Neal went on to point out that 85% of parity met more with the Farm Bureau's pleasure, if the government would only quit dumping.

Some of the most damaging testimony against fair treatment for agriculture came from Price Administrator Leon Henderson: "The President asked for legislation to repair cracks in the dam against inflation. This bill is a heavy charge of dynamite at the very base of the dam. It also lights the fuse." Here, obviously, was a man Wilken hadn't convinced.

Nor were many of the dollar-a-year men in Washington convinced, nor were the bureau people who hammered out booklets and war propaganda. On September 15, 1942 OWI's *Victory* headlined: "President Asks Curb on Farm Prices."

President Roosevelt always enjoyed the stage during that year. Congressmen were constantly being "firesided," and "I do not like to be firesided," taunted Congressman Charles L. Gifford of Massachusetts. "The microphone really endangers the existence of this legislative body." Facts had to stand on their own hind legs. In the final analysis they couldn't be put down by rhetoric and a well modulated voice. And the fact was that farm prices in July 1942 were only 54% above the 1909-1914 level, whereas the average factory workers now enjoyed an hourly wage rate 397.1 % above the 1910-1914 level, and this was well above the World War I peak of 278.7. Still the *New York Times* and the *New York Herald Tribune* hammered farmers mercilessly, and regional papers followed suit. All this stung, and it raised a question, as Congressman Gifford politely pointed out when lawmakers were being asked to vote on whether labor costs should be computed as part of parity. "Keep in mind that the President has condemned this amendment and that he has firesided you before the public as selfish and special class and, as he said, 'unpatriotic?' Ought not you farmers to be ashamed of yourselves to so embarrass your President? Can you prove to his public that he is wrong and that you are right? You have my sincere, best wishes."

The Farm Bloc believed themselves to be right, and they understood exactly how the farmer always became the "goat" in a war. The primary materials that fed and put clothes on the backs of armies were produced on farms. Everything from the farm became vital in a war, especially one in which enemy submarines suddenly cut off outside supplies, that distress prices were hard to maintain. Still, as Congressman U.S. Guyer of Kansas told the House, "The farmer is not profiteering," and the details that followed in the *Congressional Record*—either as spoken or amended remarks—chewed up column after column of print.

## [5] SENATOR GUY GILLETTE

Senator Guy Gillette in fact served up the best proof of all even before the Steagall Amendment was voted upon, and it contained Carl H. Wilken logic most of the way. After all, "70% of the new wealth is produced on the farm," he said. "And if the farmer closes his factory for the season that wealth is never produced." It was "not processed wealth," Gillette went on, "but new wealth which, in turn, is divided with the dentist, the doctor, the lawyer, the railroad man, the laborer, the factory worker, the millionaire, and the tycoon. Every one participates in that product when it is processed and made ready for use."

Gillette had no fault to find with the President's proclamation, or the practice of telling industry to proceed with production while cost-plus contracts were being written. But, he said, when that same government agent went to the farm he did not offer to figure costs and promise the farmer cost-plus.

Now consider labor. The government agent says to labor, "We are going to continue in effect our support of wages, of a wage scale, under our wage-and-hour law, which fixes a minimum. We are going to maintain the prevailing wage for your section of the country; and if you work overtime we shall see that you are paid time and a half for overtime and for Sundays and holidays. We are going to protect the purchasing power of labor."

But the farm parity idea was being hammered to death. It took unusual courage for a majority of the Congress to stick with an idea that almost all the professional economists either pooh-poohed or ignored entirely, but men such as Gillette were lawmakers with rare courage, and also men who had maintained their rapport with the problem. Guy Gillette, after all, had driven through the ranks of Milo Reno's pickets while campaigning, and then gone home to milk his own cows. He could and did recall for his colleagues the remark of an Easterner: "For heaven's sake, Guy, what is the matter with your people out there? Are they always going to be in the position of having to live out of the public treasury? I cannot understand your agricultural community. Have they not enough manhood, have they not enough stamina to stand on their own feet and conduct their own business."

This taught Gillette a lesson. People didn't understand. They did not understand that the Wagner Act and the Wages and Hour Act—as Congressman Rankin of Mississippi said—"raped the farmers.... That is exactly what these legally imposed inequalities are doing today. . . ." They did not understand, first, that without the raw material dollar there could be no labor dollar or profit dollar. All this was too much for people who hadn't spent hours in Wilken's "classes." And for this reason those who reasoned with Wilken relied less on Wilken's exact arguments, and more on common sense persuasion.

## [6] LOSING ITS FARM PRODUCTION

And common sense persuasion started with the proposition that the nation was in danger of losing its farm production. Congressman H. Carl Anderson had gathered up 42 auction bills out of one week's issue of a district newspaper. "Having Decided to Quit Farming," read the notices, or "Having Sold My Farm," or "My Sons Have been Drafted and I am Compelled to Leave the Farm," or "Moving to California."

Congressman Dewey Short of Missouri put it this way: "Common sense tells us that if the farmer cannot receive the cost of production he simply cannot produce. When the farmer does not produce, there is a scarcity and scarcity always increases the price of any commodity. The best cure of prevention of inflation is abundant production. Abundant production cannot be achieved by placing a ceiling on farm prices."

Farmers had to have parity, or food and fiber production would lag! Who could deny it? Like it or not, for the time being at least, the nation would have to pay its board bill. Experts could argue at cross purposes about inflation, but this matter of production contained its own logic, even for those who could barely endure the thought of higher farm prices.

## [7] A STABILIZATION BILL

The theory of tying commodities, wages, salaries, and the other factors entering into living costs to a date when some stability existed was illustrated by William H. Davis, Chairman of the War Labor Board, when he delivered his statement to the Banking and Currency Committee:

"As I understand it [section 6, of the bill being considered] proposes to tie industrial wages to the prices of agricultural commodities. That is, it proposes to tie together the two variables which we are jointly seeking to control. If you had one horse harnessed to a mowing machine and another horse harnessed to a farm wagon and you were threatened with a violent storm, you would not hitch the two horses to one another. You would, I think, hitch each of them to an appropriate hitching post which you knew from past experience was firm and stable enough to keep each of the horses from running away. I think that is what we do when we tie farm prices to the parity provided in your bill and tie wages to existing wage levels, with adequate provision in both cases for adjustments of substantial inequalities which result in manifest injustices."

It was all quite simple, argued Congressman Charles S. Dewey when he got the floor. "If farm prices advance over parity the wage earner's dollar will buy less, hence his real wages are lower. If, on the other hand, wages increase too rapidly, parity gets 'out of kilter' as far as the farmer is concerned because manufactured articles increase in price to cover wage raises." This kind of talk made the Steagall Amendment and parity a stabilization device in a very real sense, because full parity for six basic commodities—wheat, corn, cotton, rice, tobacco, peanuts, plus a few others would in fact determine the farm price level across the board. If not, why then farmers would shift to growing wheat, corn, cotton, rice, tobacco and peanuts faster than it took to write a farm bill. Moreover, the measure permitted the President to make adjustments for *gross inequities* that might develop.

Half of the dairy workers between 18 and 30 had walked off to take defense plant jobs or gone into service during the past year. Crops, said Congressman Clarence Cannon of Missouri, "are rotting in the fields. . . ." Preparations were underway for rationing of beef and pork, and at the same time millions of tons of beef, pork and mutton were being thrown onto the market before they were finished.

Such arguments leaned on logic that could not be ignored, not when butter rated rationing, not when stamps and coupons were fast becoming a way of life for those on the home front. But the Wilken point that came home strongest had in fact become a workday dictum in Washington. The nebulous substance of that dictum found itself lodged in the cadenced rhetoric of President Roosevelt, and though it may have been merely a platitude at that high level, down in the chambers—where Farm Bloc leaders remembered real farm hardship and real farm suffering, down where a memory of manure on boots and endless hours hadn't faded entirely, the President's words meant what they said:

"The farmer, instead of looking forward to a new collapse in farm prices at the end of the war, should be able to look forward with assurance to receiving a fair minimum price for one or two years after the war. Such a national policy could be established by legislation."

## [8] AN ANTI-INFLATION BILL

Congressman Fred L. Crawford of Michigan was a close friend of Carl Wilken. At times he loaned the hard-pressed Wilken use of staffers in doing research work, typing manuscripts and proofreading. More than most he had absorbed Wilken's fundamental proofs, and on September 22, 1942 he stood up to expound some of those proofs. "Mr. Chairman," Crawford said, "this bill is not supposed to be, in the mind of the public, a special piece of class legislation, for the benefit of any one group. It is supposed to be an anti-inflation bill. . . ."

Crawford threw down the President's own words as a gauntlet. "After all," President Roosevelt had said, "parity is, by its very definition, a fair relationship between the prices of the things farmers sell and the things they buy. Calculations of parity must include all the costs of production including the cost of labor." Crawford did a lot of "yielding" that day as debate was passed from one Congressman to the next, ring leaders of which had attended Wilken's little seminars.

Through all the farm fights, a handful of full parity supporters held out for a permanent bill, but the idea of a grace period after WWII sounded reasonable, and when the act in question came to amend the Commodity Credit Corporation Act to the extent of requiring the Secretary of Agriculture to make loans at 90% for a period of two years after the first of January "following the time when the President proclaims an end of hostilities," Farm Bloc lawmakers picked up an ear.

## [9] THAT VERY TEMPORARY VICTORY

The National Association of Commissioners, Secretaries, and Directors of Agriculture had sent over their papers, of course, but their five points also reflected something less than the lessons Wilken had talked about. Uniformly the farm groups, acting individually, or as a loose-knit coalition, pointed out that "the best protection against inflation is abundant production." They really didn't understand Wilken's economic package.

Wilken realized all this. Full parity had won by default. It had until after the war to make secure that very temporary victory.

# CHAPTER 18: WHAT THEY DIDN'T KNOW

Parity was in, but Carl Wilken could see the gathering storm. The signs had been around for several months. There was this business of divide and conquer, the very stuff Congressman Clarence Cannon of Missouri characterized as "a time-honored ruse of the enemies of agriculture," this business of having one commodity fight the others. And there was the administrative ploy, the bureau power structure that saw Price Administrator Leon Henderson clash with Agriculture Secretary Claude Wickard over lard and other oils and the production thereof because "Henderson's office saw a need for a ceiling on steamed lard, but not one for refined lard."

Southern lawmakers were disturbed about the $82 a ton top for peanuts, which was barely 55% of parity. There was a reason for all this, and the reason would one day erupt in Committee, before Congress and all of farm country, U.S.A.

"I want to take you down the road a little ways on this oil problem," argued Congressman Clevenger. "You remember the time we had 45 cents on hogs in 1940. That was about exactly the price of a pound of imported vegetable oil, plus the duty. It was about 4.5 cents that it cost to bring in palm oil and coconut oil, cottonseed oil from Brazil, and so forth. It set the price of hogs and thus the price of our corn. It brought distress and distress brought legislative panaceas. . . . Gentlemen, Henderson Field is right in the middle of Lever Brothers' coconut grove."

## [1] TOPICS WERE VARIED

The lessons were finding a mark, Wilken realized. When Congressmen got to thinking in terms of the language being spoken on the floor of the House and Senate in 1943—["You will find that the price of wheat at Liverpool was the lowest since the day of Queen Elizabeth. It was kept at 55 cents a bushel on our western farms by a subsidy averaging 28 cents per bushel in 1939."]—then this was proof that the name of the game could be explained long before the Steagall Amendment came to term.

Senator Albin Barkley already understood. Senator Richard Russell understood. Senator Young understood. The list was growing. President Roosevelt could and did veto various measures designed to iron out farm inequities, but the common denominator for prosperity couldn't be touched, not until two years after the war was over.

Wilken made speeches all year long in 1943. From the podium he was introduced as "educational director" of the National Association of Commissioners, Secretaries and Directors of Agriculture, or some such salutation that tied him to NASDA, and though his topics were varied, he always came back to a central theme—the fact that agriculture was the flywheel and the balancewheel of the economy.

Speaking before the National Food Conference at Chicago in mid-September, he scored again a foundation idea, "that raw materials, especially farm production, is the foundation of our national economy." He reviewed the production situation, the import situation, the land reclamation situation. And he ended on a note that claimed first attention during the mid-war years. ". . . if we maintain farm price parity, we cannot have a depression in the United States. We can have a solvent nation and help the rest of the world organize a prosperous economy, instead of one that exploits, booms and busts."

## [2] ROCK HARD ANSWERS

NASDA hadn't met in convention in 1942, and the war had run until November 29, 1943 before the organization met at the Statler Hotel, St. Louis. Carl Wilken had been given a spot on the program "as a representative of Dr. John Lee Coulter."

It was one of Wilken's best presentations, doubly so because at the end he fielded questions and handed out rock-hard answers. Wilken called the great American experiment *people's capitalism*. It was a form of government, he said, that had handed the right of free enterprise, the right to own homes or businesses under rules of government that protect the individual against the exploitation of a more powerful neighbor. That something awful had happened had come transparently clear during the years when equities, homes and property were wiped out by a "so-called depression." All this came about, Wilken said, because there was a general lack of understanding of the fundamental economy. It was this lack that the NASDA officials had better repair while repair was possible.

Wilken traced the origin of the American nation, not in deep charcoal lines, but in light pencil, and he explained now as he would in hundreds of other talks about "why" Congress had been given the power to issue money "and regulate the value thereof." "They realized that the power to regulate the value of the dollar automatically carried with it the power to exploit the production of our nation through the medium of low wages and low prices for goods.

"They realized that, in order to buy, the laboring men and other producers must have dollar income, the medium of exchange that the Constitution provided. By giving this power to Congress, they gave to the people the right to provide proper price levels and, in turn, sufficient money with which to exchange their products."

Here are most of the paragraphs in Wilken's NASDA speech.

## PEOPLE'S CAPITALISM

In that section of the Constitution we have the framework for distribution, the proper flow of money from production. We have the groundwork for equitable distribution of capital holdings and in turn the distribution of capital earnings. This is our system of capitalism as compared to large holdings of natural resources and exploitation of labor as prevalent throughout the rest of the world. It was money in the hands of the public that made it possible for our nation, with only 6% of the world's population, to buy 70% of the automobiles, 54% of the tin, etc. that the world produced.

In the days of our forefathers they lived on the land and over 90% of our economy was agriculture. Raw materials from the farm were processed on the farm and there was little need for trade. Hence, money was a minor item in their way of life.

They were not overwhelmed by the importance of money and believed that actual production should determine the value of money rather than to have money determine the value of wealth. To them, food, clothing and shelter were the essential things. Money, to them, was purely a medium of exchange and it was their purpose to regulate the value of the dollar so that there would not be a shortage of money, our exchange medium, with which to exchange production of goods and services.

A surplus of production was always welcome to trade for manufactured goods from the mother countries.

To protect the right of Congress in regulating the value of the dollar, the first session of Congress passed a tariff act for revenue and for the protection of the price level of goods and services in the United States. That the tariff is a monetary measure and a protection for our dollar value has been little recognized by our citizens.

At no time in our history have tariffs been abandoned as a protection for our price level. The result has been higher wages and prices in the United States than in the rest of the world.

With production turned into dollar income and, in turn, purchasing power, we had distribution of goods and developed rapidly. Manufacturing flourished with the use of abundant raw materials of all kinds. New production times price created income which translated into more capital savings available for more expansion.

Incentive of gain and ownership instilled in our citizens the desire to forge ahead and, as time passed, one new territory after another was developed and brought into use for an expanding population and consumption. Word was sent back to the mother countries concerning this land of promise and a stream of immigrants helped increase our natural growth.

Tracing through our economic history from 1850, manufacturing expanded in ratio with the growth of our agricultural areas. This was a natural result as agriculture has constantly produced the greatest part of all raw materials.

This expansion continued rapidly and by 1910 we had taken up most of the natural farm land—that with natural rainfall and soil fertility. Since that time a leveling off has taken place. The number of farms has decreased as we as the open spaces that could be had for the asking. The number of employees in manufacturing also started to level off in ratio.

In spite of the fact that since 1910 our farm acreages harvested has increased only 6% as compared to a population increase of 42%, our progress continued. With tools of production in the farm and factory, the efficiency of these two groups increased their per man production at a rapid rate.

This increase in efficiency allowed new industries to come into being. Labor, as a result of the increase in population, was drawn off into the service fields such as government, schools, medicine, dentistry, recreation, transportation, servicing of automobiles with tires, electrical appliances, gas, etc. This factor has generally been overlooked by most of our economists and they think only in terms of industrial employment, little realizing that manufacturing, as such, employs only about one out of every five laboring men. This increase in our service industries needed for a higher standard of living has a very marked effect, however, in our economy. It increased the trade turn of the initial farm dollar created by production of farm products.

In 1910, for example, each farmer was producing, roughly, enough for himself and 3.4 other families. The trade of the farm dollar, therefore, was one plus 3.4 or 4.4 times. As a result, in 1910 the national income was 4.4 times the farm income.

By 1921 this trade turn had increased to a 7-times turn. Due to the efficiency of the farmer, he was then producing enough for himself and six other families. The trade turn then became 1 plus 6 or 7. In other words, each dollar of farm income in 1921, as it passed through trade channels, created a total of six more. The average of the trade turn of the farm dollar in the period 1921-40 was approximately 7 times.

With this ratio in existence it was only natural that the income spirals up and down with the rise and fall of farm prices could become quite rapid, yes, even vicious. When translated into higher units, it means that for each loss of $1 billion of farm income, the nation will lose $7 billion of national income. Therein lies our failure to keep an even keel and maintain the distribution of goods.

## THE GROWTH OF DOLLAR INCOME

Having reached the point of natural expansion of our agricultural re-sources—those areas provided by nature with rainfall for crop produc-tion—our increase of population brought our production and consump-tion into approximate balance. No longer were we dependent on a world market for our surplus nor on a price influenced by world conditions. The law of supply and demand rapidly brought farm prices into balance with industrial wages, and for the first time in our history the farmer came into his own. In the period 1910-14, we had the first period of five years when, under normal conditions, we had equal exchange values for the products of the farm and industry. The result was tremendous prosperity and the era is often referred to as the Golden Age of Agriculture. The point of equal exchange in recent years has been used in calculating the proper value of farm crops, using the term parity prices.

This period brought into fulfillment the vision and hopes of our forefa-thers for economic equality in terms of the dollar. In this period we find that the dollar value was 100 cents and, on the average, for all groups. That, in essence, is the meaning of parity and under a people's capitalism the parity price level is the level at which we have the greatest distribu-tion of goods. The parity price level is the key to distribution. It is also the point of our maximum need for foreign goods.

Then came World War I with its increased demands for exports of farm products. The increased dollar exchange from higher farm prices and government borrowings increased the wages of labor. In our desire for more farm production we plowed up the semi-arid sections and increased our harvested acreage 12%. It was a coincidence that this increase was in line with the increase in population.

Because of the additional demand and additional income of our citi-zens, our prices advanced rapidly and a national income that had aver-aged 31 billion in the five years from 1910-14 rose by leaps and bounds.

Increased per man production on the farm and in the factory increased the trade turn and in 1920 we found ourselves with a national income of $71 billion.

The fall of 1920 was the end of the second harvest in Europe after the Armistice in 1918. They again were in production of farm products, and the economic law that goods flow to the highest market commenced to exert its influence. Our farm prices, with reduced tariffs, brought about during President Wilson's administration, started to drop in the latter part of 1920. The politicians called it coming back to normalcy.

The farm areas, and they include about 38 states in the union, exercised the power of the ballot to elect a new administration. In 1921 tariffs were revised upwards, the drop in farm prices was halted, and we started off into a higher level of national income. The new price level was approximately 169% of the 1910-14 level. With our population able to consume our own production, except in the case of wheat and cotton, again we had a new normal or parity period in 1925-29.

During this five-year period, our national income averaged approximately $78 billion instead of $31 billion in 1910-14. Part of the increase was due to the 69% increase in unit prices, and the balance was due to increased production. Because of replacement of horse power with motor power, we were able to take the acreage consumed by horses and mules and translate it into a marked increase in dairy products and vegetable production. Our basic crops of corn, wheat, oats, rye, barley and flax, which are the foundation of feed, however, remained practically constant. For example, in 1896, we produced 2,671,000,000 bushels of corn from 89 million acres, with an average of 30 bushels per acre. We have not been able to average that much in the years that followed. In 1943, we will have 94 million acres with a yield of approximately 32 bushels per acre. In other words, our corn production has become almost a constant and can be increased only through a greater use of fertilizer and more intensive farming.

With the increase in national income in the '20s, our people had the income to make the automobile a part of their living standard. This industry developed rapidly and by 1929 our factories were pouring out 4.5 million cars per year. Other items such as tires, gasoline, filling stations, became necessary and gave employment. Our petroleum industry grew apace and furnished increased demand on transportation.

The increase in income made it possible to levy fees for car licenses and taxes on gasoline, thus, we had the funds to start building one of the largest and best highway systems in the world. Many people think of 1929 as a boom period, but it was not. It was a period when, again, people's capitalism functioned in distribution; it was a period of progress, development and prosperity such as the world had never witnessed.

All through this period we maintained the basic parts of people's capitalism. In developing the great areas west of the Alleghenies, we carried out a policy of individual ownership of resources. Instead of selling the land in the middle to some capitalist, through the Homestead Laws, we provided for division of our land resources into small farms of 160 acres. This led to the springing up of over 6 million individual capitalists on our farms. It led to the building of our rural communities with their small factories and individually owned business institutions. It provided for distribution of income.

## DEPRESSION OF 1929

The Depression of 1929 was attributed to the stock market crash, but that was the finale of the show and not the opening act. The opening act was a reduction in raw material prices, starting in 1925 and culminating in 1929. The reduction in raw material prices can be attributed to our financiers' desertion of our people's capitalism in search of what they thought were higher profits in other lands.

Instead of developing the United States, they invested their money in foreign sources of raw materials, sugar plantations, mines, oil wells, and so on. After bringing their various projects into production they faced the problem of marketing and turned their eyes to the United States. Through one method and another, tariffs were reduced and evaded by depressing prices in other countries. Raw materials started to flow into the United States, destroying the foundation of our domestic income.

The drop in national income in 1930-'31-'32 ratioed approximately 7 times the drop in farm income. By 1932 our farm income had dropped from $11 billion in 1929 to $5 billion. National income had dropped from $83 billion in 1929 to $40 billion in 1932. With $45 billion less income in 1932 we had a shortage of money and all commerce was paralyzed. Our automobile industry, for example, had dropped from 4.5 million cars in 1929 to 1.26 million in 1932.

Farmers were being set out in the road by sheriffs. Angry farmers in turn were dragging judges off the bench in the northwest section of Iowa and were refusing to sell farm products. Millions were unemployed, factories were idle, and people were starving for want of food.

Yet, there had been no crop failure nor had a surplus been produced when compared with previous years. The farm production of 1932 was almost identically the same as in 1928 and 1929. Our population had increased about 4 million and any surplus that existed was created by the loss of $43 billion of purchasing power because of low farm prices. Purchasing power is determined by income. In 1932, the people, again using the power of their ballot, put out the old and elected a new administration which came in as the New Deal.

## THE NEW DEAL

The New Deal was ushered in with a deluge of promises, better prices for the farmer, social security, reduction in taxes, and a job for everyone. To bring this about, a program was initiated so contrary to people's capitalism and so contradictory of common sense and arithmetic that it was a complete revolution in economics. It was decided that we could become more prosperous by producing less and working less. Pigs were slaughtered by the millions, crops were plowed under, *thus destroying the very materials for labor to use and fashion into finished goods for trade and commerce.* Under the WPA, a disgrace to people's capitalism, men were put to work at non-productive labor that was degrading to human morals. Their wages were paid from a mortgage on tomorrow's income. We were to become prosperous through debts and government doles.

Even though this program was against all rules of economy and arithmetic, the stress of economic conditions made willing servants out of our people. Mayors from practically every small village, and the mayors from our larger cities, all started to trek to Washington to bow their knees in supplication for relief projects to be paid for by a mortgage on our citizens. After that happened, let us not say that dictatorship cannot happen here. Our people proved, like those of other nations, their willingness to accept anything under the stress of economic conditions that usually precede a dictator.

All of this occurred in spite of the fact that we had the real wealth for prosperity without a dole and without a mortgage on our children. All that we had to do was to use the foundation of our forefathers for regulating the value of the dollar under a people's capitalism. The one step that would have stopped the depression in six months—restoration of farm price to par, or regulating the dollar value at 100—was ignored with the exception of a corn loan and other commodity loans at about 52% of parity.

Thus, our nation found itself leveled off into a condition of enforced depression. Our financiers in this country and other countries had not learned a lesson from the Depression. The farm program was brought forth by them under the theory that they could better give the farmer a check to keep him satisfied than to give him a proper price. They still did not realize that he could buy only half as much with $500 for his corn crop as he could if he had received $1,000.

To pay for their exports of manufactured goods, the financiers imported many products from their acquired sources of production in other lands. These imports displaced our own farm crops which were destroyed and not produced by plowing under and curtailment.

## THE WAR AND LEND-LEASE

One of the amazing factors of our present situation is that 6% of the world's population has taken it upon itself to furnish materials for all those who have none. Our economists, who are directing the government, have a dollar complex and have asked Congress to appropriate funds in an amount that even those who ask for them cannot comprehend. As proof, I would like to point out that the Byrd Committee in July, 1943, reported that from the beginning of the war and up until July 1, 1943, the government had spent $110 billion for war purposes and that $244 billion remained unexpended. Why the unexpended balance? The answer is simple. The theorists who made the estimate of appropriations had no conception of production and thought only of appropriating money, a habit acquired prior to the war. The nation just couldn't produce the things that they wished to buy.*

These huge appropriations did much to dislocate our domestic economy, and thousands and thousands of small businessmen have been forced to close their doors because of lack of supplies. Liquidation of small businessmen, or any other owner of property, means liquidation to that extent of people's capitalism, so badly needed in the postwar era.

*The total value of all goods sold at retail in 1941 totaled $53 billion, and yet the theorists were ordering goods in terms of $100 billion per year for war purposes. And, the poor farmer was blamed for inflation.*

Of all the things we face, the one of food is the most tragic. We have promised people all over the world that we will feed them, when the facts are that we can not produce for our own use if we wish to maintain our American food standards. As I have pointed out, since 1910 we have increased our harvested acreage by 6% while our population has increased 43%. Because of the war, the imports have been shut off. Higher prices have restored the domestic buying power and our people want to buy food that is not to be had.

In spite of the fact that Nature, in 1942, gave us the most bountiful crop that we have ever had, there is not enough for them to buy. The production of 1943 has fallen off because of weather conditions that are beyond human control. Crop production has fallen off and livestock will have to be liquidated to meet the level of feed crops produced. Washington is talking of a cereal diet. Conditions actually may become that serious.

---

* See pages 358-361 for comments by Walter Bowers.

# HOW CAN A PRICE BE MAINTAINED?

It can be done by maintaining a price balance between six or seven of our basic crops such as corn, oats, wheat, barley, rye, flax, and cotton, the foundation of all farm production, and the price of finished goods as reflected in some normal period. In other words, if, in the postwar era the General Commodity Index, which reflects industrial prices, is 10% above the normal period 1925-'29, then those initial farm prices must be 10% higher than the 1925-'29 average, or vice versa.

Does it mean regimentation? No! There need be no curtailment of production. Why should there be? With each initial farm dollar creating $7 of national income, there will always be $7 to consume any additional production or to dispose of it to other nations even if required to take the extreme form of charity. In the period of 12 years, 1930-'41, we could have given away $63 billion of goods and services to other nations, and if we had maintained our price level, we still would have had $400 billion more of income than we had.

A good merchant maintains a price on his product. If he develops a surplus he has a sale and then spreads the markdown over the whole. In the same way, any cost of properly maintaining prices becomes a minor item, indeed, as compared to the loss we took because we did not maintain a proper price for our production. During the 12-year period, we could have given away all our foreign trade and charged it to profit and loss. This, of course, could not be necessary, but it is foolish to worry about foreign trade when it is such a minor part of the whole in a nation that is richer than a dream of Midas. With only 6% of the world's population, we have 25% of the available raw material supply. Why worry about foreign trade when we have everything, except a few minor items, in abundance?

Of course, we have been told that we depend on other nations, but again facts disprove mightily. Today, in 1943, we are taking care of our own 135 million people, putting into the armed forces more men than any of our allies except Russia and, at the same time, producing more war materials than all the rest of the nations together. What are we using to produce them? We are using our own raw materials, our own factories, our own labor, our own transportation, our own finances, and yes, we are even lend-leasing by the billions of dollars goods and services. Those facts cannot be denied. In like manner, in the postwar era we can produce plenty in the United States and if we price it properly we can have prosperity such as no nation in history ever had.

We may require a tariff to protect our price and the theorists will howl, "isolationists," little realizing that they themselves, through low tariffs, would bring about lower prices, lower income and in turn, less purchasing power for both domestic and imported goods.

A good example is that of rubber. In 1929 we produced 4.5 million automobiles. This required rubber for tires. In 1932 we produced only 1.25 million cars because of low prices and low income. The result was a direct curtailment of rubber purchases, not because of a tariff but because of inability to buy the cars which would have required the rubber.

## POSTWAR PRICES

If the rest of the world will adjust its price level to our parity level as a yardstick, there need be no tariffs. With our price level as a yardstick, the world can, for the first time in history, have a sound international price level and monetary system. If that should happen, the money-changers will be forced to give the people of other nations a decent wage. Then the world can have distribution of goods. Then we will have a foundation for peace. What chance is there for a Chinaman to have freedom with an annual wage of $65? What chance has he for an education? What chance has he to buy a tool of production to increase his efficiency? What opportunity do our factories have to sell him an automobile or an airplane? Yes, and finally, what chance have our missionaries to teach Christianity in the face of exploitation that is contrary to Christian doctrine?

# [3] PRICE DISLOCATION

Structured perfectly, Wilken's talk took premise after premise, proved them all, then developed his unshakable syllogism.

Wilken concluded his lecture with a long quote from Christopher Hollis' *The Breakdown of Money*. It was the passage in which Hollis pointed out that free international trade required a price dislocation between nations, and that the financiers' policy required them to "so reduce the purchasing power of the American people that they can no longer even approximately consume their own products." The rest of that quote told the story—all of it.

"As long as that purchasing power was adequate, the American manufacturer was indifferent to foreign markets. But with domestic purchasing power reduced, foreign markets become essential to him. And, the more that he could be persuaded to look abroad for this market, the easier it will be to change his whole attitude toward wages. At present he is in favor of high tariff and high wages, for he looks on the working man as his customer. But, if he can be induced to look abroad for his markets, then wages become merely an item of costs and it is to the manufacturer's interest to reduce them as low as possible. If they are reduced—and the odium for reducing them of course, allowed to fall on the manufacturer—then American industry becomes at once a much more profitable investment for the financier, while the foreign goods can flow into free trade America to pay the interest on the foreign loans."

Could Congress be persuaded? Could men who habitually gave up reading the minute they were elected be persuaded to become students again? Carl Wilken and John Lee Coulter believed the impossible was really possible if, somehow, these lessons of economies could be tied to the politician's rule of survival—knowing how to count! The NASDA members who had come to St. Louis in November were perceived to be the key. They had political ties with Senators and Representatives in each of the states. They could use their influences to make them listen, because in the final analysis most lawmakers did what they did simply because what they didn't know, they just didn't know.

That Wilken had struck fire became evident within moments after he concluded his remarks that day. Commissioner Tom Linder of Georgia led off.

"About this inflation," Linder said. "Isn't it true that the only major threat of inflation is paying out money by the government that isn't supported by the production of any civilian goods or raw materials?"

"That's right," Wilken replied. Up to the present time, November-December 1943, there had been little inflation, however. The 35 principal commodities were at 106 on the index, with 1926 as 100. "The principal reason why people seem to think we have had inflation is because that for 10 to 12 years they have been buying their groceries cheaper than they should have been able to buy them. They bought them at the expense of 10 to 12 million men out of employment." The war, in effect, had returned prices and income to levels that the nation should have maintained anyway, Wilken pointed out.

## [4] THE QUESTIONS

Here is an edited transcript of some of the questions NASDA members were asking Wilken in 1943.

VOICE. Can this [government] debt ever be paid unless we return to parity?

WILKEN. No, it cannot. You can liquidate the national debt if you operate your nation as a business and you release your national income. In the final analysis it depends on this initial foundation. In the postwar period, if you want $150 billion national income the first thing you have to do is create a raw material income. I will give you this little example. In 1929 we had a national income of $83.3 billion. Then we came up to 1942 and we have $119.7 billion. The price, however, is the same approximately as in 1929. You see, we get the difference between $83.3 billion in 1929 and $119.7 billion in 1942. We earn it by producing more units of farm products. There are two factors in income: One is the number of units, and the other is the price per unit. If you price your product properly you have money to spare and automatically exchange it with somebody else, but you must produce.

VOICE. Is there any disposition on the part of the federal government in the planning program to see that, or are they not able to see it?

WILKEN. They have a conflicting [economic theory]. They had had it since they got into power. On the one hand they were spending money to maintain the price, and they were reducing tariffs to keep the price down.

VOICE. Why should not the Directors of Agriculture of the various states realize their responsibility and assume the responsibility of writing a law and present it to Congress, and don't you think now is the proper time for the Commissioners, Secretaries and Directors to get together on such a farm program?

WILKEN. If the Congress of the United States would in the next three to four months pass a permanent parity price bill for farm products and tell the public of the United States that they are not going to have a depression, you would have the greatest wave of confidence sweep over the U.S. you have had for a long time.

VOICE. The only sure way to prevent inflation is by assuring the farmer through parity prices his fair share of the national income, or his fair share of the consumer dollar?

WILKEN. That's right.

VOICE. Mr. Wilken, will you assist the Commissioners of Agriculture in this meeting in writing up such a program to present to Congress?

WILKEN. Absolutely.

VOICE. I just want to ask another question, Mr. Wilken. Wouldn't this price subsidy that is now being considered give to the United States government all the power of price fixing? In other words we will surrender our state rights, we will in effect, say, take this now and do what you want to with it.

WILKEN. No. Let me help you think this through. One part of Mr. Thatcher's [H.K. Thatcher of Arkansas] statement pointed out we ought to combine the various credit agencies. You have a Farm Credit Administration. Part of that Farm Credit Administration is the Production Credit Association. Production Credit Association could make all the loans. Give your Production Credit Associations out here in the area under control of the farmers the power to make these loans, backed up, of course, by the government of the United States. In regard to prices, parity price is not a fixed price, never has been and never will be and your price is determined by arithmetic, not by the government. Ceiling prices of finished goods will determine relative prices of farm products. It is a matter of keeping your prices in balance. The minute the Congress of the United States passes a bill providing for 100% parity and providing for prices on basic crops, you would not have to make any loans through Commodity Credit Association. Your local banker would make the loan. You would have the government out of business. You have a law of supply and demand which says supply and demand will govern prices. You still have left out a factor, and that is the supply and demand to foreign trade. That will have to enter into there if you are going to use what we always consider the American medium of exchange, based on gold. In the postwar era if we were to take gold at $35 and we would adjust silver up to that level, which would make it about 97 cents, then take six basic world crops and maintain them on a par with gold, you would really, add those six commodities and silver to your monetary foundation. Up to the present time you have used just that one item—gold.

VOICE. Isn't it a fact that there is where the government would have to come in?

WILKEN. Your Constitution provides for that because it gives Congress power to regulate the value of the dollar. You cannot have a stable dollar or regular value of the dollar unless you have stable commodity prices all in balance one with the other.

VOICE. I have been in this fight for the commodity dollar for a good many years, ever since [it was proposed]. If you are going to change the popular sentiment of the United States away from the gold standard you are going to have to perform miracles. If we could get a committee—get Congress to appoint a committee and have this presented to Congress, we might at least have something brought in definite before Congress that we could get support for.

WILKEN. With your commodity loan, you can slip up on them. It was the best minority measure that was ever invented. You automatically establish relationship between the commodity and the dollar when you do that.

VOICE. I think there is a definite relationship between the income of agriculture and the national income, but I am at sea when it comes to how we are going to set up and stabilize parity prices to the farmer without the government perhaps entering into a subsidy program, a thing that this Association has decried definitely. I am wondering just how, or what forces are going to be responsible for setting up parity prices to agriculture without price fixing, a thing that I don't think we are altogether in favor of, and without subsidies. If we could just say that it must be done and will be done and that would turn the trick. . . . Personally, I am not clear as to how you are going to set up prices if the legislature ignores the question of supply and demand, and hold it where it ought to be. . . .

WILKEN. I would say this. . . . You forget that through your commodity loan, for example, you provide the flow of money into your channels of trade to make it possible for the law of supply and demand to work. We know we can produce 2.5 billion bushels of corn annually. Arithmetic tells us at $1 per bushel that would be $2.5 billion. At 50 cents per bushel it will mean only half that much. In those seven basic crops, if you maintain parity you could have $2.5 billion from corn, $1.5 [billion] from cotton, $1.25 [billion] from wheat, and so on. That is a definite known income you are going to produce. You establish the price through your commodity loan. If you do that and protect it with a parity tariff you cannot have a depression in the United States.

VOICE. Mr. Wilken, we would have to disregard taking care of the rest of the Americas if we adopted that plan, would we not?

WILKEN. No. It would make it possible for us to help them.

VOICE. When you determine your parity formula—I would like to see those seven or eight commodities extended to include some others. Part of our fight would be to get a basic formula that would be approved by everybody.

WILKEN. From the studies we have made, I would frankly say that—for instance, cotton—in my estimation it could be adjusted about 5 cents a pound. My reason is that cotton has always been in competition with world prices, while some of our other products have not. In all fairness, the price of cotton could be adjusted above the 1925-'29 base.

VOICE. What figures are you going to take in—to fix your parity. We have had a controversy in Washington over including farm labor. We did bring taxes in. These things have got to be settled before you can figure your actual parity on these things over a period of years. Congress, or somebody, has to determine what parity is.

WILKEN. It doesn't matter where you start. Suppose we take the 1925-'29 relative price level. Suppose Congress decides it is not high enough. We will adjust it 10% above that. Because of this trade turn, in six to nine months that 10% will automatically translate into an equivalent increase to the rest of the nation. The one factor you want to keep in mind is this, like everything else your economy has to have a beginning and if you take those seven crops which constitute 85% of your harvested acreage in the United States—take those seven basic crops and forget everything else. If after you have done that it is necessary to have some marketing agreement for other items, for the sale of milk in some areas, for instance—we have a number of things already working—but these other crop levels will adjust automatically. You talk about, for instance, the cost of hauling a ton of freight, the cost of sending a telegram. That is fixed by law. There is a minimum wage, you cannot pay a man in industry a sum below what is fixed by law. You do not have to have any CCC or OPA or any of those things. Now, we produce 12 million bales of cotton and need but 11 million bales. The New York Cotton Exchange runs the price of the whole 11 million bales down because we happen to produce a little bit more than was needed. What is the reason you couldn't fix a minimum price by statute on these commodities so that if a man didn't need a bale of cotton he wouldn't have to buy it and if he needs it and buys, he must pay the minimum price? You could do that and if Congress were to pass a bill prohibiting the sale of any product on the future market at less than parity you would cure a lot of fluctuation.

VOICE. Mr. Wilken, doesn't your plan contemplate that if there is no demand, the government will pay that parity price?

WILKEN. There is no such thing as not a demand for farm products. The demand is always there. If you keep the chips in the worker's hands you don't have to worry about him eating. Now the facts of the case are that in 1932 we didn't have overproduction of farm products. We didn't produce as much as in 1928. We had 4 million more people. We seemed to have a surplus. All we had was low prices.

VOICE. According to your statement, the agricultural dollar turns, then, when agriculture is getting its fair share of the annual national income, isn't it a fact that benefits every other essential group in the country as well as the farmer himself?

WILKEN. They cannot get it if the farmer doesn't get it. I want to make this point in closing, that 20 years of the records of the nation prove that for every 1% that your farm price has been below par you have had 1% unemployment and 1% loss of factory production and you have had 1% loss in national income; and in the period from 1930 to 1941—12 years— the United States lost $463 billion of income that it could have had without any cost to anyone and with benefit to all.

VOICE. Mr. Dumont [C. Dumont of New York] asked why you mentioned only seven or eight different commodities. Isn't it a fact that the government as a whole would be better off if each and every commodity had a true parity price for their products? It isn't your purpose to eliminate, as I understand, to eliminate and have parity prices for only those seven?

WILKEN. My purpose is to have enough of a foundation to stabilize your economy and at the same time have all the flux you can possibly have between other items. I would hesitate to put a price on any perishable product. Often, if the price goes down, you could increase consumption and increased consumption of a unit, times price, makes demand. You cannot get all the eggs out of a hen in a few days, time. They just come along one a day. A hog will put on a couple pounds of pork a day, as you feed him. Your cattle do the same. In other words, your law of supply and demand will take care of those items. When you harvest your corn crop in the fall, you have 365 days of supply and only one day of demand!

VOICE. What are some of the other crops you could include in fixing a basis to work out parity?

WILKEN. I would take corn, wheat, cotton, oats, barley, rye, flax. You could add two or three more, it wouldn't hurt.

VOICE. What about soybeans? And rice? Soybeans have become quite important.

WILKEN. Those might be added.

## [5] THE SALE OF A PACKAGE

NASDA officials remembered it as a powerful afternoon, especially those who measured *power* in terms of activity between the ears. The nation did not have to endure a depression—that much had come clear to everyone. But the sale of a package such as this one would require time, taking the breath-taking economic illiteracy in the nation into consideration. There was already talk of D-Day for Fortress Europe, and after that would come war's end. Wilken figured the NASDA officials would have about three years to sell Congress, perhaps more, certainly no less. And that meant explaining what fats and oils out of "Lever Brothers' coconut grove" had to do with the price of pork, and how come a few researchers out of the Midwest with only one Ph.D. in tow were challenging the rest of the well-credentialed academic set, those on loan to government from great trading corporations!

By the time President R.A. Trovatten had gaveled the meeting to a close, full parity had picked up important followers. But within a few days, the ranks started losing important members, also. The first was Vincent Harrington. Harrington had resigned his seat in Congress on September 5, 1942 to enter the Army Air Corps. He had been commissioned a Captain and promoted to Major. He had gone to England only a few weeks before Wilken tripped cross-country to the St. Louis NASDA meeting. Now came word that Vince Harrington had suffered a fatal heart attack.

Although Harrington died in a war, his monument, Wilken recalled later, will always be "the fight he made for full parity on the floor of the House and in the House Committees."

# CHAPTER 19:
# THE COLOR OF RAW MATERIALS INCOME

"BE IT RESOLVED that in order to stabilize our economy at the parity level, the National Association of Commissioners, Secretaries and Directors of Agriculture recommend the following steps . . ."

And with that resolution, and the seven steps that NASDA proposed, a gauntlet went into the political ring, because floor prices on seven basic crops—cotton, corn, wheat, oats, barley, soybeans and flax—would not be accepted by those dedicated to maintaining a price spread, as did the grain trade, or those in search of debt, as did the big bankers, without fighting back. The battle for the next decade was over more than Production Credit Association or Commodity Credit Corporation loans at 90% of parity and the other provisions a sound parity program required. In the final analysis the battle had to do with fantastic political maneuvers, the kind wars are fought over, the kind that topple governments and collapse empires, the kind that feed inflation and poverty, depression and chaos into a political going concern.

## [1] A MAGNA CARTA FOR AGRICULTURE

The most realistic of the NASDA members realized that the enemy would come in sheep's clothing. He would wear the cap and gown of scholarship, the robe of judicial office, and carry the leather briefcase of the businessman. And NASDA's wordy resolve to "acquaint labor leaders, industrialists, and consumer groups with the necessity of cooperating with agriculture in order to promote a sound economic policy" failed to take heed of the fact that the social sciences are unique, that there is no laboratory in which ideas can be proved by repeated experiments, that in the end each economic idea stands as a one-shot affair in terms of the human life cycle.

The very idea of parity already meant different things to different people. On the podium great leaders would declare it "a Magna Carta for agriculture," as did Secretary of Agriculture Clinton P. Anderson before the NASDA officials themselves, but such platitudes were merely soft preludes to harsher tonic.

When George Peek wrote his *Equality for Agriculture* after WWI, he defined a "fair exchange value" as the buying power a crop had during a stable and prosperous time, and this made such an era a suitable base period. So strong was the current of Peek's thinking* during the early New Deal years that Henry Wallace, Chester Davis and M.L. Wilson saw those same words written into the Agricultural Adjustment Act, and declared national policy, because to "re-establish prices to farmers at a level that will give agricultural commodities a purchasing power, with respect to articles that farmers buy, equivalent to the purchasing power of agricultural commodities in the base period" was perceived to represent high statesmanship. But even at the start, the 1910-1914 base period was viewed as somewhat inadequate, because it was good for all commodities save one—tobacco.

Certain shortfalls notwithstanding, the parity concept delivered well for agriculture—first an inch or two, then a mile, finally the whole package, or full parity. But the seed of doubt had been sown. Now, with NASDA officials making a stand for full parity as a permanent law, the question marks surfaced again.

The early effort was primitive, make-shift, critics said. If 1910-1914 was indeed a Golden Age, then surely it would be correct to note how things had changed. Look at agriculture in that Golden Age, argued Secretary Anderson—dirt roads, a horse and oats economy, jolt wagons, few tractors, no milking machines, awkward headers, few combines, no electricity. Oh, how things have changed!

And there was tobacco, a crop for which 1910-1914 seemed out of line from the start, and for which a base period of 1919-1929 had been substituted. Special concessions had to be made for soybeans, a crop all but unknown during the 1910-1914 period. In 1937, the pre-war base for milk was routinely questioned. As a result Congress gave the Secretary of Agriculture the right to decide milk prices in federal order markets. The rolling adjustments—one in 1940 that changed the base period on tobacco to 1935-1939—kept the parity concept, or at least enough of it, dancing around the center of the stage in the middle of a chorus of question marks. By 1944, USDA routinely computed parity figures for some 157 commodities. No more than 61 had 1910-1914 as a base period. Those 61 commodities, however, accounted for 82% of farm crop values. By 1944, 73 commodities had a 1919-1929 base, 21 made use of various combina-

---

* Peek, of course, was a colleague of John Lee Coulter. In fact Peek and Coulter co-authored *Alien Influences in America*, a tract published by the National Economic Council that dealt with the effect on American farm prices of farm product sales on world markets.

tions drawn from the 1920s, and two used 1935-1939.

"Are there going to be parity prices—or parity income?" became the rhetorical question out of USDA. Officially the Truman administration stayed hitched to the proposition that "the parity income goal should be agriculture's fair share of the national income under full employment, full-scale industrial activity," and the like, but plans were already being cast to take public policy in the opposite direction once the Steagall Amendment ran out.

## [2] CHARLES B. RAY

Charles B. Ray carried the ball for full parity at both the 1944 and 1945 meetings of NASDA. Ray, Coulter and Wilken realized that the education job ahead of them was breath-taking in scope, simply because "you had to start at ground level," Wilken later recalled.

"To begin at the beginning of this subject," Ray told the NASDA officials, "the farm wife and mother was the first economist and manufacturer . . ." The etymology of the term said as much. Economy came into the English language from two ancient Greek words, *oikos* (meaning the house), and *nomine* (meaning to deal out). Originally, it meant the art of managing a farm household. Accordingly, the woman of the house was the first farmer and the first manufacturer, a situation that gave rise to the old pioneer expression—"A man's work is from sun to sun, a woman's work is never done"—because the hunter husband had it much easier than his mate in the shelter.

Indeed, said Ray, most of the nation's economy still "rotates around the total annual requirements of all the homes in our nation. And as of old, food, clothing, and fuel together with outside household service, the church, schools, medicine and local government are by far the dominant facts of life in any economy. Therefore, our annual national economy is simply the sum total of the everyday needs of the nation's millions of households."

Anyone, layman or professional, could understand that much. What followed became a bit more complicated, because human beings with free wills furnished economics with an imponderable variable. But then economics was either a science or it wasn't, and if it rated attention as one, Ray opined, then "its formulas can be demonstrated over and again, systematically."

With or without human intervention, economics was subject to mathematical laws, and this—Ray insisted—required men to view the subject from the standpoint of physics and mechanics. "Annual raw material production, in the main food and fuel energy, is the power gear in our economic machine which at all times controls the volume and velocity of industry and trade as finally expressed in total national dollar income."

To make such a statement invited proof, but Ray had proof available, and he noted that on an understanding of that proof depended the future happiness, comfort and security of millions in every nation.

"Our annual total national income measured in dollars is limited to the total dollars paid for our annual new crop of raw materials of all kinds multiplied by our current annual national trade turn. The increasing pattern of the trade turn is obtained by dividing previous year's annual total raw material incomes into previous year's annual total national incomes. . . . These annual national trade and labor turns are mathematical corollaries of each other, and increase constantly and permanently as the result of technological improvement in farm, mine and factory.

"Let us make it clear here that the businessman only legally employs labor and houses and services it with machines [capital investments], but he does not hire [pay] labor, except as an agency. The various groups of labor in order of their importance—farm, mine, factory, trade, and service—through their respective production and mutual consumption of each other's product, hire and pay each other. The initial hiring and paying of all labor starts in the annual cycle with the farmer who as our largest combined capitalist and worker hires himself, hence never lacks employment or fails to produce. This initial farm-labor capital and income automatically multiplies through the rest of the groups in our national economy, at predetermined ratios. Basic agriculture, therefore, literally 'primes' our national economic pump annually and may be said to hire all ensuing or subsequent labor in the whole. *The only exception is that of labor hired and paid by new capital investment in new buildings and equipment, which only a prosperous agriculture can sustain.*"

It was this last concept that Keynes and others seized upon during the 1930's, because capital expansion took on the color of earned income—the kind turned by raw material production—and satisfied those who created money at a profit. But as Ray stated, debt that pretended to be earnings could not be sustained by anything less than a prosperous agriculture.

This all sounded like theory, physiocratic theory to be sure, but Ray, Wilken and Coulter asserted that they had proved it out. Ray started his research in 1932, and by 1936 he could predict national income with practical accuracy six months in advance. Ray found that one factor telegraphed all that was still to come. That factor was the "annual physical farm marketings, necessary for per capita growth in consumption of food and fiber crops." Accurate projections had never been possible during eras when violent fluctuations in raw materials prices prevailed. But the coming of a parity concept and the regulation of floor prices provided the missing link.

"Per capita consumption of farm crops in either depression or prosperity is the only stable factor in our national and world economy. Only speculative farm prices in the past in violent, unstable raw commodity markets the world over have made it impossible to figure future farm and national incomes with reasonable accuracy two years in advance. Annual farm income times the annual national farm trade turn (which is an annually increasing mathematical constant resultant of permanently increasing farm and factory technological improvement) determines the level of our current dollar national economy and income at any price or production level in peace time . . ."

Factory payrolls, the tabulations proved, followed farm results six months later. Ray worked out a schedule that showed the following:

|  | 1929 | 1932 | 1937 | 1947 |
|---|---|---|---|---|
| Full-time factory employment | 10.0 | 6.4 | 9.9 | 13.5 |
| Annual farm price parity | 100% | 64% | 98% | 135% |

This meant that under a permanent 100% farm price parity law, farm prices and income could be calibrated as a ratio of manufactured prices paid out by farmers. Nearly 40% of the value of a factory product came embodied as raw material cost. The rest was labor and profit.

As early as 1937, Ray predicted a decline of $1 billion in the 1939 cash farm income, and therefore a decline of $8 billion in the national income. The actual results came in a bit short of that—$7.3 billion being the actual decline in national income in 1938. In 1939 Ray again predicted national income on the basis of farm income performance. His projections pointed to a jump in national income from $69 billion to $125 billion in five years, a projection that was considered fantastic at the time because government leaders and many business officials had reconciled them selves to a "modern frontier" economy with little or no expansion, despite the fact that millions were underfed, underclothed, and undersheltered, and 9 million of them were unemployed. (In fact, Leon Henderson inaugurated OPA by stating that 1942 national income would be around $100 billion, and the standard of living would have to hover near the 1934 level.)

Ray and his associates followed their research, and by 1944 the farm trade turn came to 6.72—or $23 billion farm income, $160 billion national income. Production in mining had failed to reach the estimated figure. The 1947 and 1948 income for the nation—considering the existence of the farm parity law—simply had to preclude the possibility of a postwar depression, and on this basis Ray advised Sears, Roebuck to expand its operations at a time Montgomery Ward was pulling in its horns.

The evidence seemed conclusive to all who really listened. Parity was a requirement for maintenance of national income. A solid voice from the Senate—where only three had voted against the farm parity law—and a solid voice from the House—where only 13 voices had dissented—had made Roosevelt's threatened veto impossible! Now those voices were melting away. One word, dinned like a subliminal funeral march, wore them down. That word was *surplus*.

## [3] SURPLUS

Though the echoes were loudest in the farm press, the grain trading pits, and the bank offices of those involved in international trade, the very idea of surpluses caught hold almost everywhere. Typical of thinking then extant was expressed by Carl R. Smith, the agricultural chief of Maine. Production had been stepped up in response to war needs, he said. That much was certain. But now the boys would be coming home. ". . . we are going to have too many people on the farms. This will produce a surplus, and we cannot expect the federal government to help us out . . . If we use this labor-saving machinery as we have in the past, we will tear down our whole national economy."

Wilken had answered the "surplus" ploy in the 1944 meeting of NAS-DA: "Few people in the nation realize the ability of the American people to consume. For example in 1929, with a national income of $83.3 billion, we spent $21.7 billion for food and tobacco. This dropped to $13 billion in 1932; and in 1941 when farm prices were back at 98% of parity, we spent $25 billion. Expenditures rose to $31 billion in 1942; and in 1943 we spent $36.6 billion."

Also, there was cotton, 11 million bales of it at the end of 1945, a product that had been replaced to a large extent by rayon, nylon, spun glass and other goodies developed with tax money during the war. Could parity be maintained?

And there were enough other facts lying around, either as raw data or refined propaganda, to test the faith of Job. Generally speaking farm production had been running about 33% above pre-war production at the end of 1946, although livestock production had slackened off. These increases had resulted from mechanization, improved strains of crops and breeds of livestock, plus an added emphasis on fertilizer. All these factors were still a part of the scene, and only fertilizer application even rated attention as much of a variable. "It is extremely doubtful if a moderate decrease in prices would seriously affect this conclusion, and it is equally doubtful if even an extremely severe drop in agricultural prices would by itself substantially affect agricultural production, aside from its influence on the amount of fertilizer used," became the analysis of Oris V. Wells, Chief, Bureau of Agricultural Economics, USDA. And in an oblique way, this also added up to *surplus.*

Wilken continued to argue that food consumption was elastic, especially where there were still hungry people, and he continued to point out that farm surplus was really inventory—and a pitiful one at that. Compared to the inventory maintained by industry, any carryover of farm production hardly rated mention. And yet the nation seemed hell-bent on using a small inventory as a cudgel over the head of agriculture.

Moreover, while some voices sought to solve the farm problem by creating shortages, others operating out of the same rooms uncorked more technology to bring on more government programs proposed to raise farm prices, yet the Reciprocal Trade Agreements were designed to bring them down.

## [4] "TO PUT PARITY TO DEATH"

Wilken sometimes wondered aloud about the forces that were closing ranks "to put parity to death." Indeed, those who opposed a fair deal for farmers seemed to argue at cross purposes. Wheeler McMillen's book, *New Riches from the Soil,* was published in 1946 at exactly the time the word surplus became a staccato sound on the farm front. A long-time editor of *Farm Journal,* McMillen had become the push behind *chemurgy* during the mid-1930s, but he had never lost track of the Pew family (Sun Oil Company), which owned *Farm Journal.* Here were people who argued that the human stomach was inelastic when taken as a whole, and all of this balderdash was being supported by former Secretary of Agriculture William M. Jardine, not to mention such worthies as Colonel Frank Knox, Irenee du Pont, and Board members from firms such as American Cyanamid, General Motors, and du Pont.

## [5] THE EMPLOYMENT ACT OF 1946

There was more. There was the Employment Act of 1946, that curious measure agriculture had still to understand because it was so new.

"It is the continuing policy and responsibility of the federal government . . . to coordinate and utilize all its plans, functions, and resources for the purpose of creating and maintaining . . . conditions under which there will be afforded useful employment opportunities for those able, willing, and seeking to work."

The Act was not meant as an employment act for industry alone, but the most astute could see that an agriculture at less than full parity would bring about that precise result. As Secretary of Commerce Henry A. Wallace was later to point out, it was written so that the economy could have done with "the deadly threat of instability." But, too soon, it would rely on the fact that *labor hired and paid by new capital investment in new buildings and equipment* gave the same results as income generated by parity raw material—except that when labor groups are employed by new capital investment, investment has to be the result of savings, not debt. As Ray and Soddy and Wilken and countless others have surmised, labor groups, "through their respective production and mutual consumption of each other's products, hire and pay each other," and cannot generate the income with which to pay capital debt—and must therefore rely on a prosperous raw materials sector to sustain their activity.

Thus, Wilken pointed out, the Employment Act of 1946 could not possibly work in the long run unless the Steagall Amendment was made permanent. Those business firms that fought full parity were taking out insurance on having a debt-fueled economy, dizzy heights and collapse that could wipe away most of the private enterprise system. First, the reciprocal markets in rural America would go. Then the rural population would dwindle. New chaos would come to the cities—chaos that made full employment unavailable, and sound government impossible.

## [6] FARM INCOME AND FACTORY PAYROLLS

As early as 1944, Wilken had taken some 25 charts on the economy to Curtis Publishing Company, which then owned *Country Gentleman*. The editors and their advisers checked Wilken's figures, and E. H. Taylor prepared an article entitled "The Key to Prosperity." It turned out to be a matchless piece of journalism, the kind that made the trade turn, and the relationship between farm income and factory payrolls come clear to almost anyone.

Now Wilken, Ray and Coulter realized that they had neither the time nor the resources to go the PR route. Instead, they concentrated on those who would do the voting and the writing of any new law.

The Steagall Amendment had been so written that it would expire two full calendar years after the President declared the war emergency over. President Truman took that step December 31, 1946. This meant that 90% parity legislation would expire December 31, 1948. Obviously new legislation would have to be prepared. Obviously, Wilken and his associates would have a tough row to hoe during all of 1947 and most of 1948.

Those who had endured full parity because survival of the system required it were now ready for instant profits, hang the consequences. By early 1947 the great opinion makers were hard at work.

# CHAPTER 20: THE GREAT OPINION MAKERS

By early 1947, the great opinion makers—those who had remained somewhat submerged during the long war emergency—came out of the woodwork. Farm Bureau was the first to follow a coalition of pressure groups, even while it led. The going prosperity had erased memories of some tawdry business, such as when Senate investigators uncovered the facts about high Farm Bureau officials taking bribes from American Cyanamid to help scuttle the big Muscle Shoals fertilizer project. Also forgotten, more or less, was the bald stuff of yesteryear, such as when Farm Bureau Secretary M.S. Winder offered the entire organization to the American Steamship Owners Association as a lobby for getting ship subsidies.

I have recited something about the Farm Bureau's role in the chain store fight of the 1930's in my book, *Angry Testament,* but all this woolgathering misses its mark a mile if the point isn't made that Farm Bureau President Ed O'Neal resigned his post in 1947. O'Neal's position on farm parity had never been snowdrift pure, but it had been consistent for 16 years, and somewhat above Farm Bureau standards. Possibly because O'Neal was an Alabama Democrat, and possibly because Farm Bureau membership had dwindled to the breaking point, he supported many New Deal measures, and at one time caused Farm Bureau to turn on those "Wall Street Hayseeds"—Lammont du Pont, Alfred Sloan of General Motors, J.N. Pew of oil fame, and Winthrop Aldrich of Chase National Bank. In retirement, O'Neal walked a tight rope between Bob Taft and Dwight D. Eisenhower, finally jumping to Ike's bandwagon when the obvious became over-obvious.

## [1] WITH A WRECKING BALL

O'Neal's retirement and Allan B. Kline's election to Farm Bureau chiefdomship caused new cream to rise to the surface—and sour. Kline had headed the powerful Iowa Farm Bureau and rated recognition as a Republican. He served for seven years before retiring from office to take a position as Director of J.I. Case, the farm machinery company. Both before and after leaving the Farm Bureau presidency, Kline hammered parity, not with a hand tool, rather with a wrecking ball. "Farmers can't live very well on 60% of parity. It seems like sound public policy to protect agriculture at least on that level," he told the National Association of Food Chains.

No, the Farm Bureau didn't lead. It followed. The real leaders were of a different stripe.

There was the *Farm Journal*, for instance.

Doting on Manchester economics, *Farm Journal* had harped about "too many farmers" for years. *Too Many Farmers* in fact became the title of a book by editor Wheeler McMillen. "Too many farmers? Yes, too many, still too many after some hundreds of thousands have taken other forms of livelihood. The shift must go on. Had I the power I would hurry it up, for the good of those who will be farmers in the years to come, and for the good of the whole people."

And where were the farmers to go? Golf is sweeping the country, Mc-Millen said. There are jobs—caddying, running roadside stands, selling autos and insurance—*ad nauseam!* Circa 1947, *Farm Journal* questioned the wisdom of full parity for agriculture, and the terms used to convey this message weren't uncertain.

## [2] BOUGHT AND PAID FOR THINKING

And there was the Foundation for Economic Education.

The bought and paid for thinking in FEE was anti-parity for reasons that found full expression both before and after the Steagall Amendment had passed into history. W.M. Curtiss, a former professor of marketing at Cornell, talked the message before 1947, and wrote it down without too much varnish later on, and though these lines were written months after the first rounds had ended, they still convey something about the tornado-like thinking of the late 1940's:

"Price supports are a one-sided form of price control. Price control is a part of the more important question, namely, whether the nation shall have an economy of free markets, or whether it shall be one of a price control leading to production control, allocation of labor, and ultimately socialism. . . ."

Was this really ignorance speaking, or thoroughly informed self-interest? When the Select Committee of the House of Representatives on Lobbying Activities looked into the matter, they found that between 1946 and 1950, 51% of the Foundation for Economic Education coffers were being filled by contributions from no more than 20 biological persons. Included were the following:

W.B. Bell, President, American Cyanamid Company.

Donaldson Brown, Director, General Motors and du Pont.

W.S. Carpenter, Jr., Chairman of the Board, du Pont.

C.A. Cary, Director, du Pont.

J.E. Crane, Director, du Pont.

Lammont du Pont, Director, du Pont.

B.F. Goodrich, Goodrich Rubber Company.

D.M. Goodrich, Chairman of the Board, Goodrich Rubber Company.

E.T. Weir, Chairman of the Board, National Steel Company.

Among the business firms, behind FEE were the following: Armour & Company, Chrysler Corporation, Consolidated Edison, du Pont, General Motors, B.F. Goodrich, Gulf Oil, Kresge Foundation, Libby-Owens-Ford Glass, Eli Lilly, Marshall Field, Montgomery Ward, Republic Steel, Alfred P. Sloan Foundation, Sun Oil, U.S. Steel, the William Volker Fund, and United States Gypsum . . . to mention a few of the top firms and foundations.

There were other opinion makers, big and little, well funded and girded for a showdown fight with full parity. American Enterprise Association, Inc., was one, and the Committee for Constitutional Government—a FEE-linked and J. Howard Pew helped do-goodery—was also one, styling itself as "patriotic," which in 1947 meant "beat farm parity." They came on in waves, these groups—these tax-sheltered foundations funded by the mature fortunes. They styled themselves *board, conference, congress, forum, group, guild, institute, league, registry, society*, almost anything. Invariably they represented mature big business, *the powers that be,* and the biological persons who were really the mature fortunes, national and international. They did not want full parity in 1947 because they were now ready for their game again, international exploitation.

## [3] SINGLE FILE

As the war was ending in early 1945, the *San Antonio Evening News* carried an editorial:

ALL THE PEOPLE HAVE A STAKE IN THE FAMILY-SIZED FARMS

And, sure enough, there was Senator Arthur Capper being cited as the authority for the information that "The buying power of rural America is the motive force that keeps factory wheels turning. Take that away, and many an industrial center would become a ghost town."

This was the kind of thinking that Carl Wilken and his associates were manufacturing, and the well-funded coalition of pressure groups—with Farm Bureau as the agricultural spokesman—was determined to hammer it down.

Wilken and his associates had picked up allies, but now the enemies were marching in platoons, whereas the allies were still walking single file. Don Berry's Indianola, Iowa paper could do only so much, and the few Congressmen who favored Wilken and read his stuff into the record could do little more. Continuing support from *Country Gentleman* helped. Almost alone among the national farm magazines, *Country Gentleman* both carried the Wilken message and explained it. "A Program that Counts Everyone In" became the *Country Gentleman* appraisal for the kind of economics Wilken was selling. "For a quarter of a century the national income has averaged just about seven times the total farm income. Plainly, there is a public interest involved in sustaining farm buying power," *Country Gentleman* said.

Wilken and his associates had been working on the subject for years. In January 1946 Wilken told the National Livestock Convention in Denver a few facts about the economic riddle that hadn't been revealed before. He pointed out that retail sales would approximate 60% of the national income in the postwar period. Retailers could rely on it. As a matter of fact, the entire nation could rely on the calibrations that started with agriculture and fed the economic structure.

Wilken's message was being refined and expanded each month, either in his research office or at the podium. Wilken was behind many a mike during the mid-1940s. He was behind one on a cold February night in 1946. The occasion was the revival of the winter farm show at the Cranston Street Armory in Providence, Rhode Island, an event that had been canceled for the duration. Among those on the podium were Governor John O. Pastore. Dr. Raymond O. Bressler of the Rhode Island Agricultural Conference moderated this radio round table. On the floor farmers had been looking at more and better equipment, and many believed the government would make secure the future that had been promised. Wilken's messages were almost always the same, and yet they almost always contained a new dimension. This sample exchange tells its own story:

GOVERNOR PASTORE [to Dr. Bressler] ... I am beginning to understand what you were driving at in your annual report when you said, "Fat farms make fat factories, fat factories make fat banks, fat banks make fat citizens, and fat citizens make fat farms." I think you also said that "a nation wishing to be strong must look to the welfare of those who work with the raw materials of nature; the farms, fisheries, forests, and mines." What bothers me is how to bring about the things that Mr. Wilken suggests must be done. How can we bridge the gap between theory and action? What is the machinery for doing all this? How can the farmers be guaranteed the income you say they must have?

MR. WILKEN. The gap is already partly bridged, Mr. Governor. Let's start with the easy items first—mineral and oil resources. Of course the prices should be stabilized and in fact they have been for a great many years.

Six big oil companies control the price of crude petroleum at around 95 cents to a dollar a barrel. The Guffey Coal Act and the Wagner Labor Law, between them, have further stabilized this industry even at considerably higher base prices. Fisheries and forestry, in the main, are in the hands of commercial interests and become more a question of wages than prices. Unlike farming, most of the employees in these two industries are working for someone else. Price of the product affects them less directly. The price the farmer receives is both his salary and his profit.

Raw materials remained the linchpin for analysis by Wilken, Ray and Coulter, and it was a reasoned position that proceeded from a raw materials base.

The letters, the studies, and the mounting inventory of paperwork fairly had Wilken swimming in his own office.

"Dear Bill," read one missive—an average letter for Wilken—that was addressed to Congressman William S. Hill. "As you know, I testified before the House Committee on Agriculture relative to the wool situation." There was no farm situation that remained strange to Wilken. He understood specialties and he understood the basic storable commodities as did few others. "To alleviate the present situation of wool accumulations, I would suggest that 250 million pounds be transferred to strategic and critical stockpile for national defense, as provided by legislation in 1946." This was the Buy American Act, one of the hundreds, if not thousands that Congress managed to scoot past a roll call.

By mid-1947, laws governing the Department of Agriculture had come to be listed under 60 titles, 224 subdivisions, and codified with 270 pages of indexes—almost as if to comply with de Tocqueville's warning: "It [the lawmaking process] covers the surface of society with a network of small complicated rules, minute and uniform, through which the most original minds and the most energetic characters cannot penetrate, to rise above the crowd."

Yet Wilken and his associates were agreed that law need not stifle, that private enterprise need not lead to instability. A simple law could act as a governor for the economy without achieving de Tocqueville's syndrome.

## [4] THE OPENING GUN

Wilken fired the opening gun. Opponents of full parity drilled holes and placed sticks of dynamite. Wilken's draft of a farm bill was introduced May 18, 1947 by Representative Charles B. Hoeven of Iowa, with all Iowa Representatives joining in support. It was essentially the same measure Congressman Vince Harrington had introduced in 1937.

The 1947 version, however, called for 90% of parity loans on the seven basic farm crops—cotton, flax seed, wheat, rye, corn, oats and barley, with July 1, 1925—June 30, 1929 as the base period. It also provided for a 35% permanent reserve to protect the livestock industry against liquidation because of drought periods, and imposed a flexible tariff at parity on all farm products.

"If and when the world price is equal to the domestic parity price level," Wilken explained in a general release to the press, "the tariff would be zero. Exportable surpluses would be sold at world price levels; the difference between the parity price and world prices being assessed against the duties collected on imports of needed farm products."

Wilken's formula would have given farmers approximately 7% above the price level established under the old parity computations. Surplus disposal, if any, would have been liquidated by the collection of import duties.

Most of Wilken's proposals were at least partially provided for under existing legislation. Thus his bill merely correlated the various measures into a simple program that provided permanent parity for agriculture. All of this had been explained before the House Committee on Agriculture.

Wilken's testimony hit three points. First he nailed down fallacies. Next he proceeded to analyze the economy as a working mechanism. And then he outlined a program that would end a depression in 6 to 12 months.

The old fallacy of the early 1930's was still around, always ready to give new life to the *surplus worry*. During the Depression low prices had been blamed on surpluses that didn't exist in terms of stomachs that didn't get filled. "We merely had low prices and a shortage of income to consume what was in reality a normal supply," Wilken testified. (And as Georgia Commissioner of Agriculture Tom Linder testified, "During the period of 1933 to 1943, our excess of imports of agricultural products over our exports of agricultural products [in composite terms] amounted to about ten entire crops of wheat.")

All of Wilken's data had been updated for the 1947 Committee appearance, and with figures up to the hour Wilken marched through the "testifying" drill as he had marched through many a session before. Wilken's favorite quotation from *The Breakdown of Money* was there ["A money-lending country must be a free-trade country . . ."] as were the figures that proved beyond the shadow of doubt national income walked with farm income on a ratio of approximately 7.

Earlier, The Brookings Institution had tabulated national income and farm income for Congressman C. Knutson, who then chaired the House Ways and Means Committee. Brookings turned in the argument that the 7 times turn did not exist. Now Wilken answered. Brookings, he charged, used net farm income "and of course [it] had no relationship. We have continually stated that the gross farm income establishes the relationship. Brookings Institution ought to know better."

Wilken parked his tabulations with the Committee before he went on to explain. "The 7 times turn of gross farm income could be of very practical use to the members of Congress," he said. "Mr. Charles B. Ray, an employee of Sears, Roebuck & Company has worked out the progressive ratio and in the last eight years has predicted the national income . . . six months in advance of the United States Department of Commerce with an accuracy of 98%."

Wilken detailed these national income projections. He scoffed at Congressional leaders who worried about the cost of maintaining farm prices when they should be worrying about "the loss we will take if we don't." And then he closed with the policy pronouncements of NASDA in tow.

"As a result of our research work by the Raw Materials National Council," Wilken testified, "and that of Mr. Charles B. Ray and Dr. John Lee Coulter, the National Association of Commissioners, Secretaries and Directors of Agriculture have for the past three years advocated a seven-point program." This was the program Wilken now supported, point for point.

There were many papers read into the record in 1947, many of them mundane in the extreme. An earlier paper by Ray Iberg, Secretary Treasurer of the United Farmers of Illinois had handed out the Wilken equation and leaned on the Wilken logic, but for the most part those who came to talk about agriculture wanted lower farm prices on grounds occupied during the recent Depression—"overproduction."

## [5] ON-COMING SHILLS

Wilken had anticipated many of the Farm Bureau arguments, and the arguments pushed forward by the on-coming shills for the mature fortunes. In January 1947 he had contracted to prepare a survey for the Bureau of Reclamation. In that survey he outlined the production potential of the United States. The Bureau paid the bill, but so far nothing more had come of it. In his Reclamation report, Wilken called attention to the conjectural economies then being circulated. There was the survey which Edson Abel had prepared for the Farm Bureau, and which had been published in *The Nation's Agriculture* under the title, "Western Irrigation Agriculture and its Immediate Future." The thesis could have been stated in one word: "overproduction."

And there was the survey by Theodore Schultz now out in book form. It came copyrighted by the Committee for Economic Development (CED) and titled *Agriculture in an Unstable Economy*. After examining the CED presentation, Wilken could only second a remark by John O. Knutson, the Chairman of the Raw Materials National Council at Sioux City. "So this is the great Schultz," Knutson had said. "No wonder we are in a mess."

Nevertheless, CED was pulling big funds and delivering power-house punches. In the years to come those punches would have agriculture reeling on the ropes.

Chairman Clifford Hope ordered Wilken's Reclamation Report added to the testimony record.

Congressman Hoeven summed up both the atmosphere and the reception Wilken's fresh ideas had earned. The reception had been splendid, the questions penetrating. By any standard of platform debate, Wilken had won, hands down. But the battle wasn't being fought under the rules of debate. Rather, it was in the process of being decided according to the first law of politics, the count, and the count might lean on the lucre of mature fortunes as easily as it had once leaned on the logic of statesmanship.

## [6] PROSPERITY UNLIMITED

By early June, Wilken informed his friend, Congressman Ben F. Jensen of Iowa, that he was almost finished with a complete codification of the economic package that had required so many years of study. The work would be titled, *Prosperity Unlimited—The American Way.*

Dr. John Lee Coulter helped Wilken with some of the passages, and Charles B. Ray accomplished many of the tabulations. Congressman Fred Crawford gave the project a special assist by assigning staffers to the proofreading chore, and giving Wilken a hand with the editorial pencil.

*Prosperity Unlimited* turned out to be a short book. The text proper ran no more than 127 pages. Wilken's testimony before the Agriculture Committee and a copy of the Hoeven Bill filled out the signatures. The 31 charts included were the same ones Wilken had once exhibited to the editors of *Country Gentleman,* and they were to serve another purpose once the book had scooted its way through the bindery. As the work snailed its way to the printer, General Wood of Sears, Roebuck caused $2,500 to be sent over to help with the printing bill. It would be the last money ever to come from Sears. In terms of 1947 prices, this was probably enough to cover most of the 4,000 copies Wilken ordered.

Wilken dedicated the book to his long-time associates: Dr. John Lee Coulter, Charles B. Ray and J. Carson Adkerson.

*Prosperity Unlimited* finally was presented to each Representative and Senator, and to others who might influence the course of events. The remaining copies were sold for $3.00, and in due time the edition went out of print. As an economic text it achieved the impossible. It presented the subject in very readable form, and it stripped away the barricades behind which economists usually hide. And in hardly 127 pages it demolished the "complexity of the craft" concept that has become ego nourishment for those involved in the dismal science.

# CHAPTER 21: PROSPERITY UNLIMITED

What is free enterprise?

Wilken asked the question in the opening chapter of *Prosperity Unlimited*, but unlike many who pose such questions he stayed for an answer.

"Free enterprise is distinctly the product of the Constitution of the United States. The right of representative government to determine the laws which protect the rights of free men is the foundation upon which free enterprise is built."

## [1] EACH FARM

This much might have sounded like a polemic, but by page two of *Prosperity Unlimited* Wilken had jumped into the essence of the subject. Each farm, he wrote, had every right to be considered a business unit. The capital investment per farm was equal to the average investment in the non-agricultural business unit. As a matter of fact, agriculture accounted for approximately two-thirds of the capital invested in productive enterprise in the country. The farms were small factories. Millions of tons of grasses and feed grains were being processed through livestock into meat, dairy and poultry products each year. At the time *Prosperity Unlimited* was published, 96% of the non-agricultural business units employed no more than 19 workers.

Wilken called attention to the fact that planning was in the hands of a few in most other nations. Yet here, in the United States, planning was being carried on by 9 million individuals "with no fetters on their ability, their energy and their ambition. This simple factor of individual planning by millions rather than a few is the secret of the dynamic economy which the United States has used to outstrip the world in well being."

But private enterprise, Wilken argued, was its own worst enemy. "It lacks the coordination to maintain the stability which it must have to distribute. Competition, while it is called the life of trade, at times is unethical and so severe that it destroys our incomes and in turn our ability to consume."

Thus Wilken stated the problem. Here were 9 million independent planners who operated as an "irresistible force" in expanding operations. And yet these same individuals sometimes rushed to sell before the other fellow, and this led to chaos and a complete breakdown. "What we need is a governor to control our system of free enterprise," Wilken concluded, and the record, he said, proved the point.

Wilken had recited that record often enough, but in the opening chapter of his book he recited it again, and he concluded that "The word 'cheapness' in an economy such as ours is a fallacy. Cheap goods and cheap wages mean a cheap nation and a low standard of living."

Wilken then hammered down the idea that new technology could possibly result in lower prices. *"Technological improvement must create increased buying power through increased wages or increased capital earnings to build new industries or to expand the old, otherwise we cannot create the new jobs and consume the new product."* The italics were Wilken's because there could never be enough emphasis on this point. "Cheapness is an illusion," he went on to explain, "promoted by human selfishness. Low prices have always meant depression. Proper prices for goods have always meant periods of expansion and consumption."

Wilken's comment on cheapness fit neatly into the unfolding syllogism. "One of the principal reasons for the theory of cheapness is the thought that surpluses cannot be sold except through lower price. This theory is a fallacy. The price reduction destroys the very income needed to consume the additional production." Failure to understand this point had always condemned farmers to poverty, and nations to instability. And yet the management of so-called surpluses wasn't difficult.

"Excessive surpluses should be treated like the surplus in a mercantile store. No merchant permits a few items to destroy his entire price structure. The sale of the surplus does not make a great loss if spread over the whole." If there was a common sense ring to all this, it also led neatly into Wilken's first chapter summary. "The problem . . . of free enterprise is to stabilize farm prices and keep them at parity with finished goods. This is the governor which we need to utilize our economy to the fullest extent. It so happens that if farm prices are stabilized at parity, all groups will be stabilized to that extent." And here Wilken uncorked the first of the many equations that were to lace his text together. Retail sales, he said, would equal 60% of the national income. More important, factory payrolls, construction, transportation, indeed, all the sectors of the economy leaned on agriculture as a foundation. "With both the physical movement of goods and our income in ratio to agricultural prices and production, there is only one answer to our economic problems. We must maintain farm prices at parity if we wish to have the foundation for full employment and prosperity."

To make such a claim was not to prove it, Wilken realized, and for this reason he detailed seven reasons why agriculture was the governing factor in the national economic equation. These reasons were the cause of the effect. They provided the rationale as to why the 1:7 ratio was meaningful. Every theory has to start from reasoned premises, but a theory is meaningless if the observed facts fail to support it. Now Wilken recited the reasons why agriculture was primary. The facts and figures, he charged, supported him to the hilt.

1. Agriculture's capital investment was two-thirds that of all productive enterprise. Agriculture had over ten times more capital investment than the steel and automobile industries combined.

2. Agriculture furnished—in terms of composite figures from the previous two decades—65% * of the raw material income of the nation.

3. Past records had revealed that an increase in agricultural income invariably preceded any rise in factory payrolls and income in other segments of the economy.

4. Agriculture, because of its dependence on weather and other natural conditions, was always in full production and approximate full employment.

5. Agriculture was the foundation factor in the production of raw materials entering non-durable manufactures, all of which had a rapid turnover.

6. Agriculture had to feed and nurture the future labor force in order to make it available for human progress. Agriculture therefore, preceded the rest of the economy by at least the length of time it took to raise a child to manhood.

7. And last, agriculture was the governing factor because it owned the natural labor force known as the livestock population. Without livestock there would be little return from unimproved land.

With these premises in tow, Wilken examined the farm scene, all of it, before he led skillfully to an inevitable conclusion.

"The foundation of our agricultural economy is made up of seven basic crops: wheat, corn, oats, barley, cotton, flax and soybeans or rye. These crops make up roughly 85% of our total harvested acreage. Permanent commodity loans at 90% of parity, callable at parity, with provisions for surplus disposal, would stabilize farm income and in turn the entire economic system of the nation."

## [2] THE YARDSTICK

Wilken then recited the yardstick he had worked out with his friend, Charles B. Ray. Each segment, in terms of data available in 1947, had its own ratio. Wilken listed these ratios as follows:

---

* In later refinements of date, this percentage moved up to 70%.

- Farm income, 14% of national income.*
- Mineral production, 7% of national income.
- Transportation, 7% of national income.
- Factory payrolls, 7% of national income.
- Retail sales volume, 60% of national income.
- Value of manufactures, 80% of national income.
- Construction expenditures, 15% of national income.
- Factory production and employment in ratio to the percentage of farm parity.
- Combined farm and mine income, 20% of national income.

A footnote said simply, "Total raw material income—farm and mine—is the profit of operating the nation as a business and represents the possible earnings on all capital investment in the nation." Wilken laced his figures together, illustrated them with charts by the dozen (Chart IV, for instance, illustrated the correlation between gross farm income, national income, and bank clearings at San Francisco).

Wilken's ratios in fact became chapters, so that *Prosperity Unlimited* explained exactly what Wilken meant by mineral production at 7% of national income. Of all the chapters, the one entitled "Mineral Production" was the most difficult to bring into focus. Iron ore, lead, zinc, copper, tungsten, all rolled by in the analysis, as did all the other products that rated attention as raw commodities. "Petroleum and bituminous coal are the two prime movers in our mineral production," Wilken wrote. "Other products such as iron, copper, lead, zinc and building materials, contrary to general economic thinking, are the result of the operation of the remainder of our economy. *A prosperous operation of non-durable goods production, most of which are made from farm products, creates the profit for the purchase of durable goods, such as automobiles, houses, etc."*

## [3] PREGNANT WITH PROOF

The chapter entitled "Manufacturing" was pregnant with proof of the Wilken, Ray, Coulter thesis because it harnessed cause to effect. As the art of processing raw materials into finished goods, manufacturing had become one of the largest segments of the economy. As late as 1940 factory employment was nearly the same as that in agriculture. Many economists were arguing that manufacturing was the dog, and agriculture the tail of this economic animal, and this caused Wilken to lead off by noting that "They fail to realize the magnitude of the many industries which should, in reality, be classed as agricultural but which are listed as manufacturing."

---

* Agriculture has seldom enjoyed a proper return. Free land and free capitalization has always figured in keeping this fact from surfacing . . . hence this project figure.

Indeed, two-thirds of the manufacturing industry was simply an expansion of initial farm production. There had been a time when farmers made their own cloth, processed their own meats, and in fact performed many of the services called manufacturing. The farmer gave up these functions when efficiency made division of labor possible, as Adam Smith pointed out, and in an abstract sense the farmer hired the work done. "The farmer today employs the men in industry, indirectly, of course, and, through farm production and price, creates the income to pay the salaries of factory labor and management and capital return." Here was the proof, in Wilken's view. Proper analysis of the record revealed that all of the economy depended on agriculture for its wages and jobs. And when industry asserted its selfishness and bit the hand which fed it by underpaying agriculture, it lost in direct ratio to the damage it did to agriculture.

Wilken ladled out statistics to cover everything—the number of industrial units in the country, the fact that the steel and automobile industries employed less than 2% of the labor force at the time WWII was in the making, and all the factors extension of this idea demanded. "If our prosperity were due to automobiles, then why haven't other nations enjoyed prosperity similar to that in the United States? They, too, have known how to make cars. . . ."

Why haven't they? "It is simply that other nations did not have the wealth resulting from raw material resources and agricultural production to exchange for the cars on a scale to make mass production possible. It was the farms of America which made possible the automobile industry."

Wilken went on to make the observation noted by historians such as Arnold Toynbee, Henri Pierenne, and Will Durant, that nation after nation has fallen when it emptied its countryside and denied agriculture a "rightful place in the scheme of things."

Again, why? Because the packing plant, the textile mill, the lumber plant, the garment shop, the flour mill, the food plant, all were in reality phases of agriculture. All represented functions once done on the farms. *"In the case of severe collapse of our economic system, the farmer could revert to processing his own products, while the rest of society would be cold, naked and hungry."*

Indeed, Wilken went on to note, those parts of the economy which once belonged to agriculture are the foundation for most non-durable goods production.

## [4] CAPITAL EXPANSION

Much of Wilken's presentation came on in the form of charts, charts that revealed a striking correlation between parity and volume of manufactures, charts that related nondurable goods to the volume of farm production, charts that covered everything from farm income to bank clearings. Wilken's graphic presentation illustrated how full production of durable goods became impossible without a parity price for farm products and other raw materials. There was only one exception to this rule. It was the one Charles B. Ray had pointed out so often—that when capital expansion hires labor, the injection acts the same as income earned from raw material production and pricing. Wilken and Ray often reminded those who would listen that capital expansion required profits and savings. Wrote Wilken: "The only exception to this assumption is that any other full recovery of durable goods production must be the result of a deficit by industry, or, in the case of war, a deficit by the nation as a whole." Wilken did not stay on to point out that deficit financing by either industry or the government could not be pursued indefinitely, because the system would soon run counter to the laws of physics, and the laws of physics made compound growth of debt impossible. Yet strange as it may seem, this became the economic system of the nation almost immediately after the battle for full parity for agriculture had ended.

Wilken didn't cite Say's Law of Markets as such, but his language was somewhat the same: ". . . that markets are created through the production cycle. The law of supply and demand can function only as the consumer earns the income with which to pay." Indeed, *Each year's production of goods and services times price should create the income to operate the nation as a solvent business and consume its production.*"

## [5] FARM INCOME IS A CEILING

The metes and bounds of construction, factory payrolls and employment were also opened by the Wilken scalpel for examination. Depreciation of buildings figured in the equation, he said, but labor was more sensitive. In the end, the exchange equation dominated the picture. And the exchange equation made it impossible for factory payrolls to be increased above farm income, special legislation notwithstanding. And here again, Wilken charted his proof, proof that agreed with Allen W. Rucker's *Labor's Road to Plenty,* published in 1939, which stated "that farm income is a ceiling beyond which factory payrolls cannot go."

Again, Wilken hinted at what others might use as a solution to this dilemma. "Efficiency disemploys, and it is necessary that increased capital profits be created for expansion or investment in new industries if new jobs are to be created." That the followers of Keynes used this equation by substituting "debt" for "increased capital profits" in buying time and fabricating a synthetic prosperity was one of the points that Wilken hit time and time again in the interview I reported at the beginning of this book.

*"With full farm production,"* Wilken wrote, *"the gross income of agriculture at a parity price level provides the foundation for full employment at an income level consistent with national prosperity."* And this whiplash line was not offered without proof. Included in *Prosperity Unlimited* was a chart, prepared by Dr. John Lee Coulter, which detailed the trend of employment from 1910 to 1940. The ratios had remained somewhat the same. And the exchange equation would permit disruption of ratios only as fast as new technology benefited one industry more than it benefited the rest. Nothing less than massive overhauling of the rules for "people's capitalism" could negate what Wilken was saying. This made full employment through government impossible. "If conditions are such that private industry cannot employ the available labor, then we have reached the point of disintegration as a free and democratic people. The government has no money, and jobs created by government must be created by deficit financing, which will eventually break down our system."

Under the topic, "Labor Organizations," Wilken unloaded a point that union people must have appreciated in 1948, but no longer understand. ". . . labor must recognize . . . that low farm prices do not, as an end result, mean cheap food. Low farm prices will mean cheaper food prices, but the reduction of wages forced upon labor by low farm prices will mean less meat and other foods for the laboring man's family."*

Wilken's final caution to labor was equally profound. "Our labor cannot continue to receive an American wage, if we are willing to permit raw material products to come into the United States at less than the parity price level."

## [6] THE FLOW OF MONEY

Nothing of major importance escaped analysis in *Prosperity Unlimited*. Transportation, retail sales, services, all were scrutinized, and cemented into place with facts and figures. Finance became a searching entry. "In the cycle, Wilken pointed out, "the production of raw materials and the price per unit determines the flow of money from capital reserve to pay for the annual production of new wealth. This flow of raw material income serves as a profit to the nation, and to each group as it receives income, profit, if any, is included." These statements were not maxims. They represented reasoned approaches that complied with the observed facts of the situation. And the facts were at variance with the general concept those in finance had of themselves, because, in Wilken's words,

---

* I asked Wilken about this passage in a telephone conversation. He admitted he should have used the word "real" thus: "the reduction of real wages . . ."

"They have to come to feel that their operations govern business conditions, but they are mere servants of the public and have little effect on our economy."

Wilken must have meant this sentence in terms of a real economic cause-effect relationship, because he later admitted that the captains of finance govern manipulations, and account for malpractice in economics. It made no sense that the United States, with 6% of the world's population, and 25% of the raw material consumption, should suffer economic chaos. The Depression of the 1930s was forever an indictment of economic leadership. "Our depressions are due entirely to price dislocation, which is nothing more than a lack of parity for the products of one group as compared to another," Wilken said. "We can have a stable dollar by the simple process of maintaining a parity price relationship between farm products and finished goods. . . ." Wilken hit hard at the monetary end of the problem, because he realized that a general ignorance of coin and money by the population made manipulation possible.

"Men are put in jail because they give a person too little of this or that product in terms of pounds. Yes, we even send men out to check and inspect scales in our different business units that buy and sell goods according to weight. No one objects, for it is agreed that the public must be protected. But how long are we going to permit a monetary system that short-changes the productive cycle and brings starvation in the midst of plenty?"

Next, Wilken commented on the Federal Reserve System, the banking structure brought into being on the theory that a central money authority could stop depressions. "The theory was to curtail loans and increase interest rates when in a period of too high a price level, and to extend credit to prevent prices from going down. The theory didn't work, because a drop in raw material prices precedes a depression by at least six months and oftentimes several years."

## [7] THE INCOME OF THE WORLD

The big question, in the Wilken view, was always the same. Were people to serve the dollar, or was the dollar to serve the people. "By stabilizing the price level in the United States, we automatically stabilize 40% of the income of the world." By refusing to take that step, Wilken in effect pointed out, we make certain poverty for most of the world. And poverty starts at home all too often.

Raw materials governed, Wilken summarized. Here was a cause and effect relationship that proceeded all the way from the laws of energy to the laws of exchange. About 40 basic world raw materials determined the income of the world and the income of each nation, Wilken said, and he listed those raw materials with a weighting of each group according to the annual production worldwide:

| Wheat | Cattle | Cottonseed oil | Cotton | Pig iron | Coal | Hides |
|---|---|---|---|---|---|---|
| Barley | Calves | Olive Oil | Wool | Scrap steel | Coke | Newsprint |
| Corn | Sheep | Coffee | Silk | Zinc | Petroleum | Lumber |
| Oats | Hogs | Tea | Hemp | Tin | | Turpentine |
| Rye | Lard | Sugar | Jute | Lead | | Linseed Oil |
| Rice | Butter | | | Copper | | Nitrate of Soda |
| | | | | | | Rubber |
| | | | | | | Linseed Meal |
| 20 | 19 | 9 | 12 | 11 | 11 | 18 |

Even a casual look at these basic commodities pointed up the dominant character of agriculture, "the foundation of world income. . . ."

## [8] INTERNATIONAL MANIPULATORS

In 1935, The Brookings Institution issued a study, *Income and Economic Progress,* in which it was noted that the American nation had suffered a loss of $135 billion during the first four years of the Depression. More important, the study noted that there had been no surplus production—indeed, a marked underproduction of goods. USDA figures were cited to reveal that an adequate diet for the American people would have required 75% more by way of farm production than agriculture had accounted for.

Such studies dovetailed with what Wilken was saying, but this was not the kind of material coming out of Brookings circa 1947 and 1948. Now the studies arrived to contest the "shortage of income" thesis, and to argue that Wilken was not correct when he said farm income marched on a ratio of 1 to 7 with national income.

If anything, Wilken saw the hands of international manipulators at work. American capital owned well over half of the Cuban sugar industry. Exploitation was running rampant in India, the East Indies, South America and Africa. Now Wilken counseled those who would read by reciting Benjamin Franklin's dictum—that a nation could make profit from trade only by cheating. The English, he wrote, had never learned the quite simple fact that they could not buy cheap raw materials produced with cheap labor, and have good markets. "I do not prize the word cheap," President William McKinley had said, and Wilken reminded his readers of it; "it is not a word of comfort; it is a badge of poverty, a sign of distress. Cheap merchandise means cheap men, and cheap men mean a cheap nation."

In the end, Wilken concluded that there were three kinds of capitalism.

There was people's capitalism, or the individual ownership of property as set up by the United States Constitution. This was the natural, created form of capitalism, the kind that sprang up because people needed shelter, food and clothing.

There was state capitalism, or socialism and communism.

And there was international capitalism, a system that relied on exploitation because it placed profits first, manufacturing second, using cheap labor and cheap raw materials in the process, and relegated agriculture to a low third place.

As he concluded *Prosperity Unlimited,* Wilken pointed out the nature of the struggle. First state capitalism would fight international capitalism. International capitalism would lose in country after country because people would refuse to tolerate exploitation. The last struggle, he concluded, would be between state capitalism and the American system of people's capitalism.

Almost everything in *Prosperity Unlimited* had been printed before. Anyone viewing the body of Wilken's literature can find whole passages and pages that are repeated, but here was a complete codification. One might disagree with Wilken over whether people's capitalism would survive to see a showdown fight with state capitalism, but any serious scholar would be hard put to refute the requirement of the exchange equation and the necessity for full parity for raw materials.

## [9] THE POWERS THAT BE

Wilken took his charts and text to J.E. McDonald, Math Dahl, and Tom Linder, Commissioners of Agriculture for Texas, North Dakota and Georgia respectively. All three had gone on record against the Truman administration and its truck with the low parity idea. Of the three, Tom Linder fielded the most sarcastic language. "O democracy, democracy, what sins are committed in thy fair name." Truman's "Whole trade program, including the 23 nation treaty, has for its purpose unprecedented imports into this country," Linder charged. "Our exports to needy countries must of necessity be paid for by the taxpayers; this can only be done if we have high prices, high wages, and high salaries." Linder and his associates suspected that farm production would pay for those imports in terms of low world commodity prices, and that a "decline of 20 to 25% from present prices would be as detrimental to our economy as were the extreme low prices of 1930. . . ."

In an effort to influence Congress, Math Dahl, then a vice president of NASDA, called a meeting at the Mayflower Hotel in Washington, D.C. late in 1947. What happened in the wake of that meeting indicated that the powers that be would not tolerate prosperity unlimited.

# CHAPTER 22: OF FATS & OILS

Math Dahl, Agriculture Commissioner from North Dakota, and Vice President of NASDA, set up the Mayflower meeting. Over 300 people attended, most of them Representatives and Senators, a few of them executive assistants. Wilken had his *Prosperity Unlimited* charts in tow, and for about an hour lectured the lawmakers about the requirements of the exchange equation, covering the kind of material he had written into a book, prepared as pamphlets and caused to be inserted into the *Congressional Record*. Wilken later recalled it as a milestone meeting, because a turnout of this kind could not have been manufactured by a group without the political rapport of NASDA.

## [1] THE FATS AND OILS SITUATION

Commissioner Tom Linder of Georgia was master of ceremonies that night, and when he yielded himself the floor he literally peeled the hides off the fats and oils group—the business units that imported cheap oil, kept oil on the free tariff lists, and broke the price of lard, oil-producing grains, and finally American parity. Tung oil was one example.

Before WWI, there was no tung production in the United States. Because of its strategic nature, the government encouraged production, and by WWII tung oil production helped save the day after supplies were cut off due to the war with Japan. Now Chinese tung oil was entering the United States duty free. Even though Chinese production methods were crude and uneconomical, and the product inferior, it had become difficult for the American oil producers to compete with Chinese tung oil because Chinese tung oil was being produced by the cheapest labor in the world. As a result of these manipulations, lard was in the process of dropping from 28 cents a pound to 11 cents. Tallow was going down from 25 cents to 5 cents, and all the other fats and oils—corn oil, cottonseed oil, peanut oil—were doing the same. The process had already fed its way into the livestock market. And packers had moved to recover from low lard prices by penalizing farmers for heavy hogs and by marking up retail prices by 10 to 15 cents on pork chops. In fact, miserable, unprincipled handling of the fats and oils situation was fast becoming a prime mover in the commodity price drop.

Linder was a firebrand type of speaker, Southern drawl and all, and his every word cracked with electricity. All the institutional business arrangements were being used to take fats and oils and oil-bearing materials—lard, tallow and grease, cottonseed oil and soybeans—into a slump. Butter was heading for the support level. The U.S. had the grease and tallow, the lard and all the fats and oils. And there was a world demand. From General Clay had come word: "There is a perfectly tremendous demand for fats. The need is desperate. The fat crisis is here. We will take anything at any time that will be furnished us."

But fats and oils were kept dammed up in the U.S. because it suited Lever Brothers and the others with coconut groves to have cheap fats and oils. Administration of government controls, staffed largely by experts with business interests, first drove fats and oil prices below the OPA ceiling, then toward the pre-war price level.

## [2] THESE COCONUT GROVES

Linder clearly had the floor and would continue to have it even if torpedoes calculated to sink him were forthcoming. He could "demonstrate that whoever controls the fats and oils of the world can control the economy of the world as well as the politics of the world." A recent *Time* article had detailed exactly how international combines moved assets from one nation to another, thereby escaping taxation in their own country.

Several points in Linder's presentation challenged the very concept of government then being pushed forward. "Every American citizen is subject to fine and imprisonment for evading payment of his taxes. If Congress appropriates this money for foreign governments, then American citizens can be imprisoned for failure to pay the tax for the support of these foreign governments," Linder said.

He said a great deal more. "Congress can set up a charity commission, it can furnish money for the relief of starving people. It must handle such relief through American officials in those destitute countries. It cannot appropriate public funds to foreign governments without violating its oath of office and the Constitution."

Linder named names. There was Mr. Clayton, Mr. Armour, Mr. Luckman, men who represented great international empires. "The people of these countries are but pawns in their hands," he charged. And then he pointed out, "They are determined, through these International Trade Treaties, to reduce the people of the United States, Europe, Asia, Africa, South America and the islands of the sea to a common economic level and a common standard of living." The world "is in more peril from the operation of these stupendous combines than they were from the Germans and the Japs." This use of the public trust to betray the country, Linder charged, was being accomplished in the interest of private financial gain. These items sparked like static electricity across the big meeting room.

*Item.* Recently the President had appointed a Food Committee, and named as Chairman Charles Luckman, who was President of Lever Brothers at a salary of $300,000 per year.

*Item.* Lord Leverhulme (real name, Lever, his wife`s maiden name of Hulme being added when the title "Lord" was awarded by the crown), the son of a Lancashire grocer, started by selling scrap and by 1925 surfaced in world commerce with a mercantile empire rivaled by few for size, diversity and complexity.

*Item.* That great empire now functioned under the name of Unilever, Ltd. and Lever Brothers. A twin in the Netherlands functioned under the name of Lever Brothers and Unilever, N.V. This business empire operated in 37 countries with 400 subsidiaries and 800 factories.

*Item.* Unilever, the Netherlands twin, dominated the world's soap and margarine business. It also sold salad oil, lye, paper, candles, copra, perfume, toothpaste, vitamins, cattlecake, fertilizer.

*Item.* The great empire operated 2 million acres of palm oil plantations in the Belgian Congo, or 3,000 square miles. It also operated 300,000 acres (almost 500 square miles) of coconut plantations in the Solomon Islands.

Linder literally read the *Time* article out loud, and then he called attention to the obvious. Here was an international firm that played both ends of the trade game. In 1927, the powerful European trust, called the Margarine Union, merged with Unilever and out of the merger came Lever Brothers and Unilever, Ltd., with headquarters in London and Lever Brothers and Unilever N.V., with headquarters in Rotterdam. The London house controlled subsidiaries within the British Empire; the Rotterdam [house] controlled subsidiaries outside the British Empire, including the United States. "And the President of the United States could find no one to head the Food Committee other than the official of this great international combine."

After that Linder got what newsmen call "ugly." "I am told by an ex-service man that when United States soldiers were building air fields at Guadalcanal they saw many signs reading, 'Do not damage coconut trees for the United States Government must pay $50 each for each tree injured.'

"There American boys were giving their lives to defend these coconut groves belonging to the Dutch Company to save them from destruction by the Japanese, yet the U.S. Taxpayers were to pay $50 for each tree that our boys might injure."

In less than subtle words, Linder wanted to know just who actually ruled the United States. Who caused Charlie Luckman to be named Chairman of the Food Committee? Next Linder read out his bill of particulars.

*The Washington Times-Herald,* November 23, 1947, had carried a story that Procter and Gamble had announced, effective immediately, a 2 cent per pound rise in the price of Crisco shortening. At the moment of the announcement, a ship was unloading 7,000 tons of the appropriate raw product in the U.S. This translated into $5,600,000 being drained out of the United States, Linder said, at a time—

• When the Secretary of Agriculture was asking for unprecedented powers to prevent production of lard by forcing farmers to sell hogs at short weights.

• When the Secretary of Agriculture was compelling peanut farmers of the U.S. to vote for peanuts acreage reduction under threat of having support programs removed.

• When the Secretary of Agriculture had declared a world shortage of fats and oils, and housewives were being offered four times as much for used fats as they were paid during the war years.

• When unprecedented powers were being invoked to increase the production of oil outside of the United States.

• When the taxpayers of the United States were being called upon to furnish money and machinery to develop a gigantic peanut business in British Africa.

• When the U.S. Government was paying 100% more for vegetable oil in South America than American farmers were receiving for cottonseed, peanut and soybean oil, and when hog lard was almost without a market.

There were a few other items that alarmed Linder. "It is also a matter of deep concern when one cotton company shows profit in one year of $25 million or more while one of the largest stockholders and former President of the Company occupied the position of Assistant Secretary of State is entrusted with the making of trade agreements with foreign countries." This, Linder submitted, "is especially alarming when the records in the Commodity Credit Corporation's office show this same company [Anderson-Clayton] to have sold to the United States government 255,000 bales of cotton at a price approximately $13.75 a bale above the market price on the date of sale . . . ."

Here were Will Clayton and Charles Luckman and other internationalists "doing everything in their power to reduce the American people to the economic level of the peons and serfs of other lands. They are having no trouble in doing this because the delegates from óther nations are [of] the same stripes of international business octopuses as Mr. Clayton, Mr. Luckman and big business which they represent."

Linder spoke into the stunned silence of the place. Wilken, Adkerson and several close associates listened and nodded approval from an up-front table.

How much of this money being voted by the Congress would feed the tills of the internationalist in the several countries? "How much of it will be used to increase the profits of Lever Brothers in the United States, in Holland, in the British Empire, in the Belgian Congo, in the Malayan country, the Philippines and the Dutch East Indies? How much of it will be used to buy Anderson-Clayton cotton, cottonseed oil and other products in Brazil and other countries at $13.75 a bale above the market price? How many years of toil, suffering and sorrow must the farmers and the taxpayers endure to pay for a plan by a man [General George C. Marshall] who cannot remember where he was when the Japs attacked Pearl Harbor?"

Linder, ever dynamic, ever caustic, ever scathing, earned for himself undying enmity with lines such as these: *"The fate and fortune of the boys who fought for America as well as that of all other Americans had turned over to the tender mercies of this group of international money sharks and at their greedy hands the people of America and the people of all other lands will receive a program of destitution and slavery."*

## [3] THE ROOF FELL IN

After that, the roof fell in, and the prospect of more 300-man meetings was cancelled out for good. R.A. Trovatten of Minnesota, Math Dahl of North Dakota, Tom Linder of Georgia and J.E. McDonald of Texas together with Dr. John Lee Coulter and Carl Wilken were called in to explain why they were lobbying without registering as lobbyists. FBI men made the rounds to investigate. Wilken and Coulter were able to convince the agents that they served merely as researchers, that they made use of official government figures, and that as economists for public officials they complied with every law on the books. Grand Jury proceedings against the two Republicans, Trovatten and Dahl, were dropped. Finally Tom Linder and J.E. McDonald were indicted. McDonald retained Howard Dailey of Texas and the state's attorney general to represent him. Normally a case of this type rated dismissal on motion of counsel.

According to government theory, a cotton broker named Robert M. Harriss and a Washington lobbyist named Ralph W. Moore had conspired with the NASDA officials to raise the price of cotton. Linder and McDonald had toured the South to urge holdbacks on cotton, and the *Geor-*

*gia Farmers' Market Bulletin* calmly predicted 50 cent cotton, a happenstance futures traders on the long side liked. What *Market Bulletin* didn't know was that USDA and the Justice Department (to comply with the government's low commodities price policy) knew exactly how to pull the horns out of any bull market.

Linder was in the hospital fighting for his life when the indictment came. Later, after running a temperature that made medical history, he caused a private team to find out exactly how the roof had been caused to fall. The jury, his investigators reported, was of the "rubber stamp" type. Among the members, the report read, were government employees, several of them maintenance workers and charwomen. Linder and McDonald were specifically charged with working for legislation to raise the price of farm commodities. They were also charged with working against legislation that would lower the price of farm commodities. The Commissioners also stood accused of trying to profit in futures trading. After an all-day hearing, the initial indictment was dismissed. And the bull movement collapsed.

After the early dismissal of conspiracy charges, the Justice Department filed an "information" in the same court and charged essentially the same actions against the defendants individually. Although the "information" ran some 30 pages, only Count 9 commanded much defense attention. Here again was the charge that an attempt had been made to influence passage of legislation by the Congress that would raise farm prices and futures prices. The information on Linder, set out the following: "That for the purpose of influencing and attempting to influence the aforesaid legislation by the Congress, the defendant, Tom Linder, testified before the committees of Congress of the U.S., sent letters and telegrams to members of Congress and officials of the Executive Branch of the Government of the U.S., issued press releases to members of the Congress of the U.S. and made speeches at various functions. . . ."

Tom Linder and James E. McDonald, the information stated, "had organized a farmers commissioners council for the purpose of utilizing it in influencing and attempting to influence legislation by the Congress of the U.S. relative to farm commodities. . . ."

One item from the many legal papers attending the indictments read as follows:

"That for the further purpose of influencing the aforesaid legislation by the Congress of the United States, the defendant Harriss, between August 2, 1946, and the date of the return of this indictment, procured the services of Tom Linder by making payments of money to the said Linder and by financing and depositing money in commodity trading accounts for the benefit of said Linder with the brokerage firm of Harriss & Vose."

Linder's speech at the Mayflower Hotel was singled out, his testimony was mentioned, and there were enough specifics to prove, indeed, that Linder had tried to improve prices legislatively. All this was a crime under the Lobbying Act, a bizarre bit of legislation that had been passed because it contained a rider raising the pay of Senators and Representatives. No mention was made of the fact that the law specifically exempted public officials from the provisions of the act while in the discharge of their duties.

Linder had not stopped with his Mayflower speech. The next day, with Senator Arthur Capper presiding, he read his charges against Unilever into the record. At that time Senator Scott Lucas of Illinois objected. He wanted the footnotes, the proof, the point-by-point verification of all this "information" on Lever Brothers, and Linder in effect told Lucas to do his homework. The Senator from Illinois, in a huff, grabbed his hat and walked out of the hearings rooms.

Wrote Linder: "It is not strange that a Chicago lawyer like Scott Lucas, or the minions of internationalists in Washington, would resort to fake prosecution of public officials in the hope of intimidating them into silence." Attorneys Hugh Howell and Victor Davidson, both of Atlanta, Georgia, defended Linder for five years until charges were dropped, but NASDA officials remained moot bystanders.

"I have done nothing except what was my duty to do under the laws," defended Linder in *Georgia Farmers' Market Bulletin,* a sprightly house magazine for the Georgia Department of Agriculture that pressure on the Governor, influence with the post office, and a suit in Superior Court had failed to silence. "I have never been offered, nor would I have accepted 1 cent from any person for lobbying . . ." And in a late 1948 edition of the same publication, Linder flatly stated, "I have never in my life traded in futures," because the indictment had charged him with having a secret number for trading in cotton futures on the New York Cotton Exchange.

The case itself died a few months after Commissioner McDonald had passed away in 1952. Its epithet came styled Criminal No. 1212-49, *United States of America v. Robert M. Harriss, Ralph W. Moore, James E. McDonald, Tom Linder and National Farm Committee, Defendants.*

The case had become moot, Judge Alexander Holtzoff ruled, because *National Association of Manufacturers v. McGrath* had resulted in Section 305 of the Regulation of Lobbying Act being ruled unconstitutional.

Records of resolutions and proceedings of the NASDA organization do not suggest either interest in, or support of, the two indicted officials.

There were no more mass meetings of Representatives and Senators, however, and there were no more substantial drives for full parity from that quarter. Oris V. Wells, Chief, Bureau of Agricultural Economics, USDA, or a representative, was always on hand at NASDA meetings after that, or until the 60-90% parity provision of the Aiken Bill was allowed to go into effect in the wake of the first Eisenhower election.

If Linder's speech earned for him the double-distilled enmity of soap-makers everywhere, it also earned having fats and oils removed from the so-called positive list of commodities, at least temporarily. Unfortunately the delay had broken the back of fats and oils prices by then. And the indictment process broke up the NASDA organization as an effective lobby, and prevented it from getting a fair deal for agriculture.

## [4] A COST OF LIVING ANALYSIS

Earlier, Wilken and Coulter had prepared for R.A. Trovatten a cost of living analysis. Since neither could attend the Biloxi, Mississippi based meeting of NASDA in 1947, Trovatten presented the analysis and moved that it be made part of the minutes. There was a reason for all this. Cost of living was on every tongue, and food was being touted as the culprit. Almost all cost of living arguments compared food costs, but ignored relative wage levels, per capita consumption and the increase in taxes reflected in the cost of goods. Wilken and Coulter used the revised figures that had been published recently by the Department of Commerce under the title, *National Income*. Wilken and Coulter pointed to one of the sore spots in economics before uncorking their report—the fact of the base period. One old base period (1935-1939 = 100) was rejected because it reflected an era filled to the brim with unemployment, and because farm prices were only 82% of parity during that period in terms of 1929 = 100.

Wilken and Coulter simply pointed out that the percentage of income spent for food in the decade, 1930-1939, averaged 24.28%. In 1946 the percentage was 24.1%. In short, the cost of living in terms of food was about the same. It required 2 hours of factory labor to pay the food bill as compared to 6 hours of factory labor for the same purpose in Europe. People were eating better under full parity, and they were paying less in terms of real costs for the privilege.

The report was sophisticated, but it never once departed from common sense. "The factual record proves quite clearly that the almost hysterical concern over living costs is unwarranted. . . . The primary reason for the present price levels is the high level of both farm prices and wages. In this connection we would like to point out that our current domestic consumption is sufficient to utilize our present farm production."

". . . wages, commodity price levels . . . must be in balance," the report went on, because "Basic laws of exchange will not permit high wages and low food prices or low wages and high food prices. The producer is also the consumer, and on the basis of ability to buy our present per capita consumption of goods gives us the lowest living cost in history."

In addition to tables that detailed everything from truck crops and tobacco to granulated sugar and pink salmon, Wilken and Coulter added a reminder, "The claim of labor unions that industrial wages are not in line with living costs cannot be substantiated on the basis of a complete analysis of all factors. Farm prices a little above parity, as the result of weather conditions, is in reality a healthy condition and an incentive to full production in 1948."

There was a factor that Wilken and Coulter managed to hit with a sharp uppercut, and that was the "dislocation of lard prices." The government had forced lard prices down to 17 cents at wholesale because the powers that be in the fats and oils group demanded it. This required the packers and retailers to absorb the loss on lard by increasing the price of pork chops. As a result of this dislocation, the consumer in August 1947 was forced to pay 15 to 20 cents a pound more for pork chops. In Washington, D. C., lard dropped 10 cents a pound, and pork chops advanced 10 cents a pound. All this meant that business wasn't economics, and economics wasn't business.

## [5] NOT A CASE OF POST HOC ERGO PROPTER HOC

Hard on the heels of his appearance before the House Agriculture Committee, Wilken added a footnote, one that came to Chairman Clifford Hope in the form of a letter, Although Wilken's letter became part of the record, it was duplicated and sent to every Representative and Senator.

". . . I am very much concerned about the seemingly organized drive by the administration and industry to reduce price levels and especially the price of raw materials." There was the record, Wilken argued. There was the proof. And there were the premises that made the proof meaningful, and not another case of *post hoc ergo propter hoc*. Wilken reiterated his conclusion that the farm and mineral income constituted the profit of the annual economic cycle. He charged that "this drive to reduce raw material prices means a reduction in our national income and a reduction in our annual profit on all capital investment." A declining rate of profit, he insisted, would be the inevitable outcome of low raw materials prices— either that or an engine of credit forever winding until it exploded, possibly both.

On April 23, 1948 Wilken appeared before the Senate Agriculture Committee. His presentation was quiet and exact. The Senate was considering the Aiken Bill, and the Aiken Bill was leaning heavily on all the cost-of-living editorials that flowered from the public prints as if on signal. Wilken explained this business of cost of living, just as he explained parity and the parity equation. And then he told the Senators something few economists and almost no lawmakers realized. Parity prices, he said, *cost nothing!* *

". . . parity prices for farm products because of the 7 times turn of gross farm income into national income, do not cost society anything and do not increase the percentage of income spent for food. For example, in the 10-year period 1930-'39, with farm prices averaging about 82% of parity, 1929 as 100, we had 81% employment. The public spent 24.28% of the national income for food. . . . In other words, farm prices at parity give the public the maximum amount of units of food for the percentage of income spent for food."

Wilken explained his premises patiently. He took the proposed 60 to 90% price support level, applied it to the domestic situation, then translated the consequences to the international level. Experts, he said, had made the same mistake in promoting a world wheat agreement which established a floor at $1.10 on wheat at the end of five years. The $1.10 price was about 50% of parity, and if that price were to be permitted to become the price of wheat, it would cut in half farm income and drop national income on the ratio of 1 to 7. The American price level simply had to become the world yardstick, or worsening poverty would remain the lot of most peoples on the face of the earth. "If the rest of the world is to have a higher standard of living, they must have as a foundation a proper price for farm products. With 45% of the income of the world in the United States, the rest of the world cannot have prosperity without an average of 100% of parity for agricultural products."

Wilken then called attention to the fact that in 1947 the United States had purchased $2 billion worth of gold at a price 69% above the 1925-1929 price level for the yellow metal. If the same system were used to support the price of basic nonperishable farm products at 100% of parity, or 169% of the 1925-1929 level, "we cannot have a depression in the United States with present farm production."

But there was always the question: Which comes first, the $1 of gross

---

* The parity costs nothing observation was confirmed by House Committee on Agriculture Chairman Harold D. Cooley in *Food Costs—Farm Prices,* April 1965, Page ix: "The old farm program worked, when the great majority of farmers wanted it to work and were willing to cooperate. For 11 consecutive years prior to 1953 the average prices paid to farmers were at or above 100% of parity with the rest of the economy. This was an era of great prosperity in agriculture. The Government supported the prices of major storable crops for 20 years (1933-52, inclusive) at an actual profit of $13 million to the Government. This profit was earned by selling commodities—wheat, corn, cotton, tobacco, rice and peanuts—taken over in price-supporting operations."

farm income or the $7 of national income. Wilken challenged the Committee to permit him and John Lee Coulter to appear as often as necessary to accomplish the educational chore. He explained again as he had explained before why farm income took precedence, that approximately 70% of all consumer goods consist of food, tobacco, beverages and clothing.

## [6] THEY HAD TO RAPE THE HOUSE CONFEREES

The sanded gears of the lawmaking process finally brought the matter of a new farm bill to the floors of both chambers. By June it had become apparent that the Agriculture Committee of the House would not report out a long-range farm program. It became the judgment of the Committee, Chairman Hope said, to report out a bill that continued 90% price supports through loans, purchases and methods other than direct payments to farmers. And the House voted to accept this judgment with no more than three Representatives on record against the measure.

Then came the Aiken Bill out of the Senate with its provision for 60 to 90% of parity for agriculture. The measure was written so that it would not go into effect for 18 months, or until January 1, 1950. The timetable became all important. A Republican convention had been scheduled for Philadelphia, June 20. And the Republican-dominated 80th Congress had promised a long-range farm program, a point that stuck like undigested bone in the throats of the weary lawmakers. But the conferees refused to agree "under any circumstances" to a long-range program, any part of which would take effect as early as January 1, 1949.

The amended records of the House tell some parts of the story. "Mr. Speaker," read Congressman John W. Flannagan's remarks, "I have served in this body for 18 years, but I have gone through my strangest and most unusual experience since yesterday at 2 o'clock. . . . Thursday night about 11 o'clock the other body passed what is known as the Aiken Farm Bill. At 2 o'clock on yesterday we were called into conference, and the House conferees to a man turned down the Aiken Bill. They turned it down for the reason that they did not know what was in it. I doubt that some of the conferees from the other body knew a bit more about what was in the bill than the conferees from the House, who had not had an opportunity to examine the legislation.

"At 5:00 p.m. on Friday we were called into conference. The House conferees, because they did not know what was in the Aiken Bill, turned it down. So the conference adjourned.

"At 2 o'clock yesterday, Saturday, we were called back into conference, and the House conferees again stood pat and we adjourned. Then at 4 o'clock yesterday, we were called back into conference for the third time and the roll was called, and the House committee still stood pat . . .

"Then a strange thing happened. In order to bring the conference report back, they had to rape the House conferees. When they came back, Mr. Murray [Reid F. Murray of Wisconsin] resigned as a conferee and Dr. [George W.] Gillie was appointed in his stead; and then we met again. The Democratic members still stood pat, but the Republican members went over to the Aiken Bill."

Several House members took the floor to tell essentially the same story. The Republican convention needed a farm program, and to get it the Senate passed a bill that called for 60 to 90% of parity. As a sop to get House members to go along with it, the bill would not take effect immediately. House members could vote for it, and in turn have full parity accepted for the next year. There would be plenty of time to amend the Aiken Bill, and bring its parity formula to full strength. Everyone would get off the hook. Compromise didn't hurt, did it?

A few, such as Representative Harold D. Cooley, tried to stop the snowball. "It is neither bird nor beast nor fish nor fowl," Cooley said. "These provisions will continue a vital part of the Democratic farm program only until after the grand November election will be safely behind us and a matter of history. Then another program will go into effect and the agricultural economy of the nation will be shaken to its foundation."

The conferees, Democrats and Republicans alike, Cooley noted, objected to "having the measure rammed down our throats." So when the conferees found the bill too obnoxious, the politicians became horrified. "After secret meetings, and no doubt because of one member's unwillingness to surrender his convictions or to compromise his conscientious views, he resigned and another was appointed in his place."

Congressman Steven Pace of Georgia took up the glove. He objected to the Aiken Bill's 10-year moving average. He objected to this obvious move to abandon the parity principle. "When the Aiken Bill becomes effective a year and a half hence, the farmer will suffer a reduction in his parity price, and at the same time a reduction in his support price. Therefore he will be hit twice."

Nevertheless the question was taken, and the conference report was agreed to 147 to 70 upon division of the House. It was near 5:00 a.m. when business was completed. But Wilken realized that it was getting mighty close to midnight.

# [7] FACTORYWARD HO!

The combined House and Senate bills became law, and President Truman signed the measure that way. Almost immediately, farm prices started to slide. In 1948 and 1949, agriculture was to experience a drop of 14% on farm products because of speculator activity.

Wilken and his associates did not attend the NASDA meeting at Portland, Oregon, September 27-30, 1948. And the program did not concern itself with the ideas of Wilken, Ray and Coulter. A weak resolution called for "careful consideration and study" so that improvements in the Agricultural Act of 1948 might be forthcoming, but 90% of parity wasn't mentioned openly.

# CHAPTER 23:
# CHEAP FOOD MEANT HUNGRY PEOPLE

Harry S. Truman carried his "give 'em hell" campaign into the country-side during the fall of 1948, and in a manner of speaking he openly and convincingly abandoned the "sliding scale" and anything less than full parity. Farmers who spilled over the tracks to hear a few remarks about the outlook for farming were frequently handed a sheet of paper. It listed the prices farmers would receive for basic commodities if the Republicans won and the prices farmers would get if the Democrats won. And political historians more or less agree that Truman's lone stand in grass-rootsy America won for him an impossible election.

## [1] THE BRANNAN PLAN

Although the Aiken Bill was on the books, here was an administration seemingly dedicated to keeping it from taking effect. Secretary of Agriculture Charles E. Brannan appeared before a joint meeting of the Senate and House Agriculture Committees on April 7, 1949 to tell the lawmakers exactly how Truman's promise could be kept. And with that appearance, the Brannan Plan came into being.

The Brannan Plan, in the words of Representative August H. Andersen, "promises prosperity to farmers and cheap food for consumers, rich and poor alike. . . . It is not a new plan, for it has been used in every country where Communists and Socialists have gained control over the government by promising the people, if they vote right, all kinds of food and luxuries at low costs and prosperity for the farmers, at the expense of the taxpayers." Actually, the Brannan Plan wasn't that simple, but such was the concept that became the battle cry for "friends of agriculture" on both sides of the aisle.

Specifically, Brannan proposed a support system based on subsidy payments—direct payments in place of price supports on perishable commodities. Bluntly stated, the government would pay in cash what the market price failed to provide.

There was an emotional pitch running in Congress when Truman took office on his own after the 1948 election. There was not a little remaining bitterness over events that led to passage of the Aiken Bill. The Pace Bill included as its chief element the Brannan Plan.

Carl Wilken digested the Brannan Plan immediately and communicated his finding to Congressmen who had asked for his advice. First, Wilken argued that price supports "are not a form of socialism." The Brannan Plan, he said, was. Point by point, Wilken took the Brannan Plan apart and put it back together. It was, first, a "socialistic gimmick," one that enabled the United States to play at the game of free international trade. "Secretary Brannan and his experts, however, completely ignore this differential and ignore the need of a tariff to adjust the differences in incomes and purchasing power. Without a tariff, the United States will be forced into a position of having to support farm prices throughout the world to protect our own solvency and prosperity. Secretary Brannan seems to have a vague conception of this basic fact and, therefore, brings forth the idea of permitting prices to seek their own level. On a free trade basis this would be the world level."

There was more wrong with the Brannan Plan than that. Wilken saw the basic philosophy of the Plan similar to that of the triple-A program of the 1930's, when acreage controls and marketing quotas sought to turn business principles into macro-economics. "The principal new feature is the direct offer of cheap food to the consumer. This makes it an ideal program to get the votes. By fooling the farmer with a program of assured income, promising cheap food to the consumer and high wages to labor, he expects to get the support to put into operation a program which will socialize agriculture, the foundation of our American system."

Wilken's paper became almost nine columns of 6-point type when printed, and each line contained its own reason for being. He explained the economics of why cheap food meant hungry people, why world poverty was being manufactured by low world raw materials prices, why the cost of living could not be lowered with low food prices in terms of real costs.

Again, Wilken repeated his argument that parity prices for agriculture cost nothing, and that failure to realize this fact condemned in advance the programs being hatched by intellectuals in the employ of the powers that be. "I would like to point out," wrote Wilken, "that they are going in the same direction set out in the Aiken Farm Bill with its 60% price floor. The impossibility of the 60% price floor can be proved from the record."

Wilken was on sound ground in making this observation. As a matter of fact, both the Aiken Act and the Brannan Plan had been hatched in the same incubator. The American Farm Economic Association had sponsored a contest for papers on a new agricultural policy in 1945. The winning entry was written by Dr. William H. Nicholls, who later professored at Vanderbilt University, and at one time served as a senior economist on the Council of Economic Advisers, 1953-1954, and in foreign banking exercises.

The Farm Economic Association contest gave out $12,500 in prize money for the best papers on the subject, *A Price Policy for Agriculture, Consistent with Economic Progress, that will Promote Adequate and More Stable Income from Farming.* Some 317 papers were submitted. A composite view of the winners measures how well "theory period" instruction had influenced the thinking of those who would one day be called upon to shape farm policy. Of the 18 prize winners, fully 100% agreed that the 1910-1914 parity base represented a grossly distorted pattern, that it ignored necessary shifts of population, etc., with *etc.* meaning all the barbs that assail the parity concept once on the hour. Not one of the 18 winners accepted the idea of full parity for agriculture. The winners split over whether farm prices should be allowed to seek competitive market levels, or whether a measure of support should be forthcoming. Only one prize winner—Lawrence H. Simerl—suggested loan rates in terms of parity, but he suggested variable loan rates of 55 to 75% of revised parity, with 1935-1939 as the base. Only one—Geoffrey Shepherd—suggested storage operations to "withhold the excess over average production in good years and release it in poor years."

Prize winner Nicholls argued that price policy could not help the small farmers, hence his idea of relief checks, (that is, the Brannan approach) and the play-game called *having a go at free international trade while trying to keep the worst features from showing up domestically.*

In one critique on the winning paper, R.K. Froker of the University of Wisconsin asked the question: "Can agriculture with its full production, predominantly family-sized farms, and flexible prices operate in an economy with large corporations and national labor unions with their administered prices and wages and regulated production?" This question was not answered by Nicholls or any of the other winners, hence the generally unfavorable reception the winning papers received from farm organizations. Froker pointed out that parity prices were synonymous with parity income if the volume of production and technological developments remained constant, or changed uniformly in industry and agriculture. Technological data available for review suggested something less than the disparity policy writers thought they saw.

In a critical paper, L.H. Simerl of the Illinois Agricultural Association hit the nail on the head. Nicholls' paper "is pregnant with ideas which are sure to meet with widespread approval among the processors and distributors of farm products and among many other persons." Simerl objected to the Nicholls plan because subsidy in place of supports would make farmers dependent upon the government dole and "ever more subservient to national political machines." Simerl pointed out that "while we prepare our mathematical formulas and erect geometric figures representing our ideal world of the future, others forge the real world of tomorrow as they take positions and action on the Pace Bill, the Thomas Bill and upon literally hundreds of other important measures before the nation." Simerl objected that too often economists and national leaders have failed to foresee—a most believable statement, since Simerl himself failed to explain by what stretch of the imagination he could possibly have used 1935-1939 as a base period in his own projections, since his 55 to 75% of parity on a depression base would surely mean a *super-depression!*

The direct payment plan thus arrived.

At one time, even Allan Kline of the Farm Bureau favored the concept, and the Iowa Farm Bureau endorsed a resolution in favor of using the plan on hogs. Whether any of these gentlemen understood the implications has never been answered satisfactorily. At the time of the controversy, Wilken seemed almost alone in reading the consequences and the facts.

And Wilken recited the facts. During the five-year period, 1930-1934, agriculture received 66% of parity in terms of the parity formula being used by Brannan, or 6% more than the floor price called for by the Aiken measure. The results had become legend. During the five-year period, 1935-1939, agriculture received 84% of parity. Census figures revealed unemployment in the latter era at 8 million, or 16% of the available labor force, or 1% unemployment for each 1% farm prices remained below parity. "No program can maintain full employment and national prosperity unless it provides an average of 100% of parity for agriculture."

Wilken did not nail down the real effect of the Brannan Plan. It would tend to confuse Congress and prevent outright repeal of the Aiken Farm Bill, and finally this combination would plunge the nation into deep economic problems.

## [2] THE GROSS FARM DOLLAR

And that in fact became the outcome. Few of those who opposed the Brannan Plan did so for the right reason. Almost all wanted lower prices. Wilken alone opposed it for a reason that could be defended in terms of sound economics. Rural America needed the gross dollar, not a relief check. The farmer's end of the raw materials bill was quite small, after all. Most of the income earned by farm production fed the towns, the machinery makers, the tire factories and the trade centers that served rural

America. "If, under the Brannan program, the prices of these items are permitted to seek their own level, which as I have pointed out under a free trade program is the world level, the retail sales of these products will drop approximately 50%. . . .

"As this drop in retail sales volume takes place, the retail merchant will lose the income to pay taxes and current wages. As wages in the retail trade are reduced, under-consumption will follow. Secretary Brannan would cure this under-consumption with curtailment of production. Curtailed production will mean a reduced flow of raw materials through our economy and further unemployment will take place. This in turn will pyramid the spiral downward and we will find our economy in a regimented depression. Any attempt to collect taxes to balance the budget will give further impetus to the depression."

Almost overnight, the great farm debate became one over whether farming could best be handled with the Aiken formula of 60 to 90% price supports, or the Brannan Plan to the same economic effect. One at a time, farm groups started lining up.

## [3] BLACK HATS AND WHITE HATS

"The Brannan Plan is thoroughly bad and inherently dishonest," said Congressman Mason. Both Kline and O'Neal of the Farm Bureau fought the Brannan Plan, O'Neal calling it a "dastardly proposal." Grange leadership seemed somewhat betwixt and between. Master Herschel Newsom at one point declared himself favorable to the sliding-scale idea. At another point—somewhat later—he became disgusted with flexible supports which were not working. And to AP reporters on the White House steps he once remarked that free market prices might be better with government payments as proposed by Brannan. In the main, however, Board of Trade, Co-op Council and Farm Bureau spokesmen hit the socialism angle, and this made the choice one between black hats and white hats, between the Brannan Plan and the Aiken formula.

When Carl Wilken appeared at the Republican Farm Conference in Sioux City, Iowa in September, 1949 he tried to put sound economics and full parity back into the discussion. Wilken hit hard at two failures of both political parties.

"1. The failure to recognize the importance of agricultural income as the source of our national income. The agricultural industry produces approximately 70% of all the new wealth in the form of raw materials. In the process of using the agricultural raw materials to produce and distribute goods to society, each $1 of gross farm income generates $7 of national income. In other words, our national income is 7 times the value of our agricultural production.

"2. The failure to recognize that parity prices for our agricultural production is the natural price equation that must exist if we are to have full employment, a balanced national budget, and a national income large enough to create the purchasing power to consume our production."

Once again Wilken cited proof—figures, facts, correlations. He explained patiently why income is "lost" when farm prices are not maintained. And then he noted: "If this advice for lower farm prices were coming from Russian Communists, it would be understandable because we know that they would like to destroy our capital economy. But, the advice is coming from supposedly intelligent American citizens, who, if the record means anything, do not understand how our economy operates."

Next Wilken sounded a warning to the Republicans, a warning they would receive no better than had the Democrats: ". . . no political party can operate the economy of the United States on a basis of full employment, a balanced national budget, and pay off the national debt unless it is willing to provide such legislation as may be to maintain an average of 100% of parity at the market place for our agricultural production."

There was no excuse for ignorance. John Baker, A USDA expert, had calculated the tabulations required to illustrate how much the loss would be to national income if Congress failed to support farm prices at a proper level. Those who chose not to listen to Wilken could listen to others, well-credentialed men who had obeyed the canons of academic protocol and still arrived at the same results.

Wilken could always defend his every proposition, but many of those who he convinced couldn't! They couldn't live on the level of a thinker whose mind raced 50 to 100 years ahead of them, and they therefore fell victim to sheer puzzlement. One of the many sales jobs at the Republican Farm Conference that year came from H.E. Babcock, a Cornell product who had helped organize the Cooperative GLF Exchange at Ithaca and the Co-op Council. Babcock told the Republicans that the best "hedge against political unrest is a well-fed citizen," and he equated this with an attack on the Brannan Plan and endorsement of the Aiken Bill, which had still to bring agriculture the wonders of 60 to 90% price supports.

## [4] FRESH LAID PLANS

And this remained the name of the battle while Congress tormented itself over outright repeal of the Aiken measure, or postponement of its dubious benefits. Some of the assists to thinking came on subtly, some with all the tact of an elephant in a china shop. One of the most interesting formed under auspices of Harding College, Searcy, Arkansas, a center of learning that fielded films produced at MGM. One, *Fresh Laid Plans*, depicted an owl as the expert who had been called in to solve the economic problems of Eggville. The owl came up with the plans that ruined the economy. Cost of making the film: $80,000. Such PR efforts touted the Aiken Bill.

Wilken and his associates had no such budget, and a few lone appearances were not a match for dozens of organizations with dozens of budgets running into five and six figures.

Nevertheless, the Wilken idea had taken hold in key places. And so, in 1949, the Congress became attached to a process that really never solved anything, but kept real trouble at arm's length. First Senator Russell of Georgia and Senator Milton Young of North Dakota, a Democrat and a Republican, joined hands across the party aisle to restore 90% price supports for a year. This, in fact, became the *modus operandi*. Each year until 1954 Congress kept the full Aiken formula from being into effect. The arrival of the Korean War, more than any other factor, prompted the lawmakers to stay with the ideas that Wilken had championed for so many years. But price supports accounted for only half of the formula.

# [5] THE HIGH MARKET

During all of the parity arguments, England showed more than passing interest in the removal of American farm parity. Thus when the U.S. Congress returned to 90% price supports in 1949, English financiers must have abandoned hope of maintaining the pound at $4.05. Ever since the Roosevelt Administration jumped the price of gold to $35 an ounce, the pound had been kept in line with the old gold price of $20.67. Through the rest of the 1930s and all through World War II, England kept the pound sterling at $4.05. Some $10 billion in lend lease from the United States extended the British pound an assist in this endeavor.

Now the British pound was devalued to $2.80—or 30%. A host of lesser trading nations followed suit. This action reduced the price of goods being produced in England by 30% to the rest of the world. As a result of this devaluation, the U.S. became the high market in the world. In the five years following the devaluation of the British pound according to Wilken's computation, the U.S. imported $6 billion more in farm products than were exported. The American economy imported its surplus. As a result of the British devaluation, and as a result of imports prompted by Britain's lead in devaluing the pound, American farm raw materials were again perceived to be surplus at the time Dwight D. Eisenhower promised an end to the Korean War and inched close to the presidency.

# CHAPTER 24: THE EXPLOITATION GAME

To the perceptive student of history, the post-Employment Act of 1946 snipes at parity for agriculture did not explode in a vacuum.

## [1] ON SIGNAL

One of the few journals that read it the way it was as the Korean War opened on signal was *Pathfinder*, a Washington, D.C. based news magazine. The United States was importing 90% of the 1.5 million tons of manganese ore the steel industry required, and a U.S. manganese industry barely existed. "Russia simply put the squeeze on us," reported J. Carson Adkerson. "We leaned on her for the bulk of our manganese ore. Then, 18 months ago, she slowed down her shipments to a dribble. We were caught with our stocks down."

Adkerson had warned from as far back as 1927 that Russia was using cheap manganese as a political weapon in order to stifle American production. More recently he and Carl Wilken testified before a House Subcommittee on Mines and Mining, and that testimony brought the matter of cheap world raw materials prices around full circle, so that all who wished to look could see the folly of public policy written by the powers that be for the powers that be.

"In the United States, it would be very expensive to grow bananas or coffee, and impossible to produce tungsten," noted *Emergency Management of the National Economy*, a text used to train civilian and military personnel in 1950. Such a statement might have been a matter of simple error, but there seemed always to be enough such errors to pose grave question marks whenever men like Wilken and Adkerson testified.

They did testify, of course, and what they said went into the record well before the outbreak of hostilities in Korea. Adkerson detailed again, as he had in 1937, the name of the exploitation game. By quoting copiously from *Raw Materials in War and Peace*, a West Point text, he again showed the importance of ferro-alloy metals—chromium, manganese, molybdenum, nickel, tungsten, and vanadium—as vital to steel and iron production. And he noted the importance of antimony, asbestos, fluorspar, graphite, mercury, mica, the platinum metals, tin and uranium to a modern economy. West Point graduates knew, if others did not, that national prosperity in most of the world was tied to the world price of raw materials. In almost every case, the sovereign state had taken unto itself title to mineral lands. In many cases sovereignty fetched a good price when the colonels chose to sell it, or the internationalists chose to buy.

Through the decades, cheap raw materials coming into the U.S. had been balanced against cheap farm production moving out. In a professional manner, Adkerson proved his points. Though highly technical in nature, much of his material lacked the quiet simplicity a man like Wilken could impart.

## [2] MINES AND MINING

Adkerson had known and worked with Wilken since the first big Raw Materials National Council meeting in Sioux City, 1938. During recent months they had compared notes and structured figures that could not be dynamited apart. In the end, Wilken's appearance before the Mines and Mining Subcommittee furnished posterity with one of his finest papers, one that leaned on concepts so simple and so profound even a child could understand.

Wilken told the Congressmen: "Now this matter of steel tariffs came up at the time Abraham Lincoln was president. Abraham Lincoln was not bothered much with economists—the profession was not familiar to him at the time—but he had to reach a decision just like you people will have to reach, and the question came up as to whether we should import rails needed for the development of our railroad system, or whether we should produce our own, and Abraham Lincoln at that time stated approximately as follows: "I don't know anything about tariffs, I don't know much about rails, but here is one thing I do know; that if we buy the rails from foreign countries they will have our money and we will have the rails. If we buy the rails from ourselves, we will have both the rails and the money."

As a result the steel industry had always had a protected price, and therefore there was no justification for anything less than a support price for lead, manganese, zinc, or any other product.

Earlier, there had been testimony from a Bureau of Mines official, Elmer W. Pehrson, who stated that in case of war, failure to procure manganese would force the American nation to throw up its hands and say, "Well, we have lost the war."

There were deposits, Wilken pointed out, and there was no excuse for a man like General Eisenhower telling the National Press Club that deposits did not exist. The ores in the United States were as rich as any in the world. There was only one reason why manganese was not being produced—public policy made production impossible. First laws had to be written that made production possible, then those same laws rated enforcement, Wilken said. ". . . if in the administration of that act the departments of the government sabotage its operations," then it would be up to Congress to follow through and take the necessary steps.

There had been a Stock Piling Act in 1939, and yet 2½ years to the day later came Pearl Harbor, and still there was no stockpile. Only the inventory of strategic materials in the hands of private enterprise stood between the United States and disaster. There was criminal negligence involved because the administrative part of the government simply refused to comply with the law.

The same thing happened again in 1946. As the President signed the Buy American clause he ordered different departments to avoid recognizing it. Wilken had appeared before the Mines and Mining Subcommittee a year earlier. There was no stockpile in 1947, and there was no stockpile in 1948. The 79th Congress passed an act to pay premium prices on lead, copper, zinc, manganese and other ores. President Truman vetoed the act, and mines closed their shafts as if on signal. Rather than getting a stockpile, the measure Congress passed ended up wiping out the stockpile so that a few international companies could use blacks in the Congo to better effect.

## [3] CHEAP RAW MATERIALS PRODUCTION

Why had the United States adopted a policy antagonistic to the development of domestic minerals? According to Wilken, Congress had been sold on an economic theory that was satisfactory to the industrialists. By 1925-1929, the price level in the United States had risen to 55% of 1910-1914 level. "American industrialists felt that the raw material price in the United States and the price of labor was too high, and under the view of their economists they decided that it would be better for them to import cheap raw materials from abroad." The appropriate committee to promote the international control of minerals was set up, Wilken testified, exactly as J. Carson Adkerson had testified before. Named to chair that committee was Charles Leith, a sometime employee of American Steel Institute, and chief mineral consultant to the War Production Board in WWII, and in 1948 acting chairman of a number of subcommittees appointed from mining companies by the Secretary of Interior. It was this committee that first announced an "exploit minerals" policy and it was this committee that proposed special expense allowances so that government could assist American firms in developing minerals abroad. The committee did not seek to promote development of minerals at home.

From that day forward, American firms turned their backs on domestic development so that they could go to the four comers of the world, investing money, and contributing to cheap raw materials production worldwide.

Wilken read into the record some eight pages of material J. Carson Adkerson had supplied. Some of it tunneled back to 1929, some merely repeated the testimony of the 1937 hearing, but in the process Wilken tied the matter of metals to the matter of parity agriculture in order to point out how institutional business could not possibly write public policy, that Congress had to do the job.

"In 1941, when war broke out, the Japs immediately invaded the far east and shut off our supply of rubber, tin and other strategic materials," Wilken related. "It took my good friend, Senator Gillette of Iowa, over 12 months to unfasten the hold of the international rubber cartel on the different parts of the government and make it possible for us to produce synthetic rubber in the United States. Even though we needed it for war, and we were at war, it still took him about 12 months to get the thing under way."

Not even the war for survival of the system caused institutional business to look beyond its own interest, Wilken reminded. With cheap world tin cut off during WWII, there was bound to be a shortage. "I knew there were tin deposits in the Black Hills of South Dakota," Wilken related. "I wrote to Donald Nelson, who was Chairman of the War Production Board, and told him about these tin deposits, and as a result of that letter I was asked to meet with the Lead and Tin Division to tell them about the deposits of tin in South Dakota." As a result of the meeting a man was dispatched to the Black Hills. A few weeks later, he reported back—"No tin."

"Where did he go," Wilken wanted to know. "Did he go to the School of Mines?"

No, the gung-ho explorer hadn't gone to the School of Mines.

Wilken realized he had gone too fast and imposed too much strain on the process of ratiocination. "I want you to send out another man, and I will tell you where to send him" he said. "I want him to go up and see Dr. Andrew Karstens, South Dakota School of Mines, and Dr. Karstens will put him in his car and take him out to the tin deposits, show him the ore body and show him pieces of ore weighing 100 or 200 pounds, and get him some samples to bring back to you."

Was this a matter of ignorance, or thoroughly informed self interest? The Barium Steel Company did set up operations, but actual production of Black Hills tin became stalled. After WWII the project was dropped. There was always testimony before any committee that American production wasn't feasible. And yet there was tin in the Appalachian range, in Oregon, and in South Dakota.

"The only reason we do not produce is a matter of price. Today the only reason why they are not producing manganese and a lot of other materials in the United States is just simply a matter of price."

Why, then, didn't Barium Steel Company produce 10,000 tons as Abe Fortas, then Assistant Secretary of the Interior, advised?

"I imagine the international tin cartel had enough influence to head it off," Wilken said.

Cheap raw materials for the world was the real curse. Instead of a policy of cheap raw materials, Wilken argued, "our policy should be first to maintain a solvent and prosperous United States, and then bring the rest of the world up to our level instead of going out and reducing our price level to that of the rest of the other countries, and pushing the whole world into chaos. If you are going to carry out any kind of help for the rest of the world, we must start and maintain this one fundamental premise, American production at American price levels. This is how we won the war, and this is how we will win the peace, if we win it . . . ."

## [4] AN UNECONOMIC PRACTICE TO IMPORT

The exchange equation made it so.

"We generate two units of income and two units of labor in the process of producing raw materials, handling them, and taking them to the factories. Then we utilize roughly one unit of labor and generate one unit of income in the factory, and then we generate two units of labor and two units of income from the factory to the consumer. That is the five times turn your materials go through in being handled by labor and the turn that your dollar goes through to exchange the production about which we speak."

With this equation in tow, Wilken asked the lawmakers whether America could afford to produce ore rather than buy it abroad. The answer was self evident. When raw materials were imported, the importing nation lost that part of the economic cycle from raw material production to factory, and in the use of an imported raw material there remained only a three times turn of the national income instead of the five times turn available if raw materials were produced at home.

Imported raw materials generated one-half as much national income as domestic production. Thus it became an uneconomic practice to import raw materials that could be produced at home.

Both importation at the domestic price and at the world price violated economic common sense, Wilken pointed out. "A 10 cent per pound price on copper, for instance, would generate 50 cents of national income—the base price x the trade turn of 5. It costs us nothing to pay the additional price because the additional price will automatically generate the additional national income to sustain it."

During WWII the United States produced more materials than the rest of the world combined, and all the while the American people enjoyed a higher standard of living, more food, better clothing—even during a war. By the end of that decade, even after the war was over, the nation enjoyed a balanced budget, was paying out foreign relief from current collections, and the population was consuming 20% more per capita than had been consumed during the 1925-1929 period. The reason for all this, Wilken submitted, was price. And the fact that America enjoyed a higher price level did not make things cost more in terms of hours of labor.

But look at what happened when a nation became afraid to pay the price for production. A 20-cent pound of copper generated $1 of national income. But if public policy made it possible for industry to pay only half the price—the rest to be taken up by subsidy to the primary producer— then the exchange equation fell apart. First, only four steps in the trade turn became operative, and the national income generated by 10-cent copper became 40 cents, not 50 cents. The 10-cent subsidy had to come out of a deficit simply because 10 cent copper would not generate enough income to make a subsidy possible.

[That such reasoning wasn't transparently clear became evident when Wilken was questioned.]

MR. ENGLE. Let us take manganese. What price do you say we would have on manganese?

MR. WILKEN. I assume it would be about $1 a unit. That is the price I assume.

The $1 price represented American parity. But Representative Engle wanted to know about imports. The world price was 70 cents a pound.

MR. ENGLE. Assume it is 70 cents, and if you put a tariff on it, you would bring the price to $1, and that would be a 30 cent tariff.

MR. WILKEN. That is right.

MR. ENGLE. And the fellow shipping it in pays the tariff, and he tacks it onto the price and the consumer at the steel mill pays it. Now if you do it the other way, put a subsidy on of 30 cents, the producer pays or the consumer pays at 70 cents in effect and the government is paying the 30 cents, and instead of getting the 30 cents the government goes back and taxes everybody, including the consumer, and on an over-all basis then the difference between a subsidy and a tariff is that the consumer pays the tariff and the taxpayers pay the subsidy, is that right?

MR. WILKEN. That is true, but in the process you have a little loss. Let me illustrate. Suppose the foreign price of manganese is 70 cents, and we will put on a 30 cent a unit tariff. That would automatically force the industry to pay $1 a unit. Supposing we ship in 1,000,000 tons of manganese at 30 cents a unit . . . where does the tariff collected go? It goes into the treasury of the United States. If that money is used to pay for the cost of operating the government and reduces your taxes a fair amount, it has not cost the consumer anything particularly. If you bring it in at 70 cents and pay the consumer 30 cents, then it becomes a deficit and has to be paid out of the taxes of the government just the same, and, of course, whether the taxpayer pays it or the consumer pays it, in effect the consumer bears it anyhow.

MR. ENGLE. You get back to where you started, and it is just like the dog chasing his tail.

MR. WILKEN. That is right . . . with the exception that if you use raw materials at half price, you have one-half the national income you need, and if you pay the full price you will have all the income you need to operate at a profit and without a deficit.

MR. ENGLE. That is assuming that there is not a kink in your formula some place.

## [5] DEBASED KEYNESIANISM

Wilken had successfully defended his formula before experts and layman alike ever since the Raw Materials National Council was first formed, but there was always the question about a kink in the formula. The economists out of the colleges, with their debased Keynesianism in tow, regularly fell back on investment as the prime mover, and hardly a lawmaker questioned the system despite the fact that it ran counter to the laws of physics and pretended perpetual motion in economics. The formidable array of educated experts fairly baffled lawmakers, whereas Wilken's simple presentation seemed too easily understood or too difficult to comprehend to rate recognition. To a man, Representatives and Senators seemed obsessed with the idea that fantastic complications had to attend an explanation of the economic equation. Many must have believed that the topic was at least as difficult as nuclear physics or relativity, something that only a few masterminds could understand. Anything with as much common sense attached as what Wilken was talking about was suspect of having a kink.

Nevertheless Wilken convinced Representative Engle that a tariff made more sense than a subsidy, and that the trade turn between raw materials and national income was five, considering the state of the arts.

As it stood now, Wilken noted, America was required to support raw material prices for the entire world in order to protect its own solvency. Tariff reductions and currency devaluations made it so. Gold was being bought at 69% above the 1925-1929 level in order to be remanded into a hole in Kentucky. Why couldn't the nation apply the same thinking to strategic raw materials of the world, maintain the same price level, and force currencies up to the same level. A stockpile of strategic raw materials not only rated recognition as war insurance, it also helped insure national solvency.

Looking world economics squarely in the eye on the eve of the Korean War, Wilken pointed to an inescapable fact. Gold was at 169 on the index—or 69% above the 1925-1929 = 100 level, [100 + 69 = 169]. And sales were being made to the rest of the world on the basis of an index, 169. But the U.S. was buying back goods on an index of 120. On some $8 billion imports, America short-changed the rest of the world $4 billion— the figure that constituted handsome profits for traders of several shades. But now, circa 1948, the rest of the world was so short of dollars a Marshall Plan had to be devised to loan them money.

There would be a day, not too far away, when the exchange flow would reverse, but first agriculture and raw materials states-side had to be scaled back either to or below the world level. The machinery for all this was already on the books, floating in a nebulous limbo. The unseen hands, it seemed, were only waiting for the exact moment. And at the exact moment the principal provisions of the Aiken Bill—the 60 to 90% parity formula—would be allowed to go into effect.

Wilken recited much of the same material before the same subcommittee a year later, adding a preliminary tabulation—one that illustrated the relationship between payment for raw materials and national income for the period 1929 to 1948. The total average percentage of gross farm income to national income turned out to be 14.3%. So far each $1 of gross farm production continued to be matched by approximately $7 of national income.

# CHAPTER 25:
# FRUSTRATION ECONOMICS TRIUMPHANT

The Korean War provided something of a grace period for 90% price supports, but Wilken knew the fight was far from won. He became employed by Homer Capehart's Banking and Currency Committee because he sensed that the Steagall approach was still the best one, and that rapport with a powerful Committee might prove to be a sound anchor position for an idea that took so much explaining.

## [1] KEY TO SOUND PROSPERITY

Early in 1950, Carl Wilken scooted a 28-page booklet entitled *Key To Sound Prosperity* through the presses. Most of the material had been printed before, either as entries in *Prosperity Unlimited* or as paragraphs in talks, testimony, or *Congressional Record* inserts. The most important contribution of the booklet was its series of tables, almost all of them up-to-the-minute arrays of figures that proved out each of the several points in the Wilken dialogue.* The table that Wilken had given to the Subcommittee on Mines and Mining, one that illustrated the relationship between gross farm income, gross mineral income and the relationship to national income, was updated to include the year 1949 in terms of an estimated figure. The 1:5 ratio stood out like a brass monument.

Another table developed the relationship of salaries and wages to national income, with the near 60% level remaining constant from 1929 to 1949.

In condensed form, the many graphs in *Prosperity Unlimited* floated by again—"Comparison of Consumer Expenditures For Food, Shoes, Beverage, Clothing & Tobacco To National Income," "Comparison of Non Durable and Durable Goods to Consumer Expenditures," "Comparison of Retail Sales to Gross Farm Income," "Comparison of Imports to National Income and Ratio of Imports to Domestic Retail Sales," "Percentage of

---

* See the Interlude, pages 167-177 for an update on these several charts.

National Income Spent for Food in The United States," "Comparison of Gross National Income to Farm Proprietors and Total Wage Payments to Labor," to mention a few. Wilken and Senator Homer Capehart were agreed that a manual of sorts was needed, because too much of Wilken's thinking was being lost in the orientation process. *Key To Sound Prosperity* wrapped up the package—if only lawmakers could be induced to read and study it!

The conjectural economics of the help-yourself set was very much in evidence as the new decade of the '50s arrived. The American Manufacturers' Association was telling farmers to produce cotton cheaper, and the Committee for Economic Development was yammering about efficiency, cheaper raw materials, and the kind of frustration economics Carl Wilken had spent his life in fighting. And still, while the Steagall Amendment hung on with weakening fingers, there was the proof. The inroads being made by the gut-agriculture seers had temporarily driven wheat to 85% of parity, but by late 1950 it was back to within 2 or 3% of the proper relationship. But there was this yammering Drew Pearson telling his readers how Mike Di Salle couldn't regulate prices because farmers had obtained laws to feed themselves ever so properly. As a matter of fact, Senator Young pointed out on the Senate floor, December 19, 1950, farm prices had barely managed to stay in the squared circle while wages took two rounds. All this was workaday stuff, Wilken realized, spot dislocation, because parity was a relationship, not a price, and as long as the essence of full parity remained the law of the land a balanced income equation became the inevitable outcome.

Wilken's argument that price supports cost nothing was being challenged regularly. But there were those few friends.

Representative Charles W. Vursell: "You hear much criticism of the billions of dollars Congress has voted to support farm price. These billions were responsible for the continued prosperity we have had since the farm program became operative, and have not been lost. . . . On loans and purchasing of surplus farm products to the extent of over $8 billion by the government during the past 17 years, the balance sheet furnished me by the government up to April 30, 1950 shows a total net loss of only $212,858,871."

Figures were floating around like popcorn in a windstorm as newspapers, lawmakers and economists debated the high cost of supporting agriculture. The *Washington Post* was reporting $1 billion as a cost figure, and to this Frank Wooley, vice president of the Commodity Credit Corporation replied: "The figure of $1 billion which has been used in newspapers as the figure representing the cost of CCC price-support programs actually represents the net withdrawals of funds from the United States

Treasury during the fiscal year 1950 (about the same in 1949) for investment in loans or inventories by the Corporation." Senator Milton Young,
commenting on all this reflected that the modest cost paled when compared to the $20 billion or more spent in Europe since WWII on boon-
doggling projects.

Occasionally, and when time permitted, men like Representative Fred
Crawford recited the general wrap-up of Wilken economics, and sounded a warning. Because of the Steagall Amendment, Crawford in effect
said, "our business units were doing a larger volume of sales in 1950 on
a lower extension of credit with a comparatively smaller inventory than
in 1939." Yet credit was being restricted, and prices were being driven up,
up, up. Crawford wanted to know why? Why was the nation suddenly
pursuing a policy of creating an age of inflation?

## [2] INFLATIONARY BUYING POWER

Wilken covered these points and many more in a special report for the
National Independent Meat Packers Association. In searching terms he
pointed to the dilemma of economics, the fact that "A drop in the price
level in peacetime can leave just as much wreckage as the inflation caused
by war."

Wilken prepared for the packers a tabulation to illustrate exactly how
inflation had accompanied WWII. In substance he showed that there had
been a balance of national income above consumer expenditures of $199.1
billion during the three main war years, and that personal taxes had taken
away only $57.6 billion of this amount. Thus there was inflationary buy-
ing power of $141.5 billion at the end of the war. Price ceilings alone
could not stop inflation in WWII, and they could not stop inflation during
the Korean affair unless excess income was used to balance the national
budget.

This was the gist of what the independent packers wanted to know.
From a businessman's viewpoint, price ceilings were not something de-
voutly to be wished, but a businessman's thinking could not be passed
off as public policy unless that business rated international attention. The
independent packers weren't that big, and they knew it.

". . . price ceilings can very easily penalize some groups in our economic cycle," Wilken warned, "and prevent the very production which is
needed to supply the dollar demand from other sources." Wilken recon-
structed the several ratios of interest to meat provendors, and in the process taught them a little arithmetic. The packers had wanted to know
how prices of meats in 1939 compared to those in 1949.

On an index of 1935-1939 = 100, disposable income in 1939 was 105.

By 1949 it was 250. By dividing 105 into 250, it could be determined that a round steak could sell for 238% of 1939 prices and still be selling on the same basis as 1939. Average prices for such a cut in 51 cities in 1939 came to 36 cents. By multiplying 238 × 36, the result became 85.7 cents. Actual cost figures for 1949 were 85.3 cents.

With such a simple arithmetic, Wilken in effect taught those who would listen how to figure things out for themselves. But, always, he cautioned his "students" to consider all the facts. Some of those facts could prove elusive.

*Item.* The population in New York State was spending 50% of its personal income for goods, as compared to an expenditure of 70% for goods at retail by the people of Iowa. This made rural America roughly the market for 50% of the nation's factory production. It was for this reason that factory payrolls and gross farm income rose and fell in direct proportion.

*Item.* The low prices for fats and oils became an important factor in considering meat surplus. The removal of the tax on colored oleomargarine increased the competitive price situation between oleo and butter. Butter is the production from surplus whole milk supplies. Removal of price supports on butter could curtail dairy production and in turn meat production from that source.

*Item.* The low price of fats and oils represented a dislocation of real values. A pound of fat contains about 4,080 calories as compared to 1,275 calories in a pound of lean meat. Yet fat was selling at 25 cents a pound compared to 85 cents for round steak or lean meat.

It was in his paper for the Independent Meat Packers that Wilken best discussed the anatomy of red meat, the reality that each farm was a factory, that each cow was an unpaid labor force, that red meat production was a "technology" factor since it enabled more feed grain raw materials to be used than if the nation subsisted on mush. Some 11 tables tied Wilken's analysis together. Taken as a composite they constituted a Gordian knot the experts could hardly cut, much less unravel.

First there was the matter of capital investment. Between 1939 and 1949, the price level had increased from 77.1 % to 167.5 on an index of 1925-1929 = 100. This represented an increase of 117%. This in turn meant that future capital investment in the packing industry and other enterprises engaged in meat production would be relatively higher. When this adjustment was made, the percentage of the consumer's dollar going to farmers would decline to that extent.

Ceiling prices during WWII kept margins between farmer and consumer quite low, with resultant black markets. If black markets were to be prevented, Wilken asserted, then margins had to be maintained at "proper" levels. The equation required it. Here at the start of the Korean War, there were near 10 million biological persons, including unpaid family help, working the agricultural chore. The retail and wholesale trade, in 1949, employed a few over 11 million. "This illustrates that if these men are to receive a relative wage in our system of distribution, a proper margin must be maintained to provide the income to pay the workers in wholesale and retail trades."

Withal, it was the institutional business element that chose to upset the exchange equation, Wilken reminded again and again, and this became an easy task because so few in business and government understood how their economy operated. Thus the fats and oils cartels could visit the effects of their coconut grove dealings down to every farm, because the failure of tallow and lard to fetch a price meant that the price of steaks, hams, loins and bacon would also be affected. The pronouncements of seers in Washington could and did affect red meat prices, because conjectural economics still tolerated manipulators, future traders, and the tout sheet-fed supply and demand guessing game.

When swivel chair producers in Washington declared a tremendous pork supply increase in 1949, Wilken said, the markets responded, even though clear analysis of the situation made such pronouncements unnecessary. The killoff that followed as hogs hit 14 cents prevented needed expansion. "The packer failed to level off this excess marketing through storage, and on September 2, 1950 we find hogs selling on the Chicago market with a top of close to $25 per hundredweight or about $10 above last December."

There was only one reason for such extreme fluctuation. Traders make their profits on a swinging market. Producers make theirs on a stable market. Both results were a requirement of the exchange equation.

## [3] NO GAIN

Arithmetic, Wilken reminded again and again—as young men went to war so international cartels could profit—did not permit a change in the cost of living through a change in price levels. "When prices fall below the parity level, reducing the price of food, unemployment follows. If those who remain employed were taxed to support the unemployed there would be no gain on an individual basis." And this, indeed, became the case as the low parity crowd—inch by inch—got its way. As prices in agriculture fell too low to create the income necessary for full employment, the nostrum of choice became governmental expenditures so that all might live. The amounts needed were charged to the deficit.

To prove this point, Wilken constructed a table entitled, "Comparison of Weekly Wages with Retail Food Prices:"

Wilken summed up the subject as follows. "Labor clamors for higher wages, the farmer for higher prices, thus causing a spiral in our price level while the real cost of living remains the same. Temporarily some group has an advantage because of the submarginal factors I have mentioned or a shift in the price of some item of goods or a wage increase in some industry. But over a period of years these adjustments have to be balanced by others throughout the economy as a whole."

| Staple food items | Retail price 1939[1] cents | Retail price 1949[1] cents |
|---|---|---|
| Loaf of white bread | 7.9 | 14.0 |
| Round steak (pound) | 36.0 | 85.3 |
| Chuck roast (pound) | 23.4 | 55.5 |
| Pork chops (pound) | 30.4 | 74.3 |
| Bacon (pound) | 31.9 | 66.5 |
| Butter (pound) | 32.5 | 72.5 |
| Sugar (pound) | 5.4 | 9.5 |
| Eggs (dozen) | 32.1 | 69.6 |
| Milk (quart, fresh, delivered) | 12.2 | 21.1 |
| Lard (pound) | 11.0 | 19.2 |
| Total cost | 223.7 | 487.5 |

Parity for labor and agriculture remained forever a requirement of the system, and failure to analyze the economic mechanism could be excused at the sophomore level, and not any higher. By mid-1951 John Kenneth Galbraith had made the argument for direct controls—accompa-

---

[1] Retail prices, Bureau of Census, U.S. Department of Commerce, average price 51 leading cities.

NOTE: President's Economic Report to Congress January 1950:

| | | |
|---|---|---|
| Wage per hour 1939 in manufacturing | | $ .633 |
| Hours worked | 37.7 | |
| Wage per hour 1949 in manufacturing | | 1.40 |
| Hours worked | 39.1 | |
| Weekly wages in 1939 | | 23.86 |
| Weekly wages in 1949 | | 54.74 |
| Increase in average weekly wages 1939-49, percent | 125.0 | |
| Increase in total cost of food items, percent | 118.0 | |
| Buying power of weekly wages in 1949 as compared to 1939, percent | 117.8 | |
| Buying power of hourly wages in 1949 as compared to 1939, percent | 101.4 | |
| Time required to earn food items in 1949, 3 hours, 29 minutes | | |
| Time required to earn food items in 1939, 3 hours, 32 minutes | | |

nied by stiff taxes and tight credit—but looking over the literature from vantage point 1970 one might question whether either Galbraith or *Fortune* or the Economic Advisers really understood the name of the game.

*Fortune* headlined, "The Parity Outrage," as it castigated farmers for having jockeyed too successfully, making "stabilization of anyone else's prices or wages all but impossible." Only a highly sophisticated journal could have been as hopelessly and articulately wrong as that. *Fortune* pointed out that parity was no fixed plateau. "It is a self-hoisting device with a hair-trigger spring." *Fortune* did not point out that parity followed the other indexes, that it did not lead them. Parity for farmers did not set its own figures. The rest of the economy did. It was this confusion, manufactured by the opinion makers of the nation, that made the fight for full parity a losing game.

## [4] PRICE STABILITY OR BOOMS AND BUSTS

Through Tom Huff of Sioux City, a serum manufacturer, Wilken received repeated invitations to appear before annual meetings of the Animal Health Institute. He appeared before the group in 1951 and again in 1952. During the latter appearance he presented each of the pharmaceutical and biologic makers with a booklet, *Price Stability or Booms and Busts*. Surely, Wilken reasoned, businessmen would do what was best for their own interest if they understood. *Booms and Busts* was simple enough to be comprehensible, and yet complicated enough to retain the respect of people who dealt with facts rather than rhetoric. During the Chicago meeting of the Animal Health Institute in 1952, Wilken tied the topic of the hour, socialism, to the thesis of his booklet.

Wilken knew that the first reaction to the idea of a stable price level would be viewed as socialism, and he met the point head on. "That is because of your economic training that the law of supply and demand shall govern," he said. "You have been led to believe that it is some strange, powerful force that will bring about the payment of a proper price for production."

And then Wilken proceeded to annihilate the "conventional wisdom" that had become the businessman's copybook maxim. Failure to use government in its proper role, he said, had brought socialism to the nation's front door. "If we wish to maintain our American system, then equity of trade must exist at home and abroad." Wilken had used a quotation from Emerson before—"Our whole history appears to be a last effort of Divine Providence to help the human race"—and he used it now, but he went a bit further. The proof of the economic equation was in the record, and beyond that there could be no more proof, except that contained in the

Good Book, that "every laborer is worthy of his hire."

"Parity prices for agriculture, a fair wage for labor and an equitable profit for our business units is the very essence of our Constitution and form of government. . . . Divine Providence has given us the natural resources, the kind of government and an economic record from which to ferret out the basic steps which must be taken to replace socialism and communistic doctrine and to return to economic practices in accord with the basic concept of our forefathers and divine law."

## [5] INDUSTRY STAKE

It was an appeal that Wilken was to use with increased frequency, both because the hour was late and because there existed a real question as to whether the American people understood their birthright, the one they were about to barter away for a mess of pottage. In 1954 Wilken updated his earlier material and issued a new booklet, *Industry's Stake in Raw Materials Price Supports*. Farmers, in the main, had proved they would not listen to reason. Perhaps industry would.

Wilken wanted business to know something about the Leon Keyserling blunder, namely the one he counseled on price ceilings for OPS in 1951. The Keyserling recommendation was that operating margins be based on 85% of normal. This required a price level 15% too low and brought a cost squeeze to the doorstep of business. Faced with fixed labor costs via contracts and fixed capital costs, institutional business forced down farm prices in order to protect profits.

"After the Korean War ended, wage demands increased in ratio to any increase in the 85% price level. To generate buying power to meet wages and interest, borrowed money was used. As a result we had debt expansion at all levels. The consumer buying power was mortgaged with repayments and budgets balanced at the grocery counter, thus adding to the downward pressure on farm products."

## [6] IT'S A LONG STORY

As the election of Dwight D. Eisenhower neared, the new theory period Wilken had battled for two decades was ready to go for broke. At the time of my longest interview with Wilken the emergence of that new era was covered as follows:

Q. Institutionally and politically, how did we come to enter this debt-creation period?

WILKEN. It's a long story. I never thought the American people would be gullible enough to swallow this. You go back to 1948—we had a solvent economy, we had about an $8 billion surplus in the federal, state and local budgets, and we used about $16 billion debt to expand the economy. At that time we were reconverting from the war economy and reopening a lot of business units that had been closed because of rationing. Now we go along and the Korean War breaks out, so we move this debt expansion up from $18 to $40 billion a year. In the meantime, because of rulings under OPS limiting industry to 85% of full operating margin, the income of private enterprise started to decline. Wages and interest—the cost factors in operating the economy—kept going up. In 1953 the Korean War ended and Senator Homer Capehart was Chairman of the Committee on Currency and Banking. I served on that Committee. At that time I said that if the Republican Party doesn't restore the value of our farm production in the income of private enterprise, we're going to have a depression. He sponsored some six luncheons for Republican Senators and House members. And we invited in leading industrialists. We had the president of Dow Chemical, the president of du Pont and the vice president of Allied Chemical, and we had the president of St. Joseph Lead and Zinc, and the president of Colorado Fuel and Iron. At one of the meetings we had one of the richest oil men in the world—H.L. Hunt. We went over all of this. But nothing was done.

Q. Did you try to tell this story to any of Ike's economic advisers?

WILKEN. I spent time with Gabriel Hauge, who was Eisenhower's first Chairman of the Council of Economic Advisers. Hauge should have known about agriculture since he was from South Dakota, but it all ended with them doing nothing. So the Korean War ended. And the debt expansion dropped back from $40 billion to $30 billion. Well, that immediately took out about $25 billion in unearned income that debt creation had accounted for, and we had the 1954 depression. Then instead of correcting the situation, we suddenly injected $72 billion credit in 1955. This compared to $30 billion in 1954. And the only reason I can account for it is that Eisenhower's ghost writers in 1954 [election year 1954] prepared a speech for him in which he stated we were going to $500 billion income.

Q. Eisenhower also made a talk at Kasson, Minnesota in which he called for 100% farm parity, did he not?

WILKEN. I'll tell you how this came about. They had a meeting in Denver. And at this meeting there were Senator Frank Carlson of Kansas; Congressman Ben Jensen, of Iowa; Congressman Clifford Hope of Kansas; Earl Taylor of the *Country Gentleman;** Sherman Adams, who became

---

* *Country Gentleman* was bought by *Farm Journal* in June 1955. Earlier the *Farm Journal* had acquired *Pathfinder* and renamed it *Town Journal*, and operated it jointly with *Farm Journal*. Before they were taken over by *Farm Journal* and combined to serve the Sun Oil Company empire, both *Country Gentleman* and *Pathfinder* figured heavily in telling some parts of the story covered in this book.

Eisenhower's right hand man until he was bounced; and Anchor Nelson of Minnesota, who was vice president of the Farm Bureau up there. They debated the issue of 90% price supports, or the Farm Bureau's idea of no price supports. When they got through Eisenhower pointed to each one and asked who won the debate. The 90% boys won. So they prepared this speech which Ike gave in Minnesota and South Dakota, stating he was going to continue the 90% price supports.

Q. Why did Eisenhower abandon the idea?

WILKEN. When he got elected and after he appointed his advisers, they just completely turned him around. And one of the boys who was responsible for it was his brother, Milton Eisenhower, who was one of the original New Deal people under Wallace in the Department of Agriculture.

## [7] FROM FAR ABOVE CAYUGA'S WATERS

Many of those who turned Ike around had been waiting in the wings, having arrived from far above Cayuga's waters. Cornell was *the* agricultural college in the U.S. and the publishing center for farm opinion making. *American Agriculturist* snailed its way into the mails from Ithaca, New York, and Cooperative Grange-League-Federation Exchange (GLF for short) called Ithaca home base, having assembled its know-how and unlikely name from the New York Grange, Dairymen's League and Farm Bureau Federation. The Cornell crowd were all card-carrying members of the low-prices-for-raw-materials-set—and this penchant paid off the day international business openly captured the presidency. The cast of characters not only awed Ike, it staggered the last of those who believed in Carl H. Wilken.

Dean Myers knew a buck when he saw it. He liked directorships—in Continental Can, U.S. Industrial Chemicals, New York State Electric and Gas Corporation, L.C. Smith & Corona Typewriters, Insular Lumber, AVCO Manufacturing, Food Fair Stores and Mutual Life Insurance Company of New York. In addition to the above he made meetings as Deputy Chairman of the Federal Reserve Bank of New York, and filled in the American Bankers Association on everything they needed to know about farming. When he took office as Ike's National Agricultural Advisory Committee Chairman, the press release listed him as a *farmer*.

Dr. Earl Butz, the new Assistant Secretary of Agriculture under Benson was a comer, having gone the platform route with Farm Bureau, the Pennsylvania Bankers Association and the American Enterprise Association. Although a transplant to Purdue, original home base was Cornell.

Don Paarlberg enjoyed "bright pupil" status with Dean Myers. He could and did write, and he could and did side with the low world raw materials price thinkers. As economic adviser to Ezra Taft Benson, his role became essentially the one he suggested in a talk at West Millbury, Massachusetts in 1955—that the postwar prosperity of farmers was "a dream world, and no one expected it to last" There were those who would see to it.

Deane Waldo Malott, as President of Cornell, filled out a deep-think role, and it included a cheap raw materials philosophy. He had been assistant dean of the Harvard Business School before becoming vice president of the Hawaiian Pineapple Company. His list of credits included directorships at General Mills, Pitney-Bowes, B.F. Goodrich, Owens-Corning Fiberglass and the First National Bank if Ithaca.

Herrell DeGraff, a sometime "milk salesman" on TV, had distinguished himself as a Farm Bureau speaker and secretary of the Foundation for Economic Education, the Irvington-on-Hudson parking ground for ex-Cornell professors who could rationalize low world raw materials prices because they were paid well to do so.

Jim A. McConnell, GLF manager for 16 years, stood in the wings to serve Ezra Benson as Administrator of Commodity Stabilization Service, the office charged with management of price support programs. McConnell hated the very idea of supports. He stayed on long enough to see the new order installed, then retired back to teaching a new course, Business in Agriculture.

Victor Emanuel was always available for low raw materials counsel. Although his chief concern was AVCO Manufacturing, interests included ACF-Brill Motors, Bendix, New Idea Farm Equipment Company, and Crosley Corporation. He was a director at Republic Steel. There were other credits to spare, one of the most important being friendship with E.T. Benson. Benson used Emanuel's AVCO office in the World Center Building as headquarters prior to the inauguration.

There were others from far above Cayuga's waters—too many to list—and they all told the same story, a story as old as economic development and exploitation. And the general's tent became silent.

Both Charles Ray and John Lee Coulter were gone now. Coulter, rich with years and experience, faded from view shortly after helping Wilken complete the cost of living study for NASDA in 1947. He died in early 1959. Charles B. Ray, no longer able to keep up his massive charts and statistical arrays, retired with General Wood and passed away even before the parity concept he championed died. Only Wilken remained, a lone batsman, a tired warrior, a single solitary figure amazed but not awed by the passage of events.

Here he had the key to the economic riddle, and the key was being rejected. Like the Frenchman Turgot, Wilken couldn't believe the nation would turn its back once this truth had been given. Much as with *les economistes,* Wilken was in revolt against artificial wealth, and political artifices for wealth getting, a struggle in which he was bested by interests that found a profit in buying cheap and selling dear. Now would come the time when those same interests pulled down the whole economic structure on top of themselves.

Wilken was least able to measure accurately the powers of the vested interests—and he was least able to accept the fact that his drive had largely spent itself, leaving the old way of thinking in command of the field.

# CHAPTER 26: A BALANCE SHEET

Carl H. Wilken had defended the raw materials thesis against all comers for almost two decades before those he opposed unfolded a new approach, one that apparently negated his dire warnings about a depression, and suggested refutation of the principle that all new wealth comes from the soil.

The origin of that refutation appeared to come straight out of John Maynard Keynes. Actually, a great many "thinkers" have figured in the development of that astounding principle. John Stuart Mill often ridiculed those who wanted a tie between currency and something physical. Success of the old English system in fact depended on some confusion between debt and wealth, confusion that haunts economic reasoning to this day. H.D. MacLeod, writing in *The Theory of Credit* as early as 1893, pursued the proposition to its logical conclusion. A merchant's credit or ability to run into debt *is wealth*, MacLeod pointed out. Their credit constitutes wealth, and therefore wealth can be created out of nothing.

"How is Debt created? By the mere consent of two minds. By the mere fiat of the Human Will. When two persons have agreed to create a debt, whence does it come? Is it extracted from the materials of the globe? It is a valuable product created out of Absolute Nothing, and when it is extinguished it is a valuable product decreased into Nothing by the mere fiat of the Human Will. . . .

"Goods, Chattels, Commodities, WEALTH can be created out of Absolute Nothing and DECREATED again into the Absolute Nothing from whence they came, to the utter confusion of all the materialistic philosophers from Kapila to the present day and to the first school of Economists."

*If this reasoning were true, then Wilken and his associates rated attention as no more than talented amateurs, and a few superior minds—those capable of determining the need for new credit and those deserving of the lavish reward for creation of wealth out of nothing—were in fact prime movers, not social drones. And the price paid for raw materials didn't matter at all.*

"If we reasoned similarly in physics," commented Frederick Soddy, "we should probably discover that weights possessed the property of levitation."

Nevertheless, it was reasoning such as MacLeod's that uncorked the post-war age of inflation in America. Who would choose to decreate wealth? Create and create became the name of the game. Strange reasoning supplied a way around the laws of physics and the equation, $1 of raw material income generates approximately $5 national income.

One might be allowed to wonder how much Raymond W. Goldsmith's *A Study of Saving in the United States* figured in what was happening. For that monumental study had turned up a ratio of savings equal to $1/7$ of income in too many instances to be ignored. Arthur F. Burns, President Eisenhower's one time chairman of the Council of Economic Advisers, had been on the advisory committee for the Goldsmith study, as had Ford's (and CED's) Theodore O. Yntema, together with a fine representation of insurance, banking and money-lending folks, plus professors who had been favored with their grants.

These gentlemen had discovered, as had Ray, Coulter and Wilken, that raw materials primed the national economic pump, and they also knew that "labor hired and paid by new capital investment in new buildings and equipment" delivered national income through the medium of the multiplier. If new debt (as a substitute for profits and savings) could be kept coming, then delivery of national income more than four-fold would make it possible to re-finance each debt the day it came due. Why pay it off? *We owe it to ourselves* became copybook maxim.

Within days after Eisenhower took office, interest rates were raised on the public debt. Those who created loans called for expansion of the economy well beyond anything profits and savings permitted, and those who profited by inflation and fluctuation simply ignored the physical fact that all new wealth came from the soil, and that it couldn't be created through the medium of compounded debt.

## [1] 1946-1950 = 100

It was during the post-1954 period that Carl Wilken developed and refined a new base period—1946-1950 = 100. An audit of the best available data indicated that through 25 years, 1929 to 1953, utilization of farm products accounted for 70% of all the raw materials used in operating the economy. The remaining 30% was accounted for by all other raw materials. The breakdown for the 1946-1950 period turned out to be the same.

Wilken's worksheets for that computation revealed this inventory of facts under a head: "Income of the Six Principal Segments of the Economy and the Percentage of Each of the National Income in 1946-1950."

| | AMOUNT | PERCENTAGE |
|---|---|---|
| Total wages and salaries | $136.5 | 64.26 |
| Small business income | 21.9 | 10.31 |
| Net farm income | 15.1 | 7.12 |
| Corporate profit before taxes | 27.1 | 12.76 |
| Rentals income | 7.1 | 3.49 |
| Interest (net as used) | 4.3 | 2.02 |

Wages and interest thus averaged 66.2% of the national income, and they constituted the principal cost factor in operating the economy other than the cost of raw materials used in production.

In terms of this new base period, Wilken calculated that if gross farm income had been maintained on the same ratio to national income as it existed in 1946-1950, then gross farm income in 1955 should have been approximately $49 billion, or $16 billion more than the actual amount paid to rural America. Had agriculture been paid its full share, there would have been an increased consumer market, one that required an additional $1.5 billion worth of raw materials from mineral sources. Finally, total utilization of new wealth should have approximated $70 billion.

In terms of the average trade turn that the state of the arts had accounted for, a raw materials income of $70 billion in 1955 would have generated an earned national income of $350 billion. By adjusting national income factors to the same general balance that existed during the 1946-1950 base period, Wilken struck up figures for *what should have been:*

| | |
|---|---|
| National Income | $350.0 billion |
| Wage Payments | 226.6 " |
| Net Farm Income | 23.6 " |
| Small Business | 35.5 " |
| Rentals | 11.9 " |
| Interest | 7.5 " |
| Corporate Profit | 45.0 " |
| Durable Goods Sales | 37.0 " |
| Non-durable Goods | 156.5 " |
| Treasury Receipts | 77.0 " |

## [2] GENERATING UNEARNED INCOME

Wilken computed national income for 1955 as 166% of 1946-1950. Consumer goods sales (durable and non-durable) were computed on the basis of the average use of 55.3% of the national income, also on the basis 1946-1950 = 100.

The complete simplicity of these computations was at once apparent. Equally at ease was Wilken's explanation, including his charge that the "larger interest total of $10.5 billion in 1955 is the interest charge resulting from excessive debt increases following 1946-1950." During the previous three years, $20 billion had been added to the national debt, approximately $9 billion had been added in installment credit, and many billions had been added to the outstanding mortgages. These elements added up to an excessive increase in the total debt of about $60 billion. This, Wilken submitted, could have been avoided had the nation maintained farm prices at the 1946-1950 parity.

Point by point, Wilken analyzed the name of the game—*generating unearned income* so that it no longer looked as if farm income marched on a ratio of approximately 1 to 7 with national income. Here were corporate profits in 1955 expanded $9.4 billion over 1954, thus representing 42.5% of the increase in national income of $22.6 billion. The Treasury could thus take $4.7 billion in taxes, but the increase was being manufactured at the expense of excessive private debt. Yet if farm income had been maintained, the Treasury could have enjoyed a surplus without winding up the engine of credit.

And how would consumer sales have fared in 1955 with full parity in agriculture? They would have been $32.3 billion greater than the actual level attained, which was $161.1 billion. Actual sales for 1955 were $17.1 billion below normal in the non-durable goods field. Had farm income been maintained at full parity, total consumer goods sales should have been $193.5 billion, and these sales should have been racked up without expansion of installment credit.

Wilken's mode of analysis can best be understood after concentrated scrutiny of this "operating analysis," which was privately circulated in 1956:

"The nation utilized $52.6 billion of raw materials or new wealth in 1955, and using the 5 times turn of all raw materials into national income (the average for 1929-1953), the earned national income was $263 billion.

"The additional $60 billion generated in 1955 to bring the total up to $322.3 billion was unearned and created by the use of expected profits from tomorrow's income totaling approximately $12 billion, which turned over backwards 5 times to generate the $60 billion of *unearned national income.*"

The simple arithmetic that made the exchange equation work that way could be demonstrated with striking finality. With the nation's annual operating profit approximately 20% of the national income, a deficit could be traced to the operation of the economy in any year, 1955 included. Some $43.2 billion of capital profits had been spent for new construction—$28.3 billion for new plant and equipment, and expanded consumer credit of $6.1 billion had been logged in during 1955. Added together, these figures totalled $76.6 billion. Yet the profit on $322.3 billion national income was approximately $64.6 billion. This left a long-term deficit of approximately $12 billion.

It would require $60 billion of future income to generate the profit from which the $12 billion deficit had to be repaid. In the meantime the cost of carrying that debt became a charge against future profits through interest payments of some $600 million per year. In short, to service the debt the economy would have to earn profits from an additional $3 billion of national income the following year. "The net result of our operation in 1955," wrote Wilken, "was a loss of approximately $87 billion of earned income which could have been generated by maintaining our farm production at a parity price with 1946-1950. Approximately $60 billion of this loss was offset with the use of deficits and the balance of $27 billion was lost entirely."

## [3] THE SEEDS OF ITS OWN DESTRUCTION

That such economic management contained the seeds of its own destruction seemed too self-evident to Wilken to require explanation. In time industry would experience a declining rate of profits. In time, debt construction would funnel the wealth of the nation into a few hands. In time, compounded debt would make inflation unbearable, and poverty and inflation juxtaposed throughout the nation an ironic reality. But as the charade proceeded, the ratio of raw material income to national income would be made to sound ridiculous, because few—ever so few—understood what earned income really meant.

Why? This was the question Wilken asked then, and the question those who read his works asked later on. "Why didn't we maintain our farm production and farm prices?" Wilken knew all about manipulators, yet he always extended the benefit of doubt to those who opposed him. "Most of the leading economists in government and business almost completely ignore the agricultural segment of our economy," he wrote. They didn't understand.

The economists discussed agriculture in terms of the farm operator, rather than in terms of rural America. They did not understand that rural America was an important market for the production of industrial America.

During the 1946-1950 period, the farm operator ended up with 44% of his gross. The rest of it went to rural America, to the service centers, to the machinery makers and the suppliers. Some 70% of the farm dollar passed into circulation at retail, compared to 50% in industrial states such as New York and Pennsylvania. There had been a constant ratio of $1 of farm production with $1 of factory payrolls before WWII. During the war, a dislocation had taken place, but during the 1946-1950 period the normal 1 to 1 ratio resumed. Wilken pointed to an approximate $50 billion of factory payrolls and $33 billion gross farm income in 1955. "Unless farm income is brought up in balance, the factory payroll cannot be maintained except through further excessive increases in total debt."

All this made little sense to those who recited a litany of "surpluses" several times a day. How could men like Wilken argue in favor of 90% price supports when the nation was swimming in surpluses?

And to this Wilken answered: At the end of the 11-year price support era, six years of war and five years of peace, total stocks—at the end of 1952—approximated a mere $2.5 billion. Specifically, the inventories for three basic crops were 256 million bushels of wheat, 2.8 million bales of cotton, and 487 million bushels of corn. The corn supply was good for two months, perhaps less. The other surpluses constituted a bare inventory.

Surpluses? There were no surpluses!*

In 1953 farm prices had been permitted to drop to 92% of parity, and this had set the stage for a cut-back in the economy. It came in August 1953. Total production dropped over 8% until the low of 1954 was reached. This cut-back forced a loss of $30 billion of income that would have been created had the July 1953 production schedule been maintained. The drop in farm income levels wiped out the market to utilize potential production.

There was a new public policy. Wilken recognized it as such as he wrote out this paragraph:

"Instead of correcting the farm price situation and restoring our primary markets, those in charge of government and business instituted the credit expansion to revive the economy. Instead of helping agriculture it merely forced farm prices downward as money was diverted away from the purchase of non-durable goods, 90% of which are processed from farm products, to capital goods or goods normally purchased with savings or profits."

---

* The cry of surpluses, Wilken pointed out, has been used by the government in every era. Data from Table 715, page 656, *Statistical Abstract of the United States,* 1944-1945, indicates that between 1933 and 1943—an 11 year period—U.S. exports of farm products totaled $8,723,787,000. Imports for the same 11 years came to $12,786,725,000. In other words, the U.S. imported $4,062,938,000 more of farm production than was exported. In composite terms, the U.S. excess of imports of farm products over exports of the same products for the period amounted to about ten entire crops of wheat. The surplus ploy was used to hold farm prices down before WWII. It was used to kill parity. And it is being used to prevent the return of parity.

# [4] THE OLD CONSTITUTIONAL REPUBLICAN

Wilken had departed official Washington the moment the new administration entered, despite the fact that he was a life-long Republican. His economic thinking was no longer acceptable to the party he had supported all his life. In fact, the thinking of the old constitutional Republican wasn't acceptable at all, because a new philosophy had gained the saddle. The quite simple fact that no production × no price = no income was being refuted by the fact that men with international cunning knew how to create debt, buy time, make a profit, buy more time, scuttle the private enterprise system, buy still more time, profit from war, and depart the scene before their legacy came home to roost.

And their economic advisers, preoccupied with econometric models—each more sophisticated than the last—dealt with income statement analysis and GNP projections. And the fantastic national income being rolled up could not reflect the balance condition of the economy or what was happening to people. Fed control of the money supply, and government management of debt creation could do nothing to solve the basic problem—the problem of balance of trade between rural America and industry, between industrial America and the world, nor the attendant symptoms, inflation, high interest, and deficient liquidity. Astute business operators at first watched each successive balance sheet so that dazzling income projections would not hide a liquidity problem. Finally almost all became drugged by the lotus of the times.

And still no single balance sheet of the U.S. economy was being prepared by the government.

NASDA officials told of fantastic droughts when the agricultural chiefs from the several states met in 1954. They recited their tale of woe again in 1955. Hog prices dropped even faster than the water tables. At one point Wilken journeyed to Omaha to speak to the Nebraska Livestock Feeders Association. Secretary Ezra Taft Benson had the authority to correct hog prices by invoking the device of floor prices. Benson declined. He believed in a free market, and in the sanctity of supply and demand. He caused USDA to buy up cheap pork for use in school lunch programs, and that was all. In the meantime hog prices in Iowa dropped to a 10 cent low by December 1955.

At the tailgate, farmers recalled the passionate state of mind that prevailed during the Holiday movement—and they organized. Those were electric days, those first dozen days in Iowa when farmers styled themselves as NFO—National Farmers Organization—and threw dollar bills into a hat so that farmers might put strength behind their demand for Benson's hide.

Wilken had gone the farm organization route before. He had argued and split with Milo Reno because too many farm organizations lacked substance, a real reason for being, or goals that could be pursued fearlessly and without vacillation. In Iowa, Wilken addressed several county meetings, and then in the spring of 1956 he, a Lake View, Iowa farmer named Jake Auen, and Hartington, Nebraska banker Vince Rossiter drove down to Corning to get acquainted with leaders of the new farm movement and suggest the preparation of a national balance sheet. Later, Wilken spoke before the St. Joseph-based convention of the brash young farm organization. But it would be years before farmers understood the balance sheet.

## [5] A SOUND PROGRAM

As a result of many meetings in the midwest, Wilken prepared suggestions for a sound program to restore farm prices "within 60 days." He called on Secretary of Agriculture Benson to use the authority of the Farm Act of 1949 and previous acts to take the following steps:

1. Publicly declare to the commodity trade in the United States and the world that not one pound or bushel of farm production would be sold from storage below 100% of parity. (This would restore confidence in normal trade channels and prove to the world that there would be no profit made by waiting for cheap U.S. farm production.)

2. Restore 90% of parity price supports on all nonperishable crops— corn, wheat, cotton, flax, rice, tobacco, oats, barley, sorghum grains, peanuts, rye and wool.

3. Divert 400 million bushels of non-milling wheat into a stockpile of feed to be used in areas where drought had created a shortage of feed for livestock. (This reserve was to be used only in case of drought or shortages which had increased the normal market price of feeds above 110% of parity.)

4. Place a floor of $17 per hundredweight under hogs and agree to take from packers any inventory above a normal carryover accumulated as a result of the price floor.

5. Place a temporary floor under cattle on the basis of $30 per hundredweight for prime cattle (Chicago market).

6. Place a temporary floor under the price of fats and oils, especially lard, cotton seed oil, soybean oil, at 20 cents per pound, and by purchase remove 1 billion pounds from market supplies for export. (This step would create upward price pressure on hogs, corn, cattle, soybeans, flax, cotton seed and peanuts.)

7. Immediately announce payments on any land removed from crops

and seeded to grass for the purpose of soil conservation.

Wilken calculated that the above program would require less than $500 million and would recover a market for over $25 billion of factory goods industry was losing in rural America.

## [6] ALL NEW WEALTH COMES FROM THE SOIL

Wilken scheduled meetings by the score in 1956, and yet he realized that orientation was not the proper vehicle to explain foundation economics. The several concepts required study. With study even a high school student could understand. Wilken decided to write a new book—a very short one, still one that could be made available at a token price. He called it *All New Wealth Comes from the Soil.*

Wilken in fact wrote out the lines for that book aboard a cruise ship. Congressman Fred Crawford of Michigan, an accountant, helped him with some of the tabulations. Since the book covered all raw materials, it became necessary to structure raw material income for minerals as well as agriculture.

James White, who for five years headed the Tungsten Institute, secured figures for mineral production. Figures up to 1948 were readily available from Bureau of Mines publications. But it took a special request to get the data from 1949 to 1953. By any rule of logic, recycled raw products had to be handled the same as fresh raw materials. Starting in 1949, however, figures on mineral raw material income were changed. The value of metals obtained through resmelting of iron, copper, lead, zinc, was added to manufacturing income by the government's figure keepers.

*All New Wealth Comes from the Soil* rates as a small masterpiece. Yet its impact was as limited as 5,000 published copies imply. Its long-range impact has still to be measured.

# CHAPTER 27:
# ALL NEW WEALTH COMES FROM THE SOIL

*"La Terre est la source ou la matiere d'ou l'on tire la Richesse. . . ."* So wrote Richard Cantillon. Translated, his famous *Essai* opened thus:

"The Land is the Source or Matter from whence all Wealth is produced. The Labour of man is the Form which produces it; and Wealth in itself is nothing but the Maintenance, Conveniencies, and Superfluities of Life.

"Land produces Herbage, Roots, Corn, Flax, Cotton, Hemp, Shrubs and Timber of several kinds, with divers sorts of Fruits, Bark, and Foliage like that of the Mulberry tree for Silkworms; it supplies Mines and Minerals. To all this the Labour of man gives the form of Wealth."

When W. Stanley Jevons rediscovered Cantillon about the time Andrew Jackson was President in the U.S., he concluded that Cantillon had written no later than 1725, that his analysis of the circulation of wealth anticipated by 70 years J.B. Say's Law of Markets, that Cantillon's precept of balance of payments between country and city, between country and country, described the root of inflation and the cause of collapse. A skillful financier, Cantillon became wealthy through currency exchange during the era when John Law believed he had discovered perpetual motion in economics. For Law also believed that wealth could be created with an act of the will, and out of nothing. His printing press money is still legend.

It was Cantillon's assertion that all new wealth came from the soil, and that labor enabled its production, that made a distinction between the material cause and the formal cause (in terms of Aristotelian philosophy). Quesnay's fundamental doctrine *"a terre est l'unique source des richesses"* came straight from Cantillon's *Essai*, just as did Adam Smith's assertion that a nation was required to develop its agriculture first, its manufacturing second and its trade last.

How amazing that Cantillon's *Essai* should disappear from the face of the earth, surface again under the signature of another, then die until Jevons discovered it anew! How amazing that the French physiocrats should codify the thinking, hand it to Ben Franklin, Thomas Jefferson and a group of "Founding Fathers" in order to administer what Emerson called "the last effort of Divine Providence to help the human race."

As Jevons observed, perhaps correctly, Cantillon and the French school "is known to have formed to a considerable degree the basis of *The Wealth of Nations*, and may yet be destined to be recognized in regard to many of its doctrines, as the true scientific school of economics."

## [1] THIS FACT FLOWED LOGICALLY

Wilken had never read Cantillon's *Essai*, nor Quesnay's adaptation thereof. In the opening line of *All New Wealth Comes From the Soil*, he called attention to the fact that Thomas A. Edison had stated the "all new wealth" proposition and that philosophers through the ages had recognized that truth once it had been given. But current economic thinking, dominated by "the vastness of our industrial expansion, has apparently forgotten that new wealth in the form of raw materials has been the beginning of the economic cycle since the days of creation."

Even without a schoolbook grasp of philosophy and history, Wilken concluded that this fact flowed logically from the record. And a refinement of the record revealed that between 1921 and 1953 approximately 70% of the raw material production was derived from the renewable resource of agriculture. Furthermore, 12 storable crops became the production from 90% of the harvested acres. These basic crops could be used to "level off the unequal supply of farm products due to climatic changes." The other 30% of the raw materials emerged in Wilken's analysis as three groups:

1. Metals, such as gold, silver, lead, copper, zinc, iron, manganese, tungsten, etc.

2. Fuels, including coal, petroleum, products used to release energy placed on deposit millions of years ago, products that became power energy to supplement human energy, thus increasing per man production.

3. Non metallic raw materials, such as bauxite, rocks, sand, gravel, shale for cement production, and raw elements for production of fertilizer.

"If we were to select 40 of our principal storable raw materials in dollar value we would have the foundation of our economic cycle which determines the production of manufactured goods and through price the source of the national income. Our production and income in turn determine our standard of living. The impact of raw material production in our economic cycle precedes other economic factors."

In so few words, Wilken stated his fundamental ideas. It was the same one he had stated at the first meeting of the Raw Materials National Council, but the message seemed clearer now. Nothing could happen without raw materials. Economies could not be structured on desert islands. A group of men cast adrift could have all the technical knowledge and all the money in the world. Without raw materials they would be as helpless as babies—indeed, without the ability to feed the group all would soon perish.

*All New Wealth* unfolded the Wilken thesis inch by inch, each paragraph so pregnant that comprehensive citations become almost impossible.

Yet many of the points in *All New Wealth* had been stated before. Wilken had discussed the common error of thinking that lower price levels were the result of efficiency. Now he pointed out that between 1939 and 1955, increased per man production of 2.8% per year had resulted in an average price level increase of 6% per year. "Their wishful thinking, if carried to the point of infinity, would mean an efficiency ratio which would eventually require no price at all to create income."

Wilken had also discussed the theory that it took lower prices to sell more goods. "This is true in a competitive situation between the price of one product as compared to another. It is not true in the case of our overall consumer price level. A drop in our consumer price level of 1% will reduce our national income 1% and in turn 1% of our market for goods."

And Wilken had discussed the necessity for parity before. Still the public had been led to believe that maintenance of farm prices in line with other cost factors was a subsidy. Yet a parity price was not determined by the producer of raw materials. "It is determined by labor and industry as the result of charges added to raw materials on their way through the economic cycle and final sale at the market place."

## [2] ARITHMETIC AND MULTIPLICATION

Why the logic of all this escaped the public in general puzzled Wilken. It stood to reason that when the raw materials producer was underpaid 10%, then he in turn could buy only 90% of his share of goods at retail. Had Congress given farmers 110% of parity, then it could have been properly called a subsidy. But deliberate maintenance of farm prices 10% below parity became a subsidy to the rest of the economy, and therefore a one-way ticket to inflation or deflation.

Both of the latter could be explained by arithmetic and multiplication. ". . . if we have a 10% increase in our production at a stable price level we create 10% more income, or in direct proportion to the increase in the supply of goods. Such a happening is neither inflation nor deflation. It is sound economic expansion.

"On the other hand if we have an increase of 10% in our physical production and a 10% increase in the price level at the same time, the result is an increase of 21% in our income with only a 10% increase in the supply of goods. This result is inflation.

"In like manner if we have a 10% drop in our production we suffer a loss of 10% in our income. If a drop of 10% in our price level takes place at the same time the income drops 19% and we have serious deflation. In spirals of deflation, as income falls off, the production has to be cut back to adjust to the loss of markets, and for all practical purposes doubles the rate of the move downwards."

The last equation was the one adopted by the administration during the depression of the 1930s, and it—of course, contained its own insurance against working. It could not work because it was not subject to working.

Much of *All New Wealth* was given over to explaining the exchange equation, the flow of goods and money, and the role of technology in permitting use of more raw materials, ergo development of more income. Wilken used his 1946-1950 = 100 base period in *All New Wealth* because it was the best period of stability since 1910-1914. During the 1946-1950 period, use of farm production averaged $32.2 billion. Use of other raw materials averaged $12.8 billion. With a total raw materials intake of $45 billion, the simple division of $12.8 billion into $45 indicated that 29% of raw materials used in 1946-1950 were non-agricultural, and that 71% were of farm origin. This came close to the 1929-1953 average of 70.5% agricultural raw materials used, 29.5% coming from other sources.

In other words, for five years running five categories of consumer goods, food, clothing, shoes, beverages and tobacco were processed from farm raw materials, and these represented approximately 70% of all consumer goods. Wilken detailed consumer goods expenditures to prove that the percentage of income required to buy these products had not increased, and that at the low point of 1933 it took more to meet the consumer goods bill in terms of percentage than at the high point of 1929.

The requirement of a high consumer goods turnover was being replaced by a high turnover requirement in durable goods sales, supported by credit. It was to this point that *All New Wealth* addressed itself because there was a firming of public policy afoot, a policy that was taking 70% of the material production down so that 30% might prosper.

## [3] INCOME EQUATION

To pinpoint the dislocation, Wilken explained the balance sheet (or income equation) he had invoked before in a private audit. Needless to say, the final computation of the national income was divided into six segments. Payrolls, farm proprietor income and income of small business represented the money return for personal effort. It represented the labor income of all workers—approximately 65 million in 1955. Payrolls included all labor compensated with wages and salaries. Income for farm operators and independent business units represented returns of individuals who were self employed. Together, these three groups received 80% of the national income.

The next three brackets, rentals, interest and corporate profits, represented approximately 20% of the national income. And this 20% approximated the profit of the United States as a huge corporation. It was on this profit that the private enterprise economy was bound to rely for investment in capital goods, that is, the kind of durable to which national income was being tied via debt support.

*"It is very important to remember that only 20% of the national income is available to buy capital goods by individuals and for all other forms of construction.* The 20% of the national income translated into profits and savings becomes the new capital to be used."

This principle was as clear to Wilken as was the overly simple fact that the earth circled the sun in 365¼ days. Yet here was a managed economy, one under the apparent dictatorship of three economic advisers, embarked on a John Law-type program of borrowing future savings and profits in order to structure dizzy heights now.

A few of the consultant economists of the hour even listened to the "debt can become cumbersome" complaint, as did the American Keynesian, Lawrence R. Klein, but they invariably responded with "As long as the interest charge is a small fraction of the income, the burden is not cumbersome." Wrote Klein in *The Keynesian Revolution,* "An internally held public debt can never be a burden, because we owe it to ourselves." And to those who objected to the trite "owe-it-to-yourselves-argument," Klein could only reply that he was tired of hearing the *a fortiori* trite "burden-of-the-debt argument."

The Keynesian economists couldn't understand that the operating flow sheet of the economy was more important than the ability to regulate fiscal and credit policy. Pure inflation of money could not repair private liquidity problems and resolve over-extended debt burdens. It took a balance sheet to pinpoint the problem and suggest suitable remedial steps. Neither was possible as long as the managers did not understand something as fundamental as the fact that all new wealth came from the soil.

To illustrate his points, Wilken filled his book with tables: "Value of Mineral Production in the United States, 1929-1953"; "Total Value of Raw Material Production and Percentage of National Income"; "Comparison of Consumer Expenditures for Food, Clothing, Beverage and Tobacco to Total Consumer Goods Expenditure" and finally—among others—"Comparison of Total Value of Raw Material Production and Gross Savings."

Combined total raw material production averaged out at 20.26% of national income. And, finally, the average gross saving for 25 years turned out to be 95% of the total value of all raw materials.

It was "The 20% of income from capital return" that became the capital for new expansion. Institutional business arrangements could borrow against future earnings in order to over-industrialize or bring on new capital equipment, but in the end production and monetization of consumable wealth had to be fine-tuned to the production of capital goods, so that capital goods production proceeded only as fast as required to produce perishable wealth, or wealth that passed quickly into consumption channels.

## [4] FOUNDATION RAW MATERIALS

This requirement could be met simply by bringing stability to the price structure of foundation raw materials. The device of choice, Wilken argued, was the price support mechanism, the one tool that government could invoke to provide primary producers with power that matched the muscle of the institutional business arrangements. Also required: a tariff system.

In *All New Wealth,* Wilken listed national income by year from 1929 to 1953, and juxtaposed this column next to imports. As a percentage of national income, imports accounted for 5% in 1929, a low of 1.9% in 1943, and the going equation ranged from 3.2 to 3.5% between war's end and 1953. Yet this small percentage of income consumed by imports was allowed to dictate the price level in the United States.

". . . by buying cheap raw materials we remove any possibility of creating dollar exchange in sufficient amounts to finance the exports we may have available," Wilken summarized.

## [6] EQUITY OF TRADE

And to those who argued that international trade was the cement that held the free world together, Wilken answered: "Our foreign policy . . . must be one which contemplates a program which will make it possible for nations exporting to us to obtain a comparable price for their products as compared to the price of our exports." Wilken counseled paying for coffee in terms of an American parity, not the cheap world price. If the American nation was to import copper, then the price paid for copper should be the American price, not the low world price. The same principle had been used, he said, in raising the living standard in Cuba, Puerto Rico, Hawaii, the Philippines and the Virgin Islands. By paying the higher price for imported sugar, rather than the world price, the American market enabled exports to flow on an equitable basis.* Wilken called his international parity *equity of trade*. It was essentially the same equity of trade concept advocated by Colin Clark then, and Pope Paul VI later on.

Although it should never have gone out of print, *All New Wealth Comes from the Soil* finally passed from the scene.

In the main, its conclusions were simply restatements, albeit with italics. One towered above the rest: *"A greater use than 20% of the national income in expansion and investment creates an excessive addition to the total debt and eventually forces either inflation or deflation as a means of meeting financial obligations."*

Finally, Wilken concluded (as had Cantillon before him) that wide fluctuations in "the price of new wealth has existed for centuries, and contrary to the basic economy of the United States set forth in the Constitution, has prevented us from giving the world the leadership that they have a right to expect us to provide." It was this failure that cancelled out all of America's showy successes.

Withal, *All New Wealth Comes from the Soil* contained the premises on which Wilken's exchange equation was built. It would be impossible to understand Wilken's "balance sheet" without mastering the premises. And to this end lectures from the podium proved somewhat inadequate. Men listened, but nothing happened.

---

* Since the lion's share of the Cuban sugar plantations were owned by New York and London interests, Congress has always seen fit to pay parity to foreign producers for that product. It was a case of doing the right thing for the wrong reason, thus achieving the inevitable result.

# CHAPTER 28: OUR AMERICAN HERITAGE

Nothing happened!

Those who supported the Raw Materials National Council had been characterized as "voices in the wilderness," and yet men like Wilken were anything except that. They were always on the outlook for organized entities that could take the precepts of sound economics and run with them. Success on this order was achieved when NASDA adopted Wilken, Ray and Coulter and put the push of the organization behind full parity for agriculture. The indictments of Tom Linder and J.E. McDonald had caused the NASDA officials to lie low, and ever since Wilken had met with little success in finding another organizational powerhouse. Individual members of the National Farmers Organization (Vice President Erhard Pfingsten included) used Wilken material to recruit, but the organization figured on building collective bargaining, not the legislative lobby Wilken wanted.

*All New Wealth Comes from the Soil* didn't deliver. And now the Raw Materials National Council was moribund—no assets and no liabilities. General Wood, an on-and-off supporter, had retired, and Theodore V. Houser, the new board chairman at Sears, was being listed on CED policy papers. O.L. Brownlee of the old *Sioux City Tribune* had passed away.

## [1] NATIONAL FOUNDATION FOR ECONOMIC STABILITY

In 1959, Wilken elected to try again. With Thomas B. Huff of Sioux City, who was president of the American Serum Company, and James White, secretary of the Tungsten Institute (until American users bought enough foreign tungsten to liquidate tungsten production in the United States), Wilken incorporated the National Foundation for Economic Stability in the District of Columbia. As an old ally, Huff continued to pick up the tab for the office rent, but in the main the new organization operated hand to mouth, and almost without funds.

Wilken had analyzed the tungsten situation during the Korean War. He had prepared a report to illustrate the availability of tungsten, and calculated the price it would take to bring on production. Wilken had been ordered by the Committee to write a report and a press release by Chairman Burnet R. Maybank. "I was busy typing it off when I got word from the House side that they wanted a meeting regarding this report," Wilken recalled. Wilken detailed how he met for two days. Finally he concluded, "Boys, you don't want anything in the report to indicate that we've got these materials in the United States, or that we could produce them if we paid a price. The Committee asked me to prepare this report and I've prepared it." Wilken's taped recollection told the story. The report had been set in type and printed, but it was never distributed.

The world tungsten price seemed attractive to the policy makers. As a result James White saw the Tungsten Institute dry up and blow away. He became associated with Wilken both to share office space and to share a measure of defeat.

Earlier, in 1957, Wilken had sailed to Ireland and toured the island in a rented car. He and his wife had gone to Scotland, where they visited Glasgow, the former home of Adam Smith.

Glasgow had changed. Smog now filled the air, and the town of a few thousand in 1775 had grown into a metropolitan center. But all around there was evidence of how poverty was authored. With a scant supply of raw materials, Britain had been sentenced to become a trading nation.

As a trading nation, Britain "believed" in the magic of compound interest, or something for nothing at the expense of others. Queen Elizabeth's share from Sir Francis Drake's adventure with the *Golden Hind* came to $200,000—a staggering sum in those days. According to John Maynard Keynes, the investment of this sum in the Levant Company and in the East India Company, grew at a compound rate of $3\frac{1}{4}\%$. And it emerged as Britain's $20 billion foreign investment by 1930. Each dollar grew to become $100,000—all at a modest $3\frac{1}{4}\%$ compound interest.

## [2] THE AMERICAN SYSTEM

Wilken did not write *Our American Heritage* for some years, but the decision to issue such a booklet was born while touring the Glasgow of Adam Smith. Americans, not even those who served in Congress, understood the American system.

*Our American Heritage* became Wilken's easiest-to-understand tract. In it he pointed out that the Constitution of the United States set up three freedoms: religious freedom, political freedom and economic freedom. Under Article 1, Section 8, "our forefathers took steps to protect the economic freedom of the United States by giving to Congress, elected by the people, the power to provide a monetary system independent of the monetary systems of other countries, and to regulate the value of the dollar, adopted as our monetary unit, or measure of value. This power automatically gave to Congress the right to determine the value of United States production in terms of United States money."

In line with this authority, Congress was also given the power to protect the American price system. Indeed, the 1st Congress enacted into law the first Tariff Act, which provided price protection and price supports for certain products. As early as 1789 Congress chose to protect sugar production with a tariff—and, indeed, a tariff for the protection of sugar is still on the books. Price protection became a necessity the day the nation was organized, Wilken pointed out. "For example, we have legislation which provides for fixed contracts covering the principal and interest payments on all debts, public and private. We have legislation provided for specific wage contracts between labor and industry. We have a minimum wage law and agreements pertaining to salaries for private and public employees. We have legislation providing for an income tax upon our earnings."

Such lines brought the matter of price maintenance for farm raw materials into perspective. Even the grade school student understood that the cost of postage stamps was fixed by law, that utilities, bus fares, and transportation rates were regulated, that tolls across bridges were legislated. Unfortunately, grade school students were always being confused by terms such as *free trade* and *free markets*. Still any pupil could be made to understand that the chief purpose of the *mercantile* or *free trade* system was to secure raw materials from colonies at the lowest possible cost.

Wilken hit these points in *Our American Heritage*. He did not hit them with sledgehammer blows, but he underscored them. "Our abundant production of raw materials, and, subsequently the discovery of gold, which was adopted as a fixed yardstick for foreign obligations, made it possible for the United States to pay for the use of foreign capital; and, in addition, to earn our capital for economic expansion." And by the early part of the 20th century the American nation had, indeed, repaid its foreign debt.

## [3] POVERTY BECAME THEIR HERITAGE

The rest of the world did not fare so well. African nations, settled at the same time as the United States, fared badly, and India fared worst of all. Poverty became their heritage, whereas the wealth of the exploiters compounded itself. *"The promoters of the European system never realized that cheap raw materials acquired from their colonies established a correspondingly cheap market for their own manufactured products."* The low wage level forced on Europe brought the poverty of African and Asian colonies back home, and in effect forced migration to the United States.

The depressions that America was made to endure, Wilken noted—

such as the 1920-1921 Depression—were caused by international money manipulation, which forced lower commodity prices. Those who understood this, in 1922, fell back on the precepts of the Constitution itself. They wrote a tariff law.

## [4] TARIFFS

Wilken told the story of *Our American Heritage* in terms of the fight over tariffs and the fight over protection for the American standard. Without supports for raw material production, there was no way the nation could earn enough to operate a solvent economy. Without tariffs, there was no way of preventing importation of the commodities that newsmen could call "surpluses."

Almost as if lecturing young pupils, Wilken listed four fundamental truths:

"1. . . . the Creator set aside an area on the earth which later became known as the United States and endowed this area with resources sufficient for an almost complete economy.

"2. In the course of human events the United States established a form of government based on the general welfare of all groups in accordance with the principles of human freedom and equity of opportunity for the different segments of our economy.

"3. The United States in its production of farm products and other raw materials from the soil was blessed beyond the hopes and aspirations of many other areas of the world.

"4. In developing the economy of the United States we have compiled the most complete and detailed economic record in world history. This record points out very clearly the basic factors which can serve as yardsticks for human progress in direct proportion to the blessings inherent in soil, rainfall, and sunshine."

The record, Wilken submitted, contained the answer. And the record pointed up the requirement: production × price = income. *"It is impossible to subsidize any segments of the economy unless the price is over 100% of parity or price balance with other groups."*

## [5] A PROGRAM FOR ECONOMIC STABILITY

Early in 1959, Wilken issued *A Program for Economic Stability*, a short paper in which he switched emphasis from raw materials to the requirement of balanced economic growth.

"Our economy can be compared to a stool with three legs," he wrote. "The first and very important leg is raw material production and income.

Raw material production and income creates in rural areas the reciprocal market for factory goods which must be sold to obtain a fully operating economy.

"The second leg is the payroll or the total of all wages and salaries. It represents the market created by wage and salary payments.

"The third leg is our capital operations or the business operating units whose function is to process and distribute the finished products.

"Economic stability and a fully operating economy cannot exist unless the incomes of the three segments are in balance."

Why? "It must be remembered that price balance or a parity price for raw materials is geared to the consumer price index. It is not a rigid price, but fluctuates with the rate of capital operations and payrolls as they are reflected in the increase or decrease of consumer prices. Parity of price if properly administered is the governor that stabilizes the incomes of the three segments of our economy in balance with each other."

The record was running, Wilken pointed out. Between 1952 and 1958, the economy had been maintained by expansion of public and private debt to the tune of $192 billion. Between 1950 and 1960, the public and private debt was destined to double, Wilken in effect said, and it would double again between 1960 and 1970. After that, geometric growth of public and private debt would keep the economy on the edge of explosion and/or collapse. Both had to be avoided, or the nation would be forced to endure fantastic adjustments in its social and political arrangements.

Wilken outlined a remedy. It was the program he had outlined before. It called for a raw materials reserve, full parity, export control, and a new base period of 1946-1950 = 100.

## [6] UNHANDY SIDE EFFECTS

The Economic Advisers weren't listening. Their eyes were riveted on a higher national income and a higher GNP. They did not pause to scrutinize the balance sheet—not the one that pertained to the economy, the individual corporation, or the individual farm. Unhandy side-effects kept showing up like blips on a radar screen. A fresh inventory of programs came into being to pour oil on the sores as they appeared. No one seemed interested in the cancer itself. Late in 1957 the Fed used tight credit to cool the economy, jumping unemployment from 4 to 7% almost overnight. Then the Fed panicked and wound up the engine of credit while Eisenhower hastily unveiled a program to build $2 billion worth of post offices.

During his years in Washington, Wilken learned that most policy paper writers were really writers of their own ticket. Once before, when testifying at a hearing on cotton, Wilken had come into contact with the Cotton Council. The Council had been formed in 1939 by the biggest of the plantation owners, and the agri-business interests to which they were related: ginners, warehousemen, merchants, spinners and cottonseed crushers. The idea itself had been hatched by Oscar Johnston, then manager of the Delta and Pine Land Company of Mississippi, which was owned by English capital. Farm Bureau leaders staffed the farm end of the Council, and checkoffs financed the group. Looking back, Wilken realized that there was more to the Cotton Council than a "change your sheets at least twice a week" slogan.

The Council represented a powerhouse in politics. It was not as a result of accident that Secretary Ezra Taft Benson aired one of his first policy speeches before the 18th annual meeting of the Delta Council of Mississippi, a sister group Oscar Johnston had also helped form. There was a meeting of the minds here, Wilken pointed out.

The Council did not want excessive restrictions on importation of Mexican labor. It had supported the Taft-Hartley Act, of course, and stayed on its own side generally. In time this came to mean "splinter agriculture." By pleasing the Cotton Council, those in charge of amending farm bills were sure to fear no evil. This accounted for the fact that under the Benson administration, Brannan-type direct payments to cotton became quite acceptable, earlier worries about socialism and the loss of individual initiative among corporate members notwithstanding.

By the end of the 1950s, broad-spectrum policy papers were being bound in handsome editions, placed on library shelves and circulated to the economic profession. The best funded and most important carried a symbol, CED.

Debased pragmatism, not sound economic thinking, had taken command, and from almost any vantage point it looked as if the idea that Wilken and his associates had championed was dying.

# CHAPTER 29: THE CED REPORT

"Americans of all ages, all conditions, and all dispositions constantly form associations," wrote Alexis de Tocqueville in 1835. Over a century and a third later Carl H. Wilken, with a unique economic message in tow, decided to find one of those organizations to support research, and give to farmers a weapon on par with the one being wielded by trade interests and industrial complexes. Early in 1962 he agreed to appear before the Nebraska Wheat Growers Association on one condition: that the association provide an accountant to check the accuracy of Wilken's calculations.

Certain developments had become inescapable by 1962. *The Wall Street Journal* in December of 1961 had translated composite figures into denominators everyone could understand. Dividends on stocks had dropped from over 6% in 1950 to 3% in 1961. Now a few economists were worrying about the "declining rate of profits," almost always without developing a foundation reason for what was happening.

## [1] THE LOSS HAD BEEN MODEST

Wilken's balance sheet approach pinpointed the problem. The loss to private enterprise had been modest in 1951, he told the wheat growers, but by the end of 1961 it was $53 billion. "In 1961, in order to meet the payrolls and capital costs, we should have had $486 billion of income, but only had $430 billion. In other words," Wilken went on, "we lacked $56 billion of having enough income to meet the 1961 payroll and capital costs." In order to operate the economy without the worst effects showing up, the mortgage debt had been increased by approximately $55 billion, or $15 billion more than the increase in 1960.

Why was it necessary to harness $55 billion debt expansion to the engine of credit? There were pressures, Wilken said. Congress had increased the minimum wage. Congress had written many bills that required an increase in the public and private debt level. Certainly, there had been $13.1 billion more income in 1961 than in 1960, but some 82.5% of the increase was going to wages, salaries and interest, and very little was finding its way back to the private enterprise reservoir. The farmer got a small increase through subsidy payments, but such checks were being drawn on an empty treasury, and they too constituted an addition to the mortgage growth.

Wilken ran through his many arguments that day at Ogallala, Nebraska to point out that Nebraska had been underpaid $8 billion during the past 11 years. He covered the historical developments, the legislation that affected farmers—directly and indirectly—and finally he explained why 1946-1950 constituted an excellent base period. Wages in 1940 averaged 66 cents an hour. The average for the 1946-1950 base period was $1.329 per hour.

The complexion of the country was changing, nevertheless. Although there were less farms, the ratio to other business units remained about the same. There were 9,200,000 business units in charge of producing farm products and other raw materials, moving them to the factory, processing them, and distributing them to some 185 million people. These farms and business units had to furnish the fixed capital. They had to hire the laborers. They had to meet all the payrolls. And, finally, they had to pay out all the capital costs and other costs involved.

Wilken pointed to these facts so that the wheat growers might understand the anatomy of his procedures, and follow the simple computations that seemed to require so little and yet so much effort. Wages and salaries, together with the net interest component (which reflected the cost of the mortgage against the United States), became the focal point in Wilken's analysis. For the ten-year period—1951 to 1960—wages, salaries, and interest had averaged 74.6% more than in 1946-1950. Therefore the private enterprise components—to be in balance—had to have an increase of $74.6%. Nebraska's shortage, Wilken repeated, was $8 billion.

Wilken's points were difficult for those who had not followed his reasoning from the ground up. The net result, one Congressman told me, was that many listeners became confused. The academic economists who might have understood rejected everything Wilken was saying because he questioned a bureaucratic truth.

That bureaucratic truth was calling for farm prices at the world level, for corn at $1.20 a bushel, or barely 60% of honest parity. "What about the future? To be very frank with you, they do not intend to materially increase your farm prices, and they project farm income to remain about where it is—about $13 billion for the next ten years," Wilken said.

This observation—made in early 1962—didn't constitute soothsaying. The National Planning Association—with Walter Reuther of the United Auto Workers aboard, and with Jim Patton of Farmers Union and Eric Johnson of the motion picture trade also on tap—had issued projections. National income would be made to increase from $504 billion in 1960 to

$787 billion in 1970. But agriculture would take a 10% reduction, or a continuation of what had taken place for the past 10 years. To carry out the program, Wilken predicted, there would have to be some $70 billion of debt expansion each year for the next decade running.

## [2] THE ECONOMIC EQUATION

Either the plan writers didn't understand the economic equation, or they understood it too well. Either they understood that compounded debt expansion would bring on wild inflation and ultimate termination of the "finest economic system that any nation ever developed," or they had no idea that wages and capital costs couldn't be increased by liquidating either the farm or the industrial plant until the national economy was placed in receivership—that is, under a dictator.

Wilken didn't register well with the Nebraska Wheat Growers Association. Most of his ideas made sense, but his overall thesis wasn't really understood. Before the meeting, he had caused one wheat grower to compute parity on the place mat of an Ogallala coffee shop. The farmer complied. He computed the price of wheat from a 1910-1914 base. Then he computed parity for wheat from a 1925-1929 base, and from a 1946-1950 base. The answer came out within a penny either way.

Within a few months, farmers would be asked to buy the proposition that $1.25 wheat was better than $2.00 wheat, with the Farm Bureau equating the right to go broke with the right to make a profit. As a parting shot, Wilken warned his Nebraska and Midwest audiences that there was absolutely no way farmers could sell at world prices and keep from liquidating their farms.

## [3] ADMINISTRATIVELY CONFIDENTIAL

Nevertheless, that was the proposition seer after seer was selling. That was what Agriculture Secretary Orville Freeman's "Administratively Confidential" document was saying. Freeman's plan called for shock treatment for wheat and feed grains in order to induce deficit production so "surplus" holdings could be sold off. The plan also called for a speedy flow of rural manpower into factory jobs, elimination of thousands of small and "inefficient farms," and conversion of 34 million acres of cropland into parks, forests, grasslands, and wildlife refuges by 1969, 68 million acres by 1985.

It was not an accident that the Committee for Economic Development surfaced with essentially the same proposals during 1962. As testimony before the House Committee on Agriculture was to reveal, CED's *An*

*Adaptive Program for Agriculture* had been hatching since 1959. Backup papers had been commissioned, and steps had been taken to lock together the nation's educators of distinction with business leaders of distinction through the medium of foundation funds. Intentions were honest, Theodore O. Yntema, Vice President and Chairman of the Finance Committee, Ford Motor Company, defended. ". . . we do not regard ourselves as experts in agriculture. We do not think that we have brought down the tablets of wisdom from Mount Sinai on this subject," Yntema said before he and his associates stepped down from Mount Sinai with tablets, gospel and codification thereof.

And the CED plan became gospel and public policy, because *An Adaptive Program* expressed laws some 200 business leaders found acceptable and in compliance with the world market that their conjectural economics required.

The *Economic Report of the President* picked up added pages in 1962. For the first time an added line—"Together with the *Annual Report of the Council of Economic Advisers*"—was added to the cover, and inside, for the first time also, appeared the names of CEA members: Walter W. Heller, Kermit Gordon and James Tobin. Imperceptibly, the real public policy of the nation emerged in print.

"Many more children are born and raised on farms than will be needed to produce the nation's food and fiber. They must be educated, trained, and guided to non-agricultural employment," the *Report* said as an opener. Later, Heller and associates adopted the word form of early CED farm papers. "Objectives of agricultural policy as it develops in the future should encompass both (1) continuation of agriculture's historic role as a major contributor to national economic growth and (2) equitable distribution of gains in agricultural productivity between farmers and consumers. Achievement of these two objectives will require continued rapid transfer of labor from the farm to the nonfarm sector and reduction in resources devoted to the production, storage, and disposition of surplus production."

It was CED speaking from the nation's highest public policy podium.

## [4] THE CED REPORT

Briefly, the CED report harked back to Manchester economics and the idea of a free world market. The problems of agriculture, the report said, were several: rapidly rising productivity, diminishing use of labor rather than capital, inelastic demand, lack of response to price changes, and unsuitable flow of human resources out of agriculture. Many of those who read the CED paper recalled another era, when Marshall Plan money brought on palm oil acres, whereas at the same time farmers in the south lined up to vote themselves acreage restrictions. And many analyzed the fact that AID money bringing on red meat production for shipment to America, so cattle, sheep and hog producers could get clobbered some more.

In the main, farm economic literature supported the CED plan because the bulk of tomes by schoolmen dealt with the sophisticated juggling of numbers, prices, demand, production and population—all quantitative matters. Isolated from the mainstream of farm life, the schoolmen undertook to handle farmers as a "gross economic quantity." The words are those of Johnson D. Hill and Walter E. Stuerman, who wrote *Roots in the Soil:* "The CED argues from finances to persons, rather than from persons to finances. And they argue about finances on the basis of the myth of a *laissez faire* economy. Their program boils down to a manipulation of persons in accord with a myth which they, as businessmen—men from the urban-industrial context—cherish and seek to propagate."

That goals such as those announced for agriculture by the CED could be established for any industry was pointed out by several observers. The real question was whether the industry involved would be benefited or harmed. Had government controlled steel, frozen prices, and short-stopped steel wages, then the government could point to the steel industry's insignificance as a part of GNP.

Just as cheap world manganese prevented the establishment of an industry in the United States, so too could an adaptive program have driven the automobile industry to the wall, or remand the farm plant to a support role in the management of the economy as long as food continued to be exported cheap and imported cheap.

Carl Wilken appeared before the House Committee on Agriculture to refute the CED report on grounds that it constituted economic charlatanism. Using his balance sheet approach, he sought to show that elimination of farmers in order to turn them into factory hands did nothing to repair the income equation, that is, the inevitable requirement that private enterprise earn enough to pay the wage and capital cost bill. Indeed, were all the farms to be liquidated and turned into corporation entities, the parity requirement would still have to be met simply because the wage bill and the capital cost bill would have to be met.

Wilken pointed to the blind spot in the thinking of the CED planners. Business leaders, not being economists, believed that if price supports were eliminated, if farm prices could be reduced, thus reducing the price of food, consumers would have more money to buy manufactured goods. This, essentially, became the thesis of the CED backup papers—those being prepared by Karl Fox of Iowa State University, Vernon Ruttan of Purdue, and Lawrence Witt of Michigan State University, all under the guiding hand of Dale Hathaway, Michigan State University's farm expert whose classroom pronouncements I have called "foundations for conjectural economics."

Wilken recited the record of agriculture since the early 1930s to the House Committee in order to make the point that CED's conceptualization didn't explain "the way our economy operates." In fact, the "have-more-to-buy-manufactured-goods" thesis was static. It could not and did not explain how income was generated, distributed, and what all this had to do with the price of eggs in China. Wilken explained how price supports had maintained national income, how it happened that 6% of the people of the world enjoyed 50% of the income of the world. He pointed out, in an oblique way, why failure to develop tariff structures caused the United States to import the so-called surpluses at a time farm prices were being supported.

"Starting in 1946 and up to the present," Wilken pointed out, "we have had currency devaluations in over 30 countries, and the principal devaluation was the devaluation of the British pound in 1949 of 30%. As these currency devaluations took place, it cut back the buying power of these countries in terms of the American farm product and American goods; in other words, we lost some of our exports.

"In addition to that, it cut the price of the commodities produced by these countries in terms of American prices. And in the five years following the British devaluations we imported $6 billion more farm products than we exported. This, along with some errors of administration by the Office of Price Stabilization, broke farm prices in 1951."

Wilken told the Committee members something about debt expansion made necessary by the Korean War. "In 1953 the Korean War ended and our debt expansion dropped back from $46 billion in 1953 to $30 billion in 1954. That was not enough borrowed money to offset the operating loss due to low farm prices, and we immediately moved into the 1954 depression." Failure to restore farm prices, Wilken said, made it necessary to increase the debt injection into the economy each year, and failure to do so brought on the inevitable slump. Compounded debt injection eventually would become impossible because it outran physical possibility.

And still there was this surplus syndrome, this concept that importation of 4 or 5% of a product should be allowed to break the price structure for American producers down to the world level on grounds that surpluses existed. Wilken hit this point with hard and inescapable facts. There was a $96 billion inventory in the manufacturing, wholesale and retail trade, he said. Farm products accounted for an inventory of $8 billion. "This $96 billion surplus in the hands of American business has not been permitted to break the price. Who is paying the cost? The consumer is paying the cost because the manufacturer, the wholesaler and the retailer must recover the cost of the storage and the warehousing of the goods when he marks the price tags on what he has to sell."

Inventory in agriculture remained the nut of the problem. Business manipulation, and agriculture's failure to develop arrangements so that each farm could handle its own inventory—and institutional arrangements for agriculture as a whole marketing in an orderly manner—now made it possible for businessmen to write a policy paper that in effect told farmers to go out of business so that others could pluck the leavings.

Wilken recommended a 35% reserve of storable farm products. Ideally, he said, farmers should pay the cost of storage and the capital invested in storage, just as a businessman does on his inventory. The economy, he said, could not be operated without an inventory.

Farmers had never developed storage because the educators and Extension workers had never taught them to do so. They had never developed institutional arrangements for price administration because they still believed in an era forever gone. That was the point in all this CED policy paper business. The so-called free market was a myth, just as the auction block sale of Ford cars was a myth, even if someone turned up a case report now and then. Business wasn't handled that way. And farmers could not go to the market with a "What'll you give me?" approach and expect to recover costs in production plus a reasonable profit. Without institutional arrangements to accomplish this, there was only one possible mechanism that could link raw materials production with the value of the dollar—and that was the support price. Wilken recommended return to 90% supports on basic farm commodities, and this was exactly opposite of what CED was saying.

## [5] WILKEN'S 1946-1950 BASE PERIOD

Wilken supported his testimony with an analysis that leaned on his balance sheet approach. In Wilken's 1946-1950 base period, private enterprise—that is, agriculture, corporations, unincorporated enterprise and rentals to persons—averaged 26% of the national income. Since this period was a balanced one—with credit well within bounds—then it stood to reason that the income generating segments would have to average 26% in any period in order to pay the wages and capital costs incidental to operating the economy. Yet in 1961, Wilken pointed out, private enterprise was earning only 15% of the $487 billion of national income needed to pay 1961 wages and capital costs. And, in 1961, private enterprise was receiving only 57.7% of the income required to pay fair dividends on investments and earn new profits for expansion.

Wilken handed the figures, tables and explanations to the lawmakers. His notations were clear enough. Based on the income of private enterprise in 1961, earned national income was $280 billion. Actual income was $430 billion. The difference was due to debt expansion. Private enterprise, farming included, was receiving only 65% of its rightful share of the national income. If the shortage figure was weighted upwards by a few successful corporations, it was being weighted downwards by agriculture's poor performance—a performance being planned and executed by professors and businessmen who either knew too little or knew too much.

Congressman Charles M. Teague of California best expressed the metaphysic that demonstrated how "the process" converted the search for truth into the power to bury truth once and for all. Wilken testified as analyst for the National Foundation for Economic Stability. Teague wanted to know just who and what the National Foundation for Economic Stability was. Wilken explained.

"I want the record to show that these are really just your proposals and that you are not representing any large national organization . . . with many members," Teague said.

Those who supported CED had both reputation and academic respectability, plus money and press, and these things meant more than being right any day of the week.

In any case, Wilken's testimony wasn't intelligible to the lawmakers. They had never paid out the price of the effort needed to understand either the equation or the fundamental proposition that economics was governed by raw materials, not money creators.

# CHAPTER 30: A PRELIMINARY BALANCE SHEET

Always, there were surface statistics, and there were the subterranean rivers of statistics, and the last were telling Wilken and all who wished to see that private credit was outrunning the nation's real economic growth. A few vapors from that river surfaced now and then. By 1965 agricultural earnings had declined 18% under what they had been a decade and a half earlier. What about business?

## [1] THE FALLING RATE OF PROFIT

The First National City Bank of New York assembled data for a newsletter which revealed profits from nonfinancial institutions well below what they had been a decade earlier. Few realized that a lack of parity for agriculture had fed a reduction into the percent of profits of industrial America to the extent indicated in the table below:

|                                    | 1955 | 1965 |
|------------------------------------|------|------|
| Soft drinks                        | 8.6  | 6.8  |
| Lumber and wood products           | 9.1  | 6.3  |
| Paper and allied products          | 8.3  | 6.7  |
| Chemical products                  | 10.0 | 8.5  |
| Paint and allied products          | 6.7  | 5.7  |
| Petroleum production and refining  | 10.6 | 9.4  |
| Cement                             | 16.5 | 9.1  |
| Glass products                     | 9.0  | 7.4  |
| Iron and steel                     | 9.3  | 5.9  |
| Nonferrous metals                  | 9.5  | 8.1  |
| Automotive parts                   | 5.3  | 4.8  |
| Aircraft and space                 | 3.9  | 3.3  |
| Metal mining                       | 13.4 | 12.7 |
| Class I railroads                  | 9.2  | 8.0  |
| Shipping                           | 8.2  | 6.8  |
| Restaurants and hotels             | 3.9  | 3.4  |

There were ready explanations for such phenomena. Some invoked all the "explanations" of depression, and some expounded some rather profound observations, as did Joseph M. Gillman in *The Falling Rate of Profit* and in *Prosperity in Crisis*. Writing in the latter, Gillman saw "production and sales costs. . . . rising when the consumer market is no longer expanding," a happenstance that put to pasture the supply and demand principle that prices rise when demand outruns supply. Trade journals in almost any industry, during the late 1950s and early 1960s, reported miracles of automation, miracles that disemployed, causing Gillman to exclaim: "While the need for investment capital has been diminished, the need for unproductive expenditures has been multiplied."

Industry's answer of choice to all this continued to be "merge," because "accounting can glamorize the performance of merging firms," and the tax system in effect subsidized merger transactions. Joseph Schumpeter and John Kenneth Galbraith notwithstanding, evidence accumulated by the Federal Trade Commission suggested that merged firms were neither more inventive than smaller units nor the chief bearers of cost for modern research. They merged to hide a declining rate of profit, to structure speculative stock price rises, to harness debentures, hide investment data, save taxes, and jockey for position in an economic structure they frequently failed to understand. ". . . there is little reason to expect significant social benefits to flow from a continuation of current [merger] trends," summarized *Economic Report on Corporate Mergers,* a Federal Trade Commission staff study under the direction of Dr. Willard F. Mueller.

At year end 1968, the 200 largest industrial firms controlled 60% of the manufacturing assets in the United States, or more than the share held by the 200 largest corporations in 1950, the year when Congress was concerned enough to amend Section 7 of the Clayton Act with the Celler-Kefauver Act. Indeed, the 200 largest manufacturing firms, at year end 1968, controlled assets equal to those held by the 1,000 largest companies in 1941, when the Temporary National Economic Committee issued a prewar report.

Since they could not earn enough to pay their wages and capital costs, the leading corporations merged. They did not look to the foundation nature of their problem.

## [2] THE BALANCE SHEET

Some economists, writing in the strange jargon of the craft, caught pieces of what was happening, but they could no more communicate their findings to the public than they could ascend into space in a manner ascribed by Muslim belief to Muhammad's coffin. Working in a small office at 1757 K Street in Washington, D. C., Carl Wilken constructed tirelessly from the moment National Foundation for Economic Stability came into being. Tom Huff of Sioux City picked up the rent tab and expenses to the tune of $21,000 during that six-year period, and Carl Wilken and James White more or less donated their time. The balance sheet, Wilken reasoned, would be the bomb that would blow the farm problem and the national economic problem into the open.

With rural bankers Vince Rossiter of Hartington, Nebraska and Harry Rash of Thayer, Kansas, Wilken attended the meeting of the Independent Bankers Association in Hollywood, Florida in April 1965. There were mixed emotions about the Wilken approach then, and mixed emotions would continue to characterize the IBA view. Nevertheless, Rash was named chairman for a Sioux City Conference. Ralph Zaun, an IBA member from Wisconsin, had gone on record against anything that might inhibit rural industrial development, a proposition he had embraced with utmost zeal, if not with profound understanding.

Wilken stated the problem simply. "We have spent billions in efforts to produce more, but nothing in a study of how, through price, to translate the production into the necessary income to utilize it." Wilken used terms such as *lost income, balance, mortgage against the future income* and *balance sheet.* The bankers who listened frequently were unable to comprehend either Wilken's system or its revelations.

In order to bridge the gap, Rossiter and Rash fed Wilken's ideas to a man who could understand, and would pay out the price of the effort necessary to understand. He was Walter Bowers, former assistant to the Under-Secretary of Treasury, former Chief Fiscal Officer in the War Department, and former associate of Roger Babson, and lately a farmer and businessman at Yates Center, Kansas. Bowers concluded that the best approach would be to construct a balance sheet for agriculture first. Balance sheets for the several other sectors could follow. Finally, such a foundation might make the idea of a balance sheet for the entire economy intelligible.

Charles B. Ray's *Notes on Origin of National Consumer Income, et al.,* contained one tier of premises.

"National consumer income or what is more properly termed 'Standard of Living' of the United States in any year at any price level is always the level of physical production of agricultural and mineral raw materials. This production multiplied by the price of these raw commodities results in the sum total of ANNUAL PRIMARY NATIONAL LABOR BARTER CREDIT. This total Primary Labor Barter Credit is every year multiplied further in society by an immutable predeterminate ANNUAL NATIONAL TRADE TURN, which results in dollar expression as National Consumer Income.

"ANNUAL NATIONAL LABOR or TRADE TURN of annual total raw material labor and income increases slowly but constantly each year on account of national technological improvement of the farm, mine, and industry plus population growth. But population growth is a factor in this Trade Turn increase only if employed. This full employment of population growth can only occur as a result of and in years of PARITY RAW MATERIAL PRICES with consequent normal increasing consumer demand and consequent increased raw material production of all kinds."

It was Ray's thesis that when raw materials were below parity, a new potential labor force would remain unemployed exactly to the degree that raw materials remained below parity. If raw materials were 18% below parity, the 18% of potential labor force would be forcefully unemployed.

"This national labor turn, which as a national trade turn is expressed in dollars, is a 'moving' mathematical or economic constant—in prosperity or in depression. The ratio of the National Labor or Trade Turn to the total Raw Material Labor and Income having risen will never recede, hence can be pre-estimated or projected out at 'normal'. . . . Irrational speculative agricultural prices convert this constant prime factor into an utterly unstable income FACTOR and the whole of NATIONAL INCOME is level or ratioed to this violent speculative cycle." If Ray's paragraphs provided a second tier of premises, there was also the first tier—the laws of energy. They came first and the rest followed as night the day.

With labor and interest up, and profits in corporations down, and farm income making it necessary for farmers to consume their own capital, the only answer for the economy had been to expand private and public debt. But debt expansion had passed the point of diminishing returns.

Farms were not earning the necessary income, nor were most businesses. But low farm income had led the way. For 15 years farmers had earned less than it cost them to produce. They had consumed the fat earned from 1941 to 1951. They had lived on credit since then, and now the credit was almost gone.

## [3] WALTER A. BOWERS

The IBA Midwest Agricultural Conference was held June 18-19, 1965 at Sioux City. Walter A. Bowers ran his talk, "The American Farmer: His Balance Sheet, Good; His Profit and Loss, Bad" past the Committee with the usual schoolmaster's aplomb. As with other thinkers who saw the origin of the economic riddle in the laws of energy, Bowers called attention to this floating speck in the planetary system, this Earth, which was being swung on a gravitational string in a 300 million mile orbit around its nebular sun, wobbling slightly on its axis so that on June 21 summer would arrive, plants would grow and food would be produced.

Here was the Earth, Bowers pointed out, 8,000 miles in diameter, 25,000 miles in circumference, spinning on its axis once around every 24 hours, giving each spot an equal amount of daylight and darkness. Water covered 74% of this Earth. Only 26% was dry land. Out of this 26%, only 8% constituted farm land, and only 3% was suitable for crops. Bowers pointed out that 3 billion people were crowded into the seven bread baskets of the world—half in Asia and the South Pacific, one-fourth in Europe and Africa, and one-sixth in North and South America. By the year 2000, this population would double.

Bowers had a reason for reciting this grade school geography and social science information. He wanted to point out the inescapable fact that all was finite, that food production wasn't manna from heaven, that there were limits to everything under the sun. Cropland in the U.S., circa 1959, totaled 313,446,000 acres, or 1.5 acres per capita. By the year 2010 there would be only .75 acres per person for every man, woman and child in the world, and a scant few years beyond that hunger had to be the legacy of the composite world.

"Only by encouraging more efficient use of small acreage, by making more profitable the operation of small family-size farms, by decentralizing industry to rural areas, by restoring prosperity of rural communities, by reversing big city population flow back to small towns in rural areas and by stimulating the importance of the small town independent banker, can American farming be saved and can food shortages be delayed in the United States," Bowers reported.

This was possible, Bowers noted, because the farmer was still solvent in a bookkeeping sense.

|  | F* | R | U | M | D |
|---|---|---|---|---|---|
|  | % | % | % | % | % |
| Current Assets | 19 | 17 | 12 | 75 | 75 |
| Fixed Assets | 81 | 83 | 88 | 25 | 25 |
| Total Assets | 100 | 100 | 100 | 100 | 100 |
| Current liabilities | 8 | 14 | 8 | 10 | 14 |
| Fixed liabilities | 8 | 38 | 46 | 12 | 2 |
| Total liabilities | 16 | 52 | 54 | 22 | 16 |
| Net Worth | 84 | 48 | 46 | 78 | 84 |
| Total liabilities | 100 | 100 | 100 | 100 | 100 |

* F, farmer; R, railroads; U, utilities; M, manufacturing; D, distribution

The income and expense statement for the farmer added up a new dimension for the year Bowers covered, 1964.

|  | (billion) | Percent |
|---|---|---|
| Total assets | $230.5 | 18. |
| Gross income | 42.0 | 18. |
| Total production expense | <u>29.4</u> | <u>13.</u> |
| Net (before managers' salaries) | 12.6 | 5. |
| less 2 million managers x $2,200 | <u>4.4</u> | <u>2.</u> |
| Net after managers' salaries | 8.2 | 3. |
| Estimated annual debt payment | <u>3.8</u> | <u>1.5</u> |
| Net (after payment of debt) | 4.4 | 1.5 |
| less new machinery | <u>2.2</u> | <u>1.</u> |
| Net earnings (on capital) | 2.2 | 0.5 |

Compared to any other American business, the farmer earned the lowest return of any segment.

|  | F* | R | U | M | D |
|---|---|---|---|---|---|
|  | % | % | % | % | % |
| Capital invested | 100 | 100 | 100 | 100 | 100 |
| Income annually | 18 | 31 | 23 | 100 | 200 |
| Net earned on investment | 0.5 | 4 | 4 | 8 | 8 |

To keep the worst aspects of this from showing, the economy had elected to run deficits, and—commented Bowers—"The consumer food bills in America the past ten years . . . have been subsidized by issuing U.S. government bonds in the amount of $45 to $50 billion." Taxpayers were paying a dear price for the fiction of low food prices.

Bowers proposed public policy that would effect this comparison between the farmer and industry:

|  | F* | R | U | M | D |
|---|---|---|---|---|---|
|  | % | % | % | % | % |
| Capital invested | 100 | 100 | 100 | 100 | 100 |
| Income annually | 32 | 31 | 23 | 100 | 200 |
| Net earned on investment | 8.5 | 4 | 4 | 8 | 8 |

Such a gross annually would simply place the farmer on the same return basis as that allowed railroads by the Interstate Commerce Commission. And such a gross would net the farmer 8.5% on capital, or slightly more

---

* F, farmer; R, railroads; U, utilities; M, manufacturing; D, distribution

than was being earned by manufacturers and wholesalers and retailers on their capital investments.

Bowers recognized the role of automation. "When automation throws farm-bred workers out of their jobs in cities, they should find they can get higher wages on profitable small farms back home. Small farms are more efficient than large farms in producing higher value crops per acre and employing more manpower per acre." The efficiency of the small farm was the key in this analysis. Expensive equipment on farms had created a fiction that large farms were more efficient, but the exact opposite was true. Bowers covered the many points sound public policy should have examined, but didn't, because the business people who wrote policy saw profit in strip cities now, and didn't look into the future at all. The big operators overworked and mined the soil, "Thus civilization itself goes from surpluses—to crowded cities—to hunger."

The point in all this was that it took accounting statements to point up what was happening, or it couldn't be recognized until too late.

## [4] 40% OF SAVINGS AND PROFITS

Wilken iterated and reiterated this general concept, both in Sioux City, and in Washington when the IBA Agriculture Committee met in February 1965. Wilken started with a concept every banker presumably understood. ". . . in 1948 our debt expansion of all kinds was in ratio of 40% of savings and profits, and in the period 1951-'63, it averaged over 80%. In other words we increased the debt twice as fast in order to cover up the operating loss."

Taking the level of savings and operating profits of the economy into consideration, it took approximately $5.50 of future income to earn the profit needed to repay each dollar of excessive debt. It took the same $5.50 of future income to earn the profits needed to feed the interest mill a single dollar.

"Whether we can service this debt or are forced to repudiate it with a severe depression depends entirely upon how much goods and services we produce and the price at which it is sold in future years," Wilken told the bankers.

Wilken wanted IBA to fund the construction of a balance sheet, and take the lead in bringing certified findings to the attention of Congress. Other voices in other rooms argued against the proposal, as Rossiter was later to testify, and those voices got their direction from Farm Bureau, the funding organizations, and the powers that be.

Rejected again, Wilken nevertheless received token support from individual IBA members—rural bankers Vince Rossiter, Harry Rash, Ed Manuel—and from Granite Falls, Minnesota businessman Arnold Paulson, each contributing $400 to cover stenographic and printing costs.

# [5] THE 12 CENTRAL MIDWESTERN STATES

Wilken published *A Preliminary Balance Sheet for the 12 Central Midwestern States, 1946-1963* in 1965. Taken by itself it was the least understood of all his works. Taken as the end product of a long career, it communicated too well with the few who understood its contents, and not at all with those Wilken hoped to reach. Wilken set forth his premises, albeit in abbreviated form.

Private enterprise was the working mechanism of the economy, and private enterprise included the farms, corporations, independent business units. They had to supply the capital investment to create each job, to create the income for payrolls, capital costs and the sundry costs that attended the travels of raw materials from the ground to final sale across the counter. If the private enterprise units had to pay the labor and capital costs, then it stood to reason that the income of private enterprise had to move up in balance with any increase in wages or interest costs, the trade turn supplying the multiplier. Economists could walk away, but really, there was no other way to pay wages except by earning income. Distortions of money supply, and expanded capitalization beyond profits and savings could not absolve an economy from meeting this requirement. "This basic principle of price balance is necessary whether it is a small business grossing $100,000 of sales or a large corporation whose sales run into the billions of dollars. . . ." Wilken pointed out.

The income of private enterprise during the 1946-1950 period averaged 26% of the national income. This compared favorably to the 26.3% of national income private enterprise earned in 1929. Net farm income, with approximately two-thirds as much investment as all of the corporations, averaged 7.1 % of the national income in 1946-1950 as compared to 7.09% in 1929. The *Economic Report of the President* contained the figures, and thus there could be no argument on that score. Why were these figures meaningful?

The record had proved, Wilken submitted, that whenever the earnings of private enterprise fell below 26% of the national income, a depression resulted. Well, the income of private enterprise was well below 26% of national income, as Wilken's own shortage of income calculations revealed, but there was no depression. Why? Wilken answered that the depression was in fact here, but it was being covered up with debt creation that would explode the entire economy into receivership in the fullness of time—that is, deliver the nation into the hands of a dictatorship for management.

That was the sum and substance of *A Preliminary Balance Sheet*. Private enterprise could be computed as a sector, or it could be broken down. Each state had its own set of figures. In one table Wilken listed the income of private enterprise from 1946-1950 to 1964 to illustrate the parity of income private enterprise had received these many years, with the parity figure informing the reader exactly what part of 26% of the national income private enterprise had enjoyed. The part that hadn't been, but should have been earned, represented the "shortage" of income Wilken frequently mentioned.

INCOME OF PRIVATE ENTERPRISE FROM 1946-1950
AVERAGE $55.2 BILLIONS*
(Billions of Dollars)

| Year | Income | Increase | Parity Income of Private Enterprise |
|------|--------|----------|-------------------------------------|
| 1951 | 62.0 | 12.3% | 84.8% |
| 1952 | 59.4 | 7.6% | 75.0% |
| 1953 | 58.8 | 6.5% | 70.0% |
| 1954 | 57.3 | 3.8% | 67.4% |
| 1955 | 65.2 | 18.1% | 71.0% |
| 1956 | 67.2 | 21.7% | 67.3% |
| 1957 | 66.8 | 21.0% | 63.4% |
| 1958 | 64.8 | 17.3% | 60.7% |
| 1959 | 71.0 | 28.4% | 61.4% |
| 1960 | 69.2 | 25.3% | 56.7% |
| 1961 | 71.2 | 28.9% | 56.3% |
| 1962 | 75.8 | 37.1% | 55.9% |
| 1963 | 77.3 | 40.0% | 54.0% |
| 1964 | 83.6 | 51.4% | 54.9% |

* Income of Private Enterprise is income of Farm Operators, Small Business, and Corporate Profits after Taxes.

CONSOLIDATED BALANCE SHEET
FOR THE 12 CENTRAL MIDWESTERN STATES
(Millions of Dollars)

| | Shortage 1951 | Shortage 1963 | Shortage 1951-1963 |
|------|-----------|-----------|-----------|
| Illinois | 1,365 | 7,497 | 51,815 |
| Indiana | 26 | 1,990 | 12,099 |
| Iowa | 459 | 2,458 | 19,482 |
| Kansas | 190 | 1,121 | 7,121 |
| Michigan | 214 | 3,452 | 17,259 |
| Minnesota | 343 | 1,557 | 12,556 |
| Missouri | 425 | 2,254 | 16,891 |
| Nebraska | 212 | 1,037 | 8,159 |
| North Dakota | 173 | 614 | 5,612 |
| Ohio | 368 | 4,765 | 23,326 |
| South Dakota | 55 | 539 | 4,470 |
| Wisconsin | 90 | 1,962 | 13,150 |
| TOTAL SHORTAGE | | | 191,940 |

The Balance Sheet revealed how the steady erosion of income in the 12 states, as compared to the national increase in wages and interest, took place from 1951 to 1963. The shortage in the 13 years resulted from low farm prices which, in turn, reduced the income of rural areas in the state and the loss of markets translated into losses for farm operations, small business and corporate enterprise operating in the 12 states. This erosion of income continued in 1964, and if the planners carry out their program of eliminating another 1.5 million farms it will increase at a rapid rate.

Using 1946-1950 = 100, Wilken illustrated that the percent of national income going to wages and interest had moved from 66.4% of national income in 1946-1950 to 76.2% in 1964. "The direct result was that private enterprise could not earn a normal profit and new capital for expansion."

Although corporations and independent business units, taken as composites, were not able to earn enough to pay their wages and capital costs, it was the farm sector that fared worst of all. By failing to maintain 7.1 % of the national income, agriculture was enduring slow liquidation, as Walter Bowers had pointed out. Wilken's figures for underpayment to agriculture during the 1951 through 1964 period were as follows:

### *UNDERPAYMENT TO AGRICULTURE AS COMPARED TO WAGES AND INTEREST IN NATIONAL INCOME

| | |
|---|---|
| 1951 | $ 5.6 billion |
| 1952 | 9.7 " |
| 1953 | 14.9 " |
| 1954 | 15.9 " |
| 1955 | 20.9 " |
| 1956 | 24.2 " |
| 1957 | 26.8 " |
| 1958 | 25.0 " |
| 1959 | 30.7 " |
| 1960 | 34.1 " |
| 1961 | 34.7 " |
| 1962 | 39.07 " |
| 1963 | 42.7 " |
| 1964 | 46.9 " |
| TOTAL | $371.1 " |

---

* Underpayment in terms of gross realized farm income as compared to the increase in wages and interest component of our national income for 1946-1950. In 1946-1950 net farm income was an average of $15.1 billion, as the value of our farm production created income for others in rural areas. In 1964 the net farm income approximated $12.7 billion out of a gross farm income of approximately $42 billion. Net farm income was approximately 30% of the gross farm income while the 70% was creating income for others in rural areas.

## [6] AN ANALYSIS THAT EXPLAINED THE FACTS

Those who became acquainted with *A Preliminary Balance Sheet* frequently argued aloud and questioned the system, but when pressed to the task they could not substitute an analysis that explained the facts. That, in the final analysis, was Wilken's hole card. What he was saying explained what was happening, and what many of the other economists were selling didn't work. And still they pursued their theories, much as might "a beast of muddy brain . . . that gives itself death and wars for pence dealt out from its own stores." And when a man like Wilken arose so that this truth be given, it was the bureaucratic mind that killed him "unforgiven."

In fact industry required a parity, just as labor required parity and agriculture required parity, because parity was not a temperature, but a thermometer, not a fixed quantity, but a relationship. Those who refused to entertain Wilken's explanation continued to substitute a theory that for all its status and glory didn't work.

## [7] THE DISHONEST PENCIL

In *A Preliminary Balance Sheet,* Wilken charged that the dishonest pencil had been invoked so that the "unbelievable underpayment to agriculture" might go unnoticed. In order to make good his claim, he had asked Congressman Harold Gross of Iowa to write the USDA requesting an explanation. The letter came back as follows:

Honorable H.R. Gross
House of Representatives
Washington 25, D. C.

Dear Mr. Gross:

This is in reply to your letter of April 21 requesting data showing what the current parity price of corn would be under the old parity formula, as compared with the present formula.

The parity price of corn for March 1965 based on the old parity formula method and using the current index of prices paid would be $2.04 per bushel. This price is derived by multiplying the average price of corn for the period August 1909 through 1914 (64.2 cents per bushel) by the current index of prices paid by farmers, including interest, taxes and wage rates, of 318 (1910-1914=100). The index of prices paid by farmers used in computing parity prices by the old formula was discontinued in January 1965.

The parity price of corn as computed by the current, or modernized, formula published in *Agricultural Prices* was $1.55 per bushel for March.

I am enclosing the January issue of *Agricultural Prices* which contains more detailed information on the computation of parity prices.

> Sincerely yours,
> (Signed)
> John A. Schnittker
> Director, Agricultural Economics

Farmers had 49 cents taken off their target for corn parity with a lead pencil. In short, $1.55 corn amounted to 73.8% of honest parity. "How can Congress enact sound farm legislation with an inaccurate formula?" became Wilken's rhetorical question, and an answer was not forthcoming. Instead, USDA cranked up the age-old drive to have done with a parity formula completely.

*A Preliminary Balance Sheet* did not sell well. As an economic bomb it was too recondite for instant comprehension among farmers and ruralists. And the professionals had already made intellectual commitments to a theory period.

# CHAPTER 31: SEMINAR

Carl Wilken turned 70 as his *Preliminary Balance Sheet* hit the presses. Privately, he accepted the fact that time was running out. And yet he continued to believe in miracles. He never completely accepted the fact that the policy makers had turned their back on stability and were gearing public policy to an incredible philosophy, one composed of the frustration economics Boulding/Hathaway/Bonnen *et al.* had accounted for, and the greed economics of the international manipulators.

## [1] A TEMPORARY PROSPERITY

Yet from any logical vantage point, the economic exchange equation had to start with the price of raw materials. Raw materials had to reflect the cost of production plus a profit in ratio to overall cost factors. To this price structure had to be added the cost of handling, processing costs, capital costs, transportation, so that in the end the consumer price level reflected parity with all cost factors in balance, and a market sufficient to utilize production.

Wilken put it this way. When goods are not priced so as to reflect production costs and a profit in ratio to overall cost factors, then the sharp "buy cheap and sell dear" trader enjoys a temporary prosperity, but pays in the end when the shortage of purchasing power erodes markets, and creates overstuffed warehouses. Businessmen have always thought like businessmen—meaning, they have never looked down the road by more than a few years at a time. And, also, the business equation has never required the same kind of statesmanship demanded of those who guide public policy. Presumably, a businessman can get in there and get his—and get out—before prosperity tops out. The tragic figure of our times, Wilken pointed out, is not the businessman, but the economist.

The economic advisers now work the economic exchange equation upside down. They start their calculations at the top, with the consumer price index. After that they subtract wage costs, capital costs, transportation charges, *et al.*, from the source of production. Anything left over is assigned to the raw materials producer, including the farmer.

Obviously, the process—for this span of some 15 years that Wilken looked across—had been bankrupting farmers and eroding the economy's markets. And debt creation was having a hard go at creating artificial markets enough to keep the economic kite flying. The "gut agriculture" seers were in the saddle.

One of the back-up writers for the CED policy makers was Dale E. Hathaway, and his newspeak was called *Problems of Progress in Agricultural Economy.* "Essentially, there are four contributions that agriculture can make to a nation's economic growth. First, it can provide the food and fiber base necessary for a population growing in numbers and in wealth. However, it is important that this be done without an increase in total resources used and/or in the relative price of farm products. In fact economic growth is stimulated if farm prices decline so that [other] people will have more money to spend on other goods and services. Second, agriculture can provide workers to produce other goods and services by releasing them from the production of farm products. Third, agriculture can provide a market for non-farm goods and services enabling the gainful employment of people in their production. Finally, agriculture can provide a source of capital that may be invested in improved productive facilities in [other areas] of the economy."

Hathaway was succeeded on the Council of Economic Advisers by James Bonnen. The best of Bonnen's thinking emerged when he and Arthur Okum met with Carl Wilken and the Agriculture Committee of the Independent Bankers Association in February 1965.

"Gentlemen," Bonnen said, "if we thought there was anything wrong with agriculture, we would have a plan for it. We have no plan for agriculture. . . . However, there is the plan that the economists have been advocating for 30 years. . . ." The plan had simply been to bleed agriculture to death. The economists failed to see why this rob-Peter-to-pay-Paul prosperity contained the seeds of its own destruction.

For 15 years, Carl Wilken had followed the arithmetic position of the economic exchange equation turned upside down. Each year he constructed working statements on the imbalance that had been allowed to develop. And Wilken's balance equation pointed with grave finality to the fact that with a decline in farm income had come a decline in economic stability. The results were being hidden by new debt creation and by the income generated through war production, despite the fact that over-urbanization threatened to plunge the nation into a rock-bottom depression. In fact, the "released" population cited by Hathaway was now being "released" from industry as well, and there was no place to go.

## [2] AN EXCHANGE ECONOMY REQUIRED PARITY

Wilken's figures weren't hard to understand, not when one kept in mind the quite simple proposition that an exchange economy required parity for labor and business as well as for agriculture. The last time farm prices were hitting parity could be roughly covered by averaging the years 1946-1950, and calling the base 100. From this balanced base— when the act of producing last yielded credits across the board sufficient to consume the production—certain shortages of income had become evident. Wilken illustrated both the shortage of income caused by this imbalance, and then revealed what percentage of parity was being achieved by the various sectors of the economy.

Wilken continued to hammer out massive letters through all of 1965, explaining his balance sheet to men like Senators Jack Miller and Karl Mundt, to Congressmen he had known for three decades, to his old friend and supporter, Oscar Broyer, and to the editor of the *Sioux City Journal*.

## [3] MEASURED INTEREST

How could one calibrate the results? There were always polite letters in response, always measured interest. Gene Flaherty offered Wilken radio time for a regular series, and proposed circulation of tapes on a routine basis. Wilken didn't jump at the chance for a reason few people could understand. Wilken knew that there was little prospect of changing public policy even when backed by the powerhouse efforts of an organized group. As a lone voice in the wilderness the chance had to be rated at next to zero. Wilken did not want to be a lone voice in the wilderness.

Arnold Paulson, a businessman from the small town of Granite Falls, Minnesota, was more optimistic. After hearing Wilken, Paulson virtually dropped what he was doing—the Minnesota Business and Industrial Promotion Agency—in order to organize seminars and appear behind the podium at rural meetings. Everything Wilken was saying made sense to Paulson, and the more he studied it, the more sense it made.

Paulson and his associate, Elmo Volstad, set up a seminar for Springfield, Illinois, October 28, 1965. Wilken's address came styled, "A Balance Sheet of the United States," and that talk outlined exactly what Wilken was to sell during a season of seminars that lasted until his death. Wilken talked "shortage of income" and "failure to maintain farm prices in balance with wages and interest components of our national income." Both the Granite Falls and Springfield seminars were measured successes, albeit financial failures. Yet almost all serious students stayed an arm's length away.

Between podium appearances, Wilken wrote long letters. Each month, he pin-pointed the dislocation that was consuming the American economy. "The new farm bill just about reaches the goal of getting back to 1943 prices," he wrote Gene Flaherty, "and in balance with world prices." Wilken told his old Sioux City-based friend that there would be a duplication of 1929, only six times worse. By December 10, 1965 he had typed out a long "Message to the Citizens of the State of Iowa." Wilken listed personal income by years for Iowa, and handed out his four-point analysis, each point reiterating again the trade turn requirement, the loss being suffered, the parity it would take to put Iowa on even keel, and how the shortage could be repaired.

Wilken wanted to return to Sioux City. He wanted once more to bring the message back to its birthplace. His letters became increasingly sentimental, and yet he continued to dream impossible dreams—that Congress might wake up, that Sioux City businessmen might take hold, that the organizations that had spurned his analysis might pick it up and proceed with the educational work full understanding of his foundation concepts required. Wilken handed many of his private papers over to at least two small farm papers—*Farm Tempo U.S.A.* and the *Illinois Farmer* for publication, and in the 1966, 1967 and 1968 issues both the old and the new received added exposure. Thousands of farmers and a few rural businessmen read about Carl Wilken and learned something about his system of thought, but again "nothing happened."

There was always encouragement as seminar followed seminar. "I am glad to learn . . . that you have decided to make the direct approach to David Lawrence of *U.S. News and World Report*," wrote Senator Karl Mundt, and Mundt, of course, added his blessing to the conference.

"I would suggest that we all have a huddle and put things on tape relative to the running account of my work," Wilken wrote September 21, 1966, and when I answered the letter we arranged for a meeting at the first possible moment. That moment in fact came in January 1967, and the taped record appears in the early chapters of this book.

## [4] THE SIOUX CITY SEMINAR

Hartington, Nebraska banker Vince Rossiter opened the Sioux City Seminar that Wilken had wanted for over a year. The date was February 17, 1967. My tape transcript of that two-day meeting ran 186 pages. Between Rossiter's opener, and Arnold Paulson's long explanation of the income equation, and contributions that included words from Harry Rash, Walter Bowers, Pastor Giles Ekola, Father Dismas Treder, mining counsel Roy Harrup and several others, almost everything Wilken had ever written about was unloaded. Those who attended the seminar were required to take a tablet and a lead pencil, and compute ratios, relationships, income shortages and the exchange equation for each segment of the economy. Xerox copies of pages from the *Economic Report of the President* were used for raw data.

Every once in a while those in attendance took a break, usually to listen to lines of thought that somehow escaped the public prints. There was Walter Bowers, for instance. Bowers wanted to unload a few facts about war.

"Talk about financing the war," he said. "When the war started the generals said, 'The gravy train is in. Get your estimates on what it's going to take for a war to end quickly' . . . The totals that the generals came up with was $200 billion—to come from Congress to fight in one war, $200 billion! Well, somebody said, 'Why there's only 60 million workers in America and their wages are averaged at $2,000 each. You could hire every worker in America for less than $200 billion. That would take only $120 billion. Congress passed an appropriations bill for $200 billion when there were only 60 million workers in America. You could have hired every farmer, every man in the coal mines, every man in the steel mills for $120 billion, yet the War Department got $200 billion for one year of war.'" One of Bowers jobs turned out to be to find out the maximum that could be spent by government in any national economy. "And we found out by studying Germany and Russia and France and all of the others that 50% of the national income is all that can be spent by government for war, and the other 50% had to go for . . . clothing, food, etc. . . . ." The Constitution limited appropriations to one year. Nevertheless, said Bowers. "It was a case of renewal of appropriations—$200 billion, $200 billion, $200 billion. When the war ended they had not spent more than $150 billion out of $200 billion. The point that I want to bring out is that we can't spend more than 50% for government without bankrupting ourselves. We're now spending over 30% of our national income for that purpose." Said Bowers: "Our fathers set up our states like Iowa, Illinois, Indiana. They thought the safe amount of debt for public affairs was 5% of assessed valuation. In Iowa road bonds can't be voted over 5% of the assessed valuation. The total assessed valuation of America according to the book is about $350 billion." Bowers pointed out that the national debt was close to 70% of the nation's assessed valuation, The public and private debt, circa 1967, was $1,500 billion, or over four times the nation's assessed valuation.

This debt not being renewed, because it couldn't be renewed, became the trigger mechanism in 1929, Bowers said. Yet here was $1,500 billion debt [circa 1967] with an average life of 10 years. Every year, $150 billion had to be renewed. Without 10% renewal of that debt, the whole thing would be required to collapse. "That's what happened in 1929."

Bowers became cynical. He pointed out that in 1933 something like 30,000 people in Illinois alone refused to pay their taxes. The same thing happened in New York, where bonds sold at 80 cents on the dollar. "Our whole free enterprise system is based on credit collapses . . . Those who owe debts are 75%, perhaps 85% of the people. But 10% own everything. They're the enemies of society. So whenever our credit system collapses we then go into communism or socialism and shoot all the people that own things. Only the people in debt are allowed to survive. So the thing to do is to keep piling up debt, it'll collapse and some dictator will take over and you who have no debts will be the enemy of society. I wanted to pass that thought along."

This was the kind of thing Wilken's exchange equation could pinpoint and cause the nation to avoid. Wilken went through the relationships, and declared quite frankly that "if you don't want to lose $7 of national income for every dollar of farm income you better work out some system to bring farm prices up where they belong. And as far as private enterprise is concerned, if it becomes necessary you better get the national guard out and force these farmers to accept the program that will give them parity at the marketplace."

Wilken and Paulson taught those at the seminar to compute parity, not in the outlandish manner invoked by USDA experts, but with simple equations that related the price of fundamental commodities to any balanced base period. The base period was the key. It had to be a time in history when the several segments were "in balance."

It was over a coffee table in an informal conversation that I mentioned to Wilken that 90% support prices in effect harnessed Benjamin Graham's *Storage and Stability* without in fact creating the commodity dollar Graham had suggested. "Exactly," Wilken agreed that night, and the next morning he added this statement after Father Treder had concluded a long talk on the money changers in the American temple.

"I've never mentioned money," Wilken said, "but yesterday I gave you the 7 times turn of this new farm dollar. I gave you the trade turn of private enterprise, starting at the bottom. Now why the price support for farm products? The 90% price support monetized your farm production. It was a monetary bill. But I never called it that because I didn't want to confuse the issue. Now if we'd take 25 basic raw materials—most of them agriculture—and stabilize them at 90% of parity as the price support (and 110% ceiling), we'll have the money and we'll have the stability. And you're not going to solve this thing until you do monetize your basic raw materials. You can get the Federal Reserve Board kicked out. This is not going to give you a farm price. Now in the Constitution it says Congress will issue the money and regulate the value thereof. When you establish parity for your basic raw materials you create the flow of money that you need and you don't have to worry about financial control. You have the control in that legislation. If you monetize your raw materials through the support level you've got your monetary problem solved. And until you monetize those raw materials you're not going to solve it."

## [5] WILKEN'S ABLEST STUDENT

With Arnold Paulson at the promotional end of each seminar, Wilken toured the country during all of 1967 and most of 1968. By now, Paulson had become Wilken's ablest student. Paulson found a way of translating heady concepts into meaningful podium presentations. When the Keynesian economists argued, "We owe it to ourselves," Paulson caused the air to fairly crackle with ridicule. "We're not supposed to be concerned about this debt because we owe it to ourselves. After all, they say the wealth doesn't disappear. So we're going to take this federal debt and we're going to dump it into the ocean. We're going to mark it paid and forget it even exists. We're going to do the same with all of the debts of the 50 states. Take the debts of the 50 states and dump them in the ocean. Take the debts of every city in America—New York, Chicago, Detroit, Los Angeles—take the debts of every town and city and village, dump them in the ocean. Then take the debts of all the townships and all of the counties. And take all of the school debts and throw them in the ocean. Forget them! What have we got left? Well, we've got the debt that will bankrupt the United States, and that is the private debt. That's the debt of the people. That's your debt. Now you can't dump that one in the ocean because somebody is going to collect that debt someday, somehow, even if it means they are going to take it out of your estate after death. Now it is the private debt that causes recessions and depressions."

Paulson and Wilken tried to cram into each seminar what most colleges project into several semester courses. Few of those who attended could comprehend the staggering dimensions of what was being presented that fast—and after they left, there was no follow-up. And yet a transcription of any seminar would be worth more than a gross of textbooks now standard college fare.

Paulson conducted a series of seminars in Minnesota early in 1968, just as he had conducted seminars throughout the border states a year earlier. For the first time, laymen were introduced to the *Economic Report of the President*, to the *Survey of Current Business* and the *Economic Indicator*. For the first time the man in the street—the one who pays the bills and relies on two and two being equal to four—learned of embezzlement at the highest level, of figures being changed in the basic economic bibles of the nation, because existing figures no longer revealed what economists wanted them to reveal.

There had been a seminar at Decatur, Illinois on August 12,1966, with Bob Wilson's *Illinois Farmer* giving a mighty assist in packing the halls. Wilken traced the trade turn and put figures on the blackboard because, in his words, "the eye is 17 times as retentive as the ear," but again there was no follow-up, save Wilken's letters and the published versions thereof.

The seminars came and went, but in the end the real students remained few. Wilken had spent his life that way, always with few supporters who really understood. He had earned a living as an independent merchant of economic facts, and the customers had been few. He had prepared studies for the railroads, for the independent meat packers, for mining interests, independent petroleum producers, and a reclamation association.

The studies always tied into Wilken's basic outline on the American economy. The American Railway Association at one time paid Wilken $3,000 for a report on Class I railroads. In the railway report Wilken pointed out that with the drop of 54% of the value of farm production between 1929 and 1933, the gross operating income of the railroads fell off 53% also. There was an economist named Duncan, Wilken recalled, who scratched his head. He couldn't understand it. There had been only a 3% drop in "freight weights." And that was right. But, said Wilken, freight weight wasn't worth a tinker's dam unless it could be multiplied by miles of freight, and during that period the railroads lost 50% of their tonnage, and this cut their income 53%.

At each seminar, Wilken answered questions, and these give and take sessions were often more meaningful than erudite computations of the exchange equation because laymen understood. Those who asked understood what Wilken meant when he told about the Collins Land Company, the super farm that came to eastern Iowa during the 1925-1929 era to buy up acres, tear out fences and put in machinery. "And when the Depression hit they went broke so fast it made their heads spin."

Somehow it didn't matter how fast one knocked down the false wisdom being manufactured by the public prints. USDA told farmers that they had to produce cheap to get the markets, and yet the Common Market operating on an American parity bought 20% of American exports in 1967—"not because of price, but because the production was needed"—and invoked variable levies before allowing import production into the EEC.

# [6] A PROLIFIC LETTER WRITER

Through over three decades, Wilken had been a prolific letter writer. Some of those missives turned up in print—in the *Georgia Farmers' Market Bulletin* during the early years, in letters to the editor columns always, in the small farm papers recently, and in the *Congressional Record*. But in the main Wilken's letters went to friends, and usually a carbon copy went to each of several friends. Long drawers full of letters have been turned up, and long drawers full have been destroyed as oldsters have passed from the scene.

I did not become acquainted with the Wilken letters until early 1966, when Wilken started anew running through his economic equations for the benefit of those who had become attached to the raw materials idea in the wake of Wilken's tryst with IBA.

"The Committee started out in great style," Wilken wrote Thayer, Kansas banker Harry Rash, April 11, 1966, "and the *Independent Banker* contained articles by [Vince] Rossiter and myself that clearly set out what was happening to Rural America. But the Committee didn't work at the job of understanding what was involved and in turn therefore didn't educate the members of the IBA with facts to offset the complete program of misrepresentation as presented by the newspapers."

Wilken complained bitterly that so-called scholars and lawmakers wouldn't pay out the price of the effort necessary to understand how the American economy actually functioned. When anyone arrived who would work at gaining an understanding, Wilken instructed tirelessly. After the Springfield, Illinois seminar, a college professor came forward. He was Dr. John Forbes, a history teacher at Blackburn College, Carlinville, Illinois. Forbes could not believe what he was being told.

"Prove me wrong," Wilken challenged. It took Forbes five months to do the arithmetic and construct a ponderous tome, *The National Economy is Out of Balance*, which confirmed Wilken every inch of the way.

In letter after letter Wilken retraced the passage of events. He worked his equation from WWII forward and backward, and tied each development to historical facts. "Both the liberals and the internationalists were against taxes" during WWII, Wilken commented. "The internationalists thrive on debts, and the socialists know that cheap prices will eventually force socialism. . . . Karl Marx in 1848 in a speech on Free Trade at Brussels laid it out cold in his closing remarks when he said approximately as follows: *The protective system is conservative, the international system of free trade is destructive and for that reason and that reason alone I am for free trade because it will hasten the day of the economic revolution.*

"Every depression the United States has had since 1910 has been due to only one factor, a price of American raw materials out of balance with wage and interest costs in operating the economy."

Once, Dr. John Forbes wanted Wilken to write directly to President Johnson to explain this exchange equation. "This course would find my letter turned over to the Council of Economic Advisers, and they would not admit that they have given President Johnson the wrong direction," Wilken responded.

Wilken wrote to Senators and Representatives by the dozen. His message came on somewhat the same in each case, whether ignored in the *Congressional Record,* or ignored privately. America was already into its economic death rattle by late 1966, with the usual surface tension evident in the gold pool. Wilken recalled for Rossiter an earlier day, when Roosevelt had raised the price of gold. "The theory was that if gold was increased to $35 an ounce, an increase of 69.3%, that it would restore the 1926 commodity price level and prosperity. But other countries sold us their gold, thus removing backing for their currencies and commodity prices didn't recover."

On June 16, 1967, Wilken wrote me a long letter.

"You will find enclosed a rough draft of a paper showing what really started the current dislocation. In 1951 price ceilings were established on the basis of 85% of a normal operating margin by business. The result was to cut back the farm price and other raw materials as business tried to retain normal operating margins. In so doing they lost the market in raw material areas and have never recovered.

"I have sent a copy of the Balance Sheet to 200 corporation presidents but expect no reaction. The presidents have voted themselves a good salary and met their expansion with debt thus exploiting the stockholders by cutting back dividends in proportion to actual earned profits as determined by farm parity. To illustrate, dividends have fallen off from 6.27% to a little over 3%, or about 50% of parity. . . ."

Wilken's many letters during his last three years would fill a volume the size of this one. All rated attention, and almost all required several readings. On July 4, 1967 Wilken wrote me a long letter, and it opened thus:

"Today is Independence Day and the American people do not realize that they have lost their economic independence, without which freedom is a myth."

Wilken followed with interest the series of "interview" articles I caused to be published in *Farm Tempo U.S.A.* during 1967. Thousands were making contact with Wilken's ideas, but he exclaimed, so many "missed the impact of agriculture on rural America, private enterprise, and the economy as a whole." Wilken approved of Francis L. York using his material in his *Hot Line* newsletter, but thought York's emphasis failed the broad scope that

Wilken sought to convey. The rest of the nation's newsletters—hundreds, in fact—dealt with stock prices, monetary theory, and high finance. They didn't even consider the foundation nature of raw materials.

## [7] TO THE ATTACHED LIST

Wilken continued to appear before Congressional Committees—before the House Subcommittee on Rural Development, for instance, and before the House Subcommittee on Wheat, for instance. In each appearance Wilken unveiled his balance sheet, and before each he conveyed some of the foundation reasons why national ills accumulated when agriculture decayed.

On October 3, 1967 Wilken wrote his old friend Vince Rossiter to tell him that Leon Keyserling had been appointed to the Board of Directors of the Giant Food Stores, one of the nation's large grocery chains. "That was probably his reward for [the way in which he was] helping farmers get better prices." Wilken informed Rossiter that he had had lunch with a Herr Woelke, who was Agricultural Attache of the West Germany Embassy. How fared the German economy? Wilken detailed "how" in a few lines:

|  | West Germany 1947-1948 | West Germany 1964-1965 | Change |
|---|---|---|---|
| Cash farm income | D.M. 6.5 billion | D.M. 25.7 billion | + 395% |
| Cash expenses | D.M. 6.1 billion | D.M. 19.4 billion | + 218% |
| Net farm income | D.M. 1.6 billion | D.M. 6.4 billion | + 300% |

|  | United States 1947-1948 | United States 1964-1965 | Change |
|---|---|---|---|
| Cash farm income | $30.0 billion | $38.0 billion | + 26% |
| Cash expenses or cost of production | 17.9 billion | 30.0 billion | + 67% |
| Net farm income | 15.0 billion | 13.5 billion | + 10% |

"The effect of our domestic balance of payments problem on our fiscal policies both federal and state is serious. For example, taxes in 1967-1968 fiscal year will approximate 38% of the national income. As a result the shortage of $108 billion of national income represents a tax loss of 38% of $108 billion, or approximately $41 billion, federal, state and local. This finds all public operations with huge deficits. What is their solution? To somehow and in some way increase taxes. There is no thought of restoring the balance between private enterprise—rural buying power, etc.— and the cost factors their policies [have made necessary]."

"To restore gross farm income to parity would require an increase of about 8% in the price level, which in turn would recover the shortage of $109 billion of national income."

Wilken issued an analysis, *Operation of our Economy 1967*, early in February 1968. The analysis went to every member of Congress. It told a story of income shortage and new debt construction, a story so old it rated only a "ho-hum" from lawmakers who thought about winning the next election, not balancing the economy.

"Red Paulson," Wilken wrote to an old Iowa friend, W.W. Swain, on October 11, 1968, ". . . put his finger on the real problem. We have segregation of political and economic policies."

By October 1968, many of Wilken's letters started arriving in handwritten form. Usually he requested that I make copies for circulation "to the attached list."

". . . Note that Herschel Newsom was appointed member of Tariff Commission He is President of the Grange. He knows little about tariffs. The Grange hasn't taken a stand for import protection since Taber was President. . . .

"New Zealand is asking for more exports of beef & lamb to the United States. As I told you over the phone, slaughter steers in Australia sell for $12 to $14 per cwt. To balance with that on a free trade basis our livestock producers face a price reduction to balance with $1.05 corn. . . ."

Corn had been $1.66 a bushel in 1951. The economic planners were taking it to $1.05 and below.

The surpluses in the country, Wilken informed me over the phone, were paper surpluses. In a letter he dropped a footnote on how questionable farming techniques were pushing production higher, but one day an extra shot of sunlight or an extra dose of moisture would wipe away those gains. "From 1950-1960 the addition of 21% increase in fertilizer increased per acre production 30%. Following 1961, a 59% increase in fertilizer increased per acre production only 15%. Our economic theorists and efficiency experts have never realized that 98% of a corn crop is moisture and sunshine. With current reserves, a drought such as we had in 1934 and 1936 would find us liquidating 30% of our livestock. That would be a costly experience, but the surplus complex forces us to live dangerously."

Early in November 1968, I phoned Wilken to ask for a couple of days with him. No, he said, he was entering the Veterans' Hospital. Things did not go well after that. He continued to write letters, and lose strength. And it was from a hospital bed that he made his last presentation. He spoke via amplified phone to a pre-convention group of NFO farmers in St. Louis. The connection was poor, and the sound quality even worse—

but tape recorders captured his words, and a transcribed version was soon circulated.

"I wish Chuck Walters or Red Paulson would come in here," Wilken wrote a day later. "I have the old publications and can show how it can all be put together. Unless such steps are taken, Nixon's Economic Advisers will make the same mistakes that have been made from 1948 by the Council of Economic Advisers. They are lost in clouds of dollars without knowing how they are earned."

Arnold Paulson in fact made that trip and received from Wilken added instructions on the exchange equation, and a charge "to tell the story."

Wilken did not survive surgery. He had, however, survived most of his contemporaries, and the ideas he had defended for so long may have gained a new lease on life as the economy rushed toward death! His associate, James White, had died April 11, 1968. Tom Huff, worn slick with years, had placed his affairs in the hands of an administrator.*

Wilken had spent his life so this truth be given, and he full well knew that his lot required him to be "unforgiven."

---

* Tom Huff's administrator caused to be destroyed all of the Wilken papers that Huff had accumulated since the Raw Materials National Council was formed. "We only saved what we needed to deal with Internal Revenue," the administrator said, thereby commenting on how the mundane had become the first consideration in American life.

# CHAPTER 32: A GALE OF SILENCE

There was a fantastic problem in what Wilken wanted. Wilken himself recognized it when be stated: "It depends on . . . the intelligent coopera-tion of society."

This was the real hangup. The arguments Wilken endured were little more than rationalizations. Even those who pooh-poohed loudest knew that agriculture had more capital investment than the steel industries, the petroleum industry, railroads, automobiles, packing plants, and banks combined. When really pressed on the matter Wilken could make almost anyone admit the foundation nature of raw materials, and the fact that much of industry was an extension of factory work once accomplished on the farm. These things did not annihilate a common understanding. Misconceptions about international trade did. Misconceptions about the nature of profit did.

*If we make the rails, we'll have both the rails and the money,* Lincoln in effect said. And Wilken added: "The simple facts are that we make mon-ey out of production and not out of trade." Here was the key to the riddle. An economy made nothing out of trade. Its profit came solely from pro-duction times price.

Wilken often recited the case of Swiss watches, because hard on the heels of WWII Swiss watches were selling well below the American price level, 50% below in fact. Economists argued that to buy a $15 watch from Switzerland enabled a citizen to spend the second $15 for American goods, and that this was good economics. In practice, Wilken said, it was too costly. The economists forgot that purchase of the Swiss watch displaced the American watch and $30 of income from producing it. Thus the Swiss watch cost the economy $15 plus the $30 lost because America did not produce the watch itself—a total of $45.

Indeed, the economy made money out of production, not out of trade.

I first met Carl Wilken early in 1966. He had come to Kansas City to meet with several of his old associates, and I had arranged radio talk show time for him and Arnold Paulson. Wilken's ideas came through with the pure sound of a glass bell that night, and yet I realized that the commentator did not understand him. Wilken warned of trouble, either hard times or wild inflation, and to this the commentator answered: "If this is trouble, give us more!"

Some months later Wilken and several of his associates tripped to Manhattan, Kansas to visit with Dr. John Nordin of the economics department at Kansas State University. I went along to listen and to see the wry smile on Nordin's face as Wilken's presentation ran off into the wild blue yonder like water off a duck's back. Later that night, the same thing happened when we waded through shoe-deep carpets at Commerce Trust in Kansas City to eat expensive steaks in a private dining room and listen as Wilken's presentation ran into the ether again.

This, it seemed to me, was Wilken's lot all too often. His thinking was clearly a half century ahead of those he sought to convince. Wilken talked of stability, but he was talking to many who profited by instability, and there could be no "intelligent cooperation" from those who viewed their vested interest as deity.

What about the rest? What about the farmers and rural businessmen and lawmakers who sought to understand?

Wilken worked his equation from the ground up. He explained why division of labor and technology released farmers into other forms of enterprise. He explained how division of labor and technology enabled man to use raw materials for production, and how this created prosperity. The degree of efficiency, he pointed out, could be measured by a trade turn. Wilken generally gave his trade turn at 5 for all raw materials, and 7 for agriculture. These were ratios, nothing more. But to the unsophisticated, they became absolutes, and as such they may have damaged Wilken's case more than he realized.

Charles B. Ray included this legend on the first public presentation of the trade turn principle: "National labor or trade turn of necessity is a fundamental economic principle. In colonial days, national income was one turn of farm income, which encompassed the production of fuel (wood), manufacturing and transportation. In early periods national income was approximately 2 turns of farm income, and in 1915, 4 turns. During the past three decades, national income has increased to 6 and then to 7 turns of cash farm income. National trade turn of farm income represents dollar expression or equivalent of the labor turn. Annual increase in national labor turn represents population growth (technological improvement on the farm releasing surplus rural workers to the city) plus industrial technological improvement.

"The national trade turn," Ray pointed out, "balances to normal over any two-year period, at any price level."

During the 1930s, the movement of people into the cities came to a standstill. This caused the trade turn to fall below that of the previous decade. Shortly before WWII, there appeared an increase in the trade turn, but this was due to technological improvement in industry, which resulted in unemployment.

These observations caused Ray to conclude that the "national labor turn, which as a national trade turn is expressed in dollars, is a moving mathematical or economic constant—in prosperity or in depression."

From 1910-1914 to 1925-1929, in terms of medial five-year base periods, with 100% farm price parity, the trade turn multiple of gross farm income increased from 4.14 to 5.80, or 166 points, averaging 11 points increase annually, of 2.2%. The trend did not decline except during WWI, when war waste became an element.

From 1925-1929 to 1941, the annual trade multiple of gross farm income increased from 5.80 to 7.02, or 122 points, averaging 9.4 increase annually, or 1.5%. Again, the trend did not decline except during WWII, when a condition of war waste existed.

Between 1941 and 1947, a period of six years, one could project on the basis of the 9.4 increase annually (9.4 × 6 = 56 points) and this added to the 7.02 trade turn suggested a projected minimum future annual farm trade turn or multiple of 7.58 from 1947 onward. However, the annual increase was slowing, because technology was not affecting agriculture more favorably than it was affecting the industrial sector of the economy. Distortions were making it appear that way, but the fundamentals easily separated fact from fancy.

Wilken continued to define the farm raw materials multiple as "approximately 7," with special emphasis on the "approximately." "I didn't want to confuse the issue" was his answer when I asked him about this. Wilken had no intention of holding to a 7 times trade turn as an absolute. He knew that it adjusted to comply with the state of the arts, and that basic farm and mine incomes would slowly and permanently decrease as a percent of total annual national income. He knew that manufacturing would produce proportionately more dollar income as a result of costs made mandatory by the increasing intricacy of modern manufacturing compared to the value of crude minerals and farm raw materials. Nevertheless, the various secondary groups could not exceed ratios that were normal to basic farm group income or the combined annual national raw material income of farm and mine as progressively developed during the previous two or three years. These "normal annual trade ratios," in Ray's words, remained a mathematical moving constant because production and consumption of farm raw materials "are and always will be first and constant" and still represent the vast bulk of all raw material labor and value.

Ray formed his findings into an "Economic Law Governing Inflation and Deflation." "Inflation or deflation (except bogus scrip money issue) is due to a simple and fundamental cause. The current price level of primary basic raw materials determines the total amount of annual primary barter credit (primary buying power) in the nation and the world. Effective demand for and consumption of physical units of goods by all workers in society cannot exceed the total collective annual barter credit (total buying power). This total amount will always be in exact ratio to the total amount of annual primary raw material barter credit. Therefore, what is commonly known as inflation or deflation will always be preceded by and the result of a speculative rise or decline in levels of raw material prices, without such a rise or decline in raw material prices (x primary effective wages and demand) inflation or deflation in finished goods prices cannot occur."

Except in case of catastrophe of sufficient scope to destroy or retard the state of the arts, the ratio between raw material income and national income, having risen could not recede, and therefore could be projected, Ray pointed out.

The survival of near full parity for farm raw materials until 1954 made Wilken's extension of the Ray equation quite accurate, and use of a 7 times trade turn defensible for all practical purposes. According to the *Economic Report of the President*, 1955, output per man hour in several industries could be illustrated graphically, thus:

Needless to say, factory hours were controlled at 40 hours per week in manufacturing and mining, and unions continued to exercise a measure of control over production. At the same time, farmers continued their old trade practices, such as plowing in the dark, exploiting the labor of their families, and borrowing heavily to get bigger and efficient, beyond anything sound economics or the state of the arts could suggest.

The credit run that started in the late 1950s became tantamount to bogus money issue. It proceeded to distort the progressive trade turn so convincingly that Wilken turned to a balance sheet approach in order to explain "apparent" contradictions. Obviously, a balanced period provided the best clue for what ought to be. Taking a 1946-1950 = 100 base, Wilken concluded that normal ratios for the economy were as follows:

|  | Percent |
| --- | --- |
| Total wages and salaries | 64.26 |
| Small business income | 10.31 |
| Net farm income | 7.12 |
| Corporate profit before taxes | 12.76 |
| Rentals income | 3.49 |
| Interest | 2.02 |

The farm income-national income ratio had been arrested—as it had been during the 1930s—because farm people no longer flowed into the city as a result of genuine release from agriculture. Public policy was now forcing release through low income at the farm, and by handing out relief checks at the metro level, and continuation of both aspects, in turn was being forced by credit construction.

OUTPUT PER MAN-HOUR IN MAJOR INDUSTRIES, 1909-53

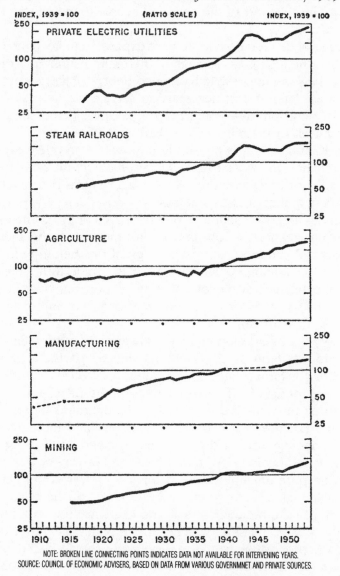

NOTE: BROKEN LINE CONNECTING POINTS INDICATES DATA NOT AVAILABLE FOR INTERVENING YEARS.
SOURCE: COUNCIL OF ECONOMIC ADVISERS, BASED ON DATA FROM VARIOUS GOVERNMNET AND PRIVATE SOURCES.

The gross public and private debt for the nation stood at near $566.4 billion in 1950. By 1960 that figure had doubled to near $1 trillion. By

1970 it had doubled again to near $2 trillion ($1,935.1 billion to be exact).

With a gross national income approximately of $796 billion at the end of the decade, and a $96 billion per annum interest tab on the gross debt, this meant that fully 12% of the national income was going to service a capital debt, and 25% serviced the capital debt and operating debt combined. In order to pour oil on the sores of the nation as they appeared, it took approximately 40% of the national income to meet local, state and federal taxes.

At decade's end, it required more debt expansion to keep the economy moving than the total gross savings of the entire nation, and this meant that it had become impossible to reduce debt a single penny, or even meet the total interest cost necessary to service the debt. On balance, debt—public and private—could not be paid at all, and simply had to compound itself by doubling in less than every ten years.

Geometric progression is physically impossible, and the only point in question remains: *at what point does it become impossible?* Analysts have gathered all sorts of data on this, but the fact remains that psychology is always a component, and psychology has no additivity—no units with equal intervals and no absolute zero. If the psychology of a nation allows geometric progression to consume its institutional arrangements, then only history will mourn. If the psychology of the nation permits distortions of the accounting system to pervert the trade turn, consume the agricultural plant, destroy the top soil of the nation, burn out the microorganisms in the soil in order to kick up production a bit more, then history becomes the final arbiter.

The history of any developing nation always tells a story. First a nation must develop its farm production capability by paying a parity price. Prosperity on the farm creates opportunities for service industries, manufacturing, transportation. The existence of opportunity and the efficiency in agriculture causes ruralists to release labor, but there must always be a finely-honed balance between those who stay and those who accept release. Technology cannot deliver a higher standard of living unless it creates increased buying power, and increased buying power cannot be created with more unemployment. Therefore, release of the farm labor force is meaningless unless new industries absorb the released labor. Curtailment of farm production is a paradox, since full farm production remains the key to full employment. Public policy has never been harnessed to the proposition that farm production should be fed into industry, as through the medium of synthetic rubber, gasoline additives and plastic production.

There was a time when low raw materials prices did not matter too much. When almost all the people lived on the farm, wheat was still wheat, and corn was corn. Farm production was used on the farm, and trade was conducted chiefly through barter. But inventions were imported and developed. The arrival of a 7 + trade turn has made stable prices mandatory. Without them, the national income is forever subject to the wide fluctuations of raw material prices. Funny money might hide the fact, but not forever. Imports might distort the fact but only for a time.

Measured words of wisdom in college texts, such as in Dale E. Hathaway's *Government and Agriculture*, almost always tell students about the market-oriented economy, and hand out the intelligence that "market prices are the primary determinant of resource allocation and returns to these resources in the economy." At the same time other professors hand out rambling, contradictory lessons to the effect that "if you are to get resources out of any occupation, you have to squeeze it." The latter quote comes from lecture notes taped by one of Ken Boulding's students at Michigan State University. ". . . the only way to get people out of agriculture is likewise to squeeze agriculture," Boulding said. "It just has to be made less profitable than other occupations. . . . A high profitability of agriculture would be a sure indication that something was definitely wrong with society. We have succeeded in progressing for over 200 years pretty well. So agriculture has been unprofitable for 200 years. People have been squeezed out of it for 200 years. It has been technically progressive for 200 years. All this is just fine."

Or, to paraphrase, public policies enunciated by the learned ones propose, and rigged market prices dispose! For if market prices really operated as a planetary system, then why the value judgment and the conjectural history that profitable agriculture leads to decay. As a matter of fact, the rhyme of history teaches something else. The empty countryside in South America has manufactured no great prosperity for the several nations, either before or after the people were squeezed out. In America excess squeezing was offset to some extent by free land on the frontier, and by real openings of industries that absorb released labor.

When real openings in the cities failed to accept the squeezed outflow from agriculture in the 1890s, cities approached a static condition and became unattractive to farmers. This condition lasted through the 1930s, when there was little shift of population between town and country. Between 1890 and 1940, there was no safety valve either way, and there was no place to go. It was and is of no use to release farm people to the city if the city cannot absorb them, and vice versa.

This became the gist of Wilken's argument. The economy now needed a governor, a man-made regulatory valve that maintained a balance between the several sectors of the economy, and allowed an orderly flow as dictated by genuine release, new inventions and industries. To artificially manufacture an outflow meant reliance on the impossibility of compound interest, containment of unused population via the degradation of relief checks, institutionalized poverty, and war.

Indeed, technology has already required the development of a giant manufacturing industry. Over two-thirds of that industry is a natural expansion of farm production, that is, food processing, meat packing, cloth and fabric making, and so on. The farmer employs industry through farm production and price, because raw material prices create the income needed to pay factory salaries and capital return. Agriculture releases labor in response to invention and technology, not in order to bring it about.

Industry has always had an important stake in agriculture. In the final analysis, farm markets, not release of farm labor, is of prime importance to continuance of factory activity.

As technology continues to release labor from either factory or farm, many of those who find market allocation for their services through the police power of the state (that is, sociologists, case workers, economists, teachers, and those who draw it more or less openly by ministering to man's spiritual needs), have developed the myth of the leisure society, a state of happiness wherein each person can designate his desires, and receive income each month, a reward for the simple process of drawing breath of life. Such an "each according to his needs" credo is no less naive than the "squeeze agriculture to achieve national prosperity" cry.

Out-migration became bogus the day debt expansion jumped from a base of 40% of profits and savings to the 1951-1953 level of 80%, a level that has since worsened. Release cannot be bullied or prescribed. It has to be earned.

As farm efficiency, and a matched factory efficiency, free workers, a large service industry becomes the vehicle for a high standard of living. Dreamers and pseudo-socialists notwithstanding, the U.S. is and will continue to be a "scarcity" economy. It was computed during Wilken's last year that by 1980 the economy would draw on some 200 billion man-hours a year, up from 165 billion in 1970. Yet this increase would have been sufficient only if new efficiency had arrived. In other words, the prospect of all the women retiring from the punch presses and the slaughter house lines, and all the janitors going home to await a free check and an improved standard of living is only a cruel vision. During the 1960s and '70s, the output of manufactured goods better than doubled, but the labor force in such industries has only increased from 28 to 29 million. Much the same was true of transportation, utilities and communications, industries in which the labor force was increased by a scant few thousand. At the same time, employment in service industries increased by 70%, or from 28 million to approximately 48 million. "Service industries" include government.

Yet service income is the end result of a prosperous production economy, Wilken said, and service industries cannot expand without proper income levels in agriculture and manufacturing. "The great forward strides made in all lines of service and education will continue if national income, maintained by production and proper price levels, will support and expand the present economy."

A service industry force fed on debt creation cannot be maintained because there will arrive the ultimate clash between mathematical ambition and physical possibility.

To repeat: the out-migration from the farm was more or less static between 1890 and 1940. War forced a new tempo, and public policy has continued to force that tempo, as Boulding of "squeeze the toothpaste" fame has pointed out. But to argue for low profitability in agriculture is also to argue for low profitability in manufacturing, a sad mistake, because production soon falls off, and this is something no amount of flippancy can resolve.

"I have been advocating around Michigan for example, that we declare automobiles an agricultural commodity," Boulding said. "It would solve our problems nicely if we could put up a parity support price on them. If we could sell them at the price, the government could stockpile them. We could ship them abroad under P.L. 480, and they could be used as chicken coops in Siam. This would be (for Michigan) the best of all possible worlds."

On the receiving end of such college fare, students the nation over have discerned a growing gap between what professors know and what they are thought to know. Even college freshmen, except for the atmosphere of intimidation under which classes commonly proceed, could point out that the entire nation subsidizes the automobile industry with taxes and war contracts. And college freshmen are fast becoming tired of having public policy play Russian roulette with their lives.

With a mile-wide credibility gap yawning in the nation's classrooms, young people have discovered Herbert Marcuse and the new leftists who would have done with a private enterprise system. Lacking elementary instruction in how the "establishment" operates, they line up to take issue with it, because—in the words of *One Dimensional Man*, men like Marcuse tell them to refuse to perform in a society—

"Which conducts its booming business on the backs of ghettos, slums and internal and external colonialism;

"Which is infested with violence and repression while demanding obedience and compliance from victims of violence and repression;

"Which in order to sustain the profitable productivity on which its hierarchy depends, utilizes its best resources for waste, destruction and an ever more methodical creation of conformist needs and satisfaction."

The most mature students see no difference between state capitalism (socialism) and the type of capitalism that is fast becoming America's heritage. And so they adopt a nihilism, and turn their backs on society at rock festivals and through the medium of juvenile exercises.

And yet those same students are the only hope of people's capitalism. They alone have the emotional pitch required to answer the questions and explain the answers. Should they by rare chance find their answers and expose the cause of the cause, then they would surely calibrate what it might take to seize Congress and restore the dignity of life in a society free both politically and economically. Wilken, before his death, had no doubt that 500 dedicated people in each congressional district could field a drive that would take the offices away from the drones and install lawmakers with common sense. As a farmer he hoped farmers would take the lead. Had he known today's caliber of students, he might have appealed to them instead.

Carl H. Wilken lived so that he could form an answer to the contradictions of the free economy and the free society. An understanding of that answer is long past due if the private enterprise economy is not to become another also ran in history's yellowed pages.

"As a broad observation," Wilken wrote, ". . . the English economy is only half as profitable as ours because as an importing nation they can have only half the trade turn on most of their economic cycle. This conclusion is borne out by the fact that Great Britain after many years of operation can pay only one half the industrial wage that we pay in the United States. It is also the reason why Great Britain is practically bankrupt and for many years has had to depend on exploitation of her colonies for the profits to maintain her position as a world power.

"We cannot afford to nor can the world prosper if we have to go back to their system of operation. The trade turn is also the reason why the United States with only 6% of the world's population has nearly one half of the income of the world.

"Without the efficiency which has resulted in the increase of the trade turn of raw material income, we would not have had the labor available to build automobiles, etc., nor would we have had the income to buy them. Other nations knew how to produce but had neither the available raw materials, the labor or the income to develop the many new industries that we have.

"Therefore instead of trying to blend our economy with the rest of the world we are forced by the laws of exchange to maintain it at full speed while we reach out and do what we can to lift the rest of the world out of their poverty with higher raw material prices and more efficient tools of production, both of which will increase the trade turn in the economic cycle of other nations. To permit our economy to be slowed up by reducing our price level below parity or by importing raw materials which we can produce will merely bring about another depression in the United States and force the rest of the world to continue its poverty and revolution against unsound economic practices. World peace requires a foundation of prosperity and that foundation can be built upon the United States if we will put into operation the program of parity prices. . . . The longer we delay putting such a program into operation, the more chaotic conditions will become and the greater will be our loss in money and goods."

*It all depends on the intelligent cooperation of society*, Wilken said. Writing in 1947, Wilken called upon every segment of the economy to set up its statistical records and calibrate its share of the national income. Industry had to realize that the producer was also the consumer, and that reduction in income for the producer meant a similar reduction in the consumer's ability to buy. Relief checks and poverty wars might mean employment for sociologists, just as real wars meant prosperity for a few industrialists, but in the end general prosperity depended on balance for every sector.

With up-to-date statistical information, it would be possible to out-predict the government. It would be possible to predict in advance the conditions for labor, automobiles, steel, transportation, everything. In fact the rate of inflation, the interest bill, the money supply—all could be projected months in advance, all on the basis of the common denominators of the Wilken system.

Wilken's prescription then remains a prescription now. The ideas he spoke of worked. The ideas being invoked at the public policy level today do not work.

Does not, then, a decent respect for the opinion of mankind require those who govern to abandon concepts that have been proved wrong? This was the question that Carl Wilken asked all his life. And he was answered with a gale of silence.

# AFTERWORD

On August 15, 1971, President Richard M. Nixon closed the gold window, thereby pretending to cancel out the last connection between physical production and money. He did more. He also pretended to reject for all time the proposition that all new wealth comes from the sea and soil, a gift of nature. Instead, it was affirmed that new wealth could be created out of absolutely nothing as a fiat of the human will. The agency for that creation was debt, compounded debt that could double and redouble itself *ad-infinitum,* or at least well beyond the lifetimes of the daring creators.

President Johnson's removal of gold backing for currency and deposits made Nixon's move necessary if a final clash of wills was to be postponed.

Wilken had predicted that public and private debt would double between 1960 and 1970, and that it would continue to double and redouble itself in less than each decade until most of the population became impoverished. The first great half-doubling arrived on schedule, approximately $1 trillion, $1.21 trillion in fact as revealed by unaudited figures. By half decades, here are the numbers:

### DEBT OF DOMESTC NONFINANCIAL SECTORS
*(Billions of Dollars)*

|      |            |
|------|------------|
| 1960 | $722.05    |
| 1965 | 1,002.10   |
| 1970 | 1,413.40   |
| 1975 | 2,250.21   |
| 1980 | 3,929.94   |
| 1985 | 7,065.63   |
| 1990 | 10,824.78  |
| 1995 | 13,694.53  |
| 2000 | 18,273.52  |

*Source: Federal Reserve Board of Governors*

Mere doubling and redoubling on a straight-line basis eluded the experts the minute the gold window came down. The spectacular increase during the Reagan-Bush watch will be noted, Reagan's token use of a tariff to save the Harley Davidson motorcycle from Japanese import invasion notwithstanding.

The Employment Act of 1946 was constructed to assure full employment of industrial America largely at the expense of agriculture. The New Deal tide was going out at that time, and with it went the Stabilization Act of 1942 and its Steagall Amendment. The physical economic indicators were in place, and the establishment of a Council of Economic Advisers assured the country that agriculture as a component of national income retained its governing position over raw materials. Nevertheless, there was the undercurrent the 80th Congress sought to block, the transfer and abandonment of national prosperity and soverigty.

Cordell Hull became honorary chairman of the blue-ribbon committee for reciprocal world trade. As during the Civil War, it was cotton that led the way. Will Clayton, cotton broker, hankered after world markets. Clayton and Hull visualized a world trade organization to police traffic the way the United Nations would police world peace.

The vast farm complex was the first to be bartered away for the benefit of free traders. For people like Clayton, there were no borders. During 1946 to 1948, Clayton carried the Richard Cobden free trade theory to Cuba, dressing down Latin American countries the way a ringmaster chastises an errant circus performer. Those who sought to curb imports to balance chronic outflow of cash were humiliated as isolationists and protectionists, demeaning terms. Cuba was the opening gun replete with many professors and theory period thinkers willing but not quite able to barter away farms in Kansas and Oklahoma for factories. The House Ways and Means Committee rejected the ITO (International Trade Organization), the forerunner of WTO (World Trade Organization), causing Harry S. Truman to characterize the 80th Congress as "the worst in history."

Most people agreed with Congress at the time.

Truman's victory over Thomas E. Dewey in 1948 got WTO going again as GATT (General Agreement on Tariffs and Trade). Agriculture was bartered away via the sliding scale parity formula described in this book. This nostrum was cemented into place when Dwight D. Eisenhower named Ezra Taft Benson as Secretary of Agriculture. Eisenhower tried to revived the free world trade idea again, but he too was rejected.

This told the one-world, International Monetary Fund pushers that plenty of spin was in order, and that bubble economics would have to be invoked to lead the *vox populi* into a deep sleep. What would be known as fast-track later on was seen as a pair of handcuffs restraining Congress in 1956.

Legal bodies that could trump the Constitution, first conceptualized in the Wilson administration, were finally achieved during the Clinton administration. WTO replaced GATT in 1994, Robert Dole and Newt Gingrich, godfathers.

As U.S. markets were thrown open during the Cold War, millions fled the farms. Commodity producers were paid and taxed into oblivion. While foreigners cut off America's world markets, domestic markets were presumed safe as long as the erosion of agriculture inched its way to year 2000.

By 1950 the very idea of tariffs was under sever attack. Americans were told they had nothing to fear because Americans were smarter than the foreigners, the could out-produce one and all with a hand tied behind their backs, U.S. Consuls were told to serve foreign traders exporting into the U.S. at least as much as they assisted U.S. nationals.

Ike, the smiling *generalissimo,* ordered a ratcheting up of open markets. The world was more important than the United States, and just about everything was more important than any farm problem. Moreover, brother Milton Eisenhower convinced Ike that Cordell Hull was right, that there were too many farmers in any case, that Kansas State University had a duty to help Extension and USDA annihilate its clientele. He was particularly worried about Japan. It was the duty of the U.S. to let Japan make a living.

Third world nations looted clean by international trade required Marshall Plans of several stripes. A Japan not allowed to swallow U.S. industries would go communist, Ike held, and thus was born the famous "domino theory." And the U.S. countryside condemned to empty.

When the U.S. Tariff Commission ruled that American money interests were being annihilated by tariff concessions to Mexico, Canada, Bolivia, Peru, Secretary of State John Foster Dulles exploded at the small-mindedness of people who didn't want to go out of business in order to achieve one world trade for oligopolies. Canada, Mexico, Peru, etc., all were entitled to their share of the U.S., Dulles held, or "they might turn to communism."

A half century of blunders have been hidden behind the terrorist attack, September 11, 2001. Yet a mature look at history reveals inflation built with the tenacity of a child building a skyscraper with an Erector set.

Well into the Kennedy administration the State Department checkmated

Congress and the Tariff Commission, and annulled the Constitution. At the time of the Reagan administration, New England fishermen—once owners of the U.S. market-held on to nearly 20% of the trade, Canada, Norway and Iceland owning 80%. New England fishermen joined western storable commodity producers in paying for America's world-running role.

Counting Truman and Eisenhower by 2002, no less than the ten administrations named above cast a proxy for the American people without once telling them where they were going, even though any historian or economist could have discovered the consequences of blunders piled on blunders for half a century. Incredibly, technology is expected to jump start the economy every few years, thus the hole card—national security. Almost anything can be excused under the imprimatur of national security, including security. Trade is being pandered as security itself.

Next, textiles and steel nosedive straight out of the country, college economists arguing that Nintendo games and dotcom companies pick up the slack. Anyone can write the rest of the story well into century 21.

## [1] CENTURY 20

By the end of century 20, agriculture was receiving less than .5%, actually 0.38491% of the national income. Academic economists charged that the Wilken 1 to 7, or 1 to 5, ratios had been annihilated, with national income riding comfortably at $7949.9 billion in 2000, $8189.6 billion in 3rd quarter 2001, supported by wealth created out of nothing—in a word, debt. That this exponentially expanding debt could not be serviced or paid was dismissed as a lack of faith.

President Wilson's dream of one-world, reaffirmed by Roosevelt, Truman, Eisenhower, Kennedy, Johnson, Nixon, Ford, Carter, Reagan, Bush, Clinton and Bush, not only exacerbated the demise of agriculture, it also promised the debasement of private enterprise, the socialization of investment and finally the withering away of American agriculture.

This last statement isn't hyperbole. Stephen Blank's book, *The End of Agriculture in the American Portfolio,* promised cheap food from abroad simply because the big agricultural fish would continue to eat the small fish and the foreign fish would swallow the American fish, releasing farm land for better uses, possibly urban sprawl.

The first President Bush promised a New World Order, now that agriculture as a provider of production that passes quietly into consumption had been dismissed, replaced to a large degree by war material easily consumed or made obsolete. This New World Order had been created carefully ever since Truman initialed the first GATT papers, the General

Agreement on Tariffs and Trade. Eisenhower ratified the Truman investiture by bringing the Republican Party into alignment with the free-trade stand of the other party, a stand that hasn't changed since it—coupled with slavery—forced Lincoln to fight the Civil War. Nixon could crow—as did Milton Friedman—that "we are all Keynesians now."

Those who have studied history could comment, "We've been here before."

## [2] NIKOLAI LENIN

When Vladimir Ilyitch Ulyanov, a.k.a. Nikolai Lenin, got off the train at Finland Station, Petrograd, in 1918, he launched the days that shook the world. His coup did more than remove the Kerensky government. It held out the greatest promise since St. Paul introduced Christianity.

Communism promised a theoretical future happiness, a withering away of the oppressive state, leisure for all, the lowest equal to the highest. There would be no hunger in the promised land, no inequality of wages.

In fact Lenin was a madman who achieved authority and he gifted that authority to another madman, Josef Stalin. Neither understood the origin of new wealth and both condemned the then new Soviet state to collapse in less than 70 years.

With more raw materials than the United States, the Soviet state opted for near zero monetization of their timber, minerals, farm commodities. The livestock industry was literally eliminated. Grain producers were starved so that seed inventories could be shipped into trade channels, priced to arrive. The raw materials were produced by prisoners of the Gulag Archipelago.

According to Aleksandr Solzhenitsyn's, *The Gulag Archipelago*, a Turkish businessman named Naftaly Frenkel closeted himself with Stalin. He explained to the dictator that free raw materials would salvage the failing Soviet economy. People had only to be arrested, made to confess, then sentenced to labor for the state. They would bring their energy into the camps and political functionaries would extract it. Such a procedure produces no social surplus, no economic profit, but then profit was a dirty word. Show trials created *Darkness at Noon* in a manner best described by Arthur Koestler in his aptly-titled novel.

With no real understanding of nature's gifts, with no awe or reverence in tow, the "future now" floundered itself into massive unemployment by the beginning of Century 21, leaving ecological devastation in its wake.

## [3] ONE-WORLD AND FREE TRADE

Free trade promises cheap products for the American malls and high wages for some four billion people elsewhere on planet Earth. The agency for this economic hocus-pocus is known variously as the World Bank, the International Monetary Fund, the World Trade Organization.

As early as the 1920s, some American economists bought into the socialist philosophy made famous by Karl Marx. Industry and business and agriculture seemed destined, he said, to merge into holding companies and super farms. Farming was trending to become an industrial procedure, never mind the laws of biology. Mass marketing, mass advertising, mass journalism and mass accumulation of people into less space. Then as now the fears that brought on the Sherman Anti-Trust Act were ignored. Then as now the combines became too large to manage or biology to abide.

Then as now the engine for economic stability was perceived to be investment, investment that bowed to the icons of *laissez faire,* greed and fear. Yet data constructed over the past century and reaffirmed now reveals that investment based on debt merely replaces savings based on earnings, always with debt transferring the wealth of the nation into the hands of a few, while underwriting an offsetting measure of bankruptcy. In summary, the shortage of income in the raw materials sector since 1950 now equals approximately the build-up of public debt. It thus seems that the academics who assert investment without supporting income as an engine are hopelessly in error.

## [4] THE INEVITABLE

It seems inevitable that such a colossal blunder should be transported to the far ends of planet Earth. Thus the World Trade Organization, the International Monetary Fund, the World Bank—all clones of each other, all dedicated to the proposition that disparity between several nations governs the royal road to profit. The promoters of the new world order, free trade, North American Free Trade Agreement (NAFTA), World Trade Organization (WTO) all have pronounced their program a moral imperative, one that could be fast-tracked into existence without troubling the electorate. Yet history suggests that these fond hopes have about the same tenure as the old Soviet state, hardly seven or eight decades.

Joe Stiglitz is a Nobel Prize winner in economics. He was formerly Chairman of the President's Council of Economic Advisers, then Chief Economist for the World Bank. With these credentials in tow, he came in out of the cold to indict WTO, IMF and World Bank as a triumvirate gone wrong.

It was to install the above-named retreats from reason that American agriculturewas sacrificed in the first place. Stiglitz was fired by the World Bank in 1999. He was not allowed the usual quiet retirement of the fallen. Treasury Secretary Larry Summers insisted that Stiglitz be carried out feet first.

Stiglitz had expressed mild dissent to the brand of globalization endorsed by both parties since Roosevelt. The World Bank is owned 51% by the U.S. Treasury. Its service to world oligopolies and as an institute for debilitation of third world countries is legend. The strategy, Stiglitz said, is to bribe the local ruler, transfer the bribe through Switzerland, rape the raw materials and assets, set up conditions for riots and IMF rescue, with an American constabulary ready to move should bombing runs become necessary. The would-be restructuring agreement is boilerplate, signatures being secured with hammerlock finesse.

Stiglitz watched with abject disbelief as U.S. backed oligopolies absconded with Russia's industrial assets, cutting national income nearly in half, with resultant depression and starvation.

World Bank and IMF know how to drain away reserves in hours and how to raise interest rates 30, 50, 80%, demolishing property values and annihilating industrial production. If collateral damage offends the oligopolies, the World Bank comes to the rescue, courtesy of the American taxpayer. U.S. banks make it big off the capital churn.

Thus the ends of the story come together.

## [5] FUTURE AS HISTORY

It can now be observed that Wilson's assault on the Constitution walked hand in hand with the aims of oligopolistic enterprise. Both hold that small business, small farms even private thoughts and nature's beauty belong to free trade. As Cardinal Spellman once pointed out, there is little difference between a Russian commisar and a capitalistic oligarchy. Oppressive measures to "fight evil" and seek good ends are indicated in either camp.

Thus politics becomes the art of handling people, showing them that the Founding Fathers were wackos, that economic protection is sinful, that ecological degradation is a small price to pay for the vast benefits of a high Dow, that war and preparation for war achieves the highest aspirations of man-indeed that religion has been replaced by the church of modern technology and denial.

The great achievement for Rome, Spain, the Soviet Union, now the United States, has been, and continues to be, hiding from the people the long-term consequences of metaphysical money and resultant free trade. Once aroused, the beast of muddy brain is quite capable of killing its tormentors or, at a bare minimum, dragging them from office.

In New York, a big sign that functions like an odometer gives pedestrians and motorists the second-by-second increase in the national debt. On the Internet, numbers for public debt outstanding on the day of your choice are supplied at www.publicdebt.treas.gov. Each click of the progression seems to say, "Have faith, dear sheeple, have faith." But people do not see what they are looking at, and so they

> ". . . give themselves death and war for pence
> doled out by kings from their own stores."

# BIBLIOGRAPHICAL ESSAY

I do not think that I can add much to this already long book by attaching an extended listing of every source. The most important sources have already been made part of this text. In almost all instances, I have been able to examine original copies, or photocopies thereof. Use of the information in this volume, and indexes of books cited will suffice when students wish to further examine a source. *Congressional Record* material is well indexed and available at depository libraries throughout the United States.

In any case, we are now living in a new "source material" era, an era in which speeches that are printed are not in fact delivered, and those delivered are never printed without editorial adjustment. Even the *Congressional Record* does not faithfully record the spoken word without giving every lawmaker a chance to "correct" his message. This is not bad necessarily. More frustrating to writers is the fact that leaders in political life nowadays pick up a phone rather than execute a memo. Great organizations and business houses take pride is seeing to it that nothing of importance goes down on paper. The *modus operandi* of the Gary Dinner is now employed at every level.

With this observation in tow, I relied heavily on the use of a tape recorder while gathering information for this book. My early chapters, in fact, are simply edited transcripts of the most fruitful conversations with Carl H. Wilken.

In addition to the Wilken tapes, my oral history entries were recorded at Wilken-Paulson seminars, in the Washington offices of lawmakers, and off telephone wires from all corners of the nation. The conversational notes on CEA adviser James Bonnen were recalled for me by banker Vince Rossiter, and confirmed by letter. Individual interviews were taped by the score, and ample citations have been made, I hope, in the text proper.

Several important bodies of information surfaced while I was on the trail of the parity story. There were the papers of the Raw Materials National Council, all of them scattered. I was able to reclaim a few. The one complete collection of Raw Materials National Council papers, possibly, was in the hands of Sioux City, Iowa serum manufacturer Tom Huff. Huff's administrator, however, caused to have burned the entire file some two months before I got to them. Withal, I have turned up many of the publications from scattered sources, and I am certain that I have missed others. Copies of *The Economic Search Light* proved difficult to come by.

The papers of Charles B. Ray have never been located. I found a few published entries, but his worksheets and files seem to have vanished. No mention was made of Ray in *Catalogues and Counters*, the history of Sears, Roebuck, and Ray documents did not survive the transfer of Sears papers to the University of Chicago. As a result, I have presented the Ray contribution essentially as it emerged in Raw Materials National Council papers, and in the proceedings of the National Association of Commissioners, Secretaries and Directors of Agriculture.

Papers of Dr. John Lee Coulter were made available to me by his son, Kirkley Coulter. Included was an extensive mimeographed treatise, *Customs Duties or Tariffs as a Source of Revenue for Central or National Government, Relationship to International Trade, Results of Study in 60 Major Nations, Original Data, Averages and Percentage Charts*. Dr. Coulter's abstracts also surfaced in the *Congressional Record*. In the main it was Coulter's thinking that became the backbone thinking of the National Association of Commissioners, Secretaries and Directors of Agriculture, and this made *Proceedings* of NASDA a prime source.

Leonard Kramp of the Illinois Department of Agriculture first helped me zero in on NASDA files, which are not available in many of the state Departments of Agriculture. *Proceedings of the National Association of Commissioners, Secretaries and Directors of Agriculture, 1916-1955*, published by the Georgia Department of Agriculture, proved helpful because of its abstract presentations. But it was not until I turned up the complete NASDA transcripts at Kansas State University, Manhattan, Kansas, that this story took on definitive form.

One of the leaders in NASDA during the Wilken years was Tom Linder, then Commissioner of Agriculture in Georgia. In Atlanta I found the incomparable files of *Georgia Farmers' Market Bulletin* to be a launching pad to further investigation. Linder gave me some of his correspondence, several legal documents, and private papers—plus taped conversations. The Georgia Department of Agriculture also handed over important papers, and loaned me the use of staffers in pursuing this research.

In cutting the Wilken tapes, the name of J. Carson Adkerson was mentioned once. I found Adkerson at Woodstock, Virginia, and during several months of correspondence and telephone traffic, the real author of the Raw Materials National Council came forward. The many documents supplied by Adkerson gave this book scope and relevance it might not have developed otherwise. It was Adkerson who called my attention to *Raw Materials in War and Peace*, and provided me with a copy of that rare document.

The Wilken Papers now fill a full sized file drawer and have been turned over to the University of Iowa. Almost all of them were gathered one at a time. One document (minutes of an anti-Reno faction meeting), for instance, turned up when an old farm house in Adams County, Iowa was being torn down. Carl Wilken's brother, Hans Wilken, wrote long letters in which he detailed the Farm Holiday movement and his brother's clash with Milo Reno. Benton Stong, an old worker in the Farmers Union vineyards, helped me pick up the anti-Wilken sentiment that still boils in the veins of those who recall the in-fighting of that era.

Carl Wilken, too, was a prolific letter writer. The letters he wrote to me would easily fill a volume the size of this one.

Gene Flaherty of KSCJ, Sioux City, Iowa gave this project an unusual assist by handing over bundles of letters and documents, and extending much needed encouragement during this manuscript's most trying hours. Carl Wilken's brothers and sisters as well as his children, of course, filled in details. Washington-based associates by the score gave an assist to this work by securing badly needed documents almost on signal, and not a few farmers who knew Wilken helped round out details when help was needed most. One additional published work deserves mention—Wesley McCune's *Who's Behind Our Farm Policy*—because of the many leads it supplied on the Wilken era. A ringing defense of the free trade idea can be found in "Richard Cobden" by Wendy Hinde.

In any case, the Wilken story was and remains the first consideration here. The times, I believe, make it a *crisis* book—one that citizens must read because there is no hope at all of getting a change in direction from the "professionals." Within this Wilken story lies not only the cause and effect of present rural and urban decay, but a way to stop it.

Finally, credit must be given to Randy Cook, President of the National Organization for Raw Materials, for statistical work exhibited in the Interlude chapter and elsewhere when extension to the year 2000 was required. NORM is internet available at www.normeconomics.org. E-mail is rccook@voyager.net.

The help of Anna Ross in putting the final touches to this manuscript is also acknowledged.

# INDEX

# *Acres U.S.A.* — books are just the beginning!

Farmers around the world are learning to grow bountiful crops profitably — without risking their own health and destroying the fertility of the soil. *Acres U.S.A.* can show you how. If you want to be on the cutting edge of eco-farming technologies, techniques, markets, news, analysis and trends, look to *Acres U.S.A.* For over 30 years, we've been the independent voice for eco-agriculture. Each oversized monthly issue is packed with practical, hands-on information you can put to work on your farm, bringing solutions to your most pressing problems. Get the advice consultants charge thousands for . . .

- Fertility management
- Non-chemical weed & insect control
- Specialty crops & marketing
- Grazing, composting, natural
- Veterinary care
- Soil's link to human & animal
- Health

For a free sample copy or to subscribe, visit us online at
**www.acresusa.com**
or call toll-free in the U.S. and Canada
**800-355-5313**
Outside U.S. & Canada call (512) 892-4400
24-hour fax (512) 892-4448
info@acresusa.com